TH

A SHORT HISTORY

BY

ADAM ALASDAIR

ISBN-978-0-9888061-1-5

TABLE OF CONTENTS

-For Janice, who is a wonderful person and a devoted cat owner.

Foreword

My approach to history is somewhat idiosyncratic, at least from my perspective as a product of the American system of higher education. In general most college history courses, especially those more general classes populated by freshmen and non-majors, are conducted within finite and usually arbitrary temporal limits. Classes are prepared and taught as discreet units, and so we order things along the lines of a history of Medieval Europe, or Rome, or Greece. Specific dates are laid down for the beginning and end of historical periods: Rome ended in 476 with the deposition of the last Western emperor (even though the East Roman or Byzantine Empire based around Constantinople would carry on until 1453 following the sacking of that city at the hands of the Ottoman Turks). The "Middle Ages" is a unit of time that begins and ends and is studied for its own sake. In too many cases history is presented in such self-contained packages as these without enough focus on how such a linear process seems alien to the organic flowing of events as they happened in the real world. When history is compartmentalized we lose the perspective that events and people and places all influence one another, that history is "alive" in a sense, that it flows and transitions along its course like a river. A picture of any history as abrupt and hard edged does a disservice to the discipline, and it takes away from the utility of history, which is to understand how the past and the present are all linked together in a long chain of events and accidents, mistakes and strokes of brilliance, horror and greed and beauty. In the college courses I've taught I eschew the arbitrary deployment of dates in the attempt to demonstrate to students how the past (even the distant past) is part of a processional linkage that leads us to the present and suggests possible futures. History is at its best, in my opinion, when it presents the ancient and ends up with the modern. Even when you study something as distant from our reality as the history of Rome (my field of specialization) there must be some thought about the ways in which that history is connected to the world we currently inhabit, and the world we might inhabit in the future. History doesn't end, and all histories have something to teach us about ourselves. To that end this volume is organized with an eye to the modern world, even though it begins in prehistory. It is not meant to be exhaustive: there are already very specialized works devoted to cats in culture, art, and mythology in a variety of times and places, many of them scholarly. The pages that follow are dedicated to presenting an overview of a number of different histories, all of them having to do with and relating to cats and people and the relationships that developed between them. I have tried to present enough history to flesh out a hopefully coherent story for the general reader, without (again hopefully) burying the main subject—cats—too far beneath the surface of the narrative. Towards the end of this volume I have allowed myself to indulge in a number of the current issues that pertain to modern cats in the present day, which takes my subject (and the reader) outside the realm of history, strictly speaking. But that is, to my mind, the whole point. A history of cats is one that shows us a lot about ourselves and the world we've created over the last five millennia. Some of it is humorous. Some of it is shocking. At its culmination it is the story of my cats and your cats and of countless generations of cats from distant ages who thought it was a good bargain to hang about.

An Introduction

This is a story about cats, as well as a story about people: it is a story of a now-ancient relationship between two very different species, one based on an element of mutual benefit. It is a tale that connects very different worlds: from the distant era of mankind's very first attempts at settled agriculture, to the increasingly urbanized and technologically complex world of the twenty-first century. The cat is an enigmatic creature, domesticated by association with man, but not so totally as with our first non-human partners, the ancestors of modern dogs. Cats have managed to retain bits of their ancient, wild selves down through the long millennia since our first association. It is probably this residual wildness that makes cats so popular with their owners. They are not nearly so eager to please as their canine counterparts. Cats do not bow and scrape to the people they live with. They live in partnership with man, but do not submit themselves to a subservient social position with the eagerness of the dog. Cats can form strong bonds with their owners, but they do not do so unequivocally: they expect to receive the same level of courtesy they would extend to others. Cats are equals, not servants.

As of the writing of this volume, the ownership of cats has eclipsed that of dogs in the United States. There are some 82 million cats kept as pets in America, versus roughly 78 million dogs. By and large these animals are housecats. Like their human friends, modern cats have been largely removed from their rural pasts. As the human population has increasingly moved towards concentration in cities, cats have gone with them. The farm cat of past centuries is relatively rare in America today. Cats, by and large, have become as urbanized as man. Despite this, cats retain their predatory instincts. Even the most pampered modern housecat will engage in play that approximates the skills needed for successful hunting. Cats allowed outside (some of them at least) will hone their hunting abilities on any unfortunate rodent or small bird they can get their paws around. In a sense, the cat connects us with our own ancient past: they have come with us since our first Neolithic associations, and they retain elements of that distant time, when hunting was not healthy exercise, but the fundamental basis of survival. Cats are fascinating creatures because they grant us glimpses of the wild past, a sort of time-capsule from the mists of history, when humans too needed to hunt to survive.

This volume follows the story of the symbiotic relationship between humans and the domesticated cat. In order to tell this story, it is necessary to go backwards in time thousands of years, before the advent of civilization. From there we must follow the cat from prehistory to the world of the classical Mediterranean, and onwards towards the dissolution of the Western Roman Empire in the fifth century BCE. From there our story will lead us onwards to the medieval world that grew out of Rome's wreckage and from there to the early modern age and ultimately the modern world. This is a story that leads us from the Middle East to Africa, to the Mediterranean, and finally to the modern globalized present. The cat, in good times and bad, has proven to be a resilient creature, and one that is widely   travelled.

Partnership

The modern domestic cat, *Felis sylvestris catus*, was first domesticated sometime around the year 8,000 BCE in what historians call the Fertile Crescent, an area which encompasses the modern states of Iraq, Syria, Lebanon and Israel. We know this from genetic and morphological evidence, as well as what archaeology can tell us about early humans. More than this, to a student of history it makes sense that cats came to live in partnership with man around 10,000 years ago, because that rough date coincides with the epochal changes associated with the rise of agriculture. Man first began to cultivate cereal grains at that time and place, though the techniques and technologies of agriculture did not occur overnight but instead were grasped only very gradually by early agriculturalists.

Agriculture wasn't agriculture at all, at least not until the end of this very long process of discovery. The first steps towards settled life took the form of hunter-gatherer bands favoring certain kinds of beneficial plants. As these bands, averaging about thirty individuals of all ages and sexes, roamed across their landscape they could take actions which would support the growth of certain species of plants which they knew to be good to eat. In the case of cereal grains the benefits were easy to see—grains were not only a good source of food but they could be stored in their raw, unprocessed state for relatively long periods of time. The problem with most wild types of grains is that they are meant to be broadcast by the action of the wind. The ripe plant is characterized by individual grains which are contained upon the end of a long stalk, which sways according to the prevailing breeze. Any attempt to harvest these stalks, as early humans realized, was made quite difficult by the fact that the ripe grains tended to easily fall off the stalk. Because of this, it seems likely that semi-nomadic humans chose to plant the seeds of these grains at known locations according to their seasonal movements through the landscape. Given enough time, this process led to the domestication of a variety of species of cereal grains, which in turn allowed nomads access to a reliable supply of food. It was a food that was good enough and reliable enough to encourage the bands to stay for longer stretches in the same location. This is probably a reasonable reconstruction of the slow processes that eventually led to settled agriculture, and civilization, writing and all the rest that we associate with humankind in the post-Neolithic world.

The changes wrought by agriculture were momentous—they transformed not only the humans who inaugurated them but eventually the face of the entire planet. There was no going back. As humans developed increasingly sophisticated and complex societies, the tiny semi-permanent villages became by turns the first city-states. The very first of these was called Uruk, located in what is now southern Iraq, near the delta region of the Tigris and Euphrates river systems. Eventually (again, transformations in this distant past happened very gradually, over huge stretches of time) other cities joined Uruk, competing with each other over natural resources as populations expanded.

Grain-based agriculture was a trade-off, of sorts. It promised a reliable food supply, certainly, and it allowed the amassing of large amounts of surplus calories. Grains store well, if kept in their raw state and not ground into flour, so food could be stored as a hedge against possible lean times. The cultivation of grains meant that the food supply could be counted upon, predicted, quantified. It allowed for the comfort of certainty. Grains also led to a population explosion. In the settled regions of the Fertile Crescent the exploitation of grain crops meant that more people could be fed off of relatively small amounts of land. Hunter-gathering gave you a varied diet, and needed little labor input, but it could support only small populations ranging over a wide area. Cereals made civilization, and they made it populous. They also created a system which was essentially impossible to abandon. There was no going back from the adoption of agriculture. Once established, there were simply too many people to feed by living off the land, as the first humans had. To survive, agriculture meant that you had to maintain and increase your agricultural output. More labor produced more surplus, which resulted in more mouths to feed, and led to a need for additional farmland. This basic (here very generalized) pattern made civilization. It made history and warfare. It also introduced us to the cat.

These first domesticated cats belonged to the species *Felis sylvestris lybica*, the African wildcat. Wild relatives of the modern housecat, they are still with us today, and they display the behaviors that mark them as wild and make them distinct from their domesticated brethren. African wildcats, like their European cousins, are shy animals who avoid human civilization and contact with humans. They are effective and mostly solitary predators who range over relatively expansive territories and prey upon small rodents, birds and other similar creatures. But 10,000 years ago in the Near East a strange thing happened—normally fearful cats began to lurk around the margins of human communities. They were attracted to these places, indirectly, by the same innovation that was transforming human interactions with nature, namely cereal agriculture.

What these ancient cats were after, of course, were other creatures who were drawn to the granaries of early agriculturalists. Rodents, especially mice and rats, were well adapted to exploiting the cereal grains that humans were now storing. These opportunistic creatures were another part of the double-edged sword of an agricultural lifestyle. With the ability to store food came the pests that would attempt to steal it. The first domestic cats were "civilized" over time through their contact with humans, and the cats were tolerated by people because of their capacity to eradicate rodent interlopers. At first it seems likely that the very first domesticated animals were particularly brazen wild specimens, who were willing to overcome their fear of humans in order to get a meal. But as time passed, the association with man led to changes in the cats themselves. With time *Felis sylvestris lybica* became *Felis sylvestris catus*, the domesticated animals we moderns are familiar with. The domestic cat was adapted to the presence of humans, which allowed them to live around human communities and take advantage of the food resources (mostly rodents) attracted by grain stocks. In giving up their wild behaviors, especially their extreme shyness around people, domestic cats made a useful evolutionary bargain. Their adaptation to tolerate the presence of humans ensured a steady food supply, since the humans weren't going to give up agriculture, and the mice weren't going to stop their raids upon the granaries kept by the humans. It was a win-win situation for all involved, except for the less lucky members of the rodent faction.

Cats were excellently adapted to the job of interdicting rodent pests. In terms of eyesight cats lag behind humans in sharp clarity of vision, especially up close. They also can't see all of the colors that human eyes (and brains) are capable of rendering. On the other hand, they possess very good peripheral vision, and they easily perceive movement, a useful ability for stalking small, quick prey animals. And of course one of the most distinguishing feature of cats large and small is the layer of cells which reflects light back through the eye in low-light conditions, enabling them to see in near darkness. Complementing their night-vision, a cat's whiskers help it to navigate through tall grass or other confining types of hunting-grounds. Cats are gifted with very precise hearing, and they can hear into registers far above what humans are capable of noting. Their sharp hearing is complemented with large ears that can move independently from one another to focus upon sounds from multiple locations, propelled by a complex series of muscles. While not as sharp as that of domestic dogs, a cat's sense of smell is many times more powerful than human olfactory abilities. This is enhanced in the cat by a "Jacobson's Organ" where scent molecules are taken into the mouth and passed over special cells for even sharper analysis of scent. Cats have powerful muscles capable of explosive bursts of speed, allowing them to catch fleet-footed prey. In terms of weaponry, retractable claws are kept lethally sharp by active honing, while their normally sheathed condition preserves them until use. Prey grasped by these razor-sharp implements is then dispatched by the biting action of dagger-like teeth, designed to pierce and sever a prey-animal's spinal column. Evolution has made the cat a very efficient predator.

Partnership with man was a good choice for the cat, speaking strictly in terms of survival. In association with man the domestic cat spread with the expansion of agriculture and settled civilization, following people and the grain and rodents that accompanied them. Uruk, as mentioned above, was for a time the only real city in the Fertile Crescent, but it was eventually followed by other cities. These settled places drew in people from the surrounding regions, their populations expanding too rapidly to be explained solely by natural increase. By 3000 BCE agriculture had spread throughout the region, and a variety of city states rose along the life-sustaining river systems that made large-scale agriculture possible.

The wild cousins of the first cats, both the European and African wildcat, were distributed over a wide area, including Europe, much of Africa, and as far east as Mongolia. Domestication, on the other hand, was initially limited to the area of the modern-day Middle East, with the newly-settled cats dependent upon humans (at least indirectly) for food. This new type of cat spread gradually along with the spread of agriculture, which while dramatic from a historian's point of view still happened very slowly.

The earliest hard evidence we have of the domestication of cats comes from an archaeological discovery by Jean-Denis Vigne of the National Museum of Natural History in Paris. In 2004 Vigne and his colleagues excavated a prehistoric grave site on the island of Cyprus in the eastern Mediterranean. Dating to about 7,500 BCE, the site contained the skeletal remnants of an adult human, gender unknown, along with stone tools and other grave goods. Directly nearby was a miniature version of the same grave site containing the remains of a young cat. The bodies of both the human and the feline were orientated in the same direction. It is difficult to know for certain that the cat in question was truly a domesticated animal or merely a tamed wild creature, but the date for feline domestication has been pushed further back as our ability to access genetic evidence has grown more sophisticated.

The firm links with the birth of agriculture and the associations between people and cats because of this suggest that the Cypriot cat may indeed have been domesticated and not merely tamed from a wild state. The find on Cyprus is important as well because we know that cats are not native to that island: the young cat from the grave site had to have been brought to Cyprus from elsewhere.

The first real city, Uruk, was founded sometime around 5000 BCE and was part of an increasing trend towards urbanization in the Fertile Crescent. Over the first millennium of its history Uruk grew from a scattered series of farming villages into an impressive city-state with a full-time bureaucracy, a standing army, and a stratified social hierarchy. At its cultural height c. 2900 BCE, Uruk was protected by expansive defensive walls enclosing an area of six square kilometers. Within those walls a population of between 50,000-80,000 people made Uruk the largest as well the most complex city of its time. Other cities sprouted throughout the Fertile Crescent as time passed, and a variety of cultures and languages developed. Facilitating the process of change was the development of writing, which took the form of wedge-shaped imprints made upon clay tablets, which were then fired. The developed script is called cuneiform, and was probably first used to record economic transactions, serving as record and receipt of exchange. Cuneiform was adapted to a variety of languages throughout the Near East over the millennia, and helped to facilitate trade and cultural contact. The picture that emerges is one of increasing social complexity over time. While there was certainly a lot of violent conflict throughout the region, with a series of empires rising and falling in succession, there was also peaceful interaction. For literally thousands of years the city-states of Mesopotamia developed their civilizations based on the exploitation of grain-based agriculture. They grew more and more complex, creating most of the things that are fundamental to human civilization—writing, religion, architecture, social hierarchy, warfare. Alongside these developments, in the alleys of mud-brick cities throughout the Near East, crept the ancestors of modern cats.

For evidence of these first domestic cats, we are forced to turn to the material objects provided by archaeological excavations. It is a commonplace among ancient historians that most of our evidence comes down to us from elites. The pen, stylus or quill that recorded most events, until very recently, was almost uniformly wielded by a wealthy or well-off hand. This phenomenon—it makes sense when you realize that subsistence farmers had neither the leisure nor the training needed to write in cuneiform, or any other ancient script—means that what evidence we have tends to record the lives of wealthy people. Thus we have the recordings of things that rich people liked, or activities they took part in. This has provided us with ample evidence, relatively speaking, of things like warfare and politics. We get stories about semi-mythical hero-kings like Gilgamesh, or law codes compiled by real world rulers like Hammurabi. We don't, generally, get much of the humbler sorts of day-to-day activities that would tell us something about grain and cats and mice. As far as the artistic representation of the first domestic felines, we're forced to look over a broad geographic and temporal area before we get anything particularly intriguing. There are plenty of depictions of another type of cat—the lion, the hunting of which was a kingly activity over many centuries—but few of the more mundane cats who populated the cities alongside humans. The bias of the evidence favors the activities of the rich, and they wanted to depict lion hunts, not mousing.

We do know that cats were around, however, and there are some early representations of domestic felines that attest to their presence in the Fertile Crescent. From the excavations of the Judean city of Lachish there is an ivory figurine that depicts a small cat, with a curled tail and impressively large ears. It dates roughly to the later second millennium BCE. The workmanship of the piece, which is rather crude, suggests that it was produced at the behest of someone of relatively modest means. This is not the valiant lion, going down to defeat under the spears of noble hunters, but is instead the sort of small cat that lived in the urban sites of the Near East. The cats in these cities likely lived in much the same way as their modern descendants do now in many cities throughout the world. Take a trip to most modern-day Italian cities, for example, and along with the succession of architectural styles your journey will introduce you to the local groups of domestic cats who form feral or semi-feral colonies there. Cats are ubiquitous in Roman period ruins—I've used them in the past to unwittingly provide scale for my photographs—lurking about in the same way that their ancient ancestors must have done in Uruk and other such cities.

The domestication of cats spread outward from the Fertile Crescent at an early date. Evidence of their footprints has been found in the ancient cities of the Harappan civilization, which flourished in northwestern India and parts of Pakistan and Afghanistan between the fourth and the second millennium BCE. One of the earliest civilizations, the Harappan people created a thriving culture centered on the Indus Valley, inhabiting mud-brick cities that sprouted to take advantage of the annual flooding that ensured bountiful harvests. These people were most certainly agriculturalists, who tilled their fields with wooden or copper-plated plows, cultivating wheat and barley. But they were also involved in a vibrant and extensive trade network that, at least in part, relied upon ocean-going vessels to carry goods back and forth through the Indian Ocean. The widely scattered archaeological footprint of the Harappan culture shows that the cities of the ancient Indus Valley were in contact with not only India in a wider sense, but also Iran, Mesopotamia and perhaps even Egypt and Cyprus farther to the west. Whether or not cats were independently domesticated in ancient India, it is sure that the extensive trade networks of the Harappan culture helped to spread the settled feline just as much as the other animals and artifacts that marked agricultural civilization.

Like the cats of the Fertile Crescent, depictions in artwork tended to focus on the more dramatic and dangerous—thus there are figurines depicting what are obviously large wild predators, who are perhaps tamed captive specimens given the presence of the collars they wear. Domesticated mousers are mostly identified by faint traces of their presence, accidentally left behind in the archaeological record. But they must have been ubiquitous in the agricultural settlements of the Indus, for the very same inducements were there in abundance: the Harappans, like other early city-state cultures, built large communal granaries, and these storehouses were potentially imperiled by the rodent prey cats were born to hunt. Thus in Harappa as in the ancient Near East the cat developed an important symbiotic relationship with settled humanity, to the mutual benefit of both species.

Testimony to the presence of domestic cats in these earliest of civilizations in many instances relies upon the identification of skeletal evidence. The finding of feline bones can tell us, obviously, that cats were present, but it doesn't necessarily provide much information about the precise relationship they enjoyed with man. It is hard to be certain that these animals were not merely seen as beneficial scavengers, who were tolerated because they were so efficient at eliminating grain-devouring pests. The much later civilization of the Romans, for example, seems not to have embraced the notion that cats were good companion animals, preferring a variety of small dogs and birds and so on. But there is good reason to believe that some of these ancient cats were viewed as beloved family pets in much the same way as they are to individual families in the modern world. Humans (or perhaps mammals in a more general sense) seem to have a predilection for the adopting of other species. If Koko the gorilla could form a close and loving bond with her pet kittens, there's no reason to expect that ancient humans living in mud-brick cities couldn't do likewise. Cats in a number of ways are predisposed to receive affection from their human neighbors, once they abandon their fear of people. Firstly, cats are the right size, approximately the same as a human infant. Their eyes are large given the size of their heads, also a characteristic that would seem to endear them to human sympathies. Speaking to their behavior, many cats will allow themselves to be picked up (the author's cat Stitch considers this an affront to his dignity, and refuses to be seized) and carried in a manner similar to human infants, and they show affection to their companions through physical contact and vocalizations that are outside the realm of spoken language. Cats, in a sense, are ideal surrogate children. Moreover, as all cat owners realize, cats are not nearly so aloof and self-centered as some popular conceptions of feline behavior would allow. Cats have wonderfully distinct personalities and are both remarkably loyal and loving to their human friends. These characteristics of the domestic cat were as prevalent in ancient India as they are in the modern world. So even without masses of solid evidence for companionship between our respective ancient ancestors, it would seem to be highly unlikely that cats did not became more than simple exterminators, from time to time, to at least some the humans they lived among.

The Nile is Life

Take a glance at a modern map, and it will show you that Egypt is a nation set in the north-east corner of Africa, roughly square in shape. To most modern day Americans this probably represents the limits of their stock of geographic knowledge about Egypt. Anything in addition to this is mostly limited, for the majority, to tidbits of trivial information about the place—Muslim, relatively non-confrontational (to the US at least), hot, big river, pyramids. The last of these features exist in a sort of touristic Orientalism, elements of an exotic "otherness" that make Egypt an interesting place to visit for the more wealthy and adventurous denizens of the West. From the perspective of the historian, however, the interplay between Egypt's unique geography and the civilization that developed there after the Neolithic are inseparable elements of a fascinating story about human adaptation.

To understand what ancient Egypt was like, you must first forget the modern borders that contain today's Egyptian nation-state. The block-like modern country is the product of European imperialism, and has little to do with the historical geographic and cultural boundaries of Egypt. In order to picture the vanished world where cats where domesticated and deified, made holy and raised for sacrifice, we have to imagine a different Egypt altogether.

Ancient Egypt of the pharaohs (and their Greek and Roman successors) was not a block on a map, but was instead a serpentine band of green snaking northwards towards the sea. Life in Egypt was made possible only by the flooding of the Nile river, which swelled over its banks every year (hopefully) to deposit from its high silt load the nutrients that made Egypt's fields among the most fertile in the ancient world. The flooding of the Nile made Egypt livable. Outside of the reach of the life-giving flood waters the desert ruled. Past the Nile valley the encroaching sands were representative of some of the driest conditions on Earth. The deadly aridity of Egypt's deserts would later prove a vast boon to modern archaeologists and historians, in that outside the reach of the Nile's periodic flooding time could be frozen by the sands. With so little rain even a few inches of sand could preserve organic material for thousands of years. As a result of this process we have incredible information locked in the archaeological record that we lack for much of the rest of the ancient world. The most famous and sensational examples of this evidence are the mummified bodies of ancient Egyptians themselves. Inextricably linked to Egyptian religious practices, the mummies left behind by the ancients can tell us (with the aid of modern technology) a host of information about the diets, diseases and lifestyles of ancient Egyptians. Less dramatically, Egypt's extreme dryness preserved pockets of written material, most famously the cache of papyrus documents discovered in an ancient garbage-pile in the city of Oxyrhynchus. In short, we know a considerable amount of information about ancient Egypt due to the peculiar environmental conditions that prevail there.

The ancient Egyptians had a close connection, practically and spiritually, with the natural world surrounding them. Domestic cats were part of this relationship, but animals in a larger sense were very important to the people of ancient Egypt, tied not only to worldly economic considerations but to the spiritual world of Egyptian religion. In part this must have been due to the obvious contrast between the life-giving river and the desert only a short distance beyond where life was impossible. In a sense, the geography of Egypt provided a very obvious and ever-present example of the fine line between life and death. The green band of the living threaded its way through an inhospitable wasteland. To the people of the Nile valley their land was an extended oasis, where life was not only possible but thriving.

We know from the paintings and carvings left by the ancients that the Nile valley and its fan-like Delta were home to an abundance of life. Egyptians represented the variety of this bounty in their artwork, with enough exactness that individual animal species can be identified. The Egyptians were very interested in the natural world around them and recorded it precisely in their artistic works.

The religion of the ancient Egyptians was a polytheistic faith, with a multitude of gods who were present in and representative of the natural world. The figure of the Pharaoh was a key component of the Egyptian belief system. Though a mortal human, the Pharaoh was considered to be born of the gods, and acted as an intermediary between the world of men and the supernatural realm of the divine. His actions, and those of Egypt's powerful priesthood, ensured that cosmic order was maintained. Over the course of Egypt's long history the Pharaoh become less important, while the power and the influence of the priests grew stronger. One sign of this transformation can be seen in the practice of mummification, itself a highly important aspect of Egypt's ancient religion. To ensure life after death the body needed to be preserved and provided with material goods that would sustain it in the afterlife. For that reason elaborate and technically complex embalming techniques were developed to halt the process of decay. At first the Pharaoh was the only beneficiary of mummification, and the only Egyptian to have access to an afterlife. This was extended gradually, so that over time all Egyptians could gain access to life after death, so long as they could afford the expensive embalming procedures.

While the Egyptians exalted the bounty and diversity of life (though they were also keen hunters who were fully capable of over-exploiting their environment), where certain animals were concerned they went a step further. Some creatures, including the domestic cat, were literally sacred beings who held an important place in the spiritual world of Egyptian religion. Entire cults developed around these animals, with massive temple

Figure 1-Mummified cats, Egypt 664-332 BCE. © RMN-Grand Palais / Art Resource, NY.

sites and their attendant priesthoods supported by the state. Temple-cities like Crocodiliopolis (as the Greeks rendered it, meaning the "city of the Crocodile") were nodes of worship for this special group of animals. The sacred site of the cat was the city of Bubastis which was situated in lower Egypt, southwest of the city of Tanis. Transcribed from the Egyptian, the name of the city was Per-Bastt, the "house of Bastet." Bubastis contained the chief temples of the goddess Bastet, to whom cats were a sacred animal. Mummified cats were entombed at Boubastis, the chief repository for their bodies in Egypt.

The religious festivals associated with the cult of Bastet were massive popular spectacles, complete with music and feasting in a manner that would have been familiar to a Greek or a Roman audience. The temple complex itself was said to be particularly beautiful, surrounded by water on two sides, with tree-lined canals and a temple building containing the image of the goddess Bastet. Associated by the Greeks with the goddess Artemis (Greeks understood foreign religions in terms of their own polytheistic faith, assuming that foreigners were mostly using different names to describe familiar deities), Bastet was depicted as having the head of a cat. While the ancient Egyptians domesticated cats according to a process similar to that of the Fertile Crescent, the sacred religious association of cats with Bastet and the city of Bubastis set them apart. In the long history of our relationship with *Felis sylvestris*, there are few times and places where cats had the cultural importance they did in ancient Egypt.

The layer of reflective cells in a cat's eyes helps to explain one particular type of feline representation in Egyptian artwork: the depiction of the God Ra as a cat. Ra was associated with the sun and the sun's light, and was opposed by the god Set. The cycle of day and night represented to Egyptians the opposition of these two gods. Because the eyes of cats reflected light after the sun went down beyond the horizon they were thought to preserve the light of the sun and so were associated with Ra. Because of this the Egyptians sometimes painted scenes of the god in the form of a cat, killing serpents and fulfilling his role as a divine protector. Cats maintained their popularity and divine associations in Egypt into the late antique period. By the fourth and fifth centuries CE Egypt had long since been absorbed by Rome and converted to Christianity, but the cats held on to their special status: no longer associated with Bastet, they were revered as destroyers of serpents, which were seen as evil creatures associated with Christian comceptions of Hell.

Though there were indeed trade contacts between the Egyptians and the cultures of the Fertile Crescent (which grew more important by the time of the New Kingdom period, in the middle of the second millennium) the domestic cat was not necessarily an import. It is quite possible that cats were tolerated, tamed and finally domesticated in roughly the same way they were further east, without any help from outsiders. The obvious reason is that Egypt too developed agriculture at an early date, based around the cultivation of cereal grains (barley and wheat). Grain crops in Egypt were gathered in and transported down the Nile, which provided a magnificent highway for travel and the transportation of goods. Taxation extracted some of the surplus from the masses of Egyptian peasants and shipped it towards the power centers in Lower Egypt (that is, north towards the sea). People and goods and food supplies would have been more or less continuously moving up and down the Nile. Surplus grain, both for local consumption and that taken for royal taxation, was stored in variously sized communal granaries just as it was in the Near East. And just as in the mud-brick cities and outlying villages of the Fertile Crescent, stockpiled grains attracted rodent pests that humans were incapable of driving off alone.

Cats came to the rescue. The first specimens were particularly (or unusually) bold members of the wild species of cats that lived along the riverine marshes or by the borderlands where desert and fertile land met. These were not domesticated animals, and populations of their wild ancestors still exist throughout Egypt, through their numbers have been affected by changes to their natural habitats.

There were two species of small wild cats in ancient Egypt—the so-called "swamp" or "marsh" cat, *Felis chaus*, and the African Wildcat, *Felis sylvestris lybica*. The swamp cats (and their descendants) were larger bodied animals who inhabited the plentiful ancient marshlands of the Nile. In modern times these animals are found only in the region of the Nile Delta, but in the ancient past they would have been more widespread, before alteration of habitat and human population increase reduced them to the territory of the Delta. Based on the study of skeletal evidence provided by feline mummies (more on these later) it seems as if nearly all of the domesticated felines roaming ancient Egyptian villages were *Felis sylvestris*. The few examples of *Felis chaus* may have been either captive wild animals or (cautiously) tamed individuals. At any rate, the predominant settlement pattern of small villages would have made it impossible to exclude contact between wild, domesticated, and semi-domesticated animals, so interbreeding must have occurred.

Egyptian tomb paintings provide a considerable amount of information about the lives of their deceased occupants. Tomb paintings from the Upper Egyptian capital of Thebes show lifelike hunting scenes with considerable accuracy regarding the wild fauna of the ancient Nile valley. One of these tombs, dating from the New Kingdom (during the reign of Amenhotep III, c. 1391-1353 BCE) displays a family pet, identifiable as *Felis sylvestris,* joining in a family hunting trip to the marshes. Such a scene should not be taken literally, due to the conventions of ancient Egyptian artwork. We shouldn't suppose that well-to-do New Kingdom families all went hunting together dressed in their finest clothes. Showing the scene this way has everything to do with artistic tastes, and not with the need to provide a factual portrayal of events. What the painting does show, importantly, is that the domestic cat, almost certainly *Felis sylvestris,* was included along with the other members of the family group. Here we have fairly strong evidence that cats were not simply beneficial pests but had become beloved members of the family. Such hunting scenes provide less evidence for the earlier Old Kingdom (c. 2649-2150 BCE) and Middle Kingdom (c. 2030-1640 BCE) periods, but it is certain that by the time of the Egyptian New Kingdom (ca. 1550-1070 BCE) the domestic cat had become a companion animal, at least among the better-off families. The Egyptian adoration of the cat continued for centuries, stretching into the period of Roman domination that came at the end of the first millennium BCE. From the late fourth century onwards Egypt was ruled by the Macedonian Ptolemaic dynasty, named after Ptolemy Soter, who had been a prominent general of Alexander the Great. After the later died in 323 BCE, Ptolemy claimed Egypt for himself and began the last phase of Egypt's independence before the Roman takeover. Near the end of Ptolemaic rule in Egypt, the Greek historian Diodorus Siculus wrote about

Figure 2-A fanciful scene, with a cat herding geese. Egypt, 19th Dynasty, 1120 BCE. Werner Forman / Art Resource, NY.

the history of Egypt and recorded what he understood of Egyptian society and culture. He noted the Egyptian reverence for certain animals, such as the crocodile, cat, hawk and ibis. All these animals were sacred to the Egyptians and it was forbidden to knowingly slay one of them. The penalty for such sacrilegious behavior was death. But some animals were held in such high esteem that anyone who killed a member of the species even accidentally would face capital punishment. The fervor of the populace was such, notes Diodorus, that violators of these laws would sometimes simply be murdered without recourse to a trial. These most sacred animals were the ibis and the cat. Diodorus tells us that if anyone killed a cat the "common people would gather in a crowd and deal with the perpetrator most cruelly."

The most famous instance of anyone being killed over the death of a cat took place in the year 60 BCE. Diodorus was in Egypt at the time, and wrote as an eyewitness to the spontaneous practice of justice. The Romans, it turns out, had sent an embassy to treat with the Egyptian King, Ptolemy (all the male line of the Ptolemaic dynasty carried the name Ptolemy). In 60 BCE Egypt was increasingly a tottering power and both the king and the populace were quite aware of their unequal relationship with the visiting Romans. It was most definitely in the interests of the Egyptians not to antagonize the Romans in any way, because Rome at the time was rich, powerful, and expansionistic. Thus everyone was supposed to be on his or her best behavior as far as the Romans were concerned. But then one of the Roman soldiers attached to the expedition killed a cat. The outraged locals formed themselves into a mob and surged towards the house where the offending Roman was quartered, intent on bringing him to justice. Diodorus relates that neither their very real fear of Rome, or the attempts by the king's ministers could stop them, and they butchered the soldier for what he had done to the unfortunate cat.

Diodorus considered it extraordinary how attached to animals the Egyptians were. As far as cats were concerned this went so far as to stretch past the bounds of life itself to include funerary practices. The people of ancient Egypt extended to cats the practice of mummification, giving cats the sacred burials that families would their human members. The occasion of a pet cat's death was a time of great sorrow, and the mourning family would react with the same sorts of emotive displays as they would for human kin. When a cat died, his or her family (based on their means) would mummify the body and treat it with fragrant oils, just as they would have done for each other.

The cat was very much a part of Egyptian family life. So many cats were mummified due to this cultural connection, for so many centuries, that by the nineteenth century European archaeologists encountered them by the tens of thousands at Egyptian archaeological sites. A well known example of this was the site at Beni Hasan, where more than 80,000 mummified cats were unearthed. Some of these were cats knowingly raised for sacrifice by Egyptian priests, intended to be offerings to the cat goddess Bastet. But as the testimony of Diodorus makes clear, the ancient Egyptians were serious about their cats, and integrated them very powerfully into their personal and spiritual lives.

Herodotus of Halicarnassus, a Greek historian who wrote in the fifth-century BCE (often called the "Father of History") also noted the importance of the cat to the Egyptian people. Herodotus' account of the Egyptians must usually be treated with a certain amount of skepticism, for he portrayed the Egyptians as the opposite of the Greeks in all things. This is taken to sometimes ludicrous and implausible lengths—if the Greeks did it, the Egyptians did the exact opposite. But in general terms his information regarding the domestic Egyptian cat is trustworthy. Most importantly, to Herodotus, was that the cat in Egypt was a sacred animal, one of the same grouping mentioned by Diodorus. Killing a member of the species, just as in Diodorus' account, was punishable by death, though Herodotus omits to mention that even the accidental death of a cat might be fatal to the offender. Fully members of the Egyptian households they belonged to, cats were taken to the sacred city of Bubastis upon death, where they would be mummified. The human members of the household, Herodotus informs us, would mourn the deaths of their feline companions, shaving off their eyebrows as an outward sign of their distress. In the event of a fire, groups of Egyptians surrounded the blaze to ensure that cats were not harmed, though Herodotus' notion that cats were somehow predisposed towards jumping into the flames seems fanciful.

In the artwork of the Egyptians cats are depicted in ways that are completely familiar to modern cat owners. Some portrayals are more faithful to reality than others. Egyptian artistic conventions included an abhorrence of empty space, and so they tended to fill these spaces on their wall paintings as a matter of habit. Since they were so fond of cats, these were often included in ways that shouldn't be taken as entirely factual. The hunting scene mentioned above is one example of this (the author's cats don't cooperate in hunting expeditions, even when the offending cockroach is shown to them). But other scenes demonstrate the realities of living with domestic felines. Cats are shown eating fish that have been procured for them. They are shown wearing what amounts to a collar and leash. They are also shown lounging around their owners or sitting on their laps, both kittens and adult animals. Associated with women (in artwork at least), artists commonly depicted seated ladies with cats underneath their chairs. The sacred nature of the animals notwithstanding, the mundane, everyday sorts of portrayals of cats should remind us that the Egyptian people loved their cats in the same way that modern cat owners care for theirs. They were family members, partners, and friends.

The first millennium BCE was a tumultuous one for Egypt. The New Kingdom fell into disorder, along with the rest of the eastern Mediterranean more generally, as part of a process that we still do not completely understand. The labors of scholars and scientists using all the finest modern archaeological techniques tell us that the city-state civilizations of the eastern Mediterranean collapsed by the year 1000 BCE. What records are available from these times suggest a period of strife and disorder marked by warfare, human migration, and destruction. In Mycenaean Greece, the city-states that had waged the semi-mythic Trojan War collapsed as the trade that sustained them was disrupted, with waves of invaders burning the palaces and displacing or killing their former occupants. Throughout the Levant, the remains of cities dating to this time show burn layers, pointing to violent destruction. Peoples set adrift from disasters elsewhere became roving bands of brigands, sailing from place to place seeking refuge and fighting against everyone they encountered. In Egypt the Pharaohs knew these invaders as the "Sea People," a motley conglomeration of all the dislocated populations and a dangerous threat. Some of the New Kingdom pharaohs mustered their soldiers and defeated the Sea

People in the Nile Delta, with their archers butchering the invaders from positions on either side of the Nile. But eventually Egypt weakened, and the New Kingdom was overthrown by Numidian kings who came from the south. For the rest of the first millennium native Egyptian dynasties alternated with periods of foreign domination, until 525 BCE, when the new and dynamic Persian Empire swept in from the east and made Egypt a province. Except for isolated and short-lived periods of rebellion, the foreigners were there to stay. When Alexander VII ("The Great") of Macedon marched into Egypt in the year 332 BCE he was treated as a liberator. From that point on Egypt was incorporated into the Macedonian conquest state that eventually stretched all the way from Greece to the borders of India. This massive empire was a fleeting thing, however, and it broke apart into several competing successor states following the death of Alexander in 323 BCE. The last period of Egyptian independence before it was absorbed by Rome resulted in a fascinating era of rule by Greco-Macedonian kings, the Ptolemaic Dynasty mentioned above. The story of the cat in what was now Ptolemaic Egypt speaks to the attractive qualities of the cat and its symbiotic place in human society.

The Egypt conquered by the Romans was a state that blended Greek and Egyptian practices, a place where the Pharaohs were Macedonian dynasts who didn't speak Egyptian but who still took pains to portray themselves according to Egyptian tradition. The Greek and Macedonian settlers who made Egypt their home during the reign of the Ptolemies enthusiastically adopted bits of Egyptian culture and religion. The cult of Bastet was especially popular and the Greeks took to the adoration of the cat just as much as the native Egyptians long had. The story of the Roman soldier described earlier in the chapter took place in the city of Alexandria, the Ptolemaic capital, whose population was largely Greek. Thus the unfortunate Roman was lynched by men and women of Greek extraction to whom the cult of Bastet was a cultural borrowing (albeit one that was quite old by the time of the story).

Into the Mediterranean

For the cultures that developed around it, the Mediterranean Sea was crucially important. It provided for trade and communication, enabled the transportation of heavy or bulky items over long distances and provided an outlet for excess people, who could travel outward to colonize new lands. The "world" of the Mediterranean was one in which the sea was both literally and figuratively the center of the world. Without the sea, there would have been no Greek efflorescence, no Roman Empire. What the Nile was to the ancient Egyptians, the Mediterranean was to the cultures of the Classical age. For our story of cats and people to continue we have to venture out into the Mediterranean, as the Greeks and Romans did, and as the Phoenicians did before them. We will follow the same pathway that ancient cats took, tracing the spidery web of maritime trade networks that crisscrossed the ancient seaways, linking city-state to city-state and enabling culture to come into conflict, contact and commerce with culture.

The ancient city-state cultures of the Mediterranean basin relied upon the sea for many things. The copper, and especially the tin, for example, that made the bronze armor and weaponry in the half-remembered Trojan War of Homer's Iliad came from afar, across the sea. Building stone, metal ores, olive oil, wines, wheat, spices, animals and slaves all moved around the Mediterranean in stubby merchant sailing vessels, for centuries on end. States grew wealthy from trade, and projected their power outwards to form empires. Small islands survived on trade, relied upon it for wealth, needed it for food supplies they could not grow themselves. The Mediterranean in a very real sense was what "made" the world of classical antiquity.

The Greeks saw themselves perched along the shoreline of the sea, in Plato's words like "frogs around a pond." The later Romans would come to call the Mediterranean *mare nostrum*, "our sea," which it in fact came to be, since the Romans gradually conquered and absorbed all the lands which surrounded it. But they were relative latecomers, for people had been exploiting and relying upon the sea and its bounty since the Bronze Age. By the Egyptian New Kingdom period there were importance trade contacts between Egypt and the Levantine coast at least as far as Syria and Lebanon. In the second millennium BCE the Minoan cities of Crete controlled an eastern Mediterranean sea-empire, a *thalassocracy* in Greek, dominating the trade of their corner of the Mediterranean and linking together Egypt, Asia Minor and the Mycenaean city-states of Greece.

After the destabilization of the eastern Mediterranean saw the downfall of Minoan power (in part through foreign conquest from Greece, in part through natural disaster and the decline of trade), the Phoenician cities of the Levant eventually filled the gap left behind, becoming the preeminent traders of the Mediterranean until well into the first millennium BCE. The Phoenicians don't usually receive the respect they deserve in history classes and popular texts, which tend to focus on the better documented societies developed by the Greeks and the Romans. We have much less written material to work with where the Phoenicians are concerned, which explains why other groups, the Athenians for example, receive the lion's share of popular interest. But the Phoenicians with their trade routes and fleets and port cities contributed much to the development of Mediterranean culture. Like the

Greeks, who were eventually rivals with the Phoenicians for control of Mediterranean trade routes, the Phoenicians relied upon the sea to transport people and things, to send out colonies of extra citizens, and to generate wealth for city-based aristocrats. Both the Greek and Phoenician city-states planted numerous colonies throughout the Mediterranean. The Greeks founded new cities along the coasts of the Black Sea, Sicily, Italy, North Africa and Southern France: the Phoenicians along the coasts of Asia Minor (modern Turkey), Africa, and Sicily (where they warred with both the Greeks and the native population, the Sicels) and the coast of Spain. In large part these colonies were independent of their mother cities. The Greek colonies of Italy and Sicily, for example, retained trade links and basic contact with their former homes, but were in all ways independent from them. Phoenician cities likewise did not form an single political entity, but were rather a loosely linked conglomeration of independent cities who shared language and culture with each other.

We know that there was a vibrant and vital sea-trade that carried bulky goods to all corners of the Mediterranean world. Grain was one of the more important of these commodities. Without the trans-Mediterranean shipment of cereal crops, life would have been much more difficult or even impossible on many of the smaller islands of the Aegean. Without such shipments there would likely have been no flowering of Greek culture at the famous city of Athens, because the Athenian territory of Attica was too small and poor on its own to host the large population of what was eventually one of the first cities of Greece. Athens would have been a smaller, poorer place, save for the grain grown around the coast of the Black Sea, which was shipped to Athens through the Sea of Marmara into the Aegean. The constant here, of course, is that where there is grain there are hungry rodents, and where there are rodents, there are cats, if there are cats to be found. This is the mechanism that exported the domestic cat into the larger realm of the Mediterranean. The trade in cereal grains moved in a yearly counter-clockwise circle around the great sea, according to the prevailing wind patterns and the accompanying technologies of ships and sails.

Egypt was a noteworthy destination along the Mediterranean sea-lanes, by Hellenistic times. After the conquest of Egypt by Alexander and the following creation of the Greco-Macedonian Ptolemaic kingdom, Egypt was tightly integrated into the political and economic life of the wider Mediterranean and Near Eastern worlds. Some of this increased contact was belligerent: the Ptolemies were rivals of the other major states that grew out of the wreckage of Alexander's conquests, and they fought frequent wars with the Seleucid Empire of Syria and Persia, and the Antigonid kingdom that controlled Greece and portions of Asia Minor. But much of it was focused on more peaceful trading relationships. Egypt, due to the flooding of the Nile, possessed what was arguable the finest agricultural land in the whole of the Mediterranean. Due to the nutrient-rich flood waters and the warm climate Egypt produced vast quantities of cereal grains. This was the major source of wealth in Egypt since ancient times, and the Ptolemaic state raised both agricultural output and taxation of said output: peasants in Egypt transported their surpluses to local weighing stations, where a portion of their grain crop was siphoned off to the royal granaries as a tax. Much of this subsequently found itself sold off and shipped around the Mediterranean. And thus the cat found itself likewise exported from Egypt, travelling around the seas on the stubby square-sailed trading vessels that supported the polyglot ancient world.

The trade in grain was extensive, more than many people would believe: by Roman times, massive grain ships sailed from Egypt, taking months to make the journey against the wind. Some of these were on the order of 200 feet in length, hauling hundreds of tons of grain to the hungry market that was the mega-city of Rome, which had an incredible population of a million people by the first century CE. Such a massive trade in rodent-attracting grain made the cat a valuable partner on sea voyages, for the rats were impossible to otherwise keep off of the ships.

The action of traders gradually introduced cats to the port cities of the Mediterranean, and from there they eventually travelled inland in partnership with humans. We know for certain than cats were present in Italy by the first century CE, because they appear as figures in Roman mosaics from that time. A famous example of this is from the "House of the Dancing Faun" in Pompey, the Roman city that was notoriously entombed by the eruption of Mt. Vesuvius in 79 CE. Buried beneath many feet of solidified ash and pumice the dead city was undisturbed until the eighteenth century when it was rediscovered by treasure hunters. The eruption, while tragic for the Pompeians, was wonderful for later archaeologists and historians since the ash fall that swallowed the city preserved mosaics and paintings that might otherwise have been lost. Pompeii is one of the most significant repositories of evidence for Roman civic life (at least for the period of the first century CE). At any rate, the mosaic in question (which is quite lifelike and well executed, a difficult thing to accomplish in an art form that is more or less painting with bits of colored glass) shows a depiction of wildlife: several ducks, some sea creatures, and in the top panel an authentic depiction of a cat catching a bird. There are other representations of domestic cats at Pompeii, telling us that they were a common enough sight that the Romans chose to depict them in works of artistic decoration around their homes. It should also be assumed that while the mosaic panels at Pompeii prove that cats were present it is by no means sure that these are the earliest examples of domestic cats in Italy. The pan-Mediterranean trade in grains and other goods was quite old by the first century CE, so it is safe to assume that cats had been travelling here and there with their human companions for some time on the day that disaster made Pompeii into a time capsule.

In Greece archaeological evidence suggests that domestic cats were present after about 400 BCE. Most likely they were brought there by seafarers who employed the animals on board their ships to keep down the numbers of errant rodents. The same method of transmission saw cats colonize southern Italy through the Greek cities of Magna Graecia, or "Great Greece" as the Romans styled the Greek settlements of southern Italy and Sicily. This occurred somewhat later than in Greece herself, around the year 270 BCE. Cats, of course, were active in colonizing new territories all on their own, without the aid of humans. Introduced to the port cities of the Mediterranean, cats managed to move inland and find an ecological niche for themselves in new areas, probably mingling with the native populations of wild *Felis sylvestris* along the way.

Roman conquests (and the trade that preceded and followed them) were responsible for spreading the domestic feline across much of Western Europe. It is likely that cats made their way into Gaul (modern France and bits of Belgium and Germany) along with the legions of Julius Caesar, who conquered the Gallic states for Rome between 58-52 BCE.

Figure 3-A cat catches a bird. Pompeii. Scala / Art Resource, NY.

The subsequent assimilation of the formerly-independent Gauls saw them quickly and eagerly adopt elements of Roman culture. Gaul was thus Romanized, becoming a fully-fledged province (actually several provinces) that stabilized the borders of Roman controlled territory along the Rhine, where it would remain until the Western Empire crumbled in the fourth and fifth centuries CE. Roman traders, settlers and soldiers migrated to the frontier regions of Rome's imperium, forming pockets of firmly Roman culture amid the native inhabitants.

Rome's soldiers, the men of the legions who conquered and sustained the Empire are at least partially responsible for the introduction of the domestic cat to Europe. Evidence for cats at legionary fortresses, mostly paw prints, is fairly common. Wet plaster for tiled flooring combined with the natural inquisitiveness of the cat to leave us with feline footprints that are frozen in time. There was a practical side to the association between cats and Roman soldiers, since the troops subsisted mainly on bread. In common with earlier feline-human partnerships the skill of the cat in fending off rodents was a prized ability, which was valued by the Roman military as much as any other human group. But cats, at least in individual cases, must have been more than this to some of the soldiers. Soldiers have been attracting pets and mascots of all kinds for as long as there have been armies. This is as true of Roman legionaries as it is of American GIs in Vietnam, for example, where my father kept a small wildcat as a pet in the late 1960s. The legionaries who garrisoned the borders of Rome's frontier took cats along with them, and some of these must have been companion animals or mascots in the fashion of soldiers from all periods of history. The cramped barracks of Roman soldiers from Britain to Syria were home to more than one species.

The link between soldiers and cats in the Roman period provides us with another novel instance of people depicting cats: as shield devices, painted upon the face of soldiers' shields. Both Roman soldiers and their non-Roman opponents from beyond the borders of Rome's dominion sometimes used the cat as a representational emblem. In the case of the Romans this was because the cat became an important symbol of *libertas*, or liberty. Anyone familiar with cats understands their particular form of independence, and the skill of certain cats as escape artists. The independent and self-sufficient nature of even very domesticated felines saw them become for the Romans a symbol of liberty, linked to the cult of the goddess Libertas.

Both the Greeks and the Romans were avid pet-owners, but the precise definition of what constituted a good pet was culturally determined and different from modern tastes. Dogs were popular as pets, and had already been bred to the point where there were considerable differences between separate breeds. Large dogs like the famous Molossian hounds of northwestern Greece were used for hunting and for guard purposes (in Pompeii there is a mosaic that reads *cave canem*, "beware of the dog," depicting such a hound). Smaller lapdogs were prized by the Romans as companion animals, leading to the condemnation that these surrogate children distracted their owners from the business of child-raising. Other pets were common as well: ferrets were kept by both the Greeks and the Romans, and there is evidence for pet goats and more exotic fare such as tamed wild cats and so forth. The Romans especially were keen on keeping birds as pets, of all varieties: in some mosaics, which depict cats seizing birds, it is not entirely clear if the purpose is to celebrate the skill of the hunter or to memorialize the death of an avian companion. Most of the surviving evidence would seem to suggest that Romans in general viewed cats as valuable working animals, and prized them for their mousing skills. The common assumption is that Roman culture favored other types of animals as pets and tolerated cats as a sort of beneficial pest that kept the rodents away. Cats were valued for their skills, not their personalities. As the note about soldiers above suggests, it is more than likely that on an individual level at least the Romans and Greeks both eventually grew fond of some members of the local mouser corps. This is all the more likely because Roman culture was not monolithic, but instead included a great many cultures with their own ideas about what types of animals made good companions. That we lack plentiful evidence for cats being beloved companions in classical antiquity does not necessarily mean that they were always and everywhere only viewed as living tools.

In Roman times the cats maintained their link with Egypt even though they travelled far beyond the borders of that land. This was because the Romans, in conquering Egypt, became fascinated with the history, culture, and particularly the religion of that place. Much that was Egyptian—works of art, pyramids, and religious cults— became something of a fad during the early Empire. In the same way as the Greeks before them, the Romans saw Egypt as representing a particular type of exotic "otherness," and they were incurably intrigued by it. Eventually the cult of the Egyptian goddess Isis would become incredibly popular among the Romans, and the "cool factor" linked to all things Egyptian rubbed off to a certain degree on domestic cats. The Greco-Roman world was more aware of and appreciative of the good qualities of domestic cats than is generally believed. The Greek author Theocritus could write in the early third century BCE, for example, that "all cats love a cushioned couch." Such a statement is perfectly understandable to modern cat owners who are quite familiar with the eagerness with which cats search out the best spots to nap in, on or under.

The Roman Empire eventually broke apart due to a combination of internal and external pressures. This happened gradually, and the popular notion of "fire and sword" is not really an accurate depiction of the process. The western portion of the Empire broke up and became a series of Romano-German kingdoms during the fifth century CE. Further east, that portion of the Empire based on the great city of Constantinople flourished for centuries as a great military and economic power. The decline of this "Byzantine Empire" was stretched out over many centuries. The absolute end of the Roman state, according to one of the standard conveniences used by historians, came in 1453 CE with the sacking of Constantinople by the Ottomans. But by then the notion of what "Rome" meant to people had transformed and been re-imagined so many times that one can argue that the Roman state never really "fell" at all. Instead, it was reborn in different ways by a succession of cultures who sought to emulate the Roman accomplishment. Thus the medieval world that was born out of the collapse of the Western Empire carried with it much that was Roman. Before we get to the medieval incarnation of European society, however, we've got to cast our gaze to the east, to view some of the events that transformed that corner of the Roman world. And, of course, cats are to be found there as well.

The Mark of Muhammad

The spread of Islam outward from the Arabian Peninsula, and the subsequent creation of Islamic empires across the Near East, Africa and Europe is one of the most important historical developments of the last two thousand years. For hundreds of years powerful Islamic states like the Abbasid and Umayyad Caliphates, and later the Ottoman Empire would alter the course of world history. The place of the cat in the spiritual and cultural life of these societies is an interesting (and relatively uplifting) chapter in our continuing story.

The history of the rise of Islam begins with the spread of that religion outward from the Arabian Peninsula beginning in the seventh century CE. Begun by the actions of the Prophet Muhammad, Islam advanced under his successors to the point that it challenged the Byzantine (or East Roman) Empire, the successor state to Rome formed out of the easternmost provinces of the formerly Mediterranean-spanning state. Islam grew through both conquest and conciliation: heavy taxation under the Byzantines made the relatively light taxation and accepting social policies of the Arabs attractive, gaining Islam willing converts and supporters. Militarily, the inspired nature of the religion helped the early Arab conquerors make up for a lack of sophisticated war material and technology. Islam gradually ate away at the East Roman Empire, swallowing up provinces one by one, until its expansion broke Byzantine power at the battle of Manzikert in 1071 CE. A disaster for the Byzantine Empire, it was inflicted by a group of Turkic people, the Seljuks, who were originally from central Asia and who had converted to Islam. In response to the defeat, which cost Constantinople (modern

Istanbul, at the time the capital of the Byzantine state) control of their provinces in what is now Turkey, the Emperor Alexios Komnenos I appealed to Pope Urban II for aid. The unintended consequence of that action was the launching of the First Crusade, which was followed by many others over the next several hundred years. The crusades resulted in violent conflict, but also trade and cultural exchange between east and west. Much classical scholarship from the Greco-Roman period entered the west as a result of this contact, as did Muslim innovations in mathematics, astronomy, medicine and science.

The reach of Islam was vast: at the height of its expansion Muslim empires controlled the entirety of the Near East, Egypt and North Africa, and much of Spain. They even invaded France before being turned back by the grandfather of the Frankish emperor, Charlemagne. Later during the fifteenth and sixteenth centuries the Ottoman Empire would launch expansionist campaigns into Europe and wage war against Russia. The vitality of these states has impacted the west in important ways, though much of this is not realized by most modern people. The system of Arabic numerals (as one example) that westerners use every day without too much thought was actually a monumental advance over the clunky Roman system that preceded its adoption. The medicine and science of the Muslim states was far advanced over that of the west for centuries. During the crusades western medicine was mostly a mixture of prayer, mysticism and nonsense, often more dangerous than the disease or injury it was called upon to cure. In contrast Muslim doctors were capable of relatively sophisticated surgery, and put their faith in a scientific understanding of the body. The more sophisticated gunpowder technology of the Ottomans spurred the west to play catch-up in order to defend itself from the military might of their opponents.

For our story about cats the differences between the cat in Catholic Christian and Islamic thought is equally striking as differences in science, medicine or technology. As detailed below, the Christian realms of Europe intermittently persecuted cats out of a misguided belief that they were in league with the forces of evil. Even though some people kept the animals as pets or working animals, until the nineteenth century there remained a latent possibility that Europeans, both individually and as groups, would kill or drive away cats due to prevailing beliefs regarding witchcraft, or fear of demons and the devil. This behavior was so ingrained in European thought patterns that the spectacle of publically slaughtering cats was not an uncommon occurrence, linked to folk beliefs and organized religion. Until relatively recently, European cats have occupied an ambiguous place in western society. This ambiguity is in general not a feature of Muslim thought about the place and role of cats.

Cats predated Islam in the Near East, and may have been considered sacred during pre-Islamic times, when the Arab tribes worshipped a polytheistic pantheon of deities. If so, Islam continued this practice in its own way, granting cats and important cultural place in the varied society of the expanding Muslim faith. Cats were certainly working animals, as elsewhere, valued for their hunting abilities. But there was more to the story of the cat in Islamic society simply than their employment as living mousetraps.

The story of the cat in the Islamic world starts with its central figure, the Prophet Muhammad. In a process somewhat analogous to the place of the gospels in Catholic tradition, the Muslim faith developed a series of stories about Muhammad that were written down in the eighth and ninth centuries. Called hadith (*aḥādīth*), these tales are ostensibly based around the sayings of Muhammad and regard his personal teachings on a variety of subjects. As far as cats are concerned the relationship between Muhammad and domestic cats is the foundation for the largely favorable view of the animals under Islam's dominion. Muhammad was by all appearances a cat lover who had a favorite cat named Muezza. Probably the most famous story regarding Muhammad and his cat is one in which the prophet was on his way to attend prayers and wished to wear a particular robe for the occasion. When he located the robe he found his beloved cat Muezza sound asleep on one of the sleeves of the robe. Rather than wake the somnolent feline he preferred instead to cut the sleeve from the robe, and leave Muezza to nap in peace. He then went to pray as he had intended. Upon his return the cat rose and bowed to him, and he stroked it upon the head.

Versions of this story and others place cats close to the prophet and end with him blessing them, and in the process bestowing upon them a number of their seemingly supernatural abilities. In one story another cat, owned by one of Muhammad's companions, acts to save the prophet from a dangerous snake. The role of cats as guardians in this way directly recalls the Egyptian view of cats as valuable protectors, capable of dealing with dangerous serpents feared by man. In gratitude for his actions against the snake, Muhammad is supposed to have again stroked the cat on its head three times, as a result of which cats gained the ability to have seven lives and land on their feet in the event of a fall. The association of Muhammad with cats is also supposed to explain the M-shaped markings found on the head of a traditional tabby cat (both of my cats display such markings, and I can see them thinking of themselves as blessed by the prophet).

Another tale concerning the treatment of cats tells the story of a certain woman who was scratched or otherwise injured by a cat and decided to punish the offending animal by leashing it and refusing to give it anything to eat. The cat was not able to hunt because of the leash, and wasn't provided with food by the woman, and at last it died. The inclusion of the story in the pages of the hadith concerns the actions of the woman, which are condemned. The reader is reminded that it is a sin to kill cats, and that the woman imprisoned the animal so that it couldn't go about the business of eradicating vermin. The scholarly opinion of the authorities concluded that the woman was doomed to hell for what she had done. This is in considerable contrast with the treatment of cats in medieval or Early Modern Europe, who were often killed due to then-contemporary understandings of Christian doctrine and folk superstition.

Modern cat lovers care a great deal about their cats, but most of us would probably not extend this quite as far as Islamic society could regarding the conjunction of cats and food. Not cats as food, mind you, but cats eating your food. Cat saliva, at least in certain Islamic texts, was not considered to be harmful or polluting so long as the mouth of the specific cat was not obviously infected or contaminated. It was permissible, that is, to eat or drink after your cat. They were allowed to partake of your food, and you could be safe in the knowledge that nothing unpleasant would take place. This is a sure sign of the important place cats held in Islamic society. There are even stories regarding Muhammad allowing cats to indulge in his own food or drink. I assume that most modern cat people would balk at this, out of fear of the danger of contamination from whatever bacteria inhabit the mouths of their cats (I would). That said, I witnessed a dog-loving friend of mine once drink water out of a cup that he had just successfully offered to a Rottweiler. Nothing bad happened to him, but I think he was pushing it. Anyway,

Figure 4-Islamic. Romance of Varqa and Gulshah. Two cats fight. Werner Forman / Art Resource, NY.

the society that lets cats eat from the same dish without fear is truly a society that likes cats.

Cats were clean animals, and were allowed to live in the home as a result, though they were supposed to be provided with adequate food and drink and allowed to roam about outside as needed. According to tradition cats were not supposed to be bought or sold, though they could be given away. As you'll see below, this tenant was not always followed, for cats would later be an important trade item in certain cities of the Islamic state of Iran, where specialized traders could buy and transport them for sale in India.

The treatment of cats (and other animals) was ideally modified by the tenants of Islamic religion, as man was supposed to demonstrate mercy to animals under its proscriptions. Most of the above evidence for the place of the cat under Islam comes to us from textual sources, which are actually quite rich due to the actions of Muslim scholars and religious authorities. But there is also the evidence of material culture, the works of art that Islamic society produced. Cats are a common image in Islamic artworks, more so than they were for the Greeks or Romans. Some of the bias of the sources comes from the prohibition against portraying the human form under Islam, but the frequency with which cats are an artistic motif goes beyond mere convenience or the need to fill space. Cats were clearly an important component of the world as envisioned by Islamic society and culture.

Another story that demonstrates the special place of the cat and how Islamic faith could intersect with the physical world revolves around a certain cleric who was eating lunch with some companions in or near a mosque. While they ate a cat crept up to them and began to beg for food. The cleric and his friends gave the animal some bits of their lunch and it went away, only to return and repeat its behavior. Several times the men fed the cat only to have it return again and again. At last the cleric decided to follow the cat as it left, and he traced it back to a nearby building. There he saw the begging cat place the morsel of food it carried at the feet of another cat, who was blind and unable to hunt for itself. The story ends with the cleric being struck by how God could provide for the blind cat through the agency of the other feline. I have a Japanese friend whose father once watched an older cat drink out of muddy puddle while allowing other cats to drink from clean water. He interpreted the behavior of the puddle drinker as noble, seeing it as an act of humility. In all likelihood the explanation of the story is that cats are not particularly picky about drinking out of puddles (at least certain cats), rather than that the cat was consciously sacrificing for the sake of the others. But maybe not: if you've been around cats long enough, you know that they have the ability to sense when one of their companions (human or otherwise) is ill or wounded. A cat might not be able to heal you, but they'll certainly stay by you in the hope that you heal yourself.

Cats have been held in high esteem by Muslim societies for centuries. While the creatures were periodically persecuted in medieval Europe, in the contemporary Islamic east the situation was quite different. A prominent example of this is the 13th century Mameluke Sultan al-Zahir Baybars (*al-Malik al-Zahir Rukn al-Din Baibars al-Bunduqdari*) who began a Mameluke dynasty controlling Egypt and Syria, and who was one of the most powerful and effective warriors of his age. Baybars, as with all Mamelukes, began as a slave (he was apparently a Kipchak, originally from the Crimean Peninsula) who was purchased and sold into bondage in Egypt, where he was trained relentlessly as a warrior. These slave soldiers were the military elites of their society, and through merit one could rise to positions of importance. Through his tenacity, ruthlessness and military competence, Baybars eventually rose to rule over Egypt and Syria. He was a famous warrior, renowned both for his victories and his ruthlessness: cities captured by his armies might be submitted to massacre as an example to others. In 1260 CE Baybars was one of the principal leaders of the Mameluke army that defeated the invading Mongols at the Battle of

Ain Jalut, a turning point in world history. Till then, the Mongol armies had swept all before them.

Baybars, besides his military skills, was also a gifted administrator. As part of his legacy he endowed a mosque on the northern outskirts of Cairo, the walls and columns of which still stand today. It was an impressive construct, meant as a form of public benefaction as well as a statement about his military triumphs. Near this mosque Baybars built his own contribution to the world history of the cat.

Baybars, besides being a ferocious and violent warrior and a cunning administrator, was also a cat lover. His battle flag at Ain Jalut had even depicted a cat, though this was most probably a lion, the same lions that decorate his mosque. The lion was perhaps a more obvious choice for proclamations of power, nobility or military glory. In the garden by the mosque, though, it was the humble domestic cat that took center stage. Elites in Baybars' society spent their wealth on public projects that benefited others. This was a means of redistributing resources, and was an important component of the socio-economic machine that ran the Mamluk state. The garden Baybars provided for was for the maintenance of destitute cats. Revenues were provided to supply the needs of the animals, and after his death the garden continued to fulfill his wishes and care for cats who had no humans to call their own. Baybars was such a powerful and prominent figure that the garden continued to operate for centuries. In the 1830s, almost six hundred years after Baybar's death, the garden was still providing for felines in need. The following comes from the account of the orientalist E.W. Lane, who wrote an *Account of the Manners and Customs of the Modern Egyptians (1836):*

"The sultan Ez-Zahir Beybars (sic) bequeathed a garden, which is called 'gheyt el-kuttah' (or the garden of the cat), near his mosque, in the north of Cairo, for the benefit of the cats: but this garden has been sold over and over again, by the trustees and purchasers: the former sold on pretence of it being too much out of order to be rendered productive, except at a considerable expense; and it now produces only a 'hekre' (or quilt-rent) of fifteen piastres a year, to be applied to the maintenance of destitute cats."

Lane noted that the garden was falling behind in its duty of maintaining the animals, as some inhabitants of Cairo would journey there to drop off unwanted cats. But that the site was still in operation almost six centuries after its foundation is testimony the place of cats in the history of Islamic Egypt.

Like many cities around the globe Cairo is home to a large population of cats. Many of these animals are owned by no one and everyone at the same time, and houses and shops leave bits of food outside for the cats. As you now know the cat was shown considerable respect in Pharaonic Egypt, and this continued into the Greco-Roman society of Egypt under the Ptolemaic Dynasty and into the period of Roman control. The coming of Islam compounded this, and cities like Cairo are quite friendly to their feline occupants. Modern Istanbul is another place where Islamic culture has created a special social space for the cat. Like Cairo, the inhabitants of Istanbul generally like cats and people leave food for them outside of their doors. This is to be expected of a society that can develop a phrase such as "If you kill a cat, you need to build a mosque to be forgiven by God."

Across the Silk Road

Felis sylvestris, as noted above, is a widespread species: it can be found from Europe to the borders of Mongolia. The efficiency of their hunting skills and their adaptability to a variety of habitats ensured them an ecological niche, and they've been exploiting it for millennia. The following section explores some of the history of the cat on the opposite end of the continent from the Greco-Roman world of the Mediterranean. After all, this volume is meant to offer the reader a "world" history of the cat, as much as is possible in a short book like this one, and it would be entirely negligent to omit the vibrant and ancient cultures at the other end of Asia.

The so-called "Silk Road" was actually composed of a number of different "roads" (trade routes) that slithered their way across central Asia and loosely linked the Roman Mediterranean with the empire of the Chinese. Along the way a whole host of cultures interacted with traders and one another in a way that created what we might refer to as a "world system." Contact between east and west was not easy or rapid, but in some ways we can speak of the ancient world as being tied together by long-distance trade and communication, even if that communication was neither easy nor particularly common. At the time of the death of Augustus Caesar, the first Emperor of the Roman Empire, very limited direct contact was established with the Chinese. The distances and difficulties of this were such that it had no particular impact on either state, but it did exist. More important was the pan-Asian trade in silk, spices and other goods that plied across the trade roads, feeding into the Mediterranean and making the cities of the

Near East wealthy. Ancient trade was by no means the globalized world economy of modern times, but the ancients were capable of impressive movements of people and things over long distances. Trade with the Indian subcontinent, for example, increased after the Roman annexation of Egypt. As a result, goods from India made their way into the Mediterranean and from there found their way to the borders of the Roman state. In Britain, evidence from Rome's northern outposts along Hadrian's Wall shows that common soldiers could routinely afford pepper, which originated in India and was once a highly expensive luxury item only available to the wealthy.

As with Egypt and the city-state cultures of the Near East, the various Chinese empires were based upon the extensive cultivation of cereal crops. China is a huge and culturally complex place, and like the Roman state contemporary Chinese emperors ruled over a diverse array of peoples. Various types of grains were cultivated by the ancient Chinese, with the most important being wheat (generally cultivated in the north) and rice, which was a staple of the south. Wet rice agriculture, in particular, was a highly efficient way to grow food: given proper irrigation and the requisite climatic conditions, relatively small amounts of land could produce huge surpluses of food, eventually supporting a large population. Like Egypt or the Near East, the cultivation of such grains was in a way a double-edged sword: it made food supplies reliable, but it also increased the population to the point where society became dependent upon agriculture. Especially in terms of rice, a large population meant that production of grain had to be maintained or increased, and grain had to be stored both for winter consumption and to provide for next season's sowing. Thus, as we've seen above, grain was stored in large granaries which were in turn irresistible targets for local rodent populations. Over time, all urban centers developed their own groups of dependent rodents, who lived exclusively off human civilization. In the modern western US this has given us a large population of city-dwelling raccoons, who would starve if not for the activities of humans. In ancient cities this similarly produced a parasitical caste of rodents who survived off the bounty inadvertently provided by man. As in the west, cats were excellently suited to the destruction of these pests.

Tombs from the Han Dynasty (206 BCE-220 CE) have yielded skeletal evidence proving the presence of domesticated cats in a period of time which roughly corresponds to the peak period of Roman power in the west. Some of these feline skeletons were clearly the pets of the entombed occupants. Cats seem to have been both pets and prized as mousers, similar to the day-to-day interactions of humans and cats in Egypt. It is likely that the cats themselves were killed to accompany their owners: going back at least to the Shang Dynasty there was a cultural tradition of burying horses and even human servants in the tombs of important people. The more extreme forms of this behavior has yielded chariots that were buried with the entire chariot team, the horses who pulled the contraption as well as the human drivers who directed them.

In a manner unlike the west, there is another type of skeletal find that illuminates an entirely different interaction between cats and people: as part of the culinary arts. The tradition of raising cats as a source of food is an ancient one in China and some parts of southern Asia. To this day cats are on the menu in major cities in China, and in countries such as Vietnam. But the practice of eating cats and viewing them as a potential food source is an ancient one in the East, with Han-period dump sites provided evidence of cat bones in a manner consistent with human consumption. The ancient Egyptians would have been horrified, presumably, though Egyptian priests did raise cats for sacrifice, if you recall.

One of the most famous and beloved types of cats familiar to modern cat owners originated in Thailand at some point after the 14th century CE. Depicted in print documents from the time, these cats were lean and long-bodied, with dark 'points' on their extremities. The cat, of course, is the Siamese, Siam being the old name for Thailand. These animals are characteristic of the "oriental" cat, as modern people understand them, with diamond-shaped faces and muscular, athletic bodies. The Siamese was eventually exported outside of the east, but this was a late development, and for most of their history they have been little known to westerners. The first examples of the Siamese to travel to the west may have been those brought to England by Edward Blencowe Gould in the 1880s. Gould had served as British Consul-General in Bangkok, and was given one of the royal cats by the king of Siam. The kittens born to this cat were exhibited by Gould's sister, and were quite popular because of their exotic coloration. Today the Siamese is one of the most popular breeds of domestic cats. In appearance the modern breed differs from the original specimens from Gould's time, with the angular characteristics and long body type the result of purposeful breeding during the 20th century. Breeders both in the U.S. and in Britain wanted to focus on the "exotic" character of the animal and accentuated these features, which are familiar to modern cat lovers ("Traditional Siamese" refers to the original, robust body type, whereas "Modern Siamese" is the term used for today's show cats). They are noted for being particularly vocal animals (my childhood cat was a Siamese with a voice that could best be described as "ear-splitting"). Siamese are generally born white, with the distinctive colored 'points' appearing as the animals mature. The coloring of the extremities, incidentally, is tied to the body temperature of the individual animal. As the cats age, their average body temperature decreases, leading to a steady darkening of their coats. The colored tail, face and paws are the coolest parts of the animals, and so as they age these dark patches tend to grow.

Cats made their way to Japan from China during the Nara period (710-794 CE), through the same sorts of trade contacts that spread them earlier throughout the Mediterranean. The animals were sometimes seen as a food source, at least among the peasantry. In pre-modern times, we should remember, animals were the source of many materials used by humans. In an age before petrochemical plastics, the bones, skins, sinews and horns of animals were put to a bewildering variety of uses. Aside from an occasional food source, cat skin was (and still is, at least in rare cases) a key material in the construction of the characteristic Japanese stringed instrument, the *samisen*. But this is not to say that the Japanese were not fond of cats: on the contrary, from an early date the cat moved from being a mouser to being a beloved pet, as in the west. During Japan's Heian Period (794-1185 CE) a cat was even given a title of nobility by imperial decree. Another story from the period involved a dog attacking a cat, whereby the Emperor became so angry he exiled the dog to an island (the dog eventually returned, probably not catching all the nuances of what 'exile' meant). Literary evidence proves that Japanese emperors kept pet cats by Heian times. In a broader sense, outside the realm of the imperial household cats were seen as harbingers of plentiful harvests.

Of course Japanese cats remained valuable in the arena of pest control. Government policies even had a hand in utilizing the hunting skills of cats against vermin. In the year 1602 the Shogun's government issued a state order prohibiting the leashing of cats: they were to be freed in order to carry out the work of rodent annihilation.

Japanese cats were guardians of more than just food staples like rice. For millennia silk production has been an important economic activity for the Japanese. It was first cultivated by the Chinese around 3,000 BCE, and the techniques of producing silk subsequently spread to Japan and Korea, and later westward to India, the Near East, and Europe. Silk was a valuable commodity that could be profitably exported. Silk weaving begins, of course, with the activities of the silkworm, which is the larvae of the domestic silk moth, *bombyx mori*. Raising silk worms and weaving silk is a delicate process. Cats come into the story of silk in regards to the apparent deliciousness of the larvae as far as mice are concerned. Rodents are voracious insect eaters under the right circumstances, and domestic silk worms were available, juicy and helpless. Domestic cats proved to be ideal guardians of the worms, which ensured the livelihood of the silk producers and allowed the worms to go on producing silk and not end up on the menu of the resident rodents. Japanese silk producers were so grateful to the cats that they erected shrines to honor them. The view of cats as valuable guardians, as they were in the case of ancient Japan, is similar in some respects to the earlier Egyptian notion of cats as protectors (in that case against both rodents and snakes, as noted above). Shrines dedicated to domestic cats are relatively common throughout Japan, a testimony to the importance of the relationship between cats and people. The so-called "Luck Cat" (maneki-neko) familiar to modern Americans from the décor in Japanese and Chinese restaurants is one tiny example of the long history of associating cats with luck, fortune or protection.

A more unusual story concerning Japanese cats and shrines dedicated to them comes from the time of the sixteenth century invasion of Korea by the Japanese warlord Toyotomi Hideyoshi. Tens of thousands of Japanese warriors (*bushi*) from throughout Japan joined this invasion and fought against both Korean and Chinese forces on Korean soil. It was a bloody and ultimately futile attempt by Hideyoshi to subjugate China, and the Japanese were finally defeated and driven out, back to their islands. Among the masses of Japanese warriors who joined the invasion fleets was a member of the powerful Shimazu clan from the southernmost island of Kyushu, a man named Shimazu Yoshihiro. He reportedly took with him on the journey to Korea a group of seven Japanese cats in lieu of bringing a clock. The idea, apparently, was that Yoshihiro would be able to tell the time of day by looking into the eyes of his cats and determining how dilated these were. Two of the original seven cats eventually survived the invasion of Korea to return to the Shimazu homeland in Kyushu, where today there is a shrine dedicated to the surviving animals in a garden belonging to the clan. We don't really know how effective they proved as time pieces, but whether or not they were the story is a memorable one.

Cats appear fairly commonly in Japanese artwork during the Tokugawa and Meiji eras. In the mid-nineteenth century the wood block prints of Utagawa Kuniyoshi depict cats standing in for people, performing human activities, wearing kimonos, practicing the three-stringed *samisen*. Kuniyoshi loved cats and kept up to ten of them at a time. His household even had a Buddhist shrine dedicated to cats who passed away. Prints by other artists show cats being rather more catlike than in many of Kuniyoshi's works. In a country heavily dependent upon the bounty of the sea, it is not surprising that cats are depicted snacking on a wide variety of foods that their modern western cousins would find exotic, including goldfish and octopi.

Modern Japan is host to a breed of cat that is not only venerable but quite characteristic. The so-called "Japanese Bobtail" is a fairly compact, powerful-looking creature with a shortened, bobbed tail. These animals can be seen depicted in Japanese painting and wood block printing going back centuries. The clear pictorial representations prove the antiquity of the breed, and they also provide evidence for the place of the cat in Japanese culture. As elsewhere, they were important working animals who kept populations of snakes and rodents at bay, but they were also beloved companions whose owners desired to immortalize them in works of art. The first specimens of the Japanese Bobtail to reach the U.S. came back with American soldiers returning from Japan after the end of the Second World War. Soldiers, be they Roman legionaries or modern American G.I.s, have a pronounced tendency to accumulate pets and mascots. Japanese Bobtails imported to America are just one piece of that larger puzzle. Opinions of these unusual cats, with their almost-nonexistent tail, were mixed at first. To contemporary American tastes, the appearance of the Bobtail was decidedly exotic. While some didn't take to the breed on this account, others found it intriguing. Today the Japanese Bobtail is a popular and well-established breed within Japan and beyond its shores.

In present day Japan cats are extremely popular as pets, maybe even more so than in the U.S., considering that most Japanese apartments are quite small by American standards and large pets are out of the question for most people. The issue of space has led to the increasing popularity of a peculiar (to Americans at least) new business: the neko cafe.

Figure 5-Woman after a bath. Meiji Period, Japan. Image copyright © The Metropolitan Museum of Art. Image source: Art Resource, NY.

Neko in Japanese means "cat," and so what you have is quite literally a cat cafe. These cafes are places where city dwelling Japanese can go and be surrounded by cats. The establishments offer coffee or tea and charge patrons a fee to be around and among a group of cats. Toys and snacks give cafe goers the chance to interact with a plethora of cats who are considered part of the staff. In a land where tiny apartments mean that many people can't even have a small pet like a cat in their homes, the cat cafes give people a chance to interact with and enjoy the company of friendly animals. The cats themselves are protected by laws designed to ensure that they aren't mistreated or overworked. The stress relief that stems from contact with cats is a powerful thing for busy Japanese. Even hardworking Japanese salarymen patronize the *neko* cafes as a means of unwinding from the strains of a hectic business schedule. The popularity of cat cafes has led to the creation of other similar animal-centered establishments: rabbit cafes are apparently gaining in popularity.

Some parts of Asia differ radically from the Japanese in terms of the cultural place of the cat. Whereas in Japan cats were prized as guardians (and at least in some circles as pets), in Korea they were seen not as protectors of the agricultural regime but as vermin, or even harbingers of bad luck and poor harvests. The notion that cats exist to harm or trick humans is still at least partially prevalent, and in one strand of thought they are bearers of disease, dangerous pests that were best eradicated. Cats were sometimes tolerated as a means of keeping down rat populations, but the notion that cats would be companion animals is a relatively recent occurrence. As with some parts of China, cats (especially in rural areas) may still be viewed as little different from domesticated farm animals, to be eaten or used to provide skins or fur. More exotically, cats served as the main ingredient for *goyang soju,* a traditional cure for rheumatism. To manufacture this medicinal product, at cat would be boiled (sometimes still alive) with dates, nuts and ginger. In recent times Western attitudes to cats have begun to take over, at least in urban areas.

It is the Chinese and Vietnamese practice of eating cats and raising them for slaughter as part of the international fur market that is most shocking to modern Western sensibilities. The cruelty of Chinese fur farms is difficult to relate in writing and in the opinion of this author they ought to be eradicated. Not only cats but dogs and an assortment of wild animals suffer through terrifying captivity and face brutal deaths, sometimes being skinned alive due to a reluctance to damage pelts. Animal rights groups have protested against the techniques used on these farms, and even the Chinese authorities have tried to reign in the more egregious practices. Urban Chinese, for their part, have also become increasingly vocal about the abuses of the fur farms. Such opposition has risen in part alongside the adoption of dogs and cats as domesticated pets. To be fair to the Chinese, humans and human civilization together have been and continue to be cruel to a wide range of animal species, not only cats. Modern feedlot production of beef and pork is fairly notorious in this regard, and the long history of using horses in war has meant the starvation and death of untold numbers of those creatures. Napoleon's invasion of Russia (1812 CE) alone caused the deaths of hundreds of thousands of draft animals and cavalry mounts (but I digress).

Sub-Continental Kitties

As we've learned, the domestic cat was introduced into the Indian subcontinent at an early date, perhaps as early as 5,000 years ago. The Harappan culture of the Indus valley, like the contemporary civilization of the Fertile Crescent, was a city-state culture where grain stocks invited hungry rodents. Thus the cat was a useful animal to have around. As with the much-later evidence of preserved paw prints found at Roman military sites, the Harappan cities also preserve fragmentary evidence of the presence of the cat: at Chanhu-daro in the late 1930s archaeologists discovered the prints of both a dog and a cat that dated from roughly 3,000 BCE. Reconstructing the evidence of the prints, it looks as though the dog was in the process of chasing after the cat, when both animals stepped on a still-wet brick, pressing their prints into its surface and locking them, as it happened, into the archaeological record for millennia. As with the Near East and Egypt, then, the cat in India has an early association with mankind.

The history of India is a massive subject, far too large to do any more than touch upon in this volume. The subcontinent is home to a rich cultural heritage that combines influences from both east and west. The Harappan civilization of the Indus Valley, introduced above, flourished between 3300-1300 BCE. The high point of this civilization was a period of about seven centuries, roughly 2600-1900 BCE. During that time the Harappans developed bronze technology and sophisticated urban sites. This came to an end with a collapse that occurred at the end of the second millennium. Following the downfall of the Harappan culture, a new power arose and conquered much of what is now modern India. Called the Mauryan Empire, this state eventually fragmented into a series of independent kingdoms that continued to be powerful and wealth despite their decentralization. For the next 1,500 years or so these states made India arguably the wealthiest and most populous place in the world by the time of the European Middle Ages.

India had a vibrant mix of cultures, producing both Buddhism and Hinduism, which subsequently spread outwards to the rest of Asia. In terms of trade contacts, India was connected to the outside world from an early date. As noted above the Harappans traded with the cities of the Fertile Crescent, and by the first century CE trade with the Roman Mediterranean was flourishing. For a period of about five hundred years from the tenth to the fifteenth centuries CE a succession of Islamic invaders conquered northwestern India and introduced the religion of Mohammed, further complicating India's already heterogeneous cultural makeup. These invasions resulted in the formation of the Mughal and Rajput states, which themselves declined and saw the rise of local powers such as the Sikhs. After the weakening of the Mughals the British East India Company was a new, and foreign imperial force throughout the subcontinent. The power and influence of the company grew (as did their annexations of territory) up to the time of the Indian rebellion of 1857. Following this, control of India reverted to the British crown, where it remained until the independence movements of the twentieth century ousted the British in 1947. All of this long and varied history means that India has not one culture, but a multitude of them, which makes generalizations problematic. Considering the place of cats, for example, the following discussion will show that in many parts of India the cat is distrusted in the name way that it is in certain regions of Korea. This statement should be taken with a generous grain of salt, though, because in other regions of India cultural differences exist to complicate our analysis. The Islamic influence on northwestern India brought along a culture that had a high opinion of cats. According to one common story, as you know, the tabby cat's characteristic M-shaped facial markings represent the blessing of the Prophet Mohammed, with the cats forever after branded with an outward sign of such blessing. A similar story exists in west, incidentally, concerning cats and Mary, the mother of Jesus. You can guess where the "M" came from in that case. And that was the medieval world of a Europe that is often supposed to have a highly negative view of felines. Beware generalizations, though I myself am guilty of making many of them in these pages.

One story from northeastern India has it that cats domesticated themselves by choice, when they saw the superior lifestyle to be had in the cities and villages of man. According to the fable, a tiger and his brother the cat lived in the forest, away from humans. When the tiger became ill, and he needed a warm fire to help him recuperate from his affliction, his brother the cat went to seek fire from a nearby village. When the cat approached the first of the houses, he found that it was empty, and no people were to be found. On his way towards the hearth to procure a flaming brand (with which to build the fire for his brother the tiger), the cat was distracted by the food in the house. After he had eaten, he grew sleepy and so he took a nap. Once he awoke, he remembered that he had a more pressing reason for being in the house, and he grabbed up a flaming branch and returned to the tiger in the forest. Once he had made the fire, he told his brother than he was going to return to the village, because it was clear that warmth and food was guaranteed there. Thus the cat of Indian folklore made a conscious decision to give up the forest and live with mankind.

In ancient India, one way of classifying animals was by analyzing the shape of the individual creature's foot. According to this process, animals which possessed five toes were not to be eaten, given that they were similar to man, who also has five toes. Though cats have only four toes on their rear feet, the front paws do indeed have five, and thus they were on the forbidden list as far as culinary matters were concerned.

Cats were not commonly kept as pets in India before modern times: indeed, even now they are relatively rare in India compared to the US. The operative word here, as with many of the other times and places touched on in this volume, is "commonly." While most Indian cats were semi-feral scavengers who roamed through the alleys and byways of city and village, certain cats <u>were</u> kept as pets. This phenomenon was probably confined for the most part to the world of the aristocrat, especially when special types of cats were imported from abroad. By the nineteenth century India was the destination for so-called "Persian" cats who came from Afghanistan and Uzbekistan via camel caravan. These long haired creatures were exotic pets, and not destined to become mere mousers. The trade in cats was important enough that individual merchants could be primarily "cat traders," specializing in the transporting and trading of cats. Cats also came into India from Iran, brought there by merchant caravans and conveyed in sacks or cages, twenty at a time. Many of these probably originated in the city of Isfahan, where nineteenth century English travelers were remarking on the beautiful cats native to the place. These were the longer haired felines who would find their way into wealthy households at the end of their journeys. The cats would be leashed during rest stops and fed with lamb meat. Through the fits and starts of the caravan trade specially-bred cats made the long journey to India.

The treatment that some of these animals received rivals that of the most outrageous stories about modern ailurophiles. A certain cat named Badri Khan, the favored cat of Naser al-Din Shah, king of Persia (1831-1896) was so loved by his owner that his behavior influenced court proceedings. According to one story, if Badri Kahn brought the name of a condemned man to the king, the pardon would be immediately granted (this required someone to tie the petition around Badri's neck, of course: the cat was only the vehicle of the request). Similarly, if the cat appeared with a note calling for the dismissal of an official, then the person in question would be sent packing. Badri ate only the finest foods and was waited on by members of the royal harem. Naser al-Din was extremely devoted to the cat and was greatly distressed when he went missing. When he was ill, both native and European physicians would be summoned to treat his ailment. The pampering of cats by wealthy individuals is not an entirely modern phenomenon.

Domestic cats in modern India do not occupy the cultural niche that they do in the US. Cats have been present in India since ancient times, but the population of domesticated cats remains far lower per capita than in today's America. Though we have a comparatively tiny population, we have the highest number of domesticated pet cats in the world. Though India contains more than 16% of the global population, the country doesn't even rank in the top ten states in terms of cat ownership. This is unfortunate in a number of ways, and not simply because the people of India are missing out on feline companionship.

India, you see, has something of a pest problem. Specifically, there are large numbers of rats in India, as you would expect considering the dense human population and the grain-based agriculture that has sustained that population since ancient times. Normally, rats are only a nuisance that you might periodically deal with, in the same way that cockroaches are an unfortunate daily reality in the American southwest. But in some regions of India rats can become much more than an occasional irritation. If the environmental conditions are right (this happens roughly every fifty years or so) then bamboo groves produce a superabundance of seeds, which Indian rats feast upon. Soon more rats feed and breed and grow larger and more numerous until a point of crisis is reached. Once the rat hordes exhaust the food supplies offered by the bamboo plants they move on to other energy sources. Eventually great numbers of rats afflict the countryside like a plague of huge fuzzy locusts, devouring everything in their path. These dramatic explosions of the rat population are dangerous to individuals, and even whole communities. Massive bodies of rodents can carry and spread disease (something not to be taken lightly, since like the American southwest areas of India are still host to the bubonic plague of Black Death fame). Aside from disease the rats are actually capable of causing famine due to their voracious eating habits. In large enough numbers, the rats are quite capable of stripping entire fields of their edible crops and wiping out stockpiled rice and other grains. An invasion of thousands and thousands of rats is nothing to sneeze at.

While cats might not be able to halt a full-blown rat tidal wave, increased numbers of cats might help India control the populations of rodents, which could prevent rodent numbers from skyrocketing. Thus it is unfortunate that modern Indians don't appreciate domesticated cats more than they do. In today's India cats occupy a social space similar to the one they inhabit in Korea: cats are seen in some regions as nothing more than vermin. The independent nature of cats, as opposed to dogs, has left the Indian cat with a reputation for being sly, tricky, and disloyal. Dogs are faithful servants and partners, but cats are potentially dangerous in the eyes of many people in modern India. They are omens of bad luck, especially black cats, which are associated with witches and witchcraft in the same manner as they were my medieval Europeans. To some, crossing paths with a cat means that you won't finish the journey you began, or complete the task you set out to accomplish. Like Korea cat owners are relatively few and veterinarians knowledgeable of and willing to treat cats are difficult to find. As with parts of China, cats are sometimes exploited as a food source, with trained dogs used to catch cats for their meat. This attitude has clearly not kept Indian cats from surviving alongside man, but it does mean that the population of domestic felines is low in relation to that of humans. All in all, it would seem to be a boon to the people of India to embrace a more accepting view of the cat, especially in areas where rat populations are a potential menace. It is likely that attitudes towards cats will gradually change, as in Korea, but for the time being cats in India exist mostly on the margins of human society. It is a role they are well adapted for.

Aside from the danger posed by periodic exponential growth of the rat population, India's rodents sometimes serve as the bearers of a more insidious danger: bubonic plague, the disease caused by the bacterium *Yesinia pestis*. Plague is endemic to some regions of India, and is spread among rodent populations by the feeding activity of fleas. The bacteria clog the feeding apparatus of the fleas as they multiply, causing the fleas to regurgitate blood into a host. When this occurs they spread the teeming bacteria into a host's bloodstream and the whole process continues anew. In 1910 in the English Medical Journal, Andrew Buchanan was already promoting domestic cats as a means of controlling the spread of plague in India. Cats were capable of controlling the rat population and could possibly avert outbreaks of the disease. Recent studies have proven that cats are themselves highly vulnerable to bubonic plague, and can easily contract the disease through the consumption of infected animals. Whereas dogs are resistant to *Yesinia pestis* and stand a good chance of surviving, cats suffer and die from bubonic plague in much the same way as humans.

Beasties & Bestiaries

Domestic cats had a tough time in medieval Europe. As with other times and places, their problems were due to the beliefs, habits and prejudices of the humans they lived among and the human society they were dependent upon. Cats were often treated like vermin, linked with the unseen forces of evil that the medieval mind tended to see all around, and even hunted and killed. Sometimes cats were murdered in ritualized public spectacles both at the level of the humble village and in the large urban centers like Paris. But there is evidence that the picture was not everywhere so bleak. Before I explain further, a little background is in order.

The medieval world of Europe was formed out of the collapse of the Western Roman Empire, which fell apart in the late fifth century CE and was replaced with a series of competing Germanic kingdoms. It's helpful to think more in terms of a process of transformation than in destruction with fire and sword. The Germans who inherited the remnants of Rome tried hard to be more Roman than the genuine article, adopting Latin and bits and pieces of the culture of the fallen superpower. Especially important was the apparatus of the Roman Catholic Church, which by the fifth century was an incredibly powerful institution that preserved the structure and many of the functions of the vanished Imperial government. The post-Roman kingdoms of Western Europe were Christian kingdoms and the Germanic "barbarians" who helped facilitate the transformation of the Roman world into its early medieval form were quick to convert. Most of the hold-out pagans would convert to Christianity around the year 1000 CE, often in order to forestall the aggression of neighboring Christian lands. Western domestic cats inhabited a world that was conditioned by the cultural and political force of the Catholic Church. Often, these forces worked to vilify the cat and contributed to a tremendous amount of cruelty and suffering.

Society in medieval Europe inherited the power structures and the settlement patterns of the late Roman state, gradually modifying them as part of a process of cultural change. As with Rome the medieval landscape was dotted with small human settlements, with the mass of the population engaged in agriculture. Settlement patterns tended to be more organized into distinct villages, with fewer individual farmsteads, but this is a generalization and the movement from one to the other was gradual and not uniform. The important thing to remember is that nearly everybody lived by farming and tending animals, and the labors of these agriculturalists made possible all the more dramatic elements of medieval life, like chivalry and feudalism or soaring architectural achievements like cathedrals and castles. Lasting from the fall of Rome to the fourteenth or fifteenth centuries CE (somewhat arbitrarily), the medieval period was a bridge between the ancient Greco-Roman civilization of the Mediterranean and the later cultural flourishing and economic expansion of the European Renaissance.

Early in the Middle Ages many of the Roman-period cities fell into decay. Rome itself, once a enormous metropolis of a million people, decayed into a largely empty shell where ten thousand inhabitants huddled amidst the ancient ruins. Once the center of the world, medieval Rome was important only because of the presence of its bishop, the Pope.

The medieval world was decentralized, with generally weak kings ruling loosely over lesser nobles who often could become effectively independent of royal power. This was especially true of the early medieval centuries, when the Church by default filled the resultant power vacuum and was more powerful (and wealthier) than the post-Roman kings and their kingdoms. It is hard to overstate the importance and the impact of Christianity and the role of the Church in shaping the history of medieval Europe. For our story about cats, the religious differences between pagan Greco-Roman antiquity and Catholic medieval Europe are important.

Pagan Rome absorbed religious influences from the Near East and Egypt (and in fact, Christianity was one such "mystery cult" as these are known to modern historians) and gained a greater appreciation of the cat in the process. The Roman fondness for all things Egyptian meant that they (at least certain individuals) also grew to have a greater appreciation for domestic cats, which were distinctly associated with Egyptian culture. As Christianity began to ascend to dominance during the later Roman Empire, it absorbed or abolished the other mystery cults one by one. The pagans resisted the expansion of Christianity for a time, but the new religion was eventually adopted by the Roman Emperors as the official state religion, which sounded the death-knell of the older pagan faiths. Mystery cults like that of Egyptian Isis, which looked favorably upon the cat were replaced with a newly powerful Christian power structure. Power was not accompanied by tolerance, and the transformation between pagan and Christian control was often accompanied with violence. Old pagan temples were attacked and desecrated, their sacred images smashed. Cats could be associated with the older pagan faiths, and because of this might find themselves targeted by religious zealots.

The basic worldview of medieval Christianity also helps explain the place of cats in Europe during the Middle Ages, as well as animals in general. While pagan religions had sometimes exalted certain types of animals as sacred (notably that of Egypt) the Christian faith placed man above the natural world that surrounded him. God had created everything and then placed man above it all, so that animal life was essentially there to be used according to the whims of mankind. Animals might be treated kindly and made pets, domesticated and made into working animals, or treated with extreme cruelty. They certainly weren't worshipped, as with the ancient Egyptians.

Worse, as the Christian church became ever more powerful, cats were often cast as servants of evil, in league with witches or the devil. These beliefs were not arbitrary, but based on aspects of feline biology that the medieval mind had no scientific basis for understanding. Firstly, cats were independent creatures who seemed to keep their own council. They were and are semi-nocturnal, which made them seem sneaky and untrustworthy to medieval Europeans. The Catholic worldview of the time was supplemented by all sorts of local folk beliefs, the remnants of pagan Roman and Germanic religious traditions. To a people who tended to associate darkness and night with unseen evil spirits, the dimly-lit prowling of domestic cats might make them guilty by association. Further, the reflective layer of cells behind a cat's retina (*tapetum lucidum*) that made them so at home in low-light conditions also gave them a potentially eerie appearance, to people already indisposed towards cats. As all cat owners know, when light conditions are just right a cat's eyes glow. The Egyptians (as you already know) looked on this feature of domestic felines as a beneficial link with the Sun and the god Ra who personified it. To medieval man, the glowing eyes of cats were more likely to be associated with malevolent supernatural forces, the evil spirits or demons that populated the medieval Christian imagination. Further proof of the sinister supernatural abilities of the cat was his or her capacity to survive falls that would easily kill a human. Again, the reason that cats can fall from great (sometimes very great) heights and live has everything to do with peculiarities of their biology and nothing to do with any sort of magical or supernatural ability. Of course medieval Europeans witnessing such feats didn't have the scientific mindset or biological understanding to explain things as we would, and so they turned to folk belief and religion to explain why it was that a cat could walk away from what would surely kill a person. Cats, you see, have highly flexible backbones, capable of bending and twisting in ways that ours cannot. Their relative light weight and flexible bone structure makes them good at absorbing the shock of falling from a height. Modern studies of falling cats have shown that they have the instinctive ability to twist themselves and land feet first, due to their flexibility and the power of their musculature. Compounding these attributes, cats seem to relax once they've accelerated to free fall. Apparently, once a falling cat feels the sensation of acceleration give way as terminal velocity is reached, he or she relaxes, which adds to the shock absorbing capacity of feline anatomy. These seemingly unnatural abilities of cats condemned them to the persecution of the superstitious and fearful. To a Christian world-view that included not only local folk belief in evil spirits but also a very potent evil force in the form of Satan (and his servants) it was easy to link the supposed unnatural characteristics of domestic cats with the evil forces of the supernatural that sought to harm man. As a result of these beliefs cats in medieval

Europe were sometimes attacked as the last pagans had been, violently persecuted by those who thought they were confronting the forces of the devil. Gruesome death was too often the lot of the medieval cat as a result of the superstitions and misconceptions of the people they lived among.

Archaeological sites provide certain types of evidence regarding the presence and place of cats in medieval Europe. Most of this evidence takes the form of skeletal remains, so a certain amount of guesswork is involved. It is fairly common for archaeologists to discover the bones of immature cats in excavations. It is probable that some (or many) of these cats were being raised for their skins, in the same manner as cats in rural China are today raised for slaughter, to supply furs to the international market. Remember that in pre-modern times, pretty much wherever you look, humans were reliant upon animals for fur, bones, skin, tendons, and other raw materials, to say nothing of the use of animals for food. At the same time, the amount and dispersal of the evidence suggests that they were also being kept as pets.

In one find from Cambridge, England the remains of seventy cats were recovered from a well. The cats had been killed and skinned, having apparently been consumed by the local inhabitants as a source of meat. This type of find should remind us that modern Western attitudes towards cats are something that only gradually developed. Medieval Europeans lived with a different understanding of animals and the natural world surrounding them than we do now, largely divorced as most of us are from nature. It might also be useful to remember that the modern world is no stranger to the cruel treatment of animals. While modern Americans don't generally eat cats, and we don't kill them during outbreaks of disease or as entertainment during harvest festivals, on balance we probably kill far more felines than medieval man ever did. In the US cats succumb to neglect, dying of disease or starvation. Huge numbers of cats (and dogs) are killed annually in animal shelters across the country. While their deaths are kinder than those of their medieval forbearers, they are no less dead in the final analysis. I include this relatively dark chapter in the history of cats not so that the reader can shake his head at the superstitious cruelty practiced by our ancestors: more profitably, the distaste we instinctively feel when we read about the death of medieval felines should be an opportunity for us to reflect on the practices of our own time, which are no less cruel (in their own way) for being largely hidden from sight.

There are numerous tales of cats being killed by medieval Europeans for a wide variety of supposed crimes and illicit associations. During the Cathar Heresy in southern France during the thirteenth century, cats were accused of being demonic minions in league with the heretics (at least according to Catholic authorities). The animals in question, where they could be caught, were killed by stoning. More mundanely, cats were linked with promiscuity, a trait they had been identified with since Roman times. This was unfortunate for the cats because medieval Christianity condemned promiscuous behavior and this tended to further bias people against cats. In certain circles it was considered good luck to bury a live cat in a newly constructed wall or building foundation. In some peasant festivals (there were myriad saint's days that punctuated the European calendar during the period) cats might be pinned to a post where villagers would try to kill the unfortunate animals. In urban areas large numbers of cats could be killed as a part of annual or semi-annual public spectacles. Sometimes this even included royalty, as in France when sacks of live cats were publically incinerated at the behest (or even the actual hand) of the French monarch. This behavior, considered barbaric to modern western sensibilities, lasted well into early modern times. Throughout history, vast numbers of cats have suffered and died as a result of the ignorance of mankind.

In the absence of germ theory, medieval man had no way of knowing what caused diseases or how they spread. Even the best doctors of the time, working off a combination of Greco-Roman and/or Islamic medical knowledge could do little to deal with infectious disease. In general, medieval Europeans suffered from poor health. Infant mortality was extremely high, as indeed it was until recent times, which made overall life expectancy much lower than it is in modern states. Parasites such as fleas, lice and bedbugs were part of life, nearly impossible to avoid given the generally unsanitary conditions of both village and city during the Middle Ages. In the countryside, peasants lived in close proximity with their animals, in many places sleeping under the same roof as their cattle and other livestock. Housing construction relied mostly upon wattle and daub for walls and straw or reeds for roofing material. Mice, rats, snakes and other unwanted creatures were always somewhere nearby. Given these conditions, disease was never far away. The grueling nature of agricultural labor, in the absence of petrochemical fuel and farm machinery, meant that the agricultural population (which means nearly everyone) was constantly strained by hard physical labor. Diets, especially for the poorer peasants, were often nutritionally deficient and limited to a few staple foods. All of these things together produced a population where disease was both rampant and totally misunderstood. Without a means to explain things rationally, people turned to folk beliefs and religion, blaming demons or spirits when somebody fell ill. Cats were sometimes seen as agents of disease during outbreaks, and were targeted by human communities because of this. Fearful people burned, impaled, drowned or otherwise murdered unknowable numbers of cats out of their misconceived notions of where disease sprang from.

In urban centers cats could suffer the same fate for similar reasons. After the fall of Rome the open and orderly Greco-Roman cities in much of Europe gave way to smaller, more cramped spaces where buildings actually arched over the narrow streets to touch one another. This was a side-effect of the breakdown of centralized control in the post-Roman world. Individual urban centers focused on defense by constructing walls and concentrating their populations within them. People thus tended to live in closer proximity in the new urban sites. Moreover, the Greco-Roman fondness for bathing was not carried over into the medieval period. In part this was religiously based, and in part it was because the sophisticated Roman plumbing to feed bath complexes was technically complex and difficult to maintain. This is not to say that medieval people never bathed, but they didn't do it with the same frequency the Romans had, and were therefore deprived of one means of combating the spread of disease. Crowded medieval cities could turn into breeding grounds for infectious diseases, and as in the countryside people searched for a scapegoat when this occurred. Too often cats were fingered for the crime.

The worst persecution of cats during the Middle Ages probably occurred during what we commonly known as the "Black Death" of the fourteenth century. The name itself is an anachronism, since the phrase "Black Death" was not used until centuries later, being coined in England. At the time, the plague epidemic we call the Black Death was referred to as "The Pest" or "The Great Pestilence," or some other formulation of the same sentiment. As with "regular" outbreaks of epidemic disease, Europeans had no way of understanding what was happening to them without turning to their faith. In medieval illustrations the plague is often shown as a series of arrows falling down upon the world from heaven. It was the judgment of God, the punishment for man's wickedness. Other than prayer, there was nothing they could do.

The disease (probably *Yesinia pestis*, the bacterium that causes bubonic plague) came to Europe from the trading ports of Italian merchants along the coast of the Black Sea. Carried back to Italy and Greece from there, it spread during the late 1340s first to the interior of Italy, and then onwards to France, Britain, Germany and Scandinavia. It was a disgusting and horrifying sickness that killed huge numbers of people. In some areas the population might be almost entirely wiped out, while other areas were spared. Overall, somewhere between one third and half of the European population died between 1346-1351 CE. In their terror, Europeans sought scapegoats to take the blame for the disaster. Jews, especially in Germany, were killed in large numbers, supposedly for poisoning wells to cause the plague. Lepers and other outcasts also suffered the same accusations, and the same fate. As for cats, they too were blamed for the spread of the disease, and like the Jews and the lepers they paid with their lives for the misunderstanding and paranoia.

Some modern writers have suggested that medieval attitudes towards cats, leading to their persecution and eradication, had a hand in the spread of the fourteenth century Black Death. The argument is based on the idea that during the Middle Ages Europeans killed so many cats that they caused a spike in the rat population, which in turn contributed to the spread of the plague as infected fleas fed upon the rats and subsequently passed the disease onto nearby humans. I am hesitant about such arguments, in part because the European population was already predisposed to outbreaks of epidemic disease. Moreover, climate fluctuations in the decades preceding the disease outbreak had led first to an explosion of the human population and then to a sustained series of crop failures and poor harvests. The population grew to its limits in the good times, and then starved (as much as 10% of the population could have starved to death in the single worst famine) during the bad. Europe right before the Black Death was filled with poorly nourished (and therefore immune compromised) people who were vulnerable to a virulent pathogen like *Yesinia pestis*. With concentrated urban populations and no prior exposure, conditions were perfect for a massive outbreak of disease. While the persecution of cats might have led to higher rodent populations in limited areas, cats could not be (and clearly were not) eradicated, and so I think it unlikely that they played a significant role positive or negative, in the apocalypse that was the Black Death.

There is a type of textual source from the period that suggests that cats were not universally despised. The medieval world developed a particular type of compendium called a "bestiary"(*bestiarum vocabulum*), which was a scholarly illustrated tome portraying various kinds of animals, many of them exotic. The illustrations of the bestiaries were accompanied by short histories of the animals in question, and often contained a moral component, meant as a lesson to be taken away by the reader. This was in part related to the Christian understanding that everything in this world was the work of God, and thus each particular creature had a place in God's ordered universe. By the twelfth century they were popular, especially in England and France.

Bestiaries, despite the Christian context, were documents that owed much to earlier classical-period works. Greek writers during the second century CE compiled the first bestiary-style texts, which were indebted to the works of earlier Greek and Roman authors, including the Roman naturalist Pliny the Elder and the Greek writer Aelian, who wrote "On the Nature of Animals" (*De Natura Animalium*) in the third century CE. The Christian authors who popularized the medieval-style bestiary were not so much interested in the factual/scientific study of the animals their works described. They were in fact much more interested in the moral or philosophical points that could be attached to the individual natural history of each species of animal. As a result of this they were free to embellish their works, resulting in all sorts of wild tales being promulgated about the animal species they wrote about. There are dozens of bestiaries surviving from the Middle Ages, and these documents allow us to have a glimpse into the medieval mind in terms of how it conceived of the animal world (at least as understood by scholars of the time). The illustrations contained within medieval bestiaries commonly portray cats in the act of catching rodents. Medieval art is highly stylized, so that the depictions of the avenging felines do not appear particularly lifelike to modern eyes. In fact the illustrations make the cats look more as if they're fuzzy policemen, arresting rodent offenders instead of seizing and devouring them. In this sense the portrayal of domestic cats from Roman-period mosaics are much more true-to-life. But nevertheless they are routinely shown performing what was considered a valuable service, one that had a direct benefit to man. Of course nobody really understood the link between rats/mice

Figure 7- A peasant dries his shoes while a cat and a dog enjoy the fire. 12th century. Kharbine-Tapabor / The Art Archive at Art Resource, NY.

and disease: they were thinking more in terms of the eradication of vermin that were attracted to the grains and other foods found in and among human habitation. In the bestiaries cats are not demons or tricksters, but working animals performing a valuable service.

As with other times and places, where cats were viewed negatively these sentiments were not universal. Even in medieval Europe, where there was so much potential distrust of cats, certain groups of people kept cats, both as insurance against rats and as pets. Millers, for example, who by the nature of their occupation were constantly surrounded by grain, commonly kept cats in order to keep away rodents. Merchants and fishermen kept cats for the same reason. As with the Romans, cats are too well adapted to life with people, and simultaneously too endowed with attributes that we consider "cute" for everyone to dislike them, no matter what society at large would   dictate.

Figure 6-13th century. Cats, apprehending rat thieves. Illustrated manuscript. HIP / Art Resource, NY.

I was reminded of this several years ago on a research trip to Sicily, where I was studying the ruins of Greek cities. Italian cities are filled with large numbers of semi-feral cats, and the half-starved and generally diseased condition of many of these animals is shocking if you are a cat lover (I eventually began to carry a five-pound bag of cat food around with me, so I would have something to leave for the strays I encountered). The attitude of the locals makes the wretched condition of these cats more distasteful, because in general people seem to ignore the masses of starving cats that live among them. By the time I encountered a stray dog sleeping on broken beer bottles in the Sicilian city of Catania my opinion of human society had sunk to a new low. One day, though, as I was trying to navigate my way back to the hotel, I came across an old woman who was unloading something from the back of small hatchback. I stopped to look because I noticed there were a number of cats nearby. As I watched, she filled a series of bowls with dry cat food and set these on the ground near her car. As she did this the cats moved closer to her to eat, and presently more cats appeared. These particular creatures were well-fed (even from a distance it was obvious) and were used to being provided with food. I realized that I was looking at a sort of "cat fairy" who fed the creatures because she liked them. The encounter made me think that pretty much anywhere, in any time, there was probably someone who liked cats, no matter what society at large thought about them.

Before we leave the medieval world behind I want to relate a story that probably isn't true. The thing is, I really wish it was. The story involves a particular breed of modern cat (actually two breeds, but we'll get to that below). The breed in question is the Maine Coon, a large and impressive long haired cat that originated in the northeastern United States. There is quite a bit that is distinctive about the Maine Coon, and not just the massive size that some of them can reach (upwards of thirty pounds for the very largest). Their personalities are almost dog-like—I am the proud owner of one, so I can attest from personal experience that they do indeed behave somewhat like dogs. At any rate, there are a number of origin stories about how the breed developed. The fanciful version has it that these cats came about through the crossing of a cat and a raccoon, which is of course genetically impossible. This tale probably has to do with the bushy tail possessed by Maine Coon cats. Another tale (also assuredly false) links the breed with Marie Antoinette, the doomed wife of Louis XVI of France, who met her end under the blade of a revolutionary guillotine in 1793. The tale has it that Marie had a ship ready to escape, and had loaded her pet Persian cats along with other belongings as she prepared to leave. Alas, Marie was captured (goes the story) before she could embark, but the ship sailed and made it to America, where the formerly royal cats escaped and blended with native tabby cats to produce the long-haired Maine Coon. But my favorite origin myth for the Maine Coon regards the discovery of Newfoundland by Scandinavian explorers from Greenland. This occurred around the year 1000 CE, and archaeologists have proved that the Greenlanders actually settled for a time in the New World before finally abandoning it, probably due to opposition from more numerous and similarly armed native inhabitants. The link between the Greenlanders and the Maine Coon is that a very similar breed of cat, the Norwegian Forest Cat, is native to parts of Scandinavia. The Scandinavian settlements on Greenland were eventually wiped out by climate change, but that didn't occur until the fourteenth century. At the time of the discovery of Newfoundland, Greenland was not isolated from Scandinavia or northern Europe, and so there is a possibility that cats from Norway were transported in stages from that country to Iceland, Greenland, and finally the New World. I like to think that my Maine Coon considers his ancestors to be Vikings (like their human companions), who came to pillage the mice of far distant lands. Whether a Scandinavian origin for these delightful cats is true or not, the physical similarities are enough to make you wonder.

In the Land of the Tsars

Russia has a complex and dramatic history, with a range of cultural influences from Asia, Europe and Scandinavia. The origins of what we know as Russia today involve the eastward expansion of Swedish Vikings (the "Rus") who conquered and blended with the native Slavic people in the region around Kiev during the early Middle Ages. The principalities of what became Russia grew wealthier and more powerful, to the point where they considered themselves the heir to Rome. This, in part, is the reason for the title "tsar," which is a variant of the term "caesar," the Roman title that developed following the death of Gaius Julius Caesar in 44 BCE. Call someone "tsar" and you're really calling them "emperor." Moreover, the Russian alphabet owes a heavy debt to the Greek alphabet, which moved north from the Greek-speaking Eastern Roman Empire centered on Constantinople through the missionary activities of Greek Orthodox clergy. If you've ever looked at the Cyrillic alphabet of Russia and thought that it looked like Greek, you were right.

The developing Russian state was dealt a savage blow by the expansion of Mongol power outwards from Asia in the twelfth century CE. The Mongols smashed in succession the armies of every European power they encountered, crushing the Poles and Hungarians. With the death of the Great Khan, Ögedei, in 1241, the victorious Mongol forces in the west retreated to take part in the succession of a new leader. In Russia, however, conquering Mongol armies did not retreat very far. While Poland and Hungary recovered from the Mongol advance, Russia would have to deal with dangerous and often oppressive Mongol overlords for hundreds of years. But it was not all fire and sword, and the Mongol state that bordered Russian territory (the "Golden Horde") helped certain Russian cities to enrich themselves through the action of the Silk Road trade routes that the Mongols protected. Due to the hundreds of years of interaction, Russian culture became heavily influenced by the Mongols, to the extent that it was a sort of amalgam of European and Asian cultural developments.

By the sixteenth and seventeenth centuries Russia was an expansionistic power, which had broken away from the tottering Golden Horde, driving back the danger posed by steppe tribesmen. From that time Russian tsars and tsarinas looked to the west, and European cultural influences began to replace the Asian customs that originated with the Mongols. From the time of the Napoleonic Wars onward Russia was a political and military force in Europe, a century-long period in which the strains of empire took their toll on Russia's people, economy, and political infrastructure. Those forces eventually culminated in the Russian Revolution and the overthrow of the ancient power of the tsars.

Buried within the larger history of Russia, there is a long and fascinating history of Russian cats. The Russian experience with the domestic cat sprang from the technologies associated with agriculture and the danger posed by mice to agricultural surpluses. But (as you've seen) the history of the cat is as varied in its own way as the history of mankind. As Russia is a Christian land, you might guess that Russian cats would have a similar history to those of contemporary Europe, with a relatively high level of distrust and periodic persecution and violence. In large part, however, Russian cats seem to have enjoyed a much easier time than their western counterparts. The place of the cat in Russian history is one that touches all levels of state and society, from humble villages and town workshops to the palaces of the tsars.

Cats were and are generally viewed positively in Russia. Some depictions of them in Russian folklore portray the cat as generally lazy and opportunistic, but they a not shown to be in league with evil forces as they were periodically in medieval Europe. As elsewhere, black cats are even today seen as bringers of bad luck: if one crosses your path you should either chose another route or let somebody else cross the area the cat passed over first, in order that the unwitting pedestrian gets the ill favor instead of you. But this is generally more than balanced by positive imagery of cats as guardians or protectors. Cats in Russia are commonly associated with prosperity or good luck, rather than the opposite.

An example of the cat's personality as understood through the medium of Russian folklore can be found in the story of the *Cat and the Fox*. According to this tale a man abandons his cat to live by his wits in a forest, because he is tired of the animal's overly-clever nature. The cat provides for himself for a time, eventually meeting a fox one day while out hunting. The cat informs the fox that he is in fact the new governor of the forest, sent there from Siberia. The lady fox takes him back to her home and feeds him, whereupon she discovers that he's a bachelor and proposes that they marry. After their marriage the fox, while out hunting, is accosted by a wolf who demands her catch. When she protests that her husband is the region's governor and will execute the wolf if he accosts her, the wolf expresses his surprise and asks to see the governor, unaware that it is only a cat. After the encounter with the wolf the fox similarly runs afoul of a bear, who like the fox is urged to journey to see the new governor of the forest, and to bring a food offering along with him. Eventually both the wolf and the bear make it to the fox's house to see the new governor, bringing gifts of food with them. Both animals hide to secretly glimpse the cat when he emerges and starts feeding on the ox brought by the bear. When the wolf moves to get a better glimpse of the cat, he rustles the leaves the bear has hidden himself under, and the cat leaps instinctively, thinking he's caught a mouse. When he lands on the wolf's head, the surprised canine is so unnerved that he flees into the forest. The bear suffers a similar surprise once the cat tries to climb the tree the bear has chosen for his vantage post. The bear leaps from the tree and lands roughly, following the wolf in flight. At the end of the tale the cat and the fox live happily ever after, and all the animals of the forest have learned to fear the cat. The tale highlights that the cat, both through his own cleaver nature and by shear good fortune manages to turn the tables on much larger and more fearsome creatures.

Cats feature prominently in Russian literature and folk tales, where the animals are roguish and independent, but portrayed in a positive light. Down through Russian history cats were linked with luck and prosperity. The sight of a well-fed cat was an outward sign of the prosperous nature of the home it came from. Cats were associated with the home, and would never be abandoned if the human occupants decided to move to a new location. Doing so would invite a loss of property. Presumably also the family members would be emotionally attached to the creature they shared their home with (sadly this custom is not prevalent in the modern world, for many of the thousands upon thousands of cats euthanized every year in the US and elsewhere are domestic pets left to fend for themselves by their owners). If a family moved to a new home, they would bring their cat with them and enter the dwelling only after allowing the cat to enter first. By allowing a cat to be the first to enter a new house the owners were ensuring that the creature would bring fortune and luck with it. Only the poorest and unluckiest households would be without a cat. Cats were seen by some as the possessors of magical abilities, and were considered special above other animals because of this. Shamanistic magic apparently held that a cat's whisker or a bit of their fur could be used to transfer these properties to potions or elixirs, and so these ingredients were included in folk alchemy.

There are a number of modern breeds of cats popularly associated with Russia. Of these probably the most well-known is the blue-gray specimen known as the Russian Blue to modern cat fanciers. It seems that these cats appeared as a distinct breed in relatively recent times, coming to Britain in the later nineteenth century aboard ships bound from the Russian port of Archangel (Arkhangelsk), which lies in northern European Russia on the coast of the White Sea. Russian blues were developed into the breed familiar to modern cat lovers by English breeders, who managed to salvage the breed after it was imperiled during WWII. Thus the Russian Blue owes at least as much to England as it does to Russia, though this is true to a certain extent for many of the modern day breeds of cat. There is another breed of domestic cat linked with Russia, one which has its roots sunk much further into the history of the medieval Russian past. This is the Russian (or Siberian) Forest Cat. These animals were native to Siberia and are similar in many respects both to the Norwegian Forest Cat and the Maine Coon. In appearance it is a large, well-muscled cat with a shaggy coat to protect it from temperature extremes. They are not very common in the US, even though they are the national cat of Russia.

First mentioned in England in the late nineteenth century, they were not brought to the United States until 1990 and remain few in number. It is only very recently that the breed has managed to achieve official recognition in international circles.

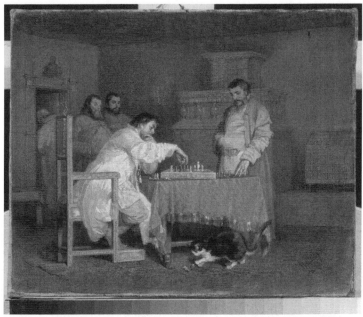

Figure 8-The Tsar plays chess, while the cat plays with fallen chess pieces. Russia. Scala / Art Resource, NY.

The history of the Russian Forest Cat stretches back as far as 1000 CE, with the animals being used to control rodent populations. Their impressive coats were an adaptation to the harsh conditions of the taiga forests they inhabited in Siberia.

With Siberian summer temperatures soaring to 100 degrees Fahrenheit and winters that were and are practically proverbial, the Russian Forest Cat needed to be capable of handling both heat and cold.   During the Middle Ages these cats were employed by Russian monks to serve as guard animals and as companions.   Later, shopkeepers kept them to safeguard stored food supplies. Well before the first modern cat shows, local Forest Cat owners would gather their animals to informally determine who had the "best" cat, with the determination being made in terms of overall size and weight (the process sounds similar to the somewhat informal judging of animals at country fairs). Like the Maine Coon, these are large and impressive animals. Their recent introduction makes them rare in the United States, but there is already a considerable amount of interest in the breed, so look for them to become more common in future.

The city of St. Petersburg actually hosts an entire museum devoted to cats, especially cats in relation to Russian history and that of the city of St. Petersburg itself. The site opened in 2008, and covers the history of cats, their presentation in artwork, and even demonstrations and showing of live cats. There is a similar museum devoted to cats and works of art depicting the creatures in the city of Moscow. It seems that as in the US cats are becoming increasingly more popular as pets, with the passage of time. The reasons are a least in part related to those already discussed for modern Japan: cats are easier and cheaper to care for than dogs, and they generally don't need as much space to house. In all probability this trend will continue, as the world's population continues to grow and concentrate itself into cities, placing a premium on personal space (but I digress)

Another, much more famous museum has a close connection with Russian cats, one that goes all the way to the eighteenth century. This is the Hermitage Museum, also in St. Petersburg, which is one of the largest museums in the world, holding a massive collection of priceless works of art. Cats first served the Russian court in an official capacity as mousers around this time: around 1745 the Empress Elizabeth ordered that large, impressive cats be gathered and brought to serve at the Winter Palace. The animals were shipped in from Khazan, and were divided into three official castes, in a manner similar to the prevailing caste system of Russia's human population. Shortly after this cats were brought to serve as guards (against mice, not people) at the Hermitage Museum. There they remained, protecting the valuable artistic works from rodent vandals. The cats of the Hermitage survived the Russian Revolution, and were kept on by the new Communist regime fulfilling their traditional duties. This state of affairs continued until the German invasion of Russia during the Second World War. Leningrad (as St. Petersburg was called at the time) was besieged by German and German-allied military forces beginning on the 8th of September, 1941. The blockade and bombardment of the city lasted for 872 days, until January of 1944. In terms of loss of life, it was the single worst siege of a city in all of human history. Perhaps 1.5 million people, both soldiers and civilians, succumbed to starvation or disease during the siege, and as many again during evacuations. Starvation was by far the largest killer in Leningrad. After all pets and domestic animals had been eaten, people started to turn on each other. Cannibalism within the city grew so prevalent that the Leningrad police organized special patrols to try and halt it. The unfortunate cats of the Hermitage fell victim to all of this in much the same way as the humans they were trapped alongside. Disease or hunger struck them down, or else they were killed by starving people for food.

Conditions were horrific within the city during the siege, an indescribable mixture of bombardment, starvation and death. Unburied corpses were common, and people grew used to the sight of them. Given the number of dead bodies, the rat population exploded during the course of the siege. The rodents had no qualms about feeding on corpses, and with no cats remaining to thin their numbers, the rodents became a menace. When the siege was finally broken and land communications were restored, the story goes that the government actually sent a special train containing cats recruited from throughout Russia in order to do battle with the plague of rodents. These cats then became the ancestors of the felines who make their home in St. Petersburg today. As for the Hermitage, with the end of the war cats could once more return to the museum and begin anew their protection of the treasures housed within. Today the cohort of feline guardians watches over the vaults of the museum as it has since the time of the tsars: visitors to the Hermitage are unlikely to encounter the cats, since they are kept away from the galleries where the museum's holdings are display. Instead they ply the basements and attics, though they do apparently have access to the gardens through the use of cat doors. Street signs in the area warn motorists of the presence of the animals. As for the cats themselves, they are taken in from the ranks of feral cats that walk the city streets. Once in the Hermitage they receive an official passport with their photograph, and a name selected to coincide with the individual's personality. Roughly sixty cats are on duty at the Hermitage at any given time, although their numbers aren't allowed to go over this limit. If there are too many cats some are retired by adopting them out to the public. They get to keep their passports from the museum as a sort of badge of service. Since no monies from the museum's budget are provided for the care of the animals, they are supported by the donations of the public at large and by funds contributed by the museum's staff. The animals have three full-time care-givers allotted for their maintenance, and the Hermitage has a basement facility for seeing to any medical problems that arise among the feline members of the staff. Each year there is a sort of "Tomcat Day," a holiday for the cats. They have become an inseparable part of the museum through their long association with the place, and today are a kind of mascot for the institution.

Not all Russian cats are as well off as the guardians of the Hermitage Museum. Russia's rocky economic situation since the collapse of the Soviet Union has meant that many pet owners are too poor to afford routine medical care for their cats, and spaying and neutering are not as common as they should be. In part, the place of animals and animal welfare in human societies is locked in a relationship with overall economic prosperity of the mass of the population. This explains some of the more egregious practices in poor rural areas around the globe in regards to the treatment of domestic animals. When people are struggling to survive themselves, cats and other domesticated creatures tend to suffer in turn. As with many of the cities in Europe, the United State's feral and semi-feral cat populations can overpopulate their environment, leading to shortages of food and the spread of diseases. There are signs that support for animal welfare in gaining ground in modern Russia. When it recently became trendy to tattoo hairless cats, making the animals in a sense living art exhibitions, there was a vocal backlash from animal rights groups, both in Russia and elsewhere. Hopefully in the future the expansion of economic stability and education concerning animal rights and welfare will continue to improve the lives of Russia's feline inhabitants.

A Cat most (Early) Modern

The designation "Early Modern Period" refers to a span of roughly three centuries between the end of the European middles ages and the beginning of the nineteenth century. This was a time of religious and political transformation. At its beginning the Early Modern world looked a lot like its medieval forbearer, but at the end many of the social and political structures that developed in the preceding centuries would be more or less familiar to modern people. In the realm of religion the period saw the weakening of church power as states become more centralized. This was exacerbated by the momentous changes of the Protestant Reformation, which split the venerable Roman Catholic Church in half and pitted Catholic against Protestant. As for states, they became modern, centralized bureaucratic entities, capable of waging war and concentrating resources in ways that far outstripped what had come before. Culturally and economically the beginnings of the Industrial Revolution began to transform humanity's relationship with the environment, beginning the process that divorced people from the land and led to the development of modern cities and mechanized industry. It also led to a general increase in wealth for large sections of the population, especially the growth of a kind of merchant class often referred to as the bourgeoisie. The bourgeoisie combined elements of what modern people think of when they contemplate the "middle class" and some of the wealth and political influence of the old nobility, which declined in importance over the course of the period. The new wealth of an expansionist Europe enriched not rural warrior aristocrats, as in the Middle

Ages, but an urban elite that based its wealth and socio-political importance upon trade and industry. This coincided with the growth of increasingly strong state structures that shifted power away from the old noble families and placed it in the hands of monarchs and (eventually) parliaments and other nascent democratic bodies.

This is not to say that everything was new in so-called Early Modern Europe. In many parts of the countryside rural life went on much as before. At the eve of the French Revolution in the late eighteenth century, for example, the economy of France was still very agrarian. Peasant farmers still predominated outside the cities, and their material and social worlds were very much as they had been for centuries. The near-total evacuation of people from rural farmsteads is a process that took place in the twentieth century, which in historical terms is practically yesterday. The history of cats in this developing world is one that is in many ways the same as it was in previous centuries. In the vibrant urban spaces that grew between the late medieval period and the French Revolution, though, cats gradually became more and more prized as pets, especially among the wealthier members of society from the middle classes on up. We have a considerable body of evidence that growing numbers of people were fond of cats and kept them as pets. Much of this comes from the ranks of the aristocracy or from artists or writers who were famous enough that later generations cared what they thought about cats (this general bias, as you now know, exists in pretty much all historical evidence since ancient times). But it still provides us with quite a bit of knowledge about what certain individuals (and perhaps groups of people) thought about cats as Europe shed it medieval past and became the forbearer to our modern world.

Prior to the nineteenth century Europe was not kind to the cat. The superstitions and stupidities of the medieval period seem to reach their apogee in and around the beginning of the Industrial Revolution. In part this was due to the peculiarities of the brand of Christianity practiced by our Early Modern ancestors. It was also due to a host of folk superstitions. In any event, the public, ritualized torture and killing of cats was a widespread practice throughout the villages and cities of Europe as the Middle Ages gave way to the modern world.

Popular notions about witches and witchcraft had a lot to do with the violence inflicted on cats. In one strand of thought cats were witches in disguise: this could be proved by beating the cat, whereupon you would later be able to identify the witch the next day by the bruises you caused the night before. Elsewhere cats were seen as the familiars of witches, or servants of the devil. They possessed dangerous magical powers, and you could interrupt these abilities by maiming the cat, which would end its supernatural associations.

The public spectacle of cat-killing was also tied to the calendar of Catholic holidays, especially the temporary inversion of the social order associated with Carnival. Drawing its inspiration from the Roman-period Saturnalia festival, Carnival was a time when the regular social order was turned on its head. It was a sort of release valve for pent up social pressures. The lower orders of society were temporarily allowed to test the normal bounds of social behavior. Carnival was accompanied by all kinds of normally prohibited behaviors, a kind of partially-controlled riot that preceded Lent, which signaled the return to the normal order of things. During Carnival it was not unusual for people to torture or kill cats in public spectacles, beating, hanging or burning them.

The historian Robert Darnton analyzed at length a peculiar incident of violence directed against cats that took place in Paris during the 1730s. The protagonists in the story were apprentice printers who worked for a cruel printing master. The master was ill-tempered and haughty, and represented the kind of social divide that was growing more severe in Europe during the period. Workers, as the Industrial Revolution advanced, were gradually seeing themselves divided from the bourgeois, the wealthy owners of capital. What happened at the printing shop involved a cruel master, disgruntled employees, and cats that the apprentices came to see as symbolic of their subjection to the master and his wife. The apprentices, first of all, were fed and housed in the worst possible conditions. Their chamber was dirty and cold, and they were fed scraps, and even rotten bits of meat that that cats wouldn't touch. In their apprenticeship they were overworked and risked running afoul of the master's harsh temper. They gradually associated these grievances with cats because the master's wife adored cats, especially a grey pet that was her favorite. The contrast between their treatment and the treatment of the household's cats was galling: while they starved and froze, the cats lived in luxury and ate fine foods. Outside their print shop the local ally cats yowled and fought and generally made it impossible to sleep. Eventually the apprentices found a way to avenge themselves on their tormentors, both feline and human. By irritating the master (with imitating the noise of yowling cats) the apprentices provoked him into ordering that the cats be gotten rid of: the apprentices then grabbed a variety of implements and hunted down every cat they could find, beating and killing them. The first victim was apparently the grey cat that was the beloved pet of their master's wife. Survivors of the orgy of violence were put on mock trial, complete with an executioner, and after found guilty were executed via hanging. The apprentices found this whole business to be practically hilarious, which is a shocking sentiment to modern audiences (especially cat lovers) who respond with horror to stories of such behavior. It should be remembered, as Darnton points out, that we must not think all pre-modern Europeans were sadistic monsters who routinely took pleasure in torturing helpless animals. The apprentices in the story were responding to a variety of social pressures, and were killing the cats as a form of symbolic revolt against what they perceived as injustice. Killing the cats was the same as killing and insulting the master and his wife.

While there are lurid stories of violence directed against cats in pre-modern Europe, there is also a large body of evidence than many people loved cats, and kept them as companions and pets. It is easy to stereotype different times and places as having this or that view of cats, but the reality is that probably in all times and places there was a mixture of cultural beliefs concerning these and other domestic animals. There are plenty of stories about the devotion of cat lovers to their pets (much of the evidence, of course, involves famous or powerful individuals, because it is their stories that are remembered). Cardinal Richelieu (1585-1642), for example, kept large numbers of cats as pets, going so far as to construct special quarters for them, employing servants to look after the animals. His care for them extended past his own lifetime: upon his death his will provided for the care of the cats and the upkeep of the servants who would look after them. Earlier the scientist and polymath Leonardo da Vinci loved cats, and thought that one day future generations of mankind would look upon the murder of animals in the same way they did the killing of humans. He often featured cats in his artwork. Alexandre Dumas, the French author who made Cardinal Richelieu an important character in "The Three Musketeers," loved cats as well as the real-life cardinal, though he didn't go to the same lengths as the churchman did with his superior resources. The stories of these and other famous cat-lovers are so numerous that should act as a check on our automatic assumption that cats were uniformly treated with hostility and fear, even in supposedly cat-averse periods like the European Middle Ages.

It is in the Early Modern Period where we encounter what would later become the United States of America. Colonized by Europeans from the early seventeenth century, the society that developed in the New World brought along with it the trappings and technologies of European societies, blending them and adopting them as necessary to local circumstances. Domestic animals were of course brought along, and cats came along with the by-then customary suite of animal associates. There they performed the same sorts of duties they did in Europe. Many New World cats would have fulfilled double duty as both pets and working animals, befriending their humans while also preying upon local rodent populations.

Cats were joined in the New World by a host of more exotic pet creatures, the taming of which became something of a fad by the eighteenth century. Squirrels were apparently especially popular in this regard, and were captured as young as possible in order that they could be tamed. Their predilection to chew (their teeth grow continually, so they are keen to gnaw on things like walnuts or expensive furniture) means that they were best confined for much of the time in metal cages. Paintings from the time period display these pet rodents with tiny golden chains around their necks, perching near (or sometimes upon) their human owners. Birds of various kinds were also popular as pets, and at least some people kept tamed deer. Obviously most of these exotic animals (and pretty much all of the ones actually depicted in painting) belonged to the wealthier strata of society.

I'm a Model

The earliest example of what we might consider a "cat show," the distant ancestor of the type of exhibition put on by the US Cat Fancier's Association (CFA), took place in Winchester England at the St. Giles Fair in the year 1598. We know relatively little about the procedures or participants of this event. We do not know how or according to what characteristics the animals were judged. But we do know that cats were present, in public, and that there was some form of quasi-official mechanism for ranking the animals and determining which one was the best one.

Cat showing (and for that matter the majority of modern cat breeds recognized by organizations like the CFA) as it is known today is distinctly British in origin. The first organized shows, like the one in Winchester, were all British. Later they would spread outward to Europe and America in the nineteenth century, but the roots of the practice are firmly English.

During the nineteenth century the increasing practice of showing cats led to a diverse and increasingly professional breeding program for the various breeds, resulting in the dozens of distinctive types now familiar with the world's cat lovers. Before the nineteenth century there was little effort put into any sort of sustained breeding, which explains some of the basic differences between modern cat breeds and those of domestic

Figure 9-Stitch is not pedigreed, but he thinks he is. Photo by author.

dogs. Not only were dogs domesticated over a longer period of time, they were actively bred to fulfill certain roles. The great physical variation displayed by modern-day dog breeds (think, for example about the contrast between the tiny shivering Chihuahua, which tips the scales at less than six pounds, while an English Mastiff might be forty times as heavy) is due to the purposeful breeding of specific traits for specific tasks. Even in antiquity there were specially "built" hunting dogs and guard dogs. The process of diverging from their lupine ancestors started early for dogs, and led to a vast diversity of sizes, shapes and coat types. The majority of dogs do not resemble wolves. In contrast most cats look much more like their ancient ancestors. Generally speaking cats demonstrate only limited evolution away from the ancestral type. The more radical departures from this generality, as for example with the nearly-hairless Sphinx or the short-legged Munchkin, are very recent twentieth century developments.

For most breeds it is only very recently that any sort of active manipulation has been undertaken by human breeders.

In America the first cat shows were concentrated in the northeastern states, with exhibitions of animals having something of the atmosphere of a country fair. During the late nineteenth century the Maine Coon was a particularly popular breed in America, until more exotic European and Asian breeds supplanted it. The archetypal long haired Maine Coon then declined in popularity until the twentieth century, when a resurgence of American interest in the breed again made it popular: at the writing of this volume the Maine Coon is one of the most well-liked breeds of cat in the US. I can speak from personal experience (being the proud owner of a catnip-loving dog-like specimen of the breed) that the current popularity of Maine Coons is entirely justified, as they are wonderful animals.

During the 1860s and 1870s cat shows because more common and steadily more popular in both England and America. In the US most of these were concentrated in the northeastern states, and they tended to be less formal than their British counterparts, with an atmosphere akin to that found at county fairs. In Britain things were about to get more formal, better organized and much more widely advertised.

In the summer of 1871, London's Crystal Palace hosted a particularly important exhibition of cats. Following a section about the restoration of the Rochester Cathedral (which apparently was "in some parts in a very bad state") the Times (London) issue of July 10th, 1871 posted an advertisement to what would be the very first modern, official, and well-organized showing of cats. The event contained nearly 150 cages of "fine and curious animals"...the advertisement mentioned some of the exotic breeds to be featured in the upcoming event, such as the Angora, Persian and one cat "of great rarity from Siam." Size was also a curiosity worth noting, with large cats (between 18-20lbs.) featured as an attraction. Organized and officiated by Harrison Weir, who not only wrote the official guidelines for judging the proceedings but also served as one of the three judges, the event was conceived as a means to promote cats to the public at large. The animals themselves were grouped according to body type into separate classes.

The conditions endured by many of the early cat-show contestants (feline, not human) would be considered animal cruelty today. In many cases the owners of pedigreed cats did not attend shows themselves, but relied upon intermediaries. Cats were crated up in various kinds of containers (boxes, wicker baskets, sacks) and shipped off, usually via rail, to the site of the show. They would often not be fed prior to arriving in order to avoid "accidents" while en route. Cats might endure having their legs bound in order to prevent them from scratching, a precaution against them damaging the coats that were so important during the judging of show contestants. From the perspective of the cats, these procedures must have been terrifying. The proximity of so many cats in close and confined spaces meant that diseases or parasites could spread from animal to animal. Show contestants also risked being harmed by humans who were not above cheating in order to win prizes. To this day some nefarious individuals resort to poisoning or otherwise sabotaging rivals of their cats, such is the human preoccupation with competition. The cats themselves surely do not understand any of this.

Cats at the show were in part grouped along class lines (perhaps expected in a society as obsessed with social class as that of Victorian England), with middle class and working class cats having their own separate divisions apart from the exotic purebred specimens put forth by the more aristocratic participants. The showing was quite popular, benefiting from a particularly Victorian attraction to public exhibitions. The English had given the world the organized cat show, and the proceedings in the Crystal Palace helped to formalize the process of showing cats. It also set a sort of standard for what was expected of such a show. For simplicity's sake the summer of 1871 can be seen as the beginning of the modern age as far as western attitudes to the domestic cat are concerned. From that point onwards they became more and more popular as pets, and the breeding and showing of cats began to develop to what we understand today. In September of 1871 the Times listed a census of cats in the city of London (how the figure was compiled was not included), noting that there were some seven hundred thousand of the animals in residence. As time went on more and more of these animals would become co-residents and family members.

The technical term for the modern practice of keeping and showing cats is "cat fancy." If you've ever gone to a pet store, you're probably familiar with the popular magazine by the same name which is devoted to cats and their care. Cat Fancy, which currently has a paid circulation of over 270,000 copies, was first published in 1965. In its modern incarnation each issue of Cat Fancy is dedicated to a single breed of cat, such as the Maine Coon volume I purchased when I found myself in possession of a specimen of that breed. The popularity of Cat Fancy is tied in part to the practices of modern cat shows, and the breeding and showing of pedigreed cats.

The American Cat Fancier's Association was founded in 1955. The goals of the organization are to promote the interests of cats and cat owners, pedigreed animals as well as non-pedigreed. Education is one of the goals of the organization. Harrison Weir would have approved of this, since his primary wish for the cat shows he inaugurated in the nineteenth century was to promote cats in general to the public at large. Later in life he grew disillusioned with cat shows as he knew them, stating that the focus for two many of the participant humans was on the competitive aspects of the shows, and the winning of prizes. Weir was more interested in championing cats than providing a venue for spectacle and competition for its own sake. In his view the humans and their interests were taking too much precedence. The ACFA, with its partial focus on educating the larger public, would have made Weir proud.

The world of the modern cat show is a distinct subculture among the larger body of cat owners. The majority of domestic cats (roughly 82 million in the US alone) are obviously not show cats. Mine are most definitely not pedigreed, and have idiosyncratic single names like most pet animals. The difference between the common house cat and the more aristocratic animals found at cat shows lies in the breeding and especially the documenting of bloodlines. Pedigree (or purebred) animals, by definition, are animals which produce like characteristics if bred together. Take two pure Siamese cats and throw them together, and you can expect to get a batch of smaller cats (after the appropriate waiting period) whose physical and behavioral traits match those of their parents. The breeding is carefully recorded, and animals with the right blood lines are highly valued creatures. The convolutions of the breeding of pedigreed felines can be seen in the lengthy official names of such animals, like Agonistes Commotion of Scrimshaw, the black male

Persian who was the victor of the Cat Fancier's Association International Cat Show held in 1996.

The CFA, or Cat Fancier's Association, is the dominant judging body for cat shows in the United States, and holds the yearly International Cat Show, which began in the mid-1990s and has continued annually to the present day. The rules for modern cats show vary slightly, with practices in England and Europe being different than those of the organizations based in the US. In CFA shows, the proceedings are extended over the course of one or two days, with a number of judges holding court in several rings at the same time. In each ring pedigreed contestants are brought forward and examined by the judge in that particular ring. Once this has been carried out the animals are returned to their cages and the next contestant can be judged. Both civilian spectators and cat owners can view the proceedings, and winners of the rings move up in the ranking until and overall champion has been declared. The list of champions of the CFA International is dominated by male Persians, indicative of the popularity of the breed's luxurious and long-admired coat.

In Britain the rules for judging cat shows differ from the general proceedings of their American counterparts. What is called "traditional" judging is sometimes combined with the ring-based judging more familiar in America. Under the "traditional" system, each cat is assigned a judge, with the animals all placed in plain cages. The judge evaluates each animal assigned to him or her and then reports back to the owners of each contestant. Judges may each select a finalist, and then these are whittled down until the eventual champion is found. This system is much more private than the spectacle that is a US ring-based show. The English counterpart of the CFA's

International show is called the "Supreme Cat Show," which is held each November in Birmingham.

As with everything else the advance of technology is introducing changes in the world of pedigreed cats and cat shows. The decreasing costs of DNA testing have resulted in a partnership between Texas A&M University and the CFA, allowing cat owners (as well as veterinarians) the ability to perform genetic screenings on their cats. As with humans, genetic testing can provide information concerning the susceptibility to diseases and genetic disorders. It also allows breeders more scientific control over the breeding of their cats, in terms of the genetic viability or desirability of potential mates for their animals. The process is just like that for humans: the cat undergoing the test is obliged to undergo an oral swabbing with a cotton swab, in order to procure cells from the inside of the mouth. In future it seems likely that further advances in genetic science and medical technology in general will revolutionize not only the breeding of pedigree cats, but the overall medical care available to all domesticated felines.

The CFA, which is the largest registry of pedigreed cats in the world, currently recognizes forty-two breeds, with the most recent addition the Burmilla, which was accepted by the organization in 2011. According to the CFA the ten most popular breeds of pedigreed cats include the following: Persian, Exotic, Maine Coon, Ragdoll, Sphinx, Siamese, Abyssinian, American Shorthair, Cornish Rex and Oriental. As noted above the CFA's annual championships have heavily favored the Persian, with that breed representing a large majority of the champions. The majority of these breeds are relative newcomers to the cat world, with specific breeding programs adding to the ranks of recognized breeds during the course of the twentieth century, or modifying the characteristics expressed by breeds of greater antiquity, as with the case of the Siamese as previously mentioned.

The CFA, in addition to providing the organizational structure for the showing of pedigreed cats and the educational support linked to this serves as an advocacy group for legislative matters pertaining to pets and pet ownership. Much of this pertains to the issue of pet overpopulation (a term the CFA disavows, preferring "population surplus") and legislation regarding the control of pet ownership. The overpopulation and euthanization of pets in general and cats specifically will be covered more fully below.

In The Greybar Hotel

The US has the dubious distinction of having the highest number of prisoners relative to population in the entire world. The state of Louisiana takes the crown as the absolute king of prisons and prisoners: for every 100,000 residents of that state, almost 900 of them are behind bars. Counting adults only, as of 2008 every thirty-first individual was a prisoner or recently released from the penal system. The prison population has exploded dramatically in the US, most of this in the last decades of the twentieth century. While the population grew almost three-fold since the 1920s, the number of prisoners is a least twenty times as large. The reasons for this are partially due to changes in the rules regarding sentencing. Most of it has to do the more-or-less misguided war on drugs, which has acted to incarcerate even minor offenders in huge numbers. There are so many prisons in the US that prison has become an industry unto itself. For many small towns scattered across the western states, prisons provided good pay in the aftermath of the collapse of American industrialization and the off shoring of manufacturing jobs. Political rhetoric often paints America as the land of opportunity, where it may be more accurate to refer to it as a land of prisons and prisoners.

This section is not meant to moralize about the state of America's correctional facilities. Instead, its purpose to tell, briefly, a particular story about prisons—the story of cats in (and around) prisons. It is a story that has elements in prisons throughout the world, and not just in the US. It includes both domesticated pets as well as feral cats in their colonies. Like much of the rest of this volume, it is a story that intertwines the histories of humans and cats in interesting and often intimate ways.

It is no fun, obviously, to be in prison. Conditions vary around the world, but generally prisons are lonely, dangerous and dehumanizing. In the United States the conditions of prisons are such that many relatively minor offenders are hardened by the experience of prison life, to the point where they become more rather than less criminal through their experience of the criminal justice system. Violence and sexual assault are difficult to stop behind the walls of prisons, and drug and alcohol abuse are widespread. If the purpose of prisons is to rehabilitate prisoners in preparation for their reintegration into civilian life outside the world of the prison, then they are largely failures. The story of the growth of US prisons is not a happy one.

Cats have probably always been at least loosely associated with prisons, in the same way that cats lurk around the margins of most human activity. Many prisons are home to (or provide the partial territory of) colonies of feral cats, who are attracted to the vermin which are in turn attracted to human activities. Prisoners often grow fond of individual cats from these colonies, although the relationship between humans and feral colonies is not always positive. The prodigious ability of cats to reproduce can very quickly lead to overpopulation, especially in areas where there is a lack of natural predation to keep the numbers of the cats in check. One women's prison in Gateville Texas was essentially overrun by hundreds of stray cats, to the point where officials were taking steps to eradicate the animals. Happily, local volunteers and animal welfare groups came to the rescue of the strays, combining their efforts in order to trap and spay/neuter the animals before releasing them back into their territories. This solution seems to work better than attempts at eradication—killing stray cats merely leaves a territorial vacuum waiting for other groups of strays to expand into. By sterilizing a colony, it is possible to stabilize its numbers. Once that occurs the colony remains in place and defends the territory, denying it other groups of cats. Elsewhere prisoners might be so fond of the strays that live around them that they resent attempts by prison authorities to remove or eliminate their feline neighbors.

Beyond the realm of stray colonies a more recent trend involves active programs that provide for the interaction of prisoners and animals of various kinds, including cats. Probably the first active promotion of a program that allowed prisoners to keep cats individually began in the mid-1980s in Switzerland, at the Saxierriet Prison for Men. The prison already had in place considerable human-animal interaction, in that the prisoners were involved in farming and caring for a variety of farm animals as part of their daily activities. The introduction of cats was designed to allow the prisoners the opportunity to take responsibility for another living creature. It was hoped that this would help provide structure for the prisoners and moderate their behavior inside the prison. Subsequent analysis of the program demonstrated that it was a success on a number of different levels. The prisoners benefited from the presence of the cats, and had something to devote their affections to while in the prison. Prison officials and guards benefited from the improved behavior of the prisoners. Similar programs have spread around the world, from Europe to America. Even South Africa has introduced cats into certain prisons, given the proven benefits of human interaction with cats.

My home state of Washington has a well-established record of integrating animals throughout its correctional facilities. Most of Washington's prisons have some form of program related to various kinds of animals, especially dogs. These efforts stretch back over several decades. More recently cats have been introduced into Washington's prisons in order to gain the benefits that they provide to all parties in the relationship.

Firstly, the cats themselves benefit from going to prison, as sad as it may be to say that. The cats selected for adoption by prisoners are routinely strays or castoffs from the teaming populations of animal control centers or private shelters. Even the best no-kill shelters struggle with having too little money and too little space for the numbers of animals that need care. Conditions are often much worse in public facilities that take in far more cats over the course of a year than they can provide for. Conditions in such shelters are crowded and psychologically disturbing for the animals incarcerated within, and the sheer numbers of animals tends to make disease inevitable. In many shelters, facilities are so limited that animals contracting simple upper respiratory ailments are euthanized due to a lack of space and the likelihood of the disease spreading to other animals. For many cats a trip to the local animal control facility is a death sentence. Thus, being sent to prison allows participant cats the opportunity to be provided for by an affectionate human and enjoy more space and less stress than they would have found in the cages of the local pound. Far fewer animals means less possibility of disease, and the cats are always monitored by prison officials in order to ensure their wellbeing. Most programs only allow prisoners access to cat ownership after demonstrating good behavior. As far as food and other expenses are concerned the funding is provided by different sources depending on the prison or the state. In some states funds are generated by donations from individuals and local animal welfare groups. In others the prisoners themselves must demonstrate the ability to pay for their animals, whether this is from money sent in by family members or by jobs held by the prisoners. Cats are usually confined by leashes of some form or another, but many have the ability to squeeze through the bars of their cages and roam to a degree around hallways and walkways. The relative confinement of cats kept by prisoners is in the end much preferable to the conditions found at most cat shelters. From the point of view of the cats, a human prison has a lot to recommend it over an animal death camp.

There are also considerable benefits to the humans involved with such programs, on both sides of the bars. The prisoners have the opportunity to care for another being—something that prisons do not generally do well. Cats are a safe and acceptable focus of attention and affection. Prisoners tend to routinely describe their cats as family members or children, and the animals serve as a moderating force on the emotions of the prisoners. Men who might be violent offenders—and many are, like the men keeping cats at Indiana State Prison, where more than two-thirds of the inmates are guilty of murder—find that having a cat forces them to control their behavior. Knowing that they have an animal to care for keeps them out of trouble.

Cats may be superior to dogs in terms of their ability to modify human behavior. While dogs are so adapted to human presence that they connect very quickly and deeply with human companions, the less-domesticated cat is a creature that has to be won over. They don't automatically demonstrate unconditional love and affections. Friendship with a cat is something that has to be worked at.

There may be some deeper scientific basis for why cats seem to be effective at moderating the behaviors of prisoners, even those serving time for violent offenses. Above and beyond the psychological effects of caring for another creature and being responsible for its life, there are the effects of the feline purr to consider. Purring is as odd sort of thing from an evolutionary point of view, and one that even today is not fully understood (despite considerable effort over many years). In Darwinian terms the act of purring seems an unlikely thing, if the only purpose of the purr is to express contentment. The act of purring uses energy that cats are otherwise loathe to waste. But observing the actual use of purring by cats shows that they use it for more than the expression of happiness. Badly injured cats also purr, which would seem to suggest that something more complex is going on. One example of this can be seen in a letter written by Ernest Hemingway in 1953, concerning the death of his cat Uncle Willie. Uncle Willie returned one day with two badly broken legs, one of them a compound fracture. The letter expresses Hemingway's' obvious pain in being forced to end his friend's life (he could tell that Uncle Willy was too badly injured to survive and therefore he ended his misery, distracting him with a bowl of milk). It also mentions, however, a certain amount of what might be astonishment (or respect for his pet's fortitude) concerning the fact that despite his horrific injuries Uncle Willie was purring. Writing in the 1950s Hemingway didn't have access to half a century of study concerning cats and why they purr, so he didn't see it for what it was. Uncle Willie's purring was not happiness or contentment, or shock, or absence of pain due to nerve damage: he was purring precisely because he was so badly injured. Recent studies have demonstrated a link between the frequency of vibration in a cat's purr (between 22-47 Hz) and a therapeutic effect on the body. Purring seems to be a function of the cat's immune system, helping to boost bone growth and spur healing. The frequency of a cat's purr even seems to have a salutary effect on nearby humans, reducing stress and possibly aiding our own healing abilities. So there is actually a real scientific basis of fact behind the contentment caused by a purring cat. The pleasant sound and sensation of purring is not something cat lovers like only because they're predisposed to loving cats. The frequency is the key, and it seems to be a lot more than simply sound and movement.

In part because of this cats are increasingly being introduced to hospital care facilities and nursing homes as therapy animals. Cats have in some instances what seems like almost paranormal intuition regarding illness and mortality (which seems intriguing considering the linkage of cats with witchcraft and the supernatural in so many societies in the course of history). One widely reported story concerns a cat named Oscar who could somehow tell when the elderly inhabitants of the nursing home he served at were near death. With a high degree of accuracy Oscar would sleep near people who were close to death, almost as if he were predicting their deaths correctly and acting to comfort them in their final moments. While the analysis of this behavior may owe much to humans "reading into" Oscar's actions, it does suggest that cats have the ability to use their much more acute senses to detect and react to wounds and illnesses. If you've ever been sick an noticed that your cat acknowledges your illness and attempts to comfort you or help you by remaining nearby, you've witnessed one aspect of this phenomenon.

Asphalt Jungle

There are some seventy million feral cats in the US, a number that approaches the number kept in captivity as pets. In some urban areas and adjacent surrounding territories the number of feral cats per square mile can rise into the hundreds. This is a much higher concentration of animals than would normally inhabit the same space given natural conditions in the wild. Cats simply breed too fast, you see, and cats which are denied contact with humans are close enough to their wild ancestors that they will go back to an essentially wild state. So the corollary with the high numbers of domesticated cats concentrated in urban spaces is that there are also great numbers of feral animals filling in the gaps between the natural and the urban.

In the wild, the numbers of cats are limited by factors such as the availability of food and the actions of predators which work to control their populations. Evolution has equipped the cat with an impressive reproductive capacity. A single female can have as many as three litters of kittens a year, and each litter might produce five new kittens that will rapidly grow to maturity and subsequently produce new kittens of their own. Technically, according to this scheme our hypothetical female could have tens of thousands of descendants within a year. Normally a lack of access to adequate food and the attacks of hungry predators limit this potential maximum. But human society has altered habitats and eliminated many of the predators, allowing

Figure 10-Feral cats and Roman-period substructure. Taormina, Sicily. Cute, but not friendly. Photo by author.

feral cat colonies to rapidly multiply if conditions are right.

A few years ago I witnessed quite a few of these feral colonies as I made my way through Italy and Sicily on a research trip. I was there to study Greek ruins and landscapes, but it was hard for me to ignore the large numbers of feral cats which lurked around the ruins and skittered their way down alleyways at my approach. Most of these cats demonstrated why it's hard to be a member of a feral colony: food is often inadequate and disease and injury are common dangers. Cats feeding on human refuse or even human leftovers put out by the well-meaning don't receive all the nutrition that they require to stay healthy. The proximity of other cats and the competition over resources mean that there are inevitably fights which result in injuries. Such problems are found among feral cat populations the world over.

Human activities contribute to the problem in another way, through the purposeful breeding of cats for the domestic pet market. Purebred cats especially are subject to this, with breeders seeing the animals as an economic opportunity. The resulting overpopulation means that many cats will find themselves in animal control shelters which do not have the staff, space or financial resources to cope with the vast numbers of animals that come through their doors each year. This means that annually millions of cats (as well as dogs) are euthanized in the US, year in and year out. According to conversations with staff members at my local pound, cats are put down if they contract upper respiratory ailments, because these can quickly spread to other animals in the confined spaces of the pound, passing silently through the gaps in the cell bars. Infirmary space is strictly limited, and cats that get sick are basically handed a death sentence. My own cat Maple was very nearly a victim of this process herself. In the US roughly twenty percent of domestic cats will find themselves in the grip of the animal control apparatus, and most of these will not return from their captivity. The problem of overpopulation is a real and cruel one.

Another serious problem is presented by cat owners who fail to spay or neuter their animals but who still allow them outside. Under those circumstances it is more or less inevitable that new litters of kittens will eventually result, and too many of them will end up with no new home to go to. Part of being a responsible cat owner is making sure that you're not contributing to the problem of overpopulation by ensuring that your cat or cats (at least) won't add new generations who have no place to go.

There is something of a war of ideas between two competing factions of animal activists. On one side are advocacy groups interested in protecting wild animals and birds, both common and endangered. On the other side are groups and individuals who seek to protect the interests and welfare of the large numbers of feral cats. Wild animal and bird activists decry what they see as an unnatural population of predatory animals wrecking havoc on wild populations of native species that are unable to defend themselves adequately from the natural skills of feral feline hunters. Their opposition is perhaps most heated where it concerns endangered populations that are already on the brink between survival and extinction, who cannot take the additional pressure of feral cats. Their opponents on the side of the feral felines argue in rebuttal that feral cats are being unfairly scapegoated for the decline of wild animal populations, especially birds, who are subject to much more than the predation of wild cat clans.

Though all cats (feral and domesticated) are blamed by some for the decline of songbird populations, cats in general do not actually catch many birds relative to the numbers of rodents that they consume. It should also not be forgotten that in urban areas most feral cats are at least partly scavengers as well as hunters. It is their adaptability in that regard that allows them to thrive, living alongside humans. The evolutionary development of cats has made them highly skilled predators mainly of rodents. In rural regions cats do not primary seek to hunt birds. If backyard cats or feral animals in urban areas take more birds than they normally would this is partly because birds are as attracted to human towns and cities as are cats and rodents. The increased population of all of these animals will then see the cats doing what they were designed by nature to do: hunt prey animals. And they will do this, to greater or lesser effect, depending on their individual skills. Many housecats, for example, are relatively poor hunters who catch prey animals only very rarely. My lone "outside" cat, despite a largely feral upbringing, is a poor hunter who catches the occasional lizard but only rarely manages a bird, despite the large numbers of birds who make their homes in Tucson for much of the year. As for my two inside-only animals, one could be an efficient hunter (he is also a rescued feral) but the other would starve if she had to rely upon hunting for her survival.

This is one of the reasons why abandoning pet cats is so cruel. Discarded on the assumption that they can fend for themselves, housecats in many cases do not have the abilities to be effective hunters if they are suddenly forced to fend for themselves. Often having been taken from their mothers at too young an age, they have not been taught the skills they need to be successful predators. My "outside" cat, Frank, seems to have a story similar to this. When I found her she (yes, she) was a starving kitten hiding beneath my house. There are a number of origins that are possible for her. Was she given as a gift, ultimately to be unwanted? Was she abandoned when someone moved (my proximity to the University of Arizona makes this a common occurrence) into a new place that did not allow pets, or returned home and found it more expedient to just jettison a pet that became suddenly difficult to host? Since Frank isn't talking anytime soon I'll likely never know, but what I can know is that she didn't find my neighborhood a bountiful place to live before she encountered me.

As a number of studies have pointed out, if cats were capable of destroying wild animal populations through their predation we should have already seen this process in action. In certain relatively rare cases there is evidence for this, mainly in terms of European expansion to locations where cats are introduced species and local

Figure 11- Skeptical alley cat, near the Roman odeon, Catania, Sicily. Photo by author.

animal populations had few or no natural predators. Such creatures never managed to develop mechanisms to cope with predation. The fate of the unfortunate Dodo bird which was exterminated on the island of Mauritius, roughly a century after its discovering 1598, is one such story. Even in that case the responsible parties included more than just cats. The cats were only one part of a multi-species assault on Dodo populations, which included pigs, dogs, rats and human sailors in addition to cats. Climate change on Mauritius came once deforestation advanced, with negative consequences for a species that may have had only a narrow band of habitation on the island. As there were no mammalian predators on Mauritius before Europeans arrived, the Dodo and other native Mauritian species had no natural defenses. Contemporary accounts of the Dodo note that the birds were entirely fearless of humans, and were easily caught by hungry sailors. Their ground-based nesting sites were easy prey for rooting pigs, and cats preyed upon young birds in their nests. At any rate, while cats did play a role in the Dodo's demise, it seems to have been a relatively minor one. It would also seem fair to note that all of the changes on Mauritius really began through the initiative of one introduced species in particular—man.

 If cats were capable of obliterating bird populations they generally should have already accomplished doing so. We can see by their inability to eradicate mice, for example, despite being specialized hunters of rodents, that cats are in fact natural predators occupying a necessary biological niche. They are not villains in a story about death and unnecessary destruction. If feline hunting behaviors are sometimes cruel, it should be remembered that nature is often cruel. This is a judgment that we humans somewhat unfairly place upon the workings of the natural world. Nature doesn't make such an analysis. It is only an equilibrium, hopefully, perpetuating itself alongside the nearly imperceptible process of evolution. Also, the deaths from feral and domestic cat populations among the ranks of wild birds pales compared to the potentially far greater numbers of birds are killed each year by means other than feline claws and jaws. Birds are killed by collisions with automobiles. They die (in massive numbers) through sudden deceleration upon meeting with man-made windows. They die through contact with power lines and human poisons and pesticides. This in particular may kill vast numbers of birds—the precise figure being unknowable—because while many are killed outright many more may be fluttering off to die secretly in the wild. Probably the biggest killer, dwarfing all the other factors, is the loss of habitat due to human activity. This affects bird populations in every country, world-wide. The loss of habitat in the tropics, due both to direct human activities (such as logging) as well as the changes caused by global warming gravely threaten migratory bird populations. Feral cats are surely responsible for inflicting some damage on wild bird and animal populations. But blaming seventy million feral cats for the decline of avian species worldwide is unfair, especially considering that cats prey on many types of creatures, and are really specialized to prey upon rodents rather than birds. An article published in the 2011 in the New York Times noted that about ten billion wild birds breed in the US every year. Perhaps it's time we stopped blaming feral felines and began to seriously look at the impact of our own activities, which are responsible for the mass slaughter of wild animals on an unprecedented scale, surpassing even the extinctions found in many of the upheavals recorded in the fossil record. Humanity should always look at itself first and then move on from there when we discuss who is responsible for unbalancing the order of the natural environment. We have an established habit of looking at dangerous creatures—lions for instance—when we think of dangerous predators, when we should easily recognize that we are by orders of magnitude the most efficient killers to ever walk the earth.

Controlling feral cat populations is a difficult task, which would remain true even if there were an abundance of money and manpower to throw at the problem, which there is not. Cats breed so quickly their numbers can practically skyrocket even in a limited area with only a few breeding animals. I once had a neighbor who consistently left his lone female cat outside, unconcerned that the cat was not fixed and male tomcats roamed the neighborhood. Within a year she was pregnant twice (that I know of) and pretty soon various kitties who bore a suspicious resemblance to our heroine began to wander around the borders of my house and sneak food from under the nose leather of my own cats. The cat population of the lot behind my house thereby expanded six-fold or so in less than a year. The math is not particularly difficult, but it is disturbing if you start to think about it.

Part of the difficultly lies in the fact that feral cats are difficult or impossible to tame if they have grown up in the wild. Perhaps because they are less removed from their wild ancestors than most people realize, cats can quickly revert to their wild state in the absence of contact with humans. Feral cat colonies are not composed of domestic cats but instead wild animals who are not amenable to attempts at domestication. Feral kittens, if they're young enough, can be taken and domesticated. These animals can then be sent through the machinery of the animal control bureaucracy to find (if they're among the lucky ones) homes and humans. The feral adults who cannot be so tamed will almost certainly find death instead. So organizations like the American Bird Conservancy, which advocates for more active (and quick) measures to control feral colonies are really calling for the slaughter of a significant number of animals. Only the youngest would be able to find homes, and there are very few resources available to house feral cats which will remain wild animals, fearful of people and not capable of adjusting to a settled life.

Probably the best means of controlling feral cat populations involves trapping the animals, spaying or neutering them to sterilize the colony, and then returning them to their territory. Their presence means that other feral cats will not move in and take over, and eventually the colony will shrink and naturally die of. This confronts the prime mechanism of growing feral populations, namely the extreme fecundity of cats, and is more humane than destroying the colony. It is not a fast process, though, since the cats in a particular territory will still inhabit it for years to come even in the absence of natural increase in their numbers. The cat people and the bird people are likely to continue their disagreement for the foreseeable future. Overpopulation in urban areas is a problem not only for feral cats but for domestic housecats as well. The unusually large numbers and micro-territories of urban cats are responsible for the spread of diseases and parasites, in much the same way it was for ancient (and not so ancient) human populations. With larger numbers of animals in smaller spaces close contact between individuals is increased, while competition for food means that individual cats are less well fed and subsequently more susceptible to disease. The large numbers of cats inadvertently caused by human civilization has meant that disease and parasitic infection are more prevalent. If you've ever seen feral cats in a large city you've probably noticed that they do not seem particularly healthy. Cats hunting in the wild have less contact with others and are less in danger of sharing diseases. This is not to suggest that living in the wild is easy, with the risk of predation and an unpredictable food supply, just that disease is less common. Leaving food and water outside for cats (your own or others) has the potential to be counterproductive, in that this is a keen way of allowing infectious diseases to pass among the local cat population. For this reason it is advisable to feed cats indoors and not leave stocks of food or water lying around. The incidence of diseases like Feline Immunodeficiency Virus (FIV) and Feline Leukemia Virus (FeLV) among feral populations, and

Figure 12-Feral female at the bus stop in Taormina, Sicily. She had been recently injured and had an open wound.

the readiness with which these may be transmitted to domestic cats makes it advisable to restrict cats to an indoor existence.

Disease and overpopulation are not, of course, the only risks faced by cats living amid human civilization. The relatively large numbers of cats in restricted spaces means that conflicts over territory or food become more common, and these can be more dangerous than many people seem to realize. All cats are territorial to a certain extent, and not just males. Female cats can be quite defensive about their personal domains and will fight to protect their access to it and to the food supplies associated with it. Despite their small size, battling cats are fully capable of inflicting serious wounds on each other.

Escaping death Row

Cats (and really all animals) owe a huge debt of gratitude to a man named Henry Bergh. Bergh was the son of a wealthy New York shipyard owner, part of a sort of Northeastern American aristocracy of the nineteenth century. His position in society was more or less guaranteed by his father's wealth. Educated and urbane, Bergh served in a diplomatic capacity in the Russian city of St. Petersburg beginning in 1862, having been appointed there by President Lincoln. In addition to his posting to Russia Bergh travelled widely throughout Europe and Asia. During his sojourns he determined to become an advocate for animal welfare, based on his experiences of the mundane everyday cruelties inflicted upon working animals as well as animal-based spectacles such as staged dogfights and bullfights. When Bergh returned to New York in the aftermath of the Civil War he worked to draft legislation aimed at protecting the basic welfare of animals. Travel in England had familiarized Bergh with the English "Royal Society for the Prevention of Cruelty to Animals," a body that provided both a model and inspiration for Bergh's activities in New York. The New York state legislature adopted and finally passed the first animal cruelty laws in the United States in 1866, after which Bergh proceeded to establish the American Society for the Prevention of Cruelty to Animals, or ASPCA. The Society grew rapidly, fed by the monetary donations of wealthy individuals and a sizeable sum donated personally by Bergh and his wife. When Bergh began his campaign to improve animal welfare no state in the newly reconstituted Union had legal protections preventing animal cruelty. The adoption by New York of such legislation in 1866 was the first of a rapidly growing list of state laws aimed at protecting the wellbeing of animals, most of them influenced by or based upon what Bergh had managed to bring about in New York State. By the time of Bergh's death in the late 1880s fully thirty-seven out of thirty-eight states had followed in New York's footsteps.

The early activities of Henry Bergh and the ASPCA were focused upon working animals rather than cats and dogs. Large nineteenth century cities like New York were in a sense carried on the backs of thousands of animal laborers who pulled carts and wagons, and otherwise provided the motive force and muscle power that would later be supplanted by fossil fuels and machine technology in the following century. Many of these workers were treated very poorly by their human masters. Animal rights activists like Bergh railed against the cruel mistreatment of mules, donkeys and horses whose labors pulled and carried the things that kept the machinery of the great cities running. Many of those animals were poorly fed and subjected to beatings and whippings in order to ensure their compliance. The ASPCA's actions improved the lives of these animals in many ways, from helping to enforce laws that prohibited physical abuse to providing for medical facilities and ambulances to care for injured animals. Bergh and the organization he founded worked tirelessly to stop illegal dog fighting, to construct fountains to provide water for working animals, and to improve conditions in slaughterhouses.

Given the number of working animals that nineteenth century society depended on it should be no surprise that the ASPCA concentrated its energies on their behalf. But dogs and cats were not ignored. Dogs actually fell under the mandate to care for the wellbeing of working creatures, since many dogs were employed in places like

New York as miniature draft animals. Often these canines were cared for in only the most rudimentary sense of the word, being left to their own devices to scavenge for food. The city of New York (and other cities) had a particularly draconian method of dealing with the many stray dogs that roamed the city's streets and alleys: they were captured by city dogcatchers and placed in metal cages, there to be drowned in the city harbors. Hundreds of such animals met their fate in this way, day in and day out. As for the dogcatchers, they were paid on a per-animal basis, and therefore the more unscrupulous were not above seizing pet animals in order to pad their incomes. Bergh and the ASPCA had their hands full in the face of such practices as this, but their continued perseverance paid increasing dividends by the end of the nineteenth century.

Cats were just as ubiquitous as ever in nineteenth century cities. New York to this day is home to a vast population of rats, by some estimates equal to the human population. The rodent inhabitants of the city provided a food source for the resident cats, who also scavenged on the castoff leftovers of human society. The ASPCA managed to improve the welfare even of these animals, one small step at a time. In the very year the ASPCA was founded a man named David Heath was given a (brief) jail sentence and slapped with a $25 fine for beating a cat to death. Such a fine was no small sum in the middle of the 19th century.

Over the course of the twentieth century the ASPCA and other animal welfare organizations shifted their focus away from working animals according to the changing nature of animal ownership. The reliance upon animals for labor power has obviously diminished greatly from the days when streetcars were driven by actual horsepower and plows were pulled by oxen. Petrochemical fuels of various kinds have radically transformed human civilization in a bewildering variety of ways. The animals in partnership with man have had their lives similarly impacted by these transitions. Many of our animals have become pets, and so animal advocacy groups now focus their time and energies on the wellbeing of these animals.

In the nineteenth century cat ownership was growing as the creatures became more popular as companion animals. But the real explosion of interest in hosting cats as household pets came in the aftermath of the Second World War. This was in large part due to the proliferation of a variety of products that made keeping cats indoors easier for the owner. Just as with the postwar boom in human consumer society that introduced processed foods and TV dinners for people, commercial cat food made it possible to feed an entirely indoor animal. Also crucial for feline maintenance was the creation of a variety of cat litters that are the dirt-substitutes used by house-bound pets. Our cats are now as dependent upon commercial society as we have become ourselves. The march of modern civilization has carried along cats the same as it has people.

From the point of view of homeless cats publically funded animal shelters are often places you go to die. The constraints of space and limited finances means that there are more animals that can be cared for, and so therefore many thousands of animals are euthanized annually. A better fate is granted to those cats which end up in so-called "no kill" cat shelters. These organizations usually operate on very limited budgets and rely upon donations and volunteer labor to operate. The best of them are fantastic places where cats are saved from an unnecessary doom. Cats are adopted out of these shelters in return for the payment of a modest fee and some basic paperwork. The atmosphere of no kill shelters is generally much better for the cats. Some animals end up staying at a particular shelter for long periods of time, since there are still too few homes for every cat that needs one. But in the no kill shelter they won't be condemned to death arbitrarily, as they very likely might at animal control facilities.

Not all no-kill shelters are created equally. The poorer examples (in several senses) suffer from overcrowding and a lack of adequate medical services. I've seen cat shelters where obviously sick animals mix freely with (up to that point) healthy individuals, likely spreading disease. Upper respiratory infections, eye diseases and various kinds of mites and other parasites can be a scourge in these places. Usually the humans in

Figure 13-Lounging alley cats, Catania, Sicily. Photo by author.

charge mean well, but are constrained by a lack of funds and insufficient labor power. As always, there are simply too many cats.

If this section can end on a moralizing note (and I think it should) I would stress the importance of adopting cats, especially adults, from out of the clutches of animal control organizations. The animal that you adopt from the local pound is one more that won't be executed because of a lack of space. Many of the people who casually allow their cat to produce a litter of kittens are actually contributing to a very serious problem of feline overpopulation. Kittens are one of the cutest things imaginable, but there are already too many cats. Pet cats should all be spayed or neutered, to help save the lives of unborn future generations who would be simply be "processed" through the machinery of local animal control facilities. If you're looking for another cat the act of checking the website of your local pound is quite simple. Every cat adopted thusly is spared the executioner's needle.

A Cat's Home is His or Her Castle

Most domestic cats in modern times are housecats. What exactly "housecat" refers to is somewhat indistinct, because many pet cats are allowed to roam outside at least some of the time. My childhood cat was more akin to a "barn" cat in terms of living predominantly outside, but most cats today spend much of their time indoors. Cats adapt well to this type of confinement, even though if left to their own devices in the wild they roam over much larger territories than they have available in the average house. This is especially true of male cats, but females too can have expansive territories in which to hunt and raise their kittens. If kept in the confined quarters of a modern home, a certain amount of adaptation is called for.

Basically, their behavior is the same but on a reduced scale: indoor cats are fully capable of determining what counts as territory belonging to them, even though this may be as limited as a particular spot on the couch. This is territorialism in miniature, and a home with multiple cats (like mine) is witness to a negotiated struggle over the bits of territory within it. Some cats are more territorial than others, and manage to share their territories without too much trouble. Others seem much more protective of their privileges, and expect rival cats to respect their ownership of certain spaces. My home has seen a number of power struggles revolving chiefly around who has hegemony over the couch: Maple owns the best spots on the back of it and does not allow access to competitors. Stitch may approach the couch and scratch it, and is allowed on the arms as long as he maintains a respectful distance. But the back belongs to Maple. In response to this Stitch has staked out his own territory in the front room of my house, and claims an area in the front closet where he sleeps on old office supplies. It is a relatively non-violent system that works well for all involved, although I sometimes feel bad for the discrimination of Maple's couch-dominance.

Introducing more than one cat into a home can be tricky depending on the nature of the cats involved. Many people have no problem adding additional cats into their clan, with unrelated animals quickly becoming inseparable friends. Other people have something more akin to my experiences. The addition of my newest cat (Stitch) caused an burst of resentment from Maple, who seemed infuriated and insulted by his presence. She was also not fond of me (at the time), and would leave the room when I came around in order to demonstrate her unhappiness. It took Maple about two weeks to get over the issue, and even now, several years later, she is at best only tolerant of Stitch's presence. My mistake (in part) was in introducing the new cat too abruptly into the territory of the resident owner (Maple). I should have quarantined Stitch until Maple was more used to his scent, which may have eased the transitionary period a bit. This is generally a good practice for anyone adding a new addition to the household. If the old cat has time to adjust to the scent of the newcomer you run less risk of hurting anyone's feelings.

Cats are not the only creatures who have to go through a period of adjustment as part of the symbiotic relationship with human housemates. People have to moderate their own behaviors in order to conform to the demands of feline co-residents. This can take a wide variety of forms depending on the personalities of both the humans and the cats. Maple has a habit of getting bored early in the morning, and she alleviates this by waking me so that I can entertain her. Maple does not work, however, so getting up in the middle of the night to play is not something that concerns her. To an academic enjoying his last minutes of sleep prior to preparing to teach an early class "cat time" is sometimes less than adorable. If you own a cat (or cats) you've got to be prepared to put up with odd sleep schedules, from time to time.

Claw-related furniture damage is a problem most cat owners will face as some point. To a cat, your brand new couch is a marvelous, cushy scratching post. Cats don't understand economics and so they don't consider the mauling of your furniture to be a problem. Humans usually don't see things in the same light. Cats can be encouraged to scratch appropriately specialized scratching posts, and a variety of products exist to help facilitate this. Double-sided tape and scented sprays can be used to ward off unwanted scratching, though some form of acceptable scratching medium has to be provided to cats or they can't hone their claws. In the wild cats scratch because doing so sloughs off the outer layers of their claws and keeps them sharp for hunting. If the cat can't scratch (of if the cat is lazy like Maple and doesn't like to scratch) then claws will eventually require trimming, which can be difficult (and painful) depending on how your cat feels about manicures. Overly long claws result in a cat that snags on the carpet. I recommend trimming by way of ambush, in which a snoozing cat has one or two claws snipped off before he or she has time to respond. Several repetitions of this and you've got a snag-free cat without any hard feelings in either direction.

The practice of declawing is used by some cat owners who seem to value their property more than their friends. If you study the process of declawing, it appears more and more like the barbarism that it is. In order to declaw a cat you're not simply trimming off their fingernails, as some humans seem to understand the process. A cat's claws are connected, in fact, to the last digit of each finger or toe. This digit is curled backwards over the preceding digit and controlled with a pair of tendons that allow the cat to uncurl and extend the claw. In order to declaw a cat this digit is surgically removed. Nobody wants someone to come by and remove the tips of all their fingers, and so cats likewise don't respond well to declawing. It is a deeply traumatic experience for cats and should never (in my opinion) be performed. If you value your furniture over your friends, then you should just hang out alone with the furniture you like so much. Cat people understand that some damage is inevitable. My own cats have managed to more or less shred my couch over the past several years: at this point I accept their behavior because it's already beyond repair. So much for a snazzy-looking

Figure 14-Regular trimming produces a snag-free cat. Photo by author.

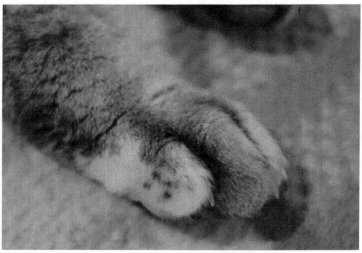

home.

Cat ownership comes with certain hazards beyond potential damage to furniture. Anyone who is already a cat owner is likely more than aware of these. For prospective cat people, they are something to bear in mind. First, owning a cat means that you'll be cleaning up after them in various ways. I don't mean litter box care, which goes without saying. Specifically, I'm referring to the connection between cats and vomit. Cats are pukers, by nature. Their digestive systems are designed with that in mind, and cats deal with digestion problems or stomach upset by means of regurgitation. The formation and expulsion of hairballs is a related subfield of the subject of vomiting cats. Cats have raspy barbed tongues, which helps them eat and drink and which they utilize as a cleaning tool to wash their fur. This is because cats are predators and are themselves subject to predation. Cleanliness is an aid both to successful hunting expeditions and a means to avoid ending up on the menu of larger carnivores. By remaining clean and odorless, the cat is protecting its own interests in several respects. The problem with this is that the combination of a rough tongue and more-or-less continual shedding means that every cat ends up ingesting various amounts of fur, depending on the severity of the shedding and the particular nature of the individual cat's coat. Cats who lick up too much fur tend to develop clots of fur, or hairballs, in their digestive tract. Some of these are passed through the digestive system without further problems, but sometimes the cat is unable to rid itself of the hair blockage in this way. The matted hair that your cat vomits up on your new living room rug after a spate of coughing and wheezing is the alternative method to watch for. Some cats produce quite a few of these, while others are only rarely afflicted with them. Regardless, most cat owners will have to get used to dealing with the various materials that their cats gack up in the course of their daily activities. Relax, this is normal, nothing to see here.

The perspective cat owner should prepare him or herself to be wounded. Seriously. Cats have a variety of weapons (fewer if the cat is declawed, but this should be avoided as I argue above) and they are not particularly shy about using them. Certain cats can react if over stimulated by their owners, and bites and especially scratches are relatively common. Again this varies from cat to cat. In my own experience cats who are socialized thoroughly from an early age are generally less subject to this, but my observable sample is based on the relatively small number of cats I've owned myself. So I could be completely wrong about this. But I suspect that this has something to do with it. The two semi-feral cats I've had were both animals that needed to be treated with care or their inner savage would come to the fore and go berserk. Even some very mild cats can get too excited if they're over stimulated (pet them too much, use the bird toy too rigorously, too much brushing, etc.) and they can respond with an application of tooth and claw. Most of the wounds that cats inflict upon their owners are quite mild, so they generally aren't something to worry too much about. Deep bites (which you shouldn't experience) should be treated with caution, because the bacteria in a cat's mouth are fully capable of causing a dangerous infection. This of course is true of other animals, including humans, so this is not meant to unfairly vilify kitties. Use your own judgment, but a deep bite (a "real" bite) should be dealt with professionally.

Nearly all of the wounds cats inflict on their owners come in the form of scratches delivered in the throes of heightened excitement. These are shallow and not generally dangerous, though they should of course be washed and cared for to insure against complications. Cat claws are not sterile, after all. This is one of the reasons that cats should be watched around toddlers and young children. Cats can respond to what they consider rude treatment with violence. The claw demands respect, as it were. It is important to remember that cats don't mean anything particularly serious by their periodic resort to violence. Observation of cats in a multi-cat home provides ample proof that they behave similarly to one another. The occasional bite or scratch is par for the course as far as cats seem to be concerned. Some small amount of clawing is only one form of communication that cats use, and play can often go overboard into the realm of wounds and temporary hurt feelings. But there is nothing unusual in this and cats don't hold grudges as humans might. The comparable behavior in human societies is called domestic abuse.

Housecats, obviously, have been removed from their natural habitat and transplanted into the artificial world of human households. One of the most fundamental changes associated with this occurrence is that modern cats have had their natural diets, which consisted variously of small rodents, birds, lizards and insects with man-made foodstuffs. On a cat-per-cat basis this is not such a bad thing. Housecats can be fed commercial-grade cat kibbles and end up living far longer in suburban captivity than feral animals who fend for themselves but who eat a more natural diet. Still, the substitution of processed cat foods is a change away from the natural, and does not come without certain complications.

Figure 15- Cats need excercise. The ball always alludes Stitch, yet he perseveres.

In essence the process of cats adopting a "civilized" diet is similar to the same ancient process by which humans gave up being hunter gatherers and took up farming. Modern feline diets (at least if you mean in developed countries where processed foods hold sway) are more monotonous and not entirely keeping with the types of foods that they would eat if left alone in the wild. The exchange, as with humans, has been a predictable and stable food supply for the variety and specific nutrition of a varied wild diet. Ancient humans made this leap thousands of years ago, gaining a larger population and a (hopefully) predictable food supply and losing the variety of food types that they would have eaten before settling down. Cats gave up the menagerie of small prey animals for kibble and canned cat food. Cats eating this food can be quite healthy, perhaps especially if higher quality processed foods are provided on a consistent basis. This is not necessarily the case with cheaper bulk cat foods: a friend's cat once quickly turned into a fuzzy white basketball when fed on cheap store-bought kibbles (better food reduced the weight gain). If possible cats should be fed the highest quality food, something that approximates as closely as possible their wild diet. Too often the foods we feed our cats (just like the foods we feed ourselves) are nutritionally poor and loaded with unwanted additives. Cat owners should pay close attention to the diets of their pets, noting that many processed cat foods are poor reproductions of what a cat would eat if left to his or her own devices in the wild.

In technical terms, cats are obligate carnivores, who consume the flesh and bones of small prey animals in the process of their daily hunting activities. A glance at the contents of cat's mouth is an excellent tutorial in the types of foods they are designed by nature to eat. Cats are not really capable of chewing as humans are, as their teeth and jaw structure are specialized to make shearing cutting motions, slicing apart their prey into bite-sized chunks that may then be swallowed. If you've ever wondered why your cat switches his or her head from side to side while he or she is eating, there is your answer. Cats are not capable of grinding their food. They normally get all the vitamins and nutrients they need from the meat, bones and skin of their prey. A cat's digestive tract is relatively short and optimized for digesting other animals. They do not normally eat plant foods, much less grain-based foods. One of the problems with mass-produced cat foods is that they commonly contain both vegetable products and grains of different kinds. It is only through processing that these types of foods are digestible by cats. Like our own food supply, what modern housecats eat on a daily basis is quite different from what evolution seems to have intended.

Opinions on the types of foods that are best for cats vary considerably. The pet food industry is large and varied in the modern US, with companies both large and small churning out dozens of different kinds of cat foods under a multitude of brand names. The diversity of types means that some are more or less expensive and more or less like what cats would eat in the wild. Many common store-bought cat foods include things that cats in nature do not eat: rice, oats, corn, and various types of vegetables. They also usually contain the by-products of human food processing, the leftover unsightly bits from industrial animal farms. Of course they also contain (as with human processed foods) various kinds of preservatives and stabilizers. All of these things may by problematic for the health of the modern housecat. One strand of thought is that cats should be fed high-quality wet cat food, rather than dry kibbles. The best of these are much more like the diets cats would eat in the wild, and it avoids possible bacterial contamination stemming from the feeding of room-temperature dry cat foods. There are also higher-end dry foods that omit most of the unnatural additives that cheaper foods contain.

The ultimate in cuisine for the modern civilized cat may be the so-called "natural" or raw-meat based diet. Such food can be bought (at least in some cities in high-end grocery or pet stores) as a prepared product, or it can be manufactured by dedicated cat owners if they are willing to put in the time and effort required. This option is more expensive than the more-processed diets, and if you make the food yourself it requires some input of labor. The aim of a raw-meat based diet is to reconstruct as closely as possible the types of foods that a cat would consume in the wild. The prospective raw-diet chef needs to acquire a quality meat grinder and source a variety of different ingredients and additives in order to prepare the food. Meat used to make cat feed must be high-quality, as fresh as possible and ideally organic. Meat and bones must be ground (cats eat the skeletons and skin of their prey) carefully, to ensure that cats get proper nutrition. Recipes vary (these can be found with a short glance at the internet) but usually include a variety of additives to make up for the fact that the meat being used does not constitute the entire animal. Advocates of the raw diet argue that it is nutritionally superior to the additive-laden commercial cat foods that are available in supermarkets and chain pet stores and provides a variety of benefits to both the cat and the owner. Cats are generally healthier and more active on such a diet, while their owners can likely expect to see a less offensive litter box odor. Thus the diet we should be feeding our cats is similar to the diet that we (in the west) should be eating ourselves: namely something more varied, more natural, less processed and chemically manipulated.

For My Cats

I've loved cats since I can remember. Literally one of my earliest memories is sitting on the curb in front of my parent's house and petting the neighbor cat which came over to investigate me. My Mom was outside raking leaves or sweeping the curb, I don't remember which: what I do remember is the neighbor lady, much less friendly than the feline, yelled at me for touching her pet. In turn I think my Mom yelled back at the neighbor, telling her that I wasn't hurting her cat. It was an early lesson in the difference between humans and cats, I think.

It was five years before I got a cat of my own. My Dad was and is more of a dog person, and we had Vizla hunting dogs who alternated between lounging around our back yard and periodically going pheasant hunting with Dad. When I was eight years old I went with my Dad and my brother to a local pet store, for what reason I can't remember. It wasn't to get a cat, I know that much. At some point my Dad found me glued to the cage of a small Siamese kitten in the dog and cat area of the store, and either succumbed to begging or could tell by looking that I really, really wanted that cat. The kitten in question spent the seven miles or so back to our house velcroed to the seat cover of our 1965 Chevrolet pickup, screaming into my Dad's right ear. He calmed down almost immediately once we got him home, and he became one of my best friends as I grew up.

Chang, as I decided to name him, lived a fairly rough existence for a domestic cat in the modern US. My Dad wasn't particularly keen on keeping animals in the house, and so Chang spent his life outside with our dogs. He didn't seem to mind so much, except during the winter cold when he would stalk by the door and dart in whenever some unexpecting human opened it, hurtling down the steps to our basement where he could bask beside our stove. He came in to eat, and I remember that he loved to wake me up in the morning: he drooled when he was happy, and I can recall him drooling and purring whenever he got a chance to serve as my alarm clock.

He wasn't a feral cat, of course, but he possessed a fairly well developed wild streak that expressed itself on the other cats in our neighborhood, as well as certain nearby dogs. Chang was a fighter, and from a young age he was determined that nobody else was allowed to set foot on his personal territory. I ended up acting as a bouncer for him, trying to intervene to break up fights and drive off the interlopers before too much damage was done. It was a losing battle, though, and by the time he was approaching old age he was covered with the evidence of a lifetime spent fighting other cats—scars crisscrossed his scalp, visible in the thin fur in front of the ears, and he had yanked out so many claws that a number of them grew crookedly. A chipped canine protruded past his lip, which added to the roughness of his appearance.

He used up what seemed like several dozen lives in the time I knew him. His constant fighting resulted in several severe infections that almost killed him. I learned first-hand the difficultly of performing medical aid on an uncooperative cat: what always seemed easy and straightforward when explained amid the characteristic odor of the vet's office tended to turn into a violent scratch-happy brawl once we were back in the living room. When he wasn't trying to kill himself in a fight he did a pretty good job of trying to do the same through poor food choices. My Dad caught him the process of eating what may have been a dead bat once, and once again we were back in the vet's emergency room trying to figure out if he'd live or not. He eventually survived the bat, but it seemed like it was curtains for a while.

Chang eventually grew close to our male dog, Trader. The relationship was sometimes parasitic, at least as I perceived it, since Chang tended to treat Trader like a big lumpy heating blanket in cold weather. But they were friends, and they spent most of their lives in each other's company. Pet owners don't need outside proof that animals have feelings and form attachments: you could tell that both cat and dog cared for one another. When trader succumbed to cancer Chang seemed to go into a depression. He was already prematurely old, I think, from all the battering of his existence. Long winters and years of fighting had taken their toll on his body.

He was twelve years old around my twentieth birthday, and I had seen less of him in recent years because of work and college. One day I came home from work and found my parents acting oddly. I found out that the cause was that Chang, sometime the previous night, had been struck by a car and killed. Uncharacteristically, he had crossed the street, a busy one, that lay to the south of our house. I'd known him from the time I was eight, and I knew that he didn't normally travel south, or go so far from his territory. My Dad later said that he thought Chang could feel his death approaching and was getting the thing over with. I do feel that Chang wasn't the type of creature to die peacefully in bed. He lived a warrior's life, and paid the cost for it, I think. I buried him myself, in a coffin my Dad made for him. He was already nailed in by the time I arrived home. I always wished that I could have seen him one last time, even though his body was broken by the impact of the car. I briefly thought about cracking the wooden vessel open, but I gave up and took my friend to find a good grave site. I have always felt that losing him was like losing a family member.

Owning a pet puts you in a position to be close to life and death and in way that we aren't often among our own species, not anymore: modern people have pushed death to the margins, in a sense, to the nursing homes and hospital beds, where we don't see and experience it first hand, not like we used to. The relationship between a beloved pet and a pet owner takes us back to a ancient relationship with mortality, to a time when we buried the dead and held wakes and sang and drank and mourned all out in the open, in the realm of the home and the community.

After Chang's death I didn't get another cat for years. My mother did, so I wasn't completely deprived of feline companionship. I found Mao Mei, as we later decided to call her, at a local pet store. I'd developed the habit, since Chang's death, of visiting pet shops to look at the cats and kittens. I don't think I was intending to actually get a cat—my thinking was more along the lines of making myself feel better by getting at least a little feline companionship.

At any rate, one day I went to look at cats and found a group of what looked to me like skinheads amusing themselves around the cat cages. I guess skinheads like cats too. As I waited for the skinheads to move along I noticed that one of them was handling an adorable Siamese kitten. When they replaced the kitten and moved on to the dogs I took a look at the kitten for myself, and I liked what I saw. We clicked, I suppose. When I got home I told my Mom about the kitten and suggested she adopt her, lest the skinheads return and condemn her to a life of rage metal, jackboots, and white supremacy.

Happily, my Mom rescued the kitten from that (purely hypothetical) fate. She was fearless as a kitten, as I remember—she was content to explore from the very moment she arrived at our house. I saw Mao Mei intermittently for most of her life, since I was off to a succession of graduate schools and busy with the jobs that helped support my academic efforts. It was always gratifying when I made periodic journeys homeward to find that Mao Mei remembered me, even after years of absence. People who think that animals are not capable of having long-term memories are wrong. Mao Mei proved that to me over and over again. She was an excellent friend and companion to my Mom through both good times and bad. Her idiosyncrasies—such as spiking a nearby human in order to steal the warm spot they were sleeping on—were all endearing, in the final analysis. Eventually, inevitably, old age caught up with Mao Mei. As she suffered through a final illness my mother made the difficult decision to end her suffering. She told me that Mao Mei relaxed as her end approached, and went to sleep in her arms. It was a good death. She will be sorely missed.

Graduate school makes most things difficult. It is a time of work, and overwork, and constant moving about, from apartment to apartment, state to state and even country to country. It's hard to have a stable life under those conditions, and this is exacerbated by the fact that graduate students are usually some of the poorest people you'll ever meet. The combination of overwork and poverty and stress tends to take a toll on both body and mind. I realized late in my career as a grad student that cats are an excellent way of relieving some of the stress, though my realization was unexpected and accidental.

The accidental part came as a result of my fondness for cats: I had offered to cat sit for a professor who was going out of town on a job interview, and who needed someone to watch a pair of cats for a few days. I agreed to this because I liked cats, and because my work at the time involved massive amounts of reading. I could take care of the cats and get my work done at the same time, which seemed like a good situation all around. On the day that I went over to learn about the specifics of the professor's cats, a tiny and obviously starved female cat jumped over a retaining wall and began to squeak for food. The professor knew the cat, and had been in the process of trying to keep it fed. It was boney, dirty and barely removed from being a kitten. In any event we fed the little cat, and I learned the instructions concerning food and feeding times and all the rest from the professor. When I left for the last time, having taken care of the official housecats, I noticed the little female hanging around the carport, so I stopped and fed her again. But it wasn't my house and I had done my duty, so to speak, so I went back to my home and my homework.

Some months passed by and the professor was in the process of leaving town for good. Adjunct professors, who are short-term employees who move about from job to job, make up a considerable percentage of the professoriate in the modern US, and this particular professor was moving on to other things. As the individual in question went through the steps of packing and preparing to leave the state, I was approached with the offer of taking the little cat that I had fed. It was a good deal, because the professor offered to have the cat spayed and updated as far as shots and associated medical care were concerned. I said yes, and shortly thereafter I was presented with the tiny female, who looked awkward with her shaved belly and bedraggled, underfed physique.

I remember that she quickly staked out my bed as the best sleeping spot. During the whole of that day she was calm and quiet, which surprised me given that she was more or less a feral cat. I decided to name her Theodora ('Theo' for short), which means 'gift from god' in Attic Greek. Theo, as it turned out, was only biding her time until I decided to go to sleep. She spent the entirety of her first night in my house screaming into my ear as I tried in vain to drift off. From her point of view she had been kidnapped by aliens and experimented on, and she wasn't happy about that or her subsequent incarceration. Sleep proved elusive.

Theodora proved to be difficult to domesticate, maybe especially because she grew up out of doors, surviving (essentially) on her own. She was grateful for the food and the hospitality, but she never really adjusted to being a completely indoor animal. At first this wasn't too much of a problem. I lived in Tucson at the time and my home was surrounded by a good sized stucco wall, which provided a safe place for Theo to roam about during the day. The problem was that pretty soon she began to disappear over the edge of the wall for longer and longer periods. Once or twice she disappeared for a day or two at a time, and I made an increased effort to make sure that I retrieved her before dark. But cats don't necessarily come when they're called, as any cat owner is aware. One day Theo simply disappeared. After the second day I started to get more and more worried, and I posted a "lost cat" sign around my neighborhood in the hope that someone had seen her. I searched the local no-kill shelters and the Tucson pound, to no avail. Eventually I began to search a larger and larger area around my home, expecting to find her body, or what might be left of it. I went out in the middle of the night to call, when I could hear better. But I never found her, or any sign of her. I can only guess what her ultimate fate was. In my opinion she was too savvy to fall victim to a sudden encounter with an automobile. What I tend to think is that on her last nocturnal excursion she ran afoul of a group of coyotes. I learned after her disappearance that Tucson has a large population of urban coyotes, who travel around the city through the system of washes and drains that funnel the runoff of the summer rains. These coyotes are wild animals who have responded to the loss of habitat by adapting to their surroundings, in this case the city that has sprawled over the desert in the course of the last fifty years. Theo was a tiny cat, and the scrub of a Tucson neighborhood didn't offer too much in the way of vertical space to use in a frantic escape attempt from a band of hungry coyotes. Her disappearance was a personal lesson of the danger that comes with allowing cats to roam unsupervised. In the wild cats lead short and often brutal lives. If you allow your cats out it needs to come with the knowledge that doing so shortens their lives considerably, at least according to what statistics would suggest.

In the aftermath of Theo's disappearance I searched my way through all of the cat shelters that I could find, hoping that she had been picked up by someone and shuttled into captivity. One day I saw a cat that at first glance made me think I'd found her. A second look at the picture told me that the animal wasn't Theo, just a cat that looked like her. The cat in question was at the Tucson pound, an organization that euthanizes huge numbers of animals annually. As it became increasingly clear that I was unlikely to find Theo, I started to think about obtaining the cat I'd seen on the pound's website. My thinking behind this, I suppose, is that I had failed to save Theo's life but I could save the life of the lookalike cat, who in all likelihood would be put down once she failed to find an owner. Adult cats stand less chance of being adopted than kittens do. So I travelled out to the pound and walked past the cages filled with howling canines (predominantly pit bulls) to the cat room at the back of the facility. A quick search through the inmates located the cat in question, a sleeping female. When I asked to see her my request was granted by a rough middle aged lady who essentially dragged the semi-conscious creature from the metal cell and thrust her into my arms. Once unleashed into the enclosed activity room she was confident and friendly and I decided to take her.

Aside from trying to claw her way through the cardboard carrier on the way home she seemed pretty accepting of her new situation. Maple, as we decided to call her, proved to be the quintessential house cat. In fact, I have never seen a more domesticated creature than Maple. She has no hunting abilities: cockroaches (a common menace in Tucson, in my experience) have little to fear from Maple. She does not lower herself to the consuming of such pedestrian fare. My time with Maple has taught me what a good evolutionary adaptation being cute really is. Based solely on the fact that Maple is fuzzy and adorable, all Maple's needs (and more) are taken care of. I've had Maple through the latter half of my time in graduate school, and I've thought on a number of occasions that she lives a better life than I do. Not to complain, of course, since her presence has kept me sane through years of too much stress and too much work. Her companionship is well worth all the times she's decided to sleep on my clean socks in the closet, or wake me at 5am because she's awake and bored and unwilling to suffer through it by herself.

Maple was joined by a little brother a year or so after I rescued her from the pound. I'd describe it as an "accident" but in reality my penchant for cats means I should stay away from pet stores or anywhere else that there are available cats. The acquisition was my fault. As it happened, I found a female kitten in a local pet food store that I liked, and I thought that it might be good for Maple to have a companion. The store was showing cats that day from a nearby no-kill animal shelter, and a day or so later (I needed time to talk myself into it) I tracked down the shelter and walked in to locate the kitten. When I asked for the cat by name, the shelter volunteer told me that somebody else had adopted the little female that morning. So I said something about fate and decided that I this was the way of the universe telling me I didn't need another cat. At the point where I was going to walk away and go back home, the clerk suggested that I look at the other cats. I figured there was no harm in that (warning: that type of thinking is an easy way to accumulate cats) and walked through the various pens, each filled with a half dozen or so felines in various stages of consciousness. The very first cat I encountered was a googly-eyed male with medium long hair. He was lying on a plastic lawn chair staring at me with his slightly-protruding eyes. He seemed nice, but then to me most cats are nice, and I made my rounds of the rest of the cages. At the end of it all I came back to the first cage and went right back to the googly male, and got the staff to give me the paperwork.

I decided to call him "Stitch," (yes, after the Disney character...it was the eyes) and he blended in right away. At least in his mind, he blended in right away. Maple was furious that I had dared to introduce another cat to her territory, and sulked for about a week. Stitch learned that Maple was in charge. What I learned was that shelter cats need immediate vet appointments, no matter what the staff members tell you about an animal's clean bill of health. At the end of Stitch's first day at my house, I noticed that he was scratching an ear to the point that he was drawing blood. When I flipped his ear over to look inside I noticed how dirty his ears were, a sign of parasites or infection, something that I should have known to look for at the shelter itself. Cats penned up together in cat shelters are at risk for parasites, such as mites, and upper respiratory infections. With so many animals sharing a small space, it's easy for them to come into contact with a sick animal, and once one catches something the others will eventually catch it too. Anyway, Stitch got hauled to the vet the next morning, where I learned all about ear mites and got the tubes of medicine to fix the problem. The stress of the mite-induced itchiness was making Stitch pull at the long hair on his tail. All in all, he wasn't comfortable. Once I got him back home he very quickly learned to flee when a human came near carrying a tube of anything. To this day he's sensitive to people bearing tubes, so that popping the cap on sunscreen or lotion sends him scuttling out of the room. But despite the indignity of being seized and having greasy paste put in his ears he got better, as the mites died off. Stitch was only about a year old when I adopted him, and he was thin from being in the shelter. As he calmed down and got better regular food he filled out and began to look more like the Maine Coon that he is. I hadn't noticed it in the shelter because he was starved and sort of sickly. Once he had time to eat and rest he filled out and produced the characteristic mane of the breed. He's proved to be a great friend: Maine Coon cats really are "dog like" in their behavior. If you've never been around one, the stories about them (at least in my experience) are true: they're more like eternal puppies than cats. He tends to wake me in the morning by licking exposed fingers or toes. Licking, in fact, seems to be one of Stitch's favored forms of interaction as far as humans are concerned. He also does not get tired of being patted. I think you could probably brush him until all his hair came off, and he would allow it.

My cats have always been some of my best friends. The relationship that I've had with cats, from the time I was young, has taught me a great deal about the nature of friendship. What friendship can and should be, perhaps. The cat that loves you does so unconditionally. Cats (and other animals, to be fair) are inherently genuine in their affections. They lack the ability and motivation for guile, duplicity, faithlessness. If you will be their friend, then they shall be yours. All people should be so lucky as to have such a relationship in their lives.

I have now come to the end of my story about people and cats. Of the shortcomings in this volume, the responsibility for them lies with me alone. I have hoped to do some justice to the multiple histories that make up the story of the cat. If I have managed to interest, intrigue or entertain the reader, then I have done what I set forth to do. May this find both you and your cats in health and happiness.

End

Index

ASPCA (American Society for the Prevention of Cruelty to Animals), 129-132

Baybars, Sultan al-Zahir, 46-47

"garden of the cat" built by, 47-48

"Black Death," 76-78

Bronze Age Collapse, 25-26, 29

cats, breeds of

Japanese Bobtail, 56-57

Maine Coon, 83-84, 104

Russian Blue, 88-89

Russian (or Siberian) Forest Cat, 90-91

Siamese, 52-53

cats, domesticated

and modern cat foods, 141-145

as surrogate children, 11-12

evidence for, 6-11, 33, 51, 60

negative views of, 58-59

overpopulation, 120

human health in, 75-76

persecution of cats in, 41, 68, 74-77

society of, 68-71

feline behavior, 135-141

feline biology, 4-5, 17-18, 71-72, 118

Felis chaus, 19

Felis sylvestris, 1,4,19-20

Felis sylvestris lybica, 3-4, 19, 49

feral cats,

colonies of, 9

controlling populations of, 125-127

impact on wildlife, 120-125

in Sicily, 82, 119

in the US, 118

Fertile Crescent, 1-3, 7-8

Harappan civilization,

evidence for cats and, 10

trade contacts of, 10

India,

cats imported by, 63

cultural complexity of, 60-62

Printed in Great Britain
by Amazon.co.uk, Ltd.,
Marston Gate.

Secr

Bosses d

Working re
into

Boardroom Brides

*Three sassy secretaries are about to
land the deal of a lifetime in these
brand-new stories from popular
Mills & Boon Romance author*

RAYE MORGAN

Winner of *Romantic Times* 2005
Reviewer's Choice Award

Raye Morgan has been writing romances for years – and fostering romance in her own family at the same time. Current score: two boys married, two more to go. Raye has published over seventy romances, and claims to have many more waiting in the wings. She still lives in Southern California, with her husband and whichever son happens to be staying at home at the moment. When not writing, she can be found feverishly working on family genealogy and scrapbooking. So many pictures – so little time!

Boardr**oo**m Brides

The Boss, the Baby and Me
Trading Places with the Boss
The Boss's Special Delivery

BY RAYE MORGAN

*M&B™ and M&B™ with the Rose Device
are trademarks of the publisher.*

*First published in Great Britain 2007
by Harlequin Mills & Boon Limited, Eton House,
18-24 Paradise Road, Richmond, Surrey TW9 1SR*

BOARDROOM BRIDES © by Harlequin Books S.A. 2007

The Boss, the Baby and Me © Helen Conrad 2005
Trading Places with the Boss © Helen Conrad 2005
The Boss's Special Delivery © Helen Conrad 2005

ISBN: 978 0 263 85546 3

009-0307

*Printed and bound in Spain
by Litografia Rosés S.A., Barcelona*

The Boss, the Baby
and Me

Chapter One

The man had to go.

Jodie Allman glared at Kurt McLaughlin, head of the marketing department of Allman Industries, as he went on talking earnestly to Mabel Norton. Office hours were long over and Mabel was on her way home, her handbag slung over her shoulder. Kurt didn't glance Jodie's way as he conversed with the director of Hospitality Services, but she knew that *he* knew she was standing there across the office floor, waiting for further instructions.

"One…two…three…" she whispered to herself, tapping her foot as she counted. Counting to ten was a primitive but well-honored way of keeping control of her temper. It was probably time she moved on to more sophisticated methods—such as finding a way to get the man out of her life.

"It's such a simple thing," she told herself for the hundredth time that week, pushing her thick, blond hair back behind her ear in a gesture of impatience. "My father owns this company. Why the heck can't I get him to announce one particular layoff?"

Of course, she hadn't actually tried. Thinking about having Kurt thrown out on his ear was infinitely satisfying. But actually watching him pack up his meager belongings in a cardboard box and carry them sadly to his truck while the female support staff sobbed helplessly and shot daggers at Jodie would be another thing entirely. She wasn't nearly the tough-as-nails independent woman she would like to pretend.

The frustrating thing was, it really seemed that no one else could see through Kurt McLaughlin the way she could. Even the others in her family didn't seem to take the threat he posed seriously. And all her co-workers around here adored him. The fact that he was over six feet tall with a build right out of a woman's fantasy and a face handsome enough to turn heads in the cafeteria didn't hurt. The auburn hair that always looked a little wind-ruffled, and the green eyes that seemed to scan a woman right down to her heart and soul, were added attractions that muddied the waters for most females. They were so busy being bowled over by his admitted charms that they didn't notice what he was up to.

She'd only been back in town and working for him for

a few weeks, but she'd gotten his number right away. Once you realized what his game was, it was just so obvious.

Suddenly she noticed he was looking up at her, though he was still talking to Mabel. And to her astonishment, he was crooking his finger in her direction. Crooking his finger!

Well, that did it. There was no way she was dashing up, like a little, woolly dog, to a man who crooked his finger at her. She wasn't going to wait around any longer, either. It was way past time to go home. The three of them were probably the only people left in this ancient building, as it was. With one last baleful look in his direction, she turned on her heel and strode for the elevator, heading back up to her office to get her things.

"Hey."

It took her a moment to realize he was coming after her. Quickly, she jabbed at the Close Door button, and the doors began to move. But he was too fast for her, stepping into the elevator, and reaching across her to jab at the "stop" button. She hit the Close Door button again, just for emphasis, and he turned to grin at her as the doors opened, closed and opened again, before finally grounding together with a screeching of gears.

His grin faded fast.

"Uh-oh," he said, turning to look at the control panel.

The elevator shot up a dozen feet or so, then shuddered to a stop, complaining loudly.

"Uh-oh," Jodie echoed, agreeing with him for the first time in recent memory.

An eerie silence reigned while they both stared at the control panel, hoping for a sign of life. Then Kurt sprang forward and tried one button after another, getting absolutely no response. Alarmed, Jodie stepped forward, as well, and did the same, pushing every button twice. There was absolutely no indication that the buttons were connected to anything.

"Look what you did," Kurt muttered darkly. "We're stuck."

"What *I* did?" she responded, throwing him a smoldering glare. "You're the one who forced your way onto my elevator ride."

"I had to do that. You were trying to escape."

"Escape!" she choked, as she fought back the retort she was tempted to make. She took a deep breath.

Calm. We must remain calm. This is, after all, your current boss. Such as he may be.

"I was standing there waiting for you, trying to catch your attention for ages, but you were talking away to Mabel Norton as though it was the most important thing you'd done all day."

"It was. The most important thing in my world, at any rate." His face softened. "I was getting some advice on finding child care for Katy."

"Oh." She winced, knowing only too well how he felt about his young daughter.

"I've been having some trouble finding someone to

care for her during the day." His look sharpened. "You wouldn't happen to know anyone who might like a baby-sitting job, would you?"

She backed away, hands out. "Sorry. I don't know much about babies. Or about those who like to care for them, for that matter."

"Yes, I realized you weren't big on babies from the first," he said dryly.

That startled her a bit. She didn't know what she'd done to give him that impression, and something about the unemotional way he'd put it made her uncomfortable. But let's face it, babies made her uncomfortable.

Still, that was hardly the point. They had larger problems at the moment. Here they were, caught together in an old elevator in a building that should have been torn down years ago. But it was considered a historic landmark by the mavens of this Texas cow-country town of Chivaree. Things like this just didn't happen. Did they?

It seemed they did. But everything had been a little out of whack ever since she'd returned to her hometown after an absence of almost ten years and found a McLaughlin in a position at Allman Industries that she never would have expected a McLaughlin to have. And then she'd been told she'd be working for him. That had certainly gone against the grain.

She'd grown up thinking of all McLaughlins as the elitist enemy, the rich people up on the hill, looking down their noses at the Allmans and their ilk. Yes, "ilk" had been a word she'd heard used about her family.

She'd never been too clear on what it meant, but she did know it was a way of being condescending toward her kind. And she knew enough about some pretty unsavory incidents in the far past that had poisoned relations between the two clans—and probably always would.

Throughout her childhood, the Allmans had always been scrambling for pennies while the McLaughlins were happily buying up the entire town. There had been times when her family might even have skimmed the edges of the law just a bit here and there. But knowing that had only hardened the resentment she'd felt when others in this town whispered that the Allmans were a shiftless rabble always out for a fast buck.

And now, miraculously, the tables had turned. Her father, Jesse Allman, had somehow managed to make a go of a business, to the surprise of even his own children. In fact, his winery had grown so quickly, it was now the major employer in town. Not many people insulted him to his face these days but prejudices weren't easy to overcome. She had a good idea what the folks of Chivaree really thought about her family.

And she thought she knew what Kurt McLaughlin's true agenda was, since she'd found him happily ensconced in the management of her father's company when she had returned. Of all people—why did it have to be him? She turned back to look at the man and found him on the intercom, trying to find help.

"Hello. Hello! We're stuck in the elevator."

They both listened for a long moment, but there was

no answer. He turned and looked at her. "There's no one in the utility room," he said, frowning.

"Obviously," she agreed, trying not to think about the fact that there was probably no one at all left in the building but the two of them. Mabel Norton would have headed for the parking lot the moment Kurt dashed off toward the elevator. And everyone else had gone long ago. Their only hope was to find a way to communicate to the outside world. "Isn't there an alarm?"

"An alarm. Of course." He reached for it, pulling the lever out. Nothing happened.

"Maybe you pulled it too slowly," she said, starting to feel real apprehension seeping in. "Try it again. Give it a good jerk."

He tried again then turned to her, the lever dangling from his fingers. "Oops," he said.

She bit her lip and forced back the comment that would have been only natural at a time like this. "Well then," she said carefully, avoiding his gaze. "Since neither of us seems to have a cell phone handy, I guess we'll just have to wait."

"Wait?" He ran a hand through his thick, auburn hair, staring at her as though he thought she might really know the answer. "Wait for what?"

"For someone to realize we're missing."

He turned away impatiently, then turned back and met her dark gaze with his own brilliant one. "Everyone's gone home," he said gruffly, as though he'd just realized that fact.

She gulped. He was right. They could be here for a long time. This was not good.

"We're stuck here until someone tries to use the elevator and it doesn't arrive," he said, making the obvious deduction. "It's just you and me, kid."

In her wildest dreams, she'd never imagined a more unexpected scenario. She reached out to steady herself against the side railing. Suddenly the air seemed too thick, and his shoulders seemed too wide, looming in her way as they filled the elevator car. And in his well-tooled cowboy boots, he seemed even taller than his normally imposing height.

"This is your worst nightmare, isn't it?" He appeared to be a mind reader among his other annoying talents, though he'd said it with a hint of amusement in his voice.

"I don't know what you're talking about," she said primly, concentrating on the inspection certificate on the wall. The official-looking document claimed all was well with this horrible machine. The document was lying.

"Don't you?" He laughed softly.

She risked a look at him and immediately regretted it. "Are you trying to tell me that you enjoy being stuck in an elevator?" she demanded.

He considered her question for a moment, one eyebrow raised. "That's not as easy to answer as you might think," he told her. "Circumstances could be the deciding factor. After all, if I was stuck with Willy from the mailroom, he'd whip out a deck of cards, and we'd be playing gin so hard we would forget about the time. Or if it was Bob from Accounting, he'd be telling me fascinating stories about his time in the Special Forces during Desert Storm. And Tiana from the art department might give me a demonstration of the new belly dancing classes she's been taking."

Jodie made a sound of impatience, hoping to keep him from going on with this. "Yes, but you're not stuck with all those wonderful, interesting people. You're stuck with me."

"Yes, you." His white teeth flashed in an impudent grin, and his gaze ran up and down the length of her, making her wish she hadn't worn the snug, blue sweater and tight, denim skirt that showed off her figure with maybe just a bit too much flare. Then he challenged her teasingly. "So what are *you* good for?"

She wanted to turn and flounce off, but that was impossible under the circumstances. A flounce like that would land her smack up against the opposite wall. So she settled for trying to look bored with it all.

"Nothing, I guess," she said, letting a tiny hint of sarcasm curdle her tone.

When he leaned his long, muscular body against the wall, her gaze was magnetically drawn to the sleek slacks molded tightly across his thighs.

"Come on, Jodie," he said. "Don't sell yourself short. The way I see it, you're certainly good for a laugh."

That startled her, and she looked at him quickly, ready to resent whatever he had to say. "What are you talking about?"

He shrugged. "Your stock in trade, of course. The McLaughlin-Allman feud. You carry it around on your shoulders as though it were still 1904, and I just stole your father's favorite broodmare."

She drew herself up. Now he was really treading on her territory. "It's the *Allman-McLaughlin* feud," she said, correcting him icily. "And I have no idea why you think it's a factor in my life."

"Oh, yes, you do." His gaze hardened and he moved restlessly. "You're one of the few, you know. Most around here have given up on it."

"That's what you think." She wished she could recall the words the moment they left her lips. Because the trouble was, she was afraid what he'd said might be true. She did seem to be one of the few who remembered the feud. What had happened to it, anyway? When she'd lived here growing up, it pervaded life in this town like nothing else had.

"So that's it, isn't it?" he said. "That's what's had you treating me like someone you need to watch around the silverware. You just can't get past the whole feud."

She gave up all pretense. "Neither can any of us," she said stoutly.

"That's not true. Look at me."

She didn't want to look at him. Looking at him was likely to get her into a lot of trouble. But she did it anyway.

And for the first time, she really saw him as the others did—not as an underhanded opponent in a quarrel that had its roots in her ancestral background, but as a man who had a really engaging grin and a dynamic presence crackling with potent masculinity. And her body reacted so intensely that her heart started to race and a quiver snaked its way down her spine. When their eyes met for a beat too long, she had the unsettling feeling he really could see inside her heart and soul.

"So you think you've changed everything?" she said, hoping he didn't notice the breathlessness in her voice.

"No." He shook his head. "No, I didn't change everything. When you come right down to it, your father was the one who changed everything."

"By hiring you, you mean?"

"Sure. I guess you know they weren't exactly cheering him in the street at the time."

He said it as though he admired Jesse Allman for crossing the line. Jodie looked up at him in consternation. Did he really think her father had done that out of the goodness of his crusty ole heart? Was he really that clueless?

No, that wasn't it; he wasn't stupid. But neither was she. She'd known from the first that Kurt had an agenda of his own. Why else would he be here, working at Allman Industries, charming the heck out of everyone in sight? He could pretend all he wanted that the past was the furthest thing from his mind. She knew better. She knew McLaughlins. It had been a McLaughlin who had almost ruined her life. But that was another story.

Still, knowing what McLaughlin men were like

meant she knew she had to get away from Kurt's influence. Taking a step into the center of the elevator, she put her hands on her hips and looked around her.

"Enough of this. I think we ought to concentrate on how we're going to get the heck out of here."

He watched her lazily. "Get out of here, eh? Great idea. What exactly do you suggest?"

"Well…" She scanned the walls and the ceiling, then saw something interesting. "Look up there. Isn't that a trapdoor to the top of the elevator unit? Maybe we could open it. Shouldn't you climb up there and see?"

She looked at him expectantly. He gave her a quizzical look, still lounging against the wall, giving every indication of being perfectly content to stay right where he was. "Me?"

"Why not *you?*" she asked a bit impatiently. "Don't men always do that in movies?"

He looked up at the supposed opening, which was more than two feet over his head, and nodded. "Sure. In movies." Looking back down, he favored her with a caustic look. "Just exactly how do you picture me getting up there? Am I supposed to sprout wings, or pull out my suction shoes for wall-walking?" He cocked an eyebrow when she didn't answer. "Pole-vault, maybe?"

She licked her lips and frowned. "I don't know. How do those men in the movies usually do it?"

He shrugged. "I could try climbing on your shoulders," he suggested mildly. "Other than that, I don't see a way up."

She didn't bother to roll her eyes, though she certainly felt like doing so. "There must be some way," she muttered, frowning as she gazed about for inspiration.

He went back to looking at the small trapdoor. "And once I got up there," he mused, "who knows what sort of electrical wiring is lurking on the other side of the door, just waiting to fry the unsuspecting adventurer." He turned to look at her with amusement. "Tell you what. I could probably lift *you* up to the opening. How about you climbing up there and seeing what can be done?"

"Are you crazy?"

He shrugged as though he were disappointed in her response. "Give the woman a chance to be a hero, and what does she do?" he murmured.

"We don't need a hero," she retorted. "What we need is some competence."

"Ouch. I suppose you consider that a direct hit."

"No. A glancing blow, maybe." She sighed, shoulders sagging. Verbal jousting with the man was all very well, but it wasn't going to get her out of the situation. "Look, I know climbing up out of this thing is probably not doable. But it's just so frustrating being stuck here. Can't you think of anything?"

His green eyes flickered with something she couldn't quite identify, but he spoke calmly. "I believe in trying to make the best of any given predicament," he said. "So I look at this as worthwhile. It's a good opportunity for us to get better acquainted."

"Better acquainted!" She gaped at him. "I don't

need to be better acquainted with you. I've known you all my life."

He shook his head. "Not true."

She threw out her hands, palms up. "What do you call knowing you from birth?"

"You've known *of* me. You haven't really known me. And I haven't known you." He gave her a slow smile. "We've been like ships passing in the night, existing side by side, but hardly paying any attention to one another. We need to get to know each other a little more intimately."

There was something in the way he said that which caused her to take a quick step backward. From her new position of security in the corner of the elevator car, she gazed at him levelly. Was this all part of his plan? Was he trying to subvert her the way he'd done with the rest of the people around here?

"I don't think we need to know each other better at all. We've got a nice, cool working relationship. Professional and businesslike. Let's leave it at that."

"Is that really what you think we have?" he asked innocently. "I thought we had a thing going where I was the boss and you were the recalcitrant, embittered employee who was always second-guessing her management."

That about nailed it, she had to admit. She lifted her chin defiantly. "Is that a problem for you?"

He laughed. "No, it's not a problem. A diversion, perhaps, but not a problem." His expression changed. "And I guess it gives you the illusion of keeping the flame going on our families' blasted feud, doesn't it?"

She wasn't going to answer that, and he knew it. Instead of prodding her, he opened a new topic.

"So tell me, Jodie. Why did you come back?"

She knew what he was asking. It was a question everyone who moved back to Chivaree got at one time or another. Most people were astonished that someone would come back to this dusty town after having made good their getaway. She decided to be frank about it.

"I came back because Matt showed up on my doorstep one day and told me that I had to."

Matt was her brother, the oldest in her family. He was even a few years older than Kurt.

"Had to?" he echoed back to her in disbelief. "And you did what someone else told you to do without a qualm?" He shook his head in wonder. "I'll have to ask him what his secret is."

She lifted her chin. "He made a compelling case."

He nodded slowly. "I see. And then you showed up in Chivaree, arrived at the office to go to work and found out you were going to have to work for me, at least for the short run."

"Yes."

"That must have been one of your darker days."

She turned and glared at him, stung by the way he was continually making fun of her. "Will you stop? It's not permanent. I'll be moving on to some other department in a month or so." It was her father's brilliant plan that she should sample each area of the business to get a solid foundation in the company. "In the meantime, I can handle it."

"Can you?" An expression of wary skepticism crossed his handsome face. "You give every indication of hating every minute of our precious time together."

"I do not." She bit her tongue. If she wasn't careful, this could turn into a silly shouting match. A new tack was called for. She took a deep breath and started on one. "But you left town before I did. Why did *you* come back?"

She'd heard the cover story, that his wife had died and left him with their baby, so he'd returned to where his extended family could help him take care of the child. But she had her doubts. And wasn't he hunting around for someone to baby-sit his daughter? That pretty much gave the lie to that excuse.

No, Kurt McLaughlin had an agenda. She was pretty sure she had a clue what it might be, too. And she could bet it had something to do with ruining things for the Allmans. After all, that was the pattern set over a hundred years ago by their great-grandfathers. The McLaughlins were always supposed to win, and the Allmans were always supposed to end up with their faces in the dirt.

"Okay, I'll tell you why I came back," he said slowly, turning his face and staring at the wall. "Believe it or not, I came back because I love this old town."

"What?" She gaped at him.

Chivaree was not one of those adorable little towns people wrote songs about. Things had improved lately,

but it was still a windswept, dusty place that the interstate bypassed years ago. People didn't flock to Chivaree. People cashed in their chips and headed out for
brighter lights as soon as they could scrape together the
carfare.

From what she'd heard, he'd spent a good number of
years in New York City. She'd noticed that his voice still
had a nice Texas drawl, but it was subtle. So he hadn't
gone completely citified.

"It's true," he went on, his voice low and gravelly.
"And when things seemed to fall apart for me out there
in the big world, the only thing I could think of was
coming back to Chivaree. Coming home."

Coming home to heal was the feeling implicit in
his voice.

For just a moment, she believed him. He sounded so
sincere, and there was some sort of emotion in his face,
a hint of pain, deep down. For just a flash, she bought it.

But she stopped herself quickly. He was smart, all
right. He was giving her exactly the story that was most
likely to touch her heart and make her believe. He was
playing with her heartstrings in a very disturbing way.
She had to get out of here before she fell for this stuff.

He'd turned back, and was pulling off his tie and
loosening the neck of his shirt, pulling open buttons as
though they were snaps. Darkly tanned skin with just a
hint of chest hair appeared before her horrified gaze.

"Is it just me," he said huskily, his eyelids drooping,
"or is it getting hot in here?"

Her pulse was racing. One moment, he set out the emotional trap. Now, the physical one was laid out in front of her, just waiting for her to step into it. And darn it all if her own traitorous body wasn't swooning like a lovesick puppy, even as she disdained the obvious way he was approaching her.

Turning away abruptly, she quickly changed the subject. "I'm not hot at all," she said with an emphasis he surely couldn't miss. "But I am hungry. For food," she added quickly. Glancing back, she was chagrined to see that his eyes were gleaming wickedly.

"Are you?" he responded.

She turned back to face him, chin-high. "Desperately. I skipped lunch to get those preliminary sketches out to the art department." She grimaced. "I wish I had my purse."

"Why?" He pretended to look about the car. "Is there a food machine here I missed?"

"No, I've got a candy bar in it."

"Hmm." He plunged a hand down into the pocket of his crisply tailored slacks. "Look what I found. A roll of peppermints."

"Oh." She looked at them longingly. She really was hungry, and her mouth was so dry.

"Here." He offered the roll to her after he'd popped one into his own mouth. She hesitated, but hunger overcame her inhibitions.

"Thanks," she said shortly, taking a mint and sighing as the sparkling sugar did its work.

"You see?" he said softly, as he watched her. "I'm even willing to share my last meal with you."

She started to say something. It was surely going to be a scathing retort, something that would knock him back on his heels for good. Unfortunately, the words themselves were lost to history, because the breath she took in to help facilitate her clever words shot what was left of the peppermint right down her throat. Now, instead of putting him in his place, she was choking.

"Here." A man of action, he took matters in hand immediately, giving her a couple of sharp thumps on the back. When that didn't seem to dislodge the little intruder, he turned her quickly and wrapped his arms around her from behind for the Heimlich maneuver.

"Hey," she protested with a cough, before he got in a good thrust. "Stop! I'm okay."

He relaxed, but for some reason his arms didn't remove themselves from around her waist. "Are you sure?" he said, his voice just a bit husky, and his face so close to hers, she could feel his warm breath on her neck.

"Yes, I'm sure." She pushed against him, but he didn't release her. "Kurt, let go!"

Turning her head, she met his gaze. And then something magical happened. It wasn't just that she suddenly noticed the golden flecks in his green eyes. It wasn't even the electric sizzle that began to spread everywhere his body was touching hers. But suddenly she was filled with a longing so deep, so overwhelming, it took her breath away. She wanted to be kissed. She wanted to be kissed by Kurt McLaughlin.

"Oh," she said softly, like a woman in a trance, her gaze fixed on his generous mouth. She tilted her head, her own lips parted, a yearning coursing through her. And for just a moment, she was sure it was going to happen.

And then he was pulling away, leaving her tottering off balance and feeling as though he'd thrown cold water on her. Feeling like a fool.

At least he didn't laugh at her. Shooting back his cuff, he looked at his wristwatch, suddenly all business.

"Oh, dammit, it is getting late. I'm way overdue for picking Katy up. We'd better get some help so we can get out of here."

Reaching behind her, she steadied herself with a hand on the railing. What was he saying? "Get some help?" she asked him, still breathless and embarrassed. "What are you talking about?"

Flipping back the tail of his suit coat, he pulled out something that had been attached to his belt. Staring openmouthed, Jodie saw a cell phone in his hand.

"I'll just make a call," he said innocently. "Hope the battery is still good. If so, we'll get out of here in no time."

She shook her head and blinked to clear her mind, then gave a sound of outrage. "You mean you've had that with you *this whole time?*" she cried. "Why didn't you say so when I asked?"

"You never actually *asked* if I had one—you just assumed I didn't," he murmured. He opened the phone and began punching in a number. "Hi, Jasper? Sorry to bother you, but we've got a problem here at the office. I'm going to have to ask you to come back in and help me get out of the elevator."

Murder. That was what was called for here. Something quick and painless, when he wasn't looking. No jury in the world would convict her. Groaning, she closed her eyes and clenched her fists at her side. If she hadn't despised him before, she now had plenty of reason to start.

But that was his plan, wasn't it? Abruptly, she opened her eyes again and glared at his pleased smile. Something had to be done about this man!

Chapter Two

Jodie sat back and looked at her family, gathered around the big, antique kitchen table where they had come together for generations. Funny how it felt so familiar and yet so strange. The main thing missing was her mother, who had died of cancer when Jodie was sixteen. Her little brother Jed was also absent, the only family member Matt and Rita hadn't managed to find and hog-tie to bring back home.

Rita had cooked an excellent meal—as she always did—of chicken and dumplings in the old style. Jodie glanced down the table at where her sister sat. She watched affectionately as the older woman blew a strand of hair back out of her eyes and looked expectantly from one person to another at the table, obviously trying to gauge how they liked what they were eating. When her gaze met her sister's, she favored her with a warm smile. At least one good thing had come out of all this. Rita was happy to have most of the family together again.

Rita took care of the house and the family the way their mother would have if she hadn't died twelve years before. She was a wonderful homemaker, and she deserved to have a loving man in her life and a family of her own. Unfortunately, you didn't meet many great, unattached men at the meat counter at the Chivaree supermarket these days. And Rita didn't often veer much farther from home than that.

Matt had been her partner in reuniting the family. But Matt didn't look happy, the way Rita did. Matt was the oldest male child in the family. He was the one who had shown up on Jodie's doorstep, in Dallas, a month before and talked her into coming back home, giving her a long spiel about how they all needed to pull together now that their father was ill. These days, he seemed to care about that almost as much as Rita did.

In many ways, Matt had been Jodie's original role model. After all, he'd been the first to defy their father and leave town, heading for medical school in Atlanta. He'd worked for years in a large urban hospital, and now he was back in his dumpy little hometown. She noted the brooding look on his handsome face and wondered what had put it there. Something was bothering him. She had no idea what it was.

But she didn't have to worry about things like that with her sunny brother David, the one she looked the most like. They both had blond hair and brown eyes and a sprinkling of freckles over short noses.

Sitting next to Matt and eating everything he could get on his plate with youthful enthusiasm, David was the one who had never really left. Someone had asked her just the other day why such a handsome, happy-go-lucky young man who looked like he should be on a surfboard in Malibu would stay in Chivaree when there was a whole world out there for him. She'd laughed and said he was too lazy to leave. But that wasn't true. She supposed she might be the only one who knew the real reason why he stayed. Love made people do strange things sometimes.

And then there was dark-eyed Rafe, the brother who was the same age as Kurt McLaughlin, the one now looking at her with a penetrating gaze that said, *Hey, Jodie, don't try to con me. I can see right through this polite little act you're putting on. I can read your mind.*

She stared right back at him with a half smile, hoping he got the message. *Mind your own business!*

"Hey, Pop," David said, greeting their father as he entered the room. "You going to try to eat something?"

Leaning on his cane, the gray-haired man shook his head as Rita jumped up to pull out a chair for him. "No. I can't eat anything. I just wanted to come out and sit with you all and look at your faces." He sat down heavily, then made a scan of the table. "My pride and joy," he muttered in a tone that could have been loving, but sounded a little sarcastic.

Glancing at him and then away, Jodie felt a stew of conflicting emotion—love, resentment, anger, pity. What could you do when you disliked your own parent almost as much as you loved him?

"So you all came back to save the farm for the old man, eh?" He laughed softly. "I guess I raised myself a bunch of good ones after all."

"Hey, Pop," Rafe said, leaning forward. "I was talking to our Dallas distributor today. Looks like we might have a shot at getting a contract with the whole Wintergreen Store chain. That could be huge for us."

Jesse Allman nodded, but he wasn't looking at Rafe. His gaze was trained on his oldest son. He'd been trying to get Matt to fulfill the role of heir apparent in the business for years, without a lot of success. Though Matt had often helped out in the old days when all they had was the tiny, struggling Allman Winery, he'd been away at college when Jesse had developed the plan to become the distributor for all the little wineries of this part of Texas hill country. That had launched all the success, and it was no secret Jesse thought Matt ought to be involved. "You got a dog in this fight, Matt?" he asked.

Matt looked surprised. "What about?"

"This Wintergreen thing."

Matt shrugged. "It's up to you, Pop. You know I'm not into the business side of things."

Jesse's eyes narrowed. "You oughta be," he said shortly.

Matt and Rafe exchanged glances. "Talk to Rafe," Matt said calmly. "He's the one who knows what's going on."

Jodie sighed. It was the same old story. Did nothing ever change? The Allman family business had grown larger, morphing into Allman Industries, and the Allman family had gotten richer, changing from the old scruffy bunch who seemed to skim along just this side of law-breaking into this vaguely respectable family that provided a good chunk of the local jobs. But the old emotions still simmered just below the surface. She was beginning to wonder if it hadn't been a big mistake for her to come back.

"What's eatin' you, missy?" her father said, looking at her accusingly. "You still trying to get me to get rid of that McLaughlin boy?"

Jodie winced and put a napkin to her lips. "I never said I wanted you to get rid of him," she protested. "I just want you to be aware of the danger he poses."

"Danger?" David looked up with a grin. "Ole Kurt McLaughlin? He's a pussycat."

"I don't trust the McLaughlins any more than you do," Matt chimed in. "But I've got to admit, Kurt is doing a fine job with marketing. We're lucky to have him."

She glanced quickly around the table, realizing with a sense of astonishment that she didn't have anyone on her side at all. Not one of them understood how dangerous it was to let a man like Kurt into the power structure of their family business.

"I know your game, missy." Jesse grinned at his daughter. "You're like me. You can't forget or forgive." He slapped the flat of his hand down on the table. "But I'm not getting rid of him. Hell, no. He's good at what he does. I don't care if he is a McLaughlin. In fact, I love that he's a McLaughlin. I love the looks on their pompous faces when I'm in town, or at the chamber of commerce meetings. I can smile at them and say, 'Your fair-haired boy is workin' for me now. Because I'm the one who's making it in this town. You McLaughlins are done for.'"

She was reminded of all the reasons why she'd run away from this man in the first place, when she was a rebellious eighteen-year-old. She'd planned never to come back. And she might have stuck to that plan if Matt hadn't found her and talked her into coming home again.

"He's old, Jodie," Matt had told her earnestly. "Old and sick. He needs us. All of us."

She noticed with a start that her father's hands were shaking, and her gaze flew to his face, searching for evidence. To her surprise, her heart began to race with something close to fear. Matt was right. He *was* old and sick. She might still be angry with him for things he'd done in the past, but he was still her father and, deep down, she cared for him. Okay, it was good that she'd come home. And despite everything, she had to stay, at least for a while.

And that meant she had to deal with Kurt McLaughlin.

A memory sailed into her head of how it had felt with

his arms around her in the elevator car, and she almost gasped aloud. She definitely had to harden herself to his lethal charm. She was stuck working for him, and maybe that was for the best. After all, somebody had to look out for the good of the family.

An hour later, she escaped from the tensions in the house and took a brisk walk toward the newly renovated downtown. The sky was velvet-blue, with a full moon rising. The air was warm and dry. She could smell newly cut hay somewhere nearby.

She'd paced these same streets when she was eighteen and trying to figure out what she was going to do. And just around the corner was the little park where she and Jeremy used to meet secretly to plot how they were going to escape from Chivaree together. That seemed so long ago.

Jeremy. Had she ever really loved him? When she looked back now, she saw more excitement than love. They had needed each other for support at the time. But that wasn't really true. She'd needed him. It turned out he hadn't needed her at all. But that was always the way with the McLaughlins, wasn't it?

Her steps slowed as she reached Cabrillo, the main street. The area was less familiar now, with new storefronts on some of the buildings, and a few new structures housing a boutique and a crafts store. It was good to see the town looking prosperous, she supposed, though it did give her a twinge to see how things had changed.

Millie's Café was just ahead, and that looked exactly the same. Maybe she would go in and have a cup of coffee and say hello to Millie, the mother of Shelley, her best friend in high school. Lights from the café spilled out onto the sidewalk, and Jodie began to anticipate how warm it was going to be once she'd gone in and snuggled into her old favorite booth.

But as she neared the corner, she got a glimpse of the people inside. It startled her to discover the place was packed. There were people crowding the entryway, waiting for seats, while others filled the booths, and still more sat at the counter. For a fraction of a moment, she got a flashing glimpse of a man who looked enough like Kurt to make her heart jump in dismay. Not wanting another possible run-in with that infuriating man, she just kept walking.

Darn! Was she really going to spend all her time reacting to Kurt? She couldn't live this way. Looking back over her shoulder, trying to see if that really was him inside the café, she stepped off the curb and started across the street.

The thing was, there had never been a stoplight on that corner when she'd lived in Chivaree before. There had never been enough traffic to warrant one. Somehow, it hadn't registered with her that there was one there now.

Brakes screeched. Fear flashed through her and she looked up, frozen for a few seconds. Then, she jumped, her whole body moving in a twitch reflex that somehow got her out of the way. But at the same time, her mind processed the fact that Kurt couldn't be in Millie's Café because that was Kurt's face behind the wheel.

Kurt! After veering to miss her, he tried to regain control of his vehicle. And she watched in horror as his truck swerved just enough to get caught by a car coming in the other direction. There was a smash, a crunch, the horrifying shriek of metal in distress.

It wasn't much more than a fender bender, but Jodie ran forward, apprehension flashing through her system, her heart in her throat. The driver of the car jumped out, swearing. But Kurt didn't move. Dread building, Jodie yanked at the handle on the truck door. It came open, and she stared at the contorted way Kurt's body lay in the cab. She gasped, and his green eyes opened.

"Hi," he said, his wide mouth twisted, obviously in pain. "Uh, Jodie? Think you could call the paramedics? Something's wrong with my leg."

She was doomed, that was all there was to it. Every time she turned around, there was Kurt McLaughlin, interfering with her peace of mind. It was enough to make her want to scream.

Or at least complain a bit. But how could you complain about a man when you'd just crippled him?

Looking at him lying in his bed in the cozy house he shared with his baby daughter, Katy, she swallowed hard and wished she were anywhere else. Her brother Matt was using an automatic sander gizmo to smooth out a rough spot in the fiberglass cast he'd applied at the town clinic an hour or so before. Her brother David, who had helped get Kurt home, was standing around with his hands shoved down in the pockets of his jeans, looking very amused with it all. And she was standing in the shadows, between the bookcase and the closet, wishing the earth would open and swallow her whole.

"I knew Jodie had it in for me," Kurt drawled, his voice half teasing, but with just enough of an edge to set her nerves twitching. "I just didn't realize how far she was prepared to go."

She moaned softly, but David couldn't resist expanding on the joke.

"You know, sis, if you really want to take a guy out, *you're* supposed to be the one in the car. He should be the one in the street, running for his life."

She ignored him. She'd spent too many years fending off the pestering of big brothers—she knew better than to rise to the bait. Besides, she did feel terrible for what had happened, and she wanted to make sure Kurt knew it.

"I just don't know how I could have been so stupid," she began, and not for the first time.

Kurt looked up at her and groaned. "Jodie, if you try to tell me how sorry you are one more time, I'm going to have your brother use that surgical tape on your mouth."

"We'd have to tape up her hands, too, or she'd be using them to give you apologies in sign language," Matt said with a smirk.

"Do that, and she'll have to resort to tapping out her pleas for forgiveness in Morse code with the toes of her shoes," David threw in teasingly. "Let me tell you something. This sister of ours doesn't give up easily."

Jodie flushed as they all laughed. It was obvious her brothers both liked Kurt. She didn't know how they could be so blind.

But another thing that stumped her was how well Kurt had taken the whole thing. She would have expected a little snarling, a few insults about watching where she was going, and a whole lot of swearing. But there had been very little of that. Maybe if he'd been grouchier about it all, she would feel better. At least then she could get mad instead of feeling so wretched.

Kurt had wanted paramedics. She only wished she could have obliged. But there were no paramedics in Chivaree. There was Old Man Cooper, who answered the phone at the fire department and then called around to the volunteers if there was a fire. He supposedly had a little first-aid training. But he certainly wasn't competent to deal with a broken leg. So she'd called Matt. After all, he was the best physician in town as far as she was concerned. He'd come right away, bringing David with him, and between them they had carried Kurt to the clinic so that Matt could X-ray the leg.

No major bone was broken, but the patella was cracked, a situation that could be very painful and required a cast that held the knee immobile.

"We'll have to keep you in the cast for a couple of

weeks," Matt had told him. "Then we'll take it off and do some X-rays to see if you can transfer to a knee brace. That will give you a lot more freedom of movement."

It had all gone pretty smoothly. They'd brought Kurt back to his house and installed him in his bedroom, where he was right now. Matt had given Kurt some sort of painkiller when he'd worked on him. Maybe that was why Kurt seemed to be taking it so calmly. Maybe he was just groggy from the medicine.

She wanted to go home. She ached to leave this behind. But she couldn't really leave. After all, the accident had been her fault.

"Jodie is a licensed physical therapist," Matt was saying. "That will be handy. She can help in your rehabilitation."

"I'd forgotten that," Kurt said. He grinned at her, knowing it would bug her. "That will be useful."

Jodie felt numb. Everything that happened seemed to tie her more firmly to this man in one way or another. As she'd said before, she was doomed.

Matt rose to get something from his bag and, to Jodie's surprise, he stopped in front of a framed picture of a cute baby girl, that was set on the top of an antique dresser.

"This your daughter?" he asked gruffly.

Kurt looked up and nodded proudly. "Yes, that's Katy. She's at my mother's for the night."

Matt was still staring at the picture in a way Jodie found a little odd. She couldn't imagine when her big brother had become a child person. Considering that none of the six siblings in her family, including herself, were married or had children, she'd assumed they all felt pretty much the way she did. She didn't dislike children, but she felt a lot more comfortable keeping them at a distance, avoiding too much up-close-and-personal interaction. Maybe she'd been wrong about Matt.

"It's a good thing the baby wasn't with you when you had the accident," Matt said with feeling.

"Yes," Kurt agreed. "That's one blessing, at least."

Jodie agreed, though she didn't say it aloud. Just imagine if she'd been responsible for hurting Kurt's baby. She shuddered, not wanting to think about it.

Still, Matt lingered, staring at the portrait. "She's a beautiful baby," he said. "About how old?"

"Sixteen months."

"A little over one year."

"Yes."

Jodie frowned, wondering what was eating her brother. This just didn't fit with the image she had of him. Then she turned to look at Kurt lying back against the pillows, and immediately wished she hadn't. All thoughts of Matt flew out the window, and unwelcome reactions to Kurt took their place.

Since he'd put on cutoff jeans, to leave his damaged leg bare for the cast, she'd wisely been avoiding looking at his beautifully sculpted good leg, which was covered with a sleek pelt of reddish-brown hair. But while she wasn't paying attention, somehow his shirt had been removed, as well, and now he was displaying a set of sexy muscles and a washboard stomach, all wrapped up in the most deliciously smooth and bronzed skin she'd ever seen.

The man was a damn Greek god! Gazing at him made her feel dangerously warm and fuzzy inside.

Realizing with a start that she'd been staring at his powerfully built chest too long, she glanced up into his bright green eyes and saw that he'd been watching her all along. Turning ten shades of red, she spun on her heel and pretended a sudden fascination with the collection of old first editions in his bookcase.

Matt and Kurt went on talking, but she didn't hear a word they were saying. Her head was buzzing with a strange vibration, and all she could think of was that his gaze had been so full of awareness of her, it was downright scary. Awareness not only of what she was feeling, but of just what she might be thinking, as well.

Had he understood just how drawn to him she was physically? Had he known she'd ached for him to kiss her in the elevator? It was all so humiliating!

She tried some even breathing, determined to get this silly blushing under control, and to avoid meeting Kurt's eyes again. And then she took a chance and escaped into the rest of the house, taking a deep breath as she did so. The cool air in the living room was a welcome relief.

She looked around the room. It was nicely furnished in a simple style, but there were toys everywhere. She winced, looking away. Funny. It had been almost ten years, but looking at baby things still brought on a wave of nausea every time. She knew it was silly and self-destructive to let that reaction rule her life, but she hadn't found a way to fight it yet. Losing a baby was hard, even if that baby hadn't been born yet at the time.

She turned toward the bookcase, refocusing her attention with a soft sigh. She couldn't help but wonder why Kurt didn't live in the old Victorian mansion up on the hill, where the other McLaughlins congregated. If he'd really come back to get help with his daughter, you would think he would have stayed there. It was supposed to be a wonderful house.

She'd never been inside the place herself, never been invited to the parties the other girls in town had attended on Sunday afternoons. In those days, Allmans weren't welcome at anything put on by a McLaughlin.

"Hey, Jodie." David came around the corner.

She jumped, startled out of her reverie. "What is it?"

"Matt's finished."

"Oh. Good."

"But Kurt wants to talk to you alone for a few minutes before we go."

"Alone?" Her hand went instinctively to her throat. "Why? What does he want to talk to me about?"

David gave her a quizzical look. "I don't know. Work, I guess." He shrugged and turned back toward the door. "Anyway, we'll be waiting in the car."

She swallowed hard. "Okay."

She made her way back into the bedroom, cringing when she saw Kurt again, looking so helpless on the bed. "Oh, gosh, I'm really…"

"Don't say it," he ordered shortly. "I know you wish it hadn't happened. So do I. But it's done now. So forget about it."

Her eyebrows rose as she noted a change in his tone. He'd put on more clothes and abandoned the easygoing attitude. What had happened to the friendly guy who'd traded jokes with her brothers just a few moments before? But the man had just broken his patella. He had to be tired, and probably the pain was coming back. She really ought to cut him a little slack.

"What we have to do now is figure out how to deal with the aftermath," he was saying.

"The aftermath?" What was there to figure out? He had an injury. Obviously, that was going to put him at a disadvantage for awhile. It might put a crimp in his plans, but it also meant she would be able to keep tabs on him more easily, when you came right down to it.

He was nodding. "Matt says I can't go back in to work for at least two weeks."

"Oh. That's too bad." She had visions of working without him around to distract her. Her spirits brightened. Maybe things were looking up after all.

"But I'm in the middle of a couple of projects that can't wait. So I'm going to have to work at home."

"At home?" she echoed, emotions switching as she

began to get a very bad feeling about what was coming next.

"Yes. I've got a computer and a fax machine right here. I won't be able to move around a lot, though. And that's where you will come in."

"I will?"

"Sure. You can come work with me here. I'll probably get twice as much done that way. It will all be for the best."

"Oh, but…"

"I've been thinking it over. You can go in to work at your regular time, clear up anything you have to do there, then bring me anything I need to deal with and work here until lunchtime. You won't have any problem with that, will you?"

What could she say? This was her fault and she had to help him any way she could. Jodie felt her head begin to ache and she bit her lip. She foresaw long mornings working with Kurt, the two of them alone, their heads together over some sticky problem, intimacy growing…. *No! Impossible!*

"You know," she said quickly, "I think it would be better if I got Paula to come over here instead." Oh, good thinking. Paula was the typist/file clerk they used. "I'm in the middle of a few things, too, you know. I'll just stay at the office to make sure everything is covered, and Paula can run back and forth, kind of a liaison between us and…"

"That won't work."

She blinked. "Why not?"

"Because I want you here."

Exactly what she was afraid of.

His gaze was dark and fathomless, and his jaw was set. He was all boss right now. He was giving orders. The problem was, she wasn't all that good at taking orders.

She stared right back at him. "Why me?" she asked.

He frowned. "Are you, or are you not, my assistant?"

"That's temporary."

"As far as work goes, let's live in the moment. Answer the question."

She wanted to say something sassy and insubordinate but she realized it was going to seem very childish if she did that. But she was having a very hard time bending to his will too easily.

Their gazes locked and held. Jodie felt a surge of anger, but she managed to keep it reined in for the moment. Still, he could tell she was unhappy. To her surprise, that brought the amusement back into his expression.

"Do all your apologies mean nothing?" he asked her softly.

The nerve!

"And I guess you casting aside all my apologies means even less?"

He laughed softly. "Jodie, calm down. This is the way I want it. You're going to have to comply."

"Or what? You'll fire me?"

"Fire you from your father's company? Never." His

grin was lopsided in a particularly infuriating way. "I could, however, begin giving the better assignments to Paula in order to leave you time for document-copying and coffee-brewing duties."

She turned away from him, furious, and tempted to head for the door. His tone said it all. *Look at this, Jodie. You laid me low, but I'm still in control.* She didn't want to give him the satisfaction of saying she would do as he wished, though she knew she was probably going to have to. But at the same time, a small part of her glowed with satisfaction. She only wished her brothers had been there to see Kurt get autocratic with her.

You see? He is underhanded. He is out to sabotage us in some way. You just wait! I'm not wrong about that.

Come to think of it, maybe it was just as well that she would be hanging around wherever Kurt was working. After all, she was the only one who was clued in to what he was up to. Someone had to keep an eye on him.

She turned back and looked at him. "All right," she said grudgingly. "I'll be here."

To her surprise, he looked relieved rather than triumphant. But before he had a chance to say anything, she added a warning.

"Kurt, just so that we understand each other. I'll come to your house. I'll do a good job for you. I'll work with you just fine, as long…as long as you don't do anything to hurt my family."

"Hurt your family?" He was going back into his innocent act. "Why would I hurt your family?"

She threw up her hands. "Oh, I don't know. Why is there air?"

"That same old, ancient feud. Is that it?"

"Bingo. Give the man the grand prize."

"I don't want any grand prize, Jodie. All I want is you…here."

Her mouth had gone dry. What was he saying? She didn't really want to find out.

"Well, you've got it," she said flippantly, turning to go. She stopped at the door and looked back. "Remember, be careful what you ask for," she reminded him. "Things have a way of turning out differently from what you expect."

"We can always hope so," he murmured.

She hesitated, wishing she had a better grip on his meaning. He was saying things that sounded strangely suggestive, and yet she had the feeling he didn't really mean them the way she was hearing them. Could it be that he was just trying to throw her off balance?

Oh, good guess, Jodie!

Still, it wouldn't hurt to make sure.

"And there will be no…romantic relationship," she said firmly.

He stared at her for a moment, then laughed.

"Ha. Listen, Jodie. Any romancing I do from now on will be strictly recreational. My 'relationship' days are only evident in my life's rearview mirror."

The bitterness in his tone startled her, but she wasn't about to let him see that. He had issues. Why not?

Everyone had issues. At least he'd had a happy marriage at one point. Some people didn't even get that much.

"That's exactly what I'm saying. I don't do recreational."

"Then we understand each other perfectly."

If only she believed that. With one last lingering glance at the man, she made her way out the door and headed for the front of the house, feeling as though she'd just avoided a dangerous trap.

But what traps would he try to spring on her tomorrow?

Chapter Three

Jodie had it all planned out by the time she pulled up in front of Kurt's house the next morning. Cool, calm and professional. That was the way she was going to play this. Dripping with efficiency and competence, but detached. Aloof.

Almost robotlike, she promised herself as she made her way up the winding walk to the front steps. *No emotions.*

She'd arranged communications with Shelley, her best friend from childhood who also worked at Allman Industries, to keep her posted on things at the office. Then she'd slicked her thick, blond hair back in a bun, and put on slacks and a tailored cotton shirt. Her dark eyes were shaded by huge sunglasses. Impersonal. Businesslike.

The shiny green door opened before she had a chance

to knock on it. Kurt stood before her wearing the suggestion of a faintly mocking grin and not much else. He was bare-chested and his biceps were swollen with the effort of using the crutches. Baggy, cotton cutoff pajama bottoms rode low on his perfectly sculpted hips. She took the sight in and blinked in surprise, taking a half step backward.

Too much male flesh, too close and too early in the morning. The shock stopped her breath in her throat, and she choked.

"You okay?" he asked, his green eyes sparkling with shafts of light from the early morning sun.

"Oh, certainly," she replied, regaining her emotional balance quickly. "I'm just worried about you. Don't you think you might catch a cold with all that bare skin hanging out?"

"'Hanging out'?" He looked down as though alarmed. "Where? I thought I was in pretty good shape."

The evidence was irrefutable, but she pretended to consider that skeptically.

"Well, 'good' is a judgment, isn't it? I suppose you could say it was in the eye of the beholder." She glanced past him into the house. "Lose your robe somewhere?"

"Robes just get in the way. It's too much trouble trying to wear clothes and use these crutches, too." He cocked an eyebrow as though a sudden thought had crossed his mind. "Are you implying that my state of undress disturbs you?"

Her eyes narrowed. "I've worked as a physical therapist for the last five years. The human body doesn't disturb me."

That blatant lie almost brought on a flush, but she managed to hold it back. The average body might not cause a blip on her radar screen, but this particular body had her equipment going haywire. She only hoped he didn't notice. In fact, the better part of valor might be in beating a hasty retreat.

"But since you don't seem to be ready to do any work, I think I'll just run over to the office and come back later." She turned, ready to make good on her threat, but he stopped her with a soft oath.

"Cut the dramatics, Jodie," he said impatiently. "I've got plenty of things waiting for your expert attention. We don't have a lot of time to waste."

She looked back, unable to ignore the way the morning light added a wonderful patina to his bronzed skin. "We don't?"

"No. Come on in. We need to get moving here."

She frowned, suspicious, but turned back in his direction. "What exactly do you have in mind?" she asked.

His bright gaze met hers, and he smiled. Her knees almost buckled. The man's smile could melt the polar ice cap. Global warming had nothing on this guy.

"Jodie, Jodie," he was saying. "You're going to have to learn to trust me."

"Trust is something you earn," she reminded him. "Right now I would rather have the facts."

"Okay Miss Sunshine. Here are the facts, and nothing but the facts. I want to go out to the vineyards today, and since I can't really drive myself, I'm going to have to count on you to do that for me."

"The vineyards?" She looked at him in surprise. "What for?"

"I'm working up concepts for a new ad campaign, and I want to go out and get some sense of what is possible. Take some pictures. Get some ideas."

Pulling off her sunglasses, she glanced at him, then looked back more intently. His expression wasn't giving anything away, but she wondered what he was up to. "Does my father know you're going out there?" she asked.

A strange look passed over his face, then disappeared as mysteriously as it had come. "Why? Do you think I need his permission?"

She hesitated, thinking exactly that, but knowing from his tone that he wouldn't like her answer. Driving all the way out to the vineyards would take up most of the day. She thought quickly, going over things that needed her attention back at the office. There really wasn't anything that couldn't wait a day. And if he was going out there, she really ought to go along, just to keep an eye on him.

"Okay, I'll drive," she said quickly. "But…" She glanced at the toys littering the carpet. "What about your baby?"

"My mother's still got her. She already brought Katy by to say hello. I can't go a morning without a couple of baby kisses, you know." He grinned, remembering, and managed to look almost endearing. "And of course, my mother needed time to give me her daily lecture," he added mostly to himself, his smile fading.

"Lecture?" Suddenly the truth dawned on her. Why hadn't she thought of this before? "Your family doesn't like you working for Allman Industries anymore than I do, do they?"

His green eyes had a way of going opaque just when she most wanted to get a glimpse of some reaction from him. But she didn't really need to see confirmation. The McLaughlins still despised the Allmans. That was all she really needed to know.

She looked at him, with his flimsy pajama bottoms and the day's worth of beard darkening his face. There was no denying he was gorgeous. The sort of gorgeous that made your heart skip a beat and the breath stop in your throat for a second. The sort of gorgeous that made you think of skin against satin sheets and long kisses—and the way a man's hand felt running down across your naked flesh.

Uh-oh. No, not going to go there. If she planned to last any time at all, she was going to have to wipe that sort of thinking out of her head.

And then she noticed something that helped take it away. He was in pain. She could see him wince as he tried to move. And for just a moment, as he stood wavering against the crutches, obviously still not used to using them, she had a rush of pure empathy. Poor guy. She wanted to reach out to him, to do something to provide a little comfort, maybe some relief. If only…

"Now there's one more thing I need your help with," he was saying calmly, masking the pain with a smooth attitude. "I want to take a shower."

Okay. There it was. Jodie pressed her lips together and looked at the wall over his shoulder, holding back a volcano's worth of protest she could have spewed at him. *No emotion,* she reminded herself. *Cool and calm.*

"I really need one," he told her with a cheerfulness that seemed a little forced. "Even my hair itches. And I need a good shampoo." He wiggled his eyebrows at her. "Maybe you could rub it in for me?"

Why not a pedicure and a deep pore treatment while he was at it? There was no point in feeling sorry for the man. He just wasn't going to allow it. Gritting her teeth, she swung her gaze back to face him.

"I'd be happy to help you go soak your head," she told him carefully. "Just as long as you keep your clothes on."

His frown had a mocking edge to it. "I thought you said you weren't afraid of a little nudity."

"I can handle nudity. What I won't tolerate is familiarity. The kind your idea of shower-sharing might bring on."

Amusement played at the corners of his eyes. "So you still don't trust me."

"What was your first clue?"

"Wait a minute. Hold on here. You're lying, aren't you?"

"What?"

He shrugged as though the point was obvious. "It's yourself you don't trust. Am I right?"

She wanted to laugh, or at the very least, throw something at his handsome head. Instead, her face flushed bright red and she cursed her circulatory system.

"I knew it," he chortled, his eyelids lowering. "You're too hot-blooded to risk it. You know your naturally passionate nature will overwhelm you and you'll find yourself—"

"Heading out the door," she told him grimly, holding her head high despite the blushing. "Just watch me."

"Wait, Jodie," he said, laughing as he snagged her by the upper arm and held her from making good on her promise, despite the fact that he was tottering dangerously on the crutches. "I was only kidding. I'll be good. You'll see." He sobered, his eyes darkening as he looked down into her rebellious face. "Don't go. I really do need you."

What a delicious opening. She could laugh at him and walk away. Why not? He deserved it. And she was tempted. She could already feel the satisfaction of striding off down the walkway, leaving him stranded on his own doorstep.

Still, he halfway expected her to do that, didn't he? So why not surprise him? After all, she'd had enough training in this sort of thing to make it just possible that she might be able to keep her cool—and her distance— while performing the very task he needed her to do.

"Okay," she said, breezing past him into the house.

"I'll help you take a shower. Why not? Cleanliness is a good thing."

He turned a bit awkwardly on his crutches. "Great," he said. "I appreciate it."

She glanced down at his pajama bottoms. They were not quite as short as boxers, but the left pant leg had been split to allow it to go over the cast. The fabric was flimsy enough to leave little to the imagination, even as it pretended to cover the good parts. Despite all that expert training, her pulse stepped up a notch.

"One condition, though," she said firmly. "The pajamas stay on."

His brow furled. "That's going to make washing myself a bit difficult."

She risked looking him full in the face and found she could do it just fine. "I thought you were the sort who laughed at adversity." She smiled coolly. "Make adjustments."

"Adjustments!"

He seemed to have more to say on the subject, but she didn't stop to chat. Spotting a sliding glass door to the backyard, she made her way there and looked out. Just what she needed—a pair of plastic outdoor chairs. Sliding open the door, she grabbed them, stacked them and toted them into the house.

"Which way to the bathroom?" she asked brightly.

He still stood where she'd left him, wavering a bit on the crutches, his expression unreadable. "What are you doing?"

"Making adjustments," she told him. "The bathroom?"

He pointed the way and followed her, watching as she set up one chair inside the shower and the other just outside.

"There," she said, turning to offer a triumphant smile. "Now let's work on your leg."

It didn't take long to get him well-wrapped in plastic. She rolled the legs of the pajamas up and clipped them so that he seemed to be wearing very short shorts. And that was the rough part. Working over the cast was not a problem, but when the backs of her fingers had to brush against his warm skin, so close to forbidden areas of major interest, areas that seemed to radiate with scorching heat, she had to work very hard to keep her reactions from showing.

Kurt didn't say a word, and since she didn't look into his face, she had no idea what he was thinking. For her part, she was trying hard not to think at all.

Just get this done, she told herself. *You can scream later.*

Her background as a practicing physical therapist held her in good stead. Very quickly she had him sitting in the shower, with his left leg angled out and resting on the other chair. She tested the water and turned it on full for him, then handed him a bar of soap.

"There you go," she said with typically detached health-worker cheer. "Give me a call when you're ready to get hauled back out of there."

Turning on her heel, she left the room, then collapsed

against the wall once she was sure she was out of his sight. What a morning.

Her amusement faded as she went back over the last ten minutes and realized something. Through the whole thing, Kurt hadn't said a word to her. What was he thinking?

She frowned. He kept up a caustic front, but sometimes his eyes gave him away. She really ought to pay more attention to that. She didn't trust him at all.

The first time Jodie remembered actually paying any attention to Kurt McLaughlin was when she was about fourteen and she watched him win a bull-riding contest. She'd had mixed feelings about him even then. She knew she was supposed to hate him. He was a McLaughlin—but even worse, he was beating both her brothers at something one or the other of them usually won. Matt had been away at college all year, so there was general consensus that he'd gotten a little rusty. But Rafe was at the top of his game; he'd been unofficially crowned the winner before he even came out of the chute. So it was with stunned amazement that the crowd watched as Kurt beat him out of his title, mastering the huge, red bull as though he'd been born to ride it.

She remembered the outrage she'd felt, and at the same time, the guilty surge of admiration. He'd looked so calm and in control. And her newly minted teenage hormones had tingled at his confident grin and the cool way his jeans fit him.

He'd seemed so much older then, mature and out of

reach for a girl her age. And, of course, a McLaughlin. But that image of him vanquishing his competition on the bull had stayed with her for a long time.

And now that same man was sitting next to her in her car while she steered it down the long, straight and mostly empty highway toward the vineyards. It hadn't been easy wedging in his leg, with its fiberglass cast, and maneuvering his bottom—now clothed in jersey shorts—into the seat. But finally they were rushing across the golden plain toward the low, rolling hills on the horizon.

She'd noticed that he'd popped a couple of pain pills before they left the house. There was still the suggestion of a white line around his mouth which told her that the effects of the medication hadn't kicked in yet. She winced for him, wishing she could do something to take away the obvious agony. Hopefully, the pills would work soon.

"You okay?" she asked him softly.

He didn't look up, but he nodded. "Sure," he said gruffly, and then fell silent again—proof that he really wasn't.

Her mind went back again to that hot, dusty day at the Chivaree Jamboree Rodeo. She and her best friend, Shelley, had sat in the stands, soaking up the attention from the males around them. That sort of thing had been very new to both of them at that point, and they were a little scared and very excited. She could even remember what she'd been wearing—white short shorts

and a skimpy, red halter top that made her really feel like
a woman for the first time ever. Watching Kurt ride that
bull made her feel even more so. And when the horn
blew and the clowns came out, and he'd swung down
and turned to the crowd, she could have sworn he sin-
gled her out. His head went back, and a half grin curled
his mouth. And she was sure he was looking right at her.

But that only lasted for seconds. Maybe she'd
dreamed it. Almost immediately, a flood of Kurt's cousins had swarmed down to gather around him protec-
tively. Everyone knew there would be a fight. There
always was when McLaughlins and Allmans bumped up
against each other in the claustrophobic Chivaree world
of those days. And since the McLaughlin boys outnumbered the Allmans two to one, it was her brothers who
usually came home with blackened eyes and split lips.

The hills coming into range snapped her out of her
reverie.

"Where are we headed exactly?" she asked, glancing sideways at Kurt. "The Allman fields?"

"That's right. The ones the company owns outright."

She nodded. "How are the vineyards doing these
days?"

"Not as well as we could want," he admitted. "We're
still depending on crops from other suppliers for about
eighty percent of the grapes."

The business had started small, just Jesse cultivating
a small yield from a vineyard the Allmans had owned
since the twenties. But through pure brass, her father

had built it up. Now, they owned or had contracts with vineyards all over Texas hill country, and they bottled under a number of different names.

Kurt went on, talking about company business, and she was glad to see that he was feeling better. But when the facts and figures kept pouring out of him, she began to frown. Why did he seem to be so informed about all the ins and outs of her father's business dealings? For a marketing guy, he seemed awfully interested in the production numbers.

"Take the old Boca de Vaca Road turnoff up around the next bend," he told her. "We'll take it on out to Casa Azul."

That made her smile. "My father's old original vineyard?"

"Right." She could sense him studying her. "I'll bet you spent time there as a kid, didn't you?"

"Too much time." She groaned, remembering the long, fall days picking grapes when Allman Industries was just a dream her father was working toward. "Is anyone living in the old house?"

"Yes, the field manager. Who, I think, is an old friend of yours. Manny Cruz."

"Manny!" She laughed softly. Manny had been a good friend of Rafe's, and one of the few boys in town who was always ready to show up to help the Allman boys in any fight they got themselves into. "Good old Manny. It'll be great to see him again."

"He married Pam Kramer. They've got a couple of kids, from what I hear."

"Manny and Pam." She drew in a deep breath. "Wow. Time flies."

A shadow passed over her thoughts. So many old friends were married now and had children. A part of her hated that things had to change.

"Now this is what I love," Kurt said suddenly, startling her. "Look out there. Can you find a sky like that anywhere else? Can you see as far? Does anywhere else look this golden?" He turned to smile at her, pushing his Stetson back on his head. "That's why I came back. Texas is home."

She felt the same way, only she hadn't ever lived in any other state. But she knew what he meant. Texas was a place where there was room to breathe. Good thing, too, because once she took in that smile, the one thing she needed was more air.

They wound their way into the hills, and suddenly, vineyards covered the landscape, each vine newly leafed out and flowing with graceful promise.

"These through here belong to the Newcombs," Kurt told her. "And just up there past that stand of cottonwoods, the Allman property begins."

Fascinating. Ownership of this acreage had expanded a lot since the days when she and her brothers and sister had been forced to work the harvest. But once again she had to wonder why Kurt was taking such an active interest in these things that would seem to be beyond his need to know.

"Go slow through here," he said, pulling out his camera. "I want to take a few shots."

"Do you want me to stop?"

"Not yet. I'll tell you when."

He leaned out the open window as best he could, being tethered by his cast, taking one shot after another as she slowed.

"You said you were working on an idea for an ad campaign?" she asked.

"Right," he said shortly.

She waited a moment, but he didn't volunteer any more information. She frowned, looking out at the perfectly ordinary rows of grapevines he was taking pictures of, wondering what he could possibly have in mind. Whatever it was, he didn't seem to want to share.

"Pull down this dirt road," he said at last. "Let's go back in and stop. I want to get a closer look at these vines."

She did as he ordered, then pulled over and turned off the engine. "Are you sure you want to do this?" she asked, thinking of the trouble they'd had getting him into the car. "I don't know how often you're going to want to drag that cast in and out of this cramped space."

"I'm okay," he told her. "There's something I really need to see here."

She helped him out, and he did much better than he had before. He was starting to get the hang of it. Either that, or his mind was so thoroughly involved with whatever it was he was investigating, he had forgotten the pain.

The crutches sank into the rich loam, but he didn't

seem to notice. She followed behind, glad she'd worn slacks today, but trying to avoid getting sand in her shoes.

"This is really an impressive sight, isn't it?" he said. "Row upon row of these brave little soldiers."

Gee, that was almost poetry. He'd said the last softly, as though he didn't really mean for her to hear. She looked at him, wondering what went on inside that handsome head. Whatever it was, she wished there was a better way to get a hint of it.

Starting off, he led her to a vine that didn't look quite as healthy as the others. Leaning on one crutch, he reached out and plucked a few leaves, studying them intently.

"You see that?" he said, holding out one leaf.

She stared, biting her lip. "It looks okay to me."

He shook his head. "No. Something is definitely wrong. And look at those." He gestured toward a row of vines. "The vines just aren't bearing the way they should be. We've got to figure out what's going on here."

She watched him, surprised he was so absorbed in this. It hardly seemed to be something a marketing guy would want to immerse himself in.

"Listen," she said. "Why don't you leave this to the growers to worry about? Or have Manny call out the Department of Agriculture. I thought we came out here to take pictures."

"We did." He frowned. "Do me a favor," he said. "Pick a few more leaves, just randomly, but keep them separate. I want to take them back and get some opinions."

"Keep them separate?" She gazed at him, bewildered. "How am I supposed to do that?"

"You've got pockets, don't you?"

"Pockets," she muttered, but she began to do as he'd asked. She had three pockets in her dark blue slacks and two in the light, checkered shirt she wore. Once she'd stuffed each of them full, she began to feel like a pack animal.

The sound of a vehicle, traveling fast, distracted her. "Oh, look. Someone's coming."

A bright red pickup truck was barreling along an access road toward where they stood among the vines. They both stopped and looked up. Jodie frowned. There was something menacing about the way the truck was hurtling toward them—something she didn't like. She began to edge closer to where Kurt was standing, instinctively looking to him for protection.

Suddenly, the unmistakable sound of gunfire split the air.

Chapter Four

"What the hell?"

The words tore out of Kurt as he grabbed Jodie, pushed her down into the dirt and threw himself on top of her. His hat flew off, and the cast fell heavily against her leg, but she hardly noticed. The rest of his body was pressing her into the earth, and she had a weird sensation of drowning.

"Lie still," he barked at her. "That damned idiot."

"Who?" she tried to ask, struggling for breath. "What's going on?"

The pickup came to a gravel-crunching stop very near them. She could hear the cab door open, but she couldn't raise her head enough to look up and see what was happening. The smell and taste of dirt filled her nose and mouth.

"McLaughlin!" The shout came from the pickup. "Get off this land."

Kurt swore softly and raised his upper body. "Manny, are you crazy?" he shouted back. "You trying to kill somebody?"

"I only wish." Jodie heard a sound of disgust coming from the man in the truck. "Don't worry, McLaughlin. I didn't aim nowhere near you. This time."

The sound of a shotgun being cocked hit Jodie like a clap of thunder.

"But I could. Like I told you before, get back in your car and get your damned McLaughlin butt off this land. This here is Allman property and—"

"Manny Cruz."

Kurt had moved enough to let Jodie wiggle her way out from under him. She pushed up into a sitting position. "Manny, this is one heck of a way to welcome me home. You're as crazy as you ever were, aren't you?"

"Jodie?" Manny stared for a moment, then a wide grin broke out on his dark, handsome face. "Hey, Jodie! I haven't seen you since…since…"

"For a long time," she said, helping him out. She rose shakily to her feet and waved at him. "So, how've you been?"

"Hey, great." He looked pleased as punch. "Did you know Pam Kramer and I got hitched?"

"I heard."

"And we've got two kids. You got to come out to the house and see them."

Jodie swallowed and managed a smile, wiping her face with her sleeve. "I'd love to. You won't shoot us, will you?"

Manny looked shocked. He glanced at the shotgun still resting in his hands and quickly put it down against the truck as though he had no further use for it.

"Hell, no. That was just a warning for this McLaughlin punk." His face changed along with his tone of voice. "Hey, what are you doing with this guy, anyway?"

"That's a question I've asked myself a few times today," she told him, giving Kurt a sideways glance. "Dad hired him, though, so I guess you'd better not shoot him."

Manny shook his head. "I'd heard that, but I didn't want to believe it." His tone conveyed his deep distaste. "McLaughlins don't work for Allmans. Or the other way round, either. It just ain't natural."

"I'll tell you what ain't natural," Kurt countered, starting toward the man, his voice hard with anger. "It ain't natural or legal or right for you to shoot at people. If you've got a problem with me, let's take care of it right now."

Both men bristled with belligerence, but then Manny's face changed as he took in the cast on Kurt's leg. Kurt seemed to have forgotten about it. He was rushing toward Manny, even though he'd lost his crutches, hopping on his good foot, his anger giving him the strength to make the charge. Manny looked confused. How was he going to fight a man with a broken leg?

Suddenly, Jodie began to laugh.

"This isn't funny," Kurt said, pausing to glare back at her.

"Oh, yes it is," she said, laughing harder. "This is the funniest thing I ever saw. Us hitting the dirt, and Manny driving up in his truck, and you trying to fight him with only one good leg." She sank back down to sit on the ground, and laughed until her sides hurt.

The two men stood glaring at her, both with hands balled into fists at their sides. But the need to fight seemed to have evaporated, at least for now. And for that, she was grateful.

The old sky-blue farmhouse didn't look quite the way it had when Jodie and her family had come out here years before. A small, pink oleander bush stood next to the porch, petunias brightened a window box, and the roof looked new. A cute little pond shimmered in the sunlight where there once had been a mud hole from a leaky faucet. Jodie pulled the car up beside the driveway and came around to help Kurt. Manny had sent them on ahead while he went to take a few workers to another field.

Meanwhile, Kurt was telling her about his last visit to the vineyards a few weeks before.

"I didn't see Manny, but some of his workers followed me everywhere I went. They stayed just out of reach, but communicated with their boss on walkie-talkies, letting him know what I was doing."

She'd been moving his bad leg out of the car, but now she stopped to look him in the face. "What *were* you doing?"

His smile was guileless. "Looking things over."

She gave him a penetrating look. There was no point in hiding the fact that she had her suspicions about him. "I see."

But he seemed oblivious. "And the next day there was a message left on my desk. Something about McLaughlins staying off Allman land."

"Or what?" she said, handing him his crutches as he made his way onto his feet.

He shrugged. "There were a few nasty suggestions as to what might happen to me, but I won't bore you with the details."

She nodded. "So you decided to trot right back out here and give him the old nah-nah-nah-nah, huh?"

"Of course." He looked bemused that she would expect anything else. "He had no right to try to keep me away."

She spread out her hands as though explaining to the heavens. "Of course."

As they started up the walkway, a small child came rocketing out the front door. His lower lip stuck out with stark determination, the tyke was heading away as fast as his chubby little legs would take him. From inside the house, a voice came sailing after him.

"Lenny, you get back here! Don't you dare go down there by that pond!"

Kurt handed Jodie one of his crutches and took a side

step to intercept the little fellow, scooping him up and dangling him at eye level.

"Hi," Kurt said to the child, whose mouth was hanging open in astonishment. "Where you goin' so fast?"

The little boy struggled for a moment, but Kurt's wide grin seemed to mesmerize him, and soon he was grinning back.

"Oh, my, how did you catch him?" A pretty, young woman with bright red hair appeared in the doorway, a baby on her hip. "Thanks so much. He keeps running down to the pond and jumping right in, and then I have to wash the frog's eggs out of his hair."

"I've got one about this age myself," Kurt told her pleasantly, carrying the little one toward the house. "I know what they're like."

Jodie would have marveled at how well he was learning to maneuver with his crutches—or without them—but her attention was riveted on the children. She usually tried to avoid being around kids this young. Even after all these years, it still hurt so much. Turning away from babies the way some turned away from the sight of blood, she tried to focus on her old friend instead.

"Pam?" she said, waiting for the young woman to turn her gaze in her direction.

The woman gasped. "No way! Jodie! Jodie Allman! I heard you were back. It's been years!"

Jodie exchanged hugs with Pam, carefully avoiding the baby she still held to her body. Pam chattered happily, escorting them into her house as though she'd been expecting them.

"You're just in time for lunch. Come on in. I'll put another couple of plates on the table."

"Oh, we couldn't impose."

"Are you kidding? I always cook enough for all the hands, and I just got word that somebody's girlfriend made a run into town and showed up with a big sack of Mickey D's, so I was going to have good food going to waste. You'll be doing me a favor. Come on in and sit down. It'll be ready in no time at all. Where's Manny? Has he seen you yet? He's going to be thrilled! All he ever talks about is the old days and how much fun it was fighting McLaughlins."

She cast a covert glance at Kurt. "I guess you're one of them, though, ain't you? I seem to remember you." She rolled her eyes as though anyone could see that was a joke. Remember Kurt? Who could forget? "Jodie and I were in class with your sister, Tracy, until she left to go to that private boarding school." She gave Jodie a significant look. "Remember that? I don't know if we were more jealous or outraged at the time. But it sure did cause a stir. Boarding school, of all things!"

"A lot of people go to boarding school," Kurt protested.

"Not around here they don't."

Jodie made formal introductions and explained that they had seen Manny out in the fields. While Pam kept up a running monologue, she got the table set, food served, Lenny into a high chair and the baby into a little recliner. Jodie was in awe.

"Pam," she said at last. "I remember when you couldn't get your Latin homework done because you had to paint your toenails one night. Now you're multitasking. What happened?"

Pam shook back her red curls and laughed. "I grew up, Jodie. Surely you did, too."

Had she? Jodie wasn't so sure.

"Having kids really changes you, you know? It starts when you're pregnant. You just become a different person when you start thinking about the life you're creating."

Pam turned to look into Jodie's face. "But maybe you do know. For all I know, you've been married and had a dozen kids by now." She grinned at her old friend. "Or at least one. You've got that look. How about it, honey? Do you have any kids?"

Jodie's mouth was dry and her heart pounded in her chest. This was just so stupid. Pam hadn't meant anything; she was just being friendly. There was no way she could have known about the baby Jodie had lost all those years ago.

Hopefully, no one in Chivaree knew.

Luckily she didn't have to answer, because Pam's youngest started to fuss, and Kurt picked her up to comfort her in the most natural way possible. Jodie envied him his ease with little ones. If she could just get control of herself, maybe she could get to be that comfortable. It was way past time for her to work on it. More and more of her old friends were going to be thrusting their children at her. She couldn't keep acting like a vampire seeing the sun. It was ridiculous.

Still, she moved across the room and started helping Pam, just to make sure Kurt didn't try to get her to hold the baby, as well.

And then Manny appeared in the doorway, taking off his straw hat and scowling just as darkly as he had out in the vineyard when he saw Kurt holding his child.

"Here," he said gruffly, reaching for her.

Pam took in the tension in a glance and began chattering again, getting everyone to sit down at the table and taking the baby back to the bedroom to put her into her crib. Manny and Kurt stared at each other until Pam called Kurt to come back to the baby's room to see the new train set she'd ordered for Lenny, thinking he'd be interested because of his own little one.

Once Kurt was out of the room, Manny looked Jodie in the eye, shaking his head.

"Will you explain to me what your dad is doing hirin' this bum?" he said in a low voice, his dark eyes flashing. "You can tell he's up to no good."

Jodie felt jolted. Finally someone agreed with her. She looked eagerly into his gaze. "You feel it, too?"

"Sure." He shrugged as though he thought it was a no-brainer. "He's a McLaughlin, ain't he?"

She frowned. It was more than that. Was this just a knee-jerk reaction Manny had? For that matter, were her own feelings about Kurt just as blind?

"Well, my brothers seem to think he's doing a good job," she pointed out, wanting to be fair.

Manny grunted. "Around here, we don't call a man a cowboy 'til we seen him ride."

Pam and Kurt came back and sat down to eat. Manny brought out a handful of glasses and a bottle of Allman Vineyards Chardonnay.

"You'll like this one," he said, giving them a little background on the vintage as he began to pour out the golden liquid into each glass. "It's fruity, but so light you'd almost swear it had some natural carbonation to it."

Jodie smiled. She could remember when Manny was a guy who spent most of his free time working on cars, and now here he was, a wine connoisseur. She watched as Kurt put his hand over his glass.

"None for me, thanks," he said.

Manny's face darkened. He'd obviously decided to take that as an insult. Jodie winced, then realized Kurt was turning down the alcohol because of the pain pills he'd taken. But the conversation had moved on, and it was too late to tell Manny that.

Jodie and Pam did most of the talking during the meal, dredging up old times and laughing over old incidents. Manny and Kurt were mostly silent. Now and then, Jodie looked over at Kurt, wishing he would join in on the conversation. But finally she realized he was thinking about something and not really listening to the chattering.

Manny's thoughts were written on his face. He detested Kurt. But she was pretty sure Kurt wasn't think-ing about Manny at all. He had something else on his mind and he was giving her no hints as to what it was.

Jodie helped clear away the dishes, and Manny went to hold Lenny while Pam cut them each a sliver of rich lemon cake for dessert. Kurt didn't look up when Jodie placed his piece in front of him, and she was about to give him a kick under the table when he suddenly pulled out a handful of the leaves he'd taken from the grape-vines and began to arrange them on the tabletop.

"What the hell are you doin'?" Manny demanded.

Kurt looked up as though he was surprised to see any-one else there. "I've been thinking. Listen, about the problem with the vines…"

"We had the guy from the Department of Agriculture out here three times," Manny told him dismissively. "If he can't figure out what's wrong, what makes you think you can?"

"I'm no expert, but—"

Manny snorted. "Damn right. You're a McLaughlin, ain't ya? Ever done anything right?"

Jodie looked quickly at Kurt. In the old days, those would have been fighting words. She could already pic-ture the two men rolling around on the linoleum floor, trading insults and punches in the old traditional dance of hatred between the two sides. She fully expected to see Kurt's face flush and his eyes gleam with anger. In-stead, he seemed more impatient with the nonsense Manny was spewing than anything.

"Listen, this is important. There's something about these leaves that keeps reminding me of something, and I'm not sure what it is. But I did my undergraduate work in botany at the university, and I still have ties to some professors there. I'm going to send them these leaves and see if they can come up with anything."

Manny's face didn't change, but he dropped the antagonistic insults. "I don't suppose they'll come up with anything new," he said, as he watched Kurt's face.

"You never know. They are developing new ways to diagnose this stuff all the time. If anyone knows the latest, my old professor Willard Charlton will have the scoop. He loves keeping up with the cutting-edge research."

Manny still looked suspicious, but what Kurt had said had definitely engaged his interest.

"What do you think it is?" he asked.

"I don't know. But look here on the back of the leaves. There are little clusters of tiny shot holes. You see?" He held the leaves up to the light so Manny could see them. "You really have to look close to notice them. I'm thinking some sort of new fungus or parasite is attacking the plants, something so small, we don't detect it easily."

Manny took one of the leaves and stared at it, looking from one way and then another. "We've tried fungicides," he said gruffly. "And I spray all the time. If it was a parasite…"

"If it was anything we could recognize, we'd know it by now."

Kurt asked Jodie for the leaves he'd had her set aside, and put them out in a line across from the infected leaves. He went on talking, showing things to Manny, and Jodie watched as the vineyard manager's belligerence died, and reluctant respect took over. Soon they were talking together like regular acquaintances, if not actual friends.

And just like that he was winning over Manny. Jodie shook her head with a tinge of resentment. She couldn't believe it. This was always happening around the man!

"How come you go out of your way to charm everybody except for me?" Jodie asked Kurt later, as they were driving home.

"You?" Obviously surprised by her comment, he grinned at her. "I know you're too smart for me, Jodie. I wouldn't insult you by trying to charm you."

Watching the road, she waved at the driver of a long cow trailer as she passed him. She couldn't help nursing feelings just this side of being hurt. Which was ridiculous, of course. Still, she was only human.

"Somehow you manage to get everyone else on your side. It's like you have this fine sense of exactly what will bring them around, and you play your cards just right. But all you do is needle me." She glanced over at where he sat. Oh, lord, she was whining, wasn't she? "So tell me why."

He sighed and leaned back. He didn't say anything for a long moment, and she began to think he was going to ignore her question. Finally, he responded.

"I can't tell you that, Miss Jodie Allman," he drawled in his best Texas accent. "With you, I'm just doin' what comes naturally, I guess."

"So you have a natural antagonism for me," she ventured.

"Could be."

Oh, he wasn't even trying! A flash of anger shot through her. "Either that," she snapped, "or your natural state is pretty Neanderthal."

"Hey, that hurts. I consider myself a real gentleman."

Okay, he was teasing. No need for her to take anything he said seriously.

"Of the old school," she shot back. "Circa 1210 in Outer Mongolia."

He chuckled. The way he was sitting, she could tell that he was completely relaxed. Well, that was one thing anyway. At least he didn't hate her so much that she made him tense up.

He'd taken more pain medication before they'd left Manny and Pam's ranch house. By the time they had walked out the door and piled back into the car, he and Manny had been exchanging e-mail addresses, and Pam had been planning to set up play dates for her little Lenny and Kurt's Katy.

It was infuriating how he seemed to stay in control of every situation all the time. She was going to do her best to find some way to get under his skin. It would be interesting to see him lose that finely honed sense of command.

"I was just remembering the first time I really knew you existed," he said all at once, out of the blue.

"At the Chivaree rodeo?" she asked before she could stop herself. A vision of how he'd looked as he triumphantly swung down off that bull and seemed to catch her eye in the stands flashed back like a delicious shock of sensation. But she immediately regretted saying anything and bit her tongue.

"The rodeo?" He frowned as though he had no idea what she was talking about, then shook his head.

She groaned inside, knowing she'd been a little too obvious. But maybe he hadn't noticed.

"No, not that. It was when we were both pretty young."

Even though she wasn't looking at him, she could feel him studying her profile as she drove. Her cheeks began to heat up, and she cursed silently. She wasn't usually self-conscious with men. Why did she keep doing this whenever Kurt paid a little too much attention to her?

"Do you remember," he said softly, "the time my sister had a birthday party at Sam Houston Park, and you were hanging around on the outskirts, watching it?" There was a warm hint of amusement in his voice. "I think I was twelve, so you must have been about seven or eight."

She frowned. That was a bit early for major recollections. She tried to think.

"I saw you watching the proceedings like a waif with

her nose pressed to the glass. I thought you were a cute little thing, so I decided to get you to join in. I went down by the merry-go-round, where you were lurking, and I invited you to come on up. But you scowled at me and shook your head."

He laughed aloud. "You still have that look a lot today—that look that says, 'Don't tempt me. I won't be compromised!'"

She wasn't about to dignify his silliness with a response, so she pressed her lips together.

"Anyway, I went back up and got you an ice-cream cone and brought it down to you. Looking back, it was like offering a piece of meat to a wolf puppy—holding it there, talking soothingly to you, watching you come warily forward to get the cone. Like a little wild child." He paused, remembering. "When you think about it, you Allman kids often seemed like little beasts in those days."

"Oh, for heaven's sake!" She'd had about enough of this. She didn't want to hear it, didn't want to think of how it had been back then. "We did not. Things like that were all in your head, and you McLaughlins spent so much time spreading that nonsense, it was like a giant propaganda campaign. You were the ones who started calling us the Allman Gang. We knew you were doing it, and we resented it!"

"I held the cone out," he went on as though she hadn't spoken. "You came closer and closer, your eyes glued to that ice cream. Oh, you wanted it, all right. And finally, you took it from my hand and looked up at me and almost smiled."

"Almost?"

He nodded. "Almost."

She waited for him to go on, and fleeting memories of the birthday flooded through her. She recalled skulking around the edges of the festivities, feeling like an outcast, wishing she would be invited in.

"You took that cone and you were getting ready to taste it. I was getting ready to enjoy you tasting it. And then you looked up, and suddenly, everything changed. You yelled a name at me, threw the cone down in the dirt, turned on your heel and took off, racing across the park with your pigtails flying." He looked at her as though that reaction still puzzled him. "Do you remember that?"

She tried. She remembered parts, but only vaguely. And she surely didn't remember throwing the ice cream cone in the dirt. Actually, knowing the way she'd felt about ice cream as a kid, she found that part a bit hard to believe.

But now that he'd mentioned it, she could remember a boy standing there holding the cone, looking at her. Yes, the picture became clearer. Was that really Kurt? She didn't think she could have named him at the time. She could remember feeling embarrassed and gratified all at once. And she thought she recalled a sense of guilt. What was that for?

"My young male ego was very affronted at what you

did," he told her lightly. "I guess that's why I still have it in my mind after all these years."

She thought about that for a long moment, then shook her head. "How do you know it was me?"

"I knew you were an Allman. That was obvious. And I asked my sister who you were."

Jodie frowned. "Tracy was watching all this?"

He shrugged. "She was around. It was her birthday party."

Wait. Yes, she remembered now. She could see the cone lying in the dirt, ice cream flying from it. She must have thrown it down, just as he'd said. But why?

"Looks like we're almost home," Kurt said. "Why don't you just drop me at the curb and go on in to the office to see if anything needs my attention. You can call me from there if anything does." He winced, moving his leg. "But make sure it's important. It's almost quitting time."

"Fine," she said, her voice a little strained, as she pulled in front of his house. Turning off the engine, she started to get out to help him, but he stopped her.

"I can get it," he said. "You just go on."

"Okay," she said reluctantly. "I guess I'll see you tomorrow."

"That's the plan," he said, reaching for the door handle.

"Kurt, wait." She was nuts. Completely nuts. He was going to see that she was desperately trying to think of reasons to delay him getting out of the car.

And why was she doing that? Oh, yeah. It was because she was nuts.

"Uh... how does your leg feel?" she asked quickly.

"Not too bad."

"You were much too hard on it today," she fretted. "I hope it hasn't set back your recovery."

One eyebrow rose sardonically. "Are you actually concerned about my welfare?"

"Of course I am."

"Ah. Just as one human being to another, no doubt."

"No." She was being an idiot, but she couldn't stop herself. "Kurt, I..." She winced and looked away, biting her lip. "I do care. Actually, I...I kind of like you. Whenever I can forget the McLaughlin part of you," she added hastily.

He laughed gruffly, and she looked up in time to see him reach out and touch her cheek, his fingers leaving a trail of sweet sensation.

"I'm so tempted to kiss you right now," he said softly, his eyes glowing. "If you weren't an Allman, I might actually do it."

This was all wrong and exactly what she'd been so determined to guard against. So why did she find herself smiling at him and feeling kind of shy? And why was her heart thumping in her chest like a wild thing? She was actually leaning toward him as though she was being pulled by some irresistible force.

And he was leaning toward her.

She closed her eyes and his lips touched hers. Just barely. The gesture was quick, almost casual, like the salute of a friend rather than a lover, but it made its mark. A wave of warm pleasure surged through her as the full, male essence of him swept over her—his wide shoulders, warm, masculine scent and smooth, tanned skin. All of this filled her with a deep yearning and she sighed as he pulled away again.

Her eyes flew open in horror. Had he noticed the sigh? She saw quick surprise flash in his gaze, and then a half smile before he leaned toward her again. This time the gentle touch was gone and she tasted raw male desire that made her heart stop.

But once again he drew back so quickly that she was left off balance, blinking up at him with her lips parted. He hesitated, his gaze caressing her mouth for just a moment before he began pulling himself out of the car. At first it was a bit awkward for him, and she had to stifle the urge to help. But once he got his bearings, he seemed to be fine. She watched as he made his way up the walkway toward his front door. He didn't even look back.

And why did that bring something that felt almost like a lump to her throat? She wanted him to turn, didn't she? She wanted him to smile at her, give her a wink, maybe—something personal. Let her know that he was going to miss her while they were apart. Let her know that he had enjoyed her company for the day and was looking forward to seeing her tomorrow. Maybe even let her know that he didn't regret the kiss.

Because the truth was, that was how she was feeling. Yup, the verdict was in. She was nuts.

Chapter Five

"I am not helping you take another shower."

Jodie was at Kurt's door again, and he was dressed the same way he had been the morning before—in almost nothing. But this time, his hair was wet and he had a towel hanging over his shoulders. So when he said, "I already took care of that," she believed him and felt a distinct sense of relief.

Still, she had a feeling he'd remained at this level of undress just to provoke her. Today she vowed to be unprovokeable.

She'd spent a sleepless night worrying about the kiss. And then she'd had her morning cup of coffee, looked at herself in the mirror and wondered what all the anguish had been about. As a kiss, it had been pretty quick and uneventful. Nothing to get herself in a dither about.

And she almost had herself convinced—until she'd remembered how she'd practically gone into a swoon and had let out that sigh full of longing. What would she have done if he'd actually taken her into his arms? She had a sinking feeling that she would have gotten swept away by the moment.

Oh, well. Good thing she recognized the danger signals. That should help her keep her guard up from now on. And as she made herself meet his gaze with a cool look, she was glad to see he didn't seem to be anxious to bring up the kiss himself.

"Good," she said briskly, coming right in and dropping a stack of manila folders on the table. "Now all we have to do is get some decent clothes on you."

He turned on his crutches, following her progress through his house. "What is this annoying obsession you have with hiding human body parts?" he teased.

"It's *my* obsession, and I'm standing by it," she retorted.

No, indeed, he wasn't going to get her goat today. She glanced down the hall toward his bedroom. She'd already raided it the day before, getting him ready for the trip to the vineyards, so she would feel right at home visiting it again. The only trouble was, the way he was standing was right in the path she had to take.

She gazed at him challengingly. "Make way. I'm going to get you dressed."

He didn't move, and one eyebrow rose quizzically.

"You wouldn't take advantage of a man on crutches, would you?"

"Heavens, no." She smiled at him, her chin high. "I'd knock him off them first."

He nodded, grinning. "Of that I have no doubt."

But he shuffled out of her way, and she went into his room and came back with sweatpants and a polo shirt.

"You really are going to have to work harder on maintaining a businesslike appearance, you know," she scolded. "Otherwise, people are going to get the wrong idea about what is going on here."

"What *is* going on here?" he asked, as she handed him the shirt. He dropped one crutch and began fumbling with the opening until she sighed and reached out to help him. "Is there any hope it might turn into something interesting?"

"That depends on your definition of interesting," she said, as she pulled his shirt over his head. Her fingers lingered on his skin, and she was glad his face was under cloth so he couldn't see her reaction. Her eyes closed for just a moment as she soaked in the pure maleness of him. "I very much doubt we would have definitions that agreed," she added a bit breathlessly.

"You might be right." He scrunched into the shirt and, as his head cleared the opening, she found herself staring right into his eyes. Suddenly, his free hand was sliding into the hair at the back of her head, and somehow he managed to pull her close enough so that her body was touching his in all the wrong places.

"For instance, I'd say this qualifies," he said, his voice rough in a deep way that seemed to resonate inside her.

She stared back into his gaze, her heart in her throat. If he knew how much she liked this, she would be in big trouble. Best to pretend it was no big deal. But how did she do that when every fiber of her being wanted to feel him tight and hard against her? Still, it had to be done. Gathering her strength, she pulled away from him.

True to form, he laughed. *You see?* his laughter said. *I'm just kidding around. This is no big deal.*

She bit her lip, wishing she didn't feel this overwhelming attraction to the man. What was she going to do to stop from melting into another kiss with him? Too much of this and she was going to surrender.

"Hey, don't look so sad," he teased. "I can take the shirt back off."

She reacted instinctively, reaching out to give him a whack in the shoulder, and he caught her hand, pulling her close again.

"This could be considered sexual harassment," she said stoutly, firmly determined not to let herself notice how good he smelled, all freshly showered and clean and smooth…

He raised one dark eyebrow. "What are you going to do? Turn me in to the big boss?"

"Why not? You deserve it." She licked her dry lips. "And he is my father. He'll do whatever I ask, don't you think?"

Kurt laughed again, looking quizzical. "In a word, no." But he let her go.

"That's the problem," she said, straightening her cotton shirt and managing to keep her cool, though her senses were reeling. "I need more clout so you'll listen to my threats."

He noticed she was still holding the sweatpants and looking doubtful, and he took them from her. "Don't worry. I'll sit down and put these on myself."

She almost thanked him, but she stopped herself in time. That would be pathetic, wouldn't it?

Things had changed a lot between them in the last two days. She still didn't trust him, but she had to admit, she was starting to enjoy being with him. Oh, danger, danger! She was going to have to toughen her defenses here. Hadn't she been down this road with a McLaughlin before?

And that was from where she would draw her strength. All she had to do was remember how his cousin Jeremy had abandoned her when she'd needed him most. That ought to keep her from letting another McLaughlin get into her heart.

The toys were driving her crazy.

Ignore them. Pretend they're rocks. Keep your head down and work.

But no matter what she was doing, she could see them out of the corner of her eye. Fuzzy little stuffed animals, a pink stuffed horse, two dolls with purple hair, a silver ball, a tall, skinny monster with green scales. They were crowding out everything else with the essence of *baby*. This was not how she wanted to waste her day.

She and Kurt had spent two hours working on his plan for a new ad campaign. They'd spent half the time brainstorming, and now were high-grading the results and blocking out a proposal. Once they had this down cold, it would go to the ad agency Allman Industries worked with, and the agency would come back with its own ideas.

And truth be told—they worked well together. Kurt was definitely in charge, but he listened to her without condescension and often took her advice to heart. She felt like a respected member of a team rather than hired help.

The phone rang, and Kurt hobbled into the hall to take the call. Jodie saw her chance and rose from the table, scooping up the toys, one after another, dumping them onto a corner of the couch. Now, to cover them with something. Gazing about the room, she didn't see anything better than one of the big, flat pillows from the couch itself, and she picked one up for the purpose.

Kurt came back into the room just as she was placing the pillow. She flushed when she realized he'd seen her. She put it down with relish, like a wicked stepmother out to smother the poor little toys. She turned, knowing she looked guilty. He frowned, looking puzzled, but he didn't ask for an explanation.

"That was Pam," he said. "She's going to bring

Lenny over to play with Katy on Saturday when they come into town to do some shopping."

"Saturday? Oh. Great." She couldn't keep the relief out of her voice. "I won't be here."

He frowned, looking back at the couch, where the toys were peeking out from under the pillow like forlorn refugees.

"Why do you hate children?" he asked.

The word *hate* made her cringe. "I don't hate children," she protested.

"I saw how you were yesterday at Lenny and Pam's. You would have thought the kids had something you were afraid you might catch."

So he'd noticed that.

"Oh, please." She sat back down at the table and shuffled some papers. "I've never been around kids much. So I'm just not comfortable interacting with them." She risked a look at his face. He was still frowning. "They just don't figure in my life, that's all."

"How tragic for you."

"Not at all," she said defensively. "I like it that way."

He sat down across from her, looking concerned. "You don't want to ever have children?"

She shook her head, dismissing his concerns. "It just works out that way for some people, you know."

She knew it was silly to have this anxiety about kids, but she couldn't help it. Why couldn't people respect that and leave her alone?

Once people had children, they seemed to think that

everyone else should want to drool over them all day, too. So far, she'd been lucky to avoid Kurt's baby, but she had no doubt her luck couldn't hold forever. She had plans made, excuses to use, just in case anyone tried to get her to do anything with the baby. It wasn't that she couldn't handle holding a little one like that. She just didn't want to.

Kurt seemed to have given up on scrutinizing her mind-set and gone back to his own problems.

"I'm afraid I'm going to have some trouble where Katy is concerned," he said, absently playing with his pencil. "My sister has been taking care of her most days, along with my mother. And Tracy is talking about leaving town very soon."

"Oh?"

He nodded and grimaced. "Tracy thinks she's found the love of her life," he said wryly.

"Maybe she has."

"Maybe. But since this is perfect lover number—oh, I don't know, about four hundred and fifty—I'd say the odds are against it." His smile was sad and fleeting. "Talk about someone who never gives up hope. A real optimist is our Tracy. She's already got two divorces under her belt. Looks like she's aiming for number three."

"You know, you're being much too cynical." She couldn't believe she was actually defending his sister after the cruel way she'd taunted Jodie when they were kids. Maybe it was the feminine right to change her mind she was standing up for. "She may really have found the right one this time."

His sexy mouth tilted in a smile. "You mean, as in 'Even a stopped clock is right twice a day'?"

"That wasn't exactly what I meant, but it will do."

He shook his head. "I might have more hope if she would start looking for a mate in places where nice guys hang out. Instead, she picks the scene that caters to jerks."

"Bars and pool halls?" Jodie asked sympathetically.

He glanced up, his gaze guileless. "No. The law firm where she works."

"Kurt!"

"I'm not kidding. Every man she brings home wants to be my legal and financial advisor and, in the course of conversation, it usually turns out he's got some great business idea that is a sure thing and he only needs a small business loan to get it off the ground."

She made a face. "Scam artists?"

"To one degree or another. Dreamers, too. They're as optimistic as she is."

She studied his face. He was frustrated with his sister's bad judgment, but worried about her, as well. That much was surely evident. And from what she remembered of Tracy, worrying was probably justified.

"It's good to dream," she said softly, holding out hope.

"Sure. As long as you do something to back it up. Dreams aren't much use without some muscle behind them."

He went on, but she was only listening lightly. She'd recalled something during the night, lying in her bed and staring at the ceiling. The whole scene where Kurt—only she hadn't realized it was him at the time—had handed her the ice cream cone and she'd thrown it in the dirt had come to her while she was dozing. She remembered what had made her throw his generous gesture back at him.

She'd reached out, and the cone was in her hand. Anticipation trembled in her. The Allmans were dirt poor in those days, and ice cream cones didn't grow on trees. She'd looked up at the boy—Kurt—to say "thank you," as her mama had taught her to do. But what she'd seen behind Kurt had changed everything.

There was Tracy, along with a few of her friends, all laughing and making faces at Jodie. It suddenly became very clear that she was in the position of the poor, little beggar girl, and they were mocking her for it. She hadn't been invited to the party and they knew it. Even at seven years of age, Jodie had learned the hard way that pride was sometimes more important to the psyche than shame, even if it cost her the thing she wanted most. That was the Allman way. So she'd thrown the cone in the mud and run off, tears making trails through the dirt on her little-girl face. But they were tears that Tracy and her friends would never see.

Should she tell Kurt about it?

Maybe. Someday. Not now.

He'd been the only one to acquit himself in the incident. Gazing at him now, that gave her a glow. He was actually a pretty good person. And that was rare for a McLaughlin.

Still, there was this odd situation with him working for the Allmans. She just couldn't reconcile that with the antagonisms of the past. What had made him do it?

Kurt chose that moment to bring up the new production numbers, and that gave Jodie the opening she needed to do a little digging.

"Tell me why you're so interested in everything that has to do with Allman Industries," she said, leaning across the table and studying his reaction.

He gazed at her levelly, totally aware of why she was asking.

"I work there," he said simply.

She narrowed her gaze, pinning him to the wall—or, at least, trying to. "You don't seem to treat your job like an everyday worker would. You seem much too involved in what's going on behind the scenes."

"Behind the scenes?" He used a mockingly dramatic voice. "Are you sniffing out a conspiracy here?"

"All I know is," she said, jabbing at him with a finger, "you fit the picture of someone who is thinking about trying to take over the company."

He looked Cheshire-cat smug. "Do I?"

He didn't deny it! What did that mean? How arrogant!

"Is that your plan? Is that *it*?"

She was beginning to think it actually might be true. Glaring at him, she went on. "Is this just another chapter in the same old feud? I know you'll deny it, but why else would you come to work for my father? You were raised to hate us." She shook her head. "It seems like the only logical explanation."

He watched her as though bemused. "Wow. Once you get rolling, you forget all about the brakes, don't you?" he said.

"Kurt—"

He held up a hand. "My turn. Jodie, I will tell you exactly why I signed on at Allman Industries."

She took a deep breath and nodded. "Okay. Go ahead."

"It was the best job I could find."

She waited, but there didn't seem to be any more information coming.

"That's it?" she asked in disbelief.

"That's it." He seemed to enjoy her consternation, but finally he relented and told her more.

"I worked in management at a major multinational corporation in New York for a few years and did pretty well. Made a good salary. When I came back to Chivaree, I knew I was going to be taking a pay cut no matter what I did. But when I found out the only openings were at Pete's garage and the busboy position at Millie's café, I decided I had to get creative. Allman Industries was the only large and thriving business in town. So I went to see your father."

Despite herself, she was impressed—if he was really on the level with her. Could she believe him?

The only alternative was to go on thinking he was somehow working to undermine her father's business. And when you came right down to it, that was beginning to look a little silly, even to her. Why would he bother? She was starting to think his innocent act was pretty convincing. Everyone else believed him. She felt very much alone clinging to her suspicions.

"I think I'm doing a pretty good job, Jodie," he told her earnestly. "I'm definitely committed to Allman Industries. I've told you before that I love this little town, and your father's company is making things better here for everyone. We all win."

Maybe he was right.

But then she remembered hints he'd given about his own family. "I know your mother isn't happy about you working for us. What about the rest of your family?"

"My father doesn't have an opinion. He hasn't been seen for six months. You did know he is taking an extended tour of Europe?"

"I'd heard that." She'd also heard that he and his father didn't get along, but that was hardly unusual.

"Tracy feels the same way my mother does. My uncle wanted me to come work the ranch with him, but…" He shook his head, his green eyes haunted. "No, I couldn't do it. That was not for me. Especially not working with my cousin Josh."

She made a face. It was strange to think of his family this way.

"I always thought of the McLaughlins as a sort of monolith," she said slowly. "I didn't know you all had disagreements among yourselves." She grinned suddenly. "I would have thought you'd have used up all that energy fighting with us all those years."

"You and all those brothers," he agreed with a nod.

"Yeah. And you with all those cousins." A picture of Jeremy flashed in her mind, but she pushed it away. "You outnumbered us two to one."

"Possible." His smile was teasing. "But we were the kind, magnanimous, open ones and you were the crafty, sneaking, back-biting—"

She brandished a small fist his way. "Watch it, McLaughlin. I can feud with the best of them."

His gaze seemed to glow, and he drawled out, "Oh, I'll just bet you can, Jodie Allman."

She found herself smiling into his eyes, and the moment held a few beats too long, until she was almost embarrassed, and looked back down at her work.

But it was hard to get her mind back on it again. Her thoughts were full of McLaughlins and Allmans—of Jeremy, and their secret, forbidden romance…of her father, and how hard he'd worked to get the business up and running in order to prove something to the McLaughlins…of her mother, and how she'd died much too young. Officially her mother had succumbed to cancer. But Jodie had always suspected she'd been vulnerable to illness because she'd been so worn down by the feud. The fight between the two families had colored all their lives for over a hundred years. And now here was Kurt, ready to bury it.

Did that make him a hero? Or a fool?

They wrapped up work in the early afternoon. Kurt had packed up the samples they'd taken from the grapevines, for shipment to the university, and Jodie was taking the package to the post office before swinging back by the office. He walked her to the door on his crutches.

"I haven't noticed you taking any pain pills today," she mentioned, hesitating on the doorstep. "Does that mean the pain has eased?"

He looked surprised. "Yeah, I forgot all about it. I did take a couple this morning, but I haven't needed anything since."

"Good." She still felt horribly guilty for having put him in this situation. But that didn't mean she was going to let up on him in other areas. "Now listen. When I get here tomorrow, I expect to see you fully dressed. Okay?"

He pretended to think that over. "Tell you what. I'll dress the way you want me to if you'll dress the way I want *you* to."

She couldn't help but laugh. "Why do I even bother to ask?" she beseeched of the heavens. But she did it anyway. "And what, pray tell, do you want me to dress in?"

"I've got a great idea," he said, eyes sparkling. "Remember that red halter top you used to wear? Is that still around?"

She stared at him. He remembered her in the red hal-

ter top. She felt her face turn as red as that piece of clothing had been, and she stammered something inane. He
remembered. He *had* been looking at her. It wasn't her
imagination. Reality seemed to ebb and flow around
her, but the sound of a car in the driveway brought her
quickly back to earth.

Chapter Six

"Oh," Kurt said in surprise. "We must be running late. It's my mother bringing Katy back."

Uh-oh. Jodie swallowed hard. She had to get out of here.

"Okay," she said, moving quickly. "I'll see you to-morrow."

"Jodie?" he called, but she didn't stop. She had to get to her car before someone tried to make her meet Katy. Her heart in her throat, she realized she was going to have to pass right by Kurt's mother.

Oh, well. If it had to be done, she'd better do it fast.

"Mrs. McLaughlin." She nodded with mock formality to the tall, handsome woman who had blackballed her from Junior Helpers League and who'd made sure she never got invited to any of the teenage parties everyone else in town attended at the McLaughlin mansion. Jodie didn't think she would ever warm up to this woman, especially after that time she'd heard her call the Allmans "trash" in that holier-than-thou tone.

"How are you?" she added, though she didn't pause in her determined trek toward her own car.

"It's Jodie Allman, isn't it?" the older woman said coolly, lifting her dark glasses to get a better look. "I'm fine, my dear. Thank you for asking."

Just as Jodie came even with the car, the woman turned and pulled Katy from the back. Jodie got a flash of blond hair and saw a chubby little hand wave in the air. The image stayed with her as she slid behind the wheel of her car and started the engine, trying to catch her breath.

Kurt's baby. A McLaughlin baby. That put an ache in the center of her being. Somehow it was just too close to home.

Dinner around the Allman table was loud and cheerful that evening, which was just what she needed to get her mind off Kurt and his child. It was one of those nights when her sister seemed extra loving, and her brothers were so funny she could hardly eat for laughing.

And then her father came down to join them. The laughter died away and everyone began to concentrate on finishing up so they could leave the table.

Jesse Allman went around the group, making comments that caused a lot of eyes to roll. And finally he fixed on Jodie.

"Well, missy," he said. "When I said you had to work with the McLaughlin boy, I didn't think you were going to move in with him."

She stiffened. "I didn't move in with him. We're just working together. I only go over for a few hours every day."

He frowned darkly. "I don't like it. I think you should stay at the office."

She'd thought exactly the same thing when all this had begun. But things had changed. She no longer thought that way.

"Dad, I can handle things. I'm an adult, you know."

He stared at her and she stared right back, until he began to chuckle.

Rafe rose from his place, giving her a significant look and taking his plate to the sink. "Dad, did you want to talk over some of those numbers from the Houston proposal?"

"Yes, I'm fixin' to do that as soon as you all are done here. Matt, I want you in on this."

"Sorry, Dad." Matt rose with a quick smile and followed Rafe to the sink. "I've got to get over to the Simpsons'. Their baby has a temperature and I said I'd come over and take a look."

Jesse scowled and Jodie hid a grin. No matter how much he tried to pretend otherwise, he had a son who was a physician. No matter how much he tried to push him, Matt would never be as interested in the family business as he was in his patients' health.

Too bad, Dad, she said to herself.

And then the phone rang, and she took that opportunity to make her own escape, hurrying out to the hall where the old, dial telephone was located.

"Jodie?"

The voice in the receiver was Kurt's, and her heart jumped. He was the last person she'd expected to hear from.

"Listen, if you're not busy….I'm going stir-crazy here. What about we go for a ride or something?"

"A ride?" It took a moment to process the unexpected request. "Oh, in my car?"

"Unless you've got a horse you need to exercise," he said dryly. "Yes, in your car. I can't drive."

"But…what about your baby?"

"Tracy took Katy with her to a friend's house. They have little kids. So I'm on my own."

She could hear it in his voice, a caged-in quality, as though he really needed to get out of the house. She could sympathize.

"I'll be over in twenty minutes," she said. As she hung up the phone, she got that old feeling of dread and regret. She was walking into a trap again, wasn't she? With her eyes wide open, her mind full of doubts—and her heart full of anticipation.

They didn't drive for long. It took only moments to decide to stop at Millie's for coffee.

"Are you sure you want to do this?" she asked, as

they prepared to go in. "You know people are going to talk."

"Sticks and stones," he said, a bit obliquely. "Who cares?"

Well, she did, for starters. But she swallowed her misgivings and held the door for him as he made his way in on crutches. He looked even better in the evening lighting than he did in sunlight. The hunter green sweater he wore emphasized his muscular form, and his thick hair was tousled by an evening wind blowing in off the plains. He was "to die for" great-looking and familiarity was breeding the opposite of contempt. Just catching his gaze made her pulse speed up.

"Besides," he said, looking around the half-empty restaurant, "there are so many new people in town, there probably won't be anyone here who remembers that McLaughlins and Allmans don't mix."

"You might be right," she said, but she was dubious.

There was definitely a different look to the place. The old Formica tabletops and red Naugahyde seat covers had given way to chrome and blond wood. Plants hung from the rafters where old hunting trophies had once glared down on the patrons. But Millie was still there to meet them, her face lighting up when she saw her daughter's best friend.

"Jodie!" she cried, rushing forward to give the younger woman a bear hug. "It's about time you came by to say hi."

After Jodie's own mother died when she was sixteen,

Millie had served as a substitute, of sorts, when times got tough to bear. They chatted warmly for a few moments, and then it was time for the big decision.

"Which side?" Millie asked, looking from one of them to the other.

Kurt and Jodie looked at each other. The side by the windows had always been McLaughlin territory. A smaller area toward the back had been staked out by the partisans of the Allman boys. The town was divided right down the middle, and so was the restaurant. Millie had her hands full in the old days, making sure that each faction kept to their own side and that the hostilities didn't spill over into real fighting in her establishment.

Jodie laughed and looked at Millie. "People don't still divide down the center line, do they?" she asked, incredulous.

Millie shrugged, a twinkle in her eye. "Some do. What about you two?"

"We'll take the booth in the middle," Kurt said smoothly. "Our relationship is a compromise, isn't it?"

"Absolutely."

Millie seated them and went to get their coffee. Jodie looked around the place, remembering coming here after football games, when the room was packed with friends and enemies. Two teenage girls passed the table, their gazes falling on Kurt. Their immediate reactions were almost comical, and their giggles echoed through the air as they made their way to the restroom in back.

Jodie hid a smile behind a napkin. "I didn't know you had groupies," she said, raising her eyebrows.

He grinned back at her. "It's a new thing. I don't like to advertise it."

She shook her head. "I'd be careful if I were you. It's pretty dangerous to depend on the fickle affections of the crowd."

"So what's new? Depending on the fickle affections of grown women isn't much better."

Jodie did a double take, wondering at the cynicism in his tone. But he'd already moved on to another topic, and Millie was serving the coffee.

A couple of people stopped by to say hello. The teenage girls passed again, giggling all the way. And Jodie began to feel as though she'd really come home. Funny that it took coming to Millie's with a McLaughlin to make that happen.

"I wish you'd stayed for another moment this afternoon," he said, as he sipped his black coffee. "I wanted to introduce you to Katy."

"Well, I thought it best if I…got going.…"

"Yeah, I know. You and my mother have never been on the best of terms."

Jodie wrapped her fingers around her cup, soaking in the heat. "That's putting it mildly. Your mother hates me."

"Hates you?" He reacted automatically to the word, as though he were going to deny it vehemently. But then he reconsidered. "Well, only because you're an Allman."

"Exactly."

Their gazes met, locked and they both laughed. He reached out to take her hand in his, but she pulled it away quickly.

"No you don't," she said, looking around the room from under her lashes. "Just us having coffee together is enough to rile the town. If we start holding hands…"

He looked almost abashed. "I wasn't going to hold your hand."

"Really?" She didn't believe him for a moment. She picked up that very same hand and looked at it. "What were you planning to do with it, then?"

He shrugged, amusement lurking in his eyes. "Nibble on your fingers a little, maybe."

She gave him a withering look. "Better order a piece of pie if you're hungry."

But she was warmed by his flirting. And she thought again about how he'd noticed her in the red halter top all those years ago…and actually remembered it! She'd never forget that summer—coming into Millie's with her friends and sneaking glances at the college-bound boys, singling out Kurt every time and getting breathless just by catching sight of him. Had he been looking at her, too? She got breathless again, just thinking of it.

He had gone off to college at the end of that summer, and she hadn't seen him again until the day she walked into his office at Allman Industries and announced she'd come to work for him. By then, there had been a lot of water under the bridge.

Kurt was talking about his mother again, and the problems he was having with the child care for his baby. Things weren't going smoothly, and he was trying to figure out a way to improve the situation.

"Here's my big dilemma," he was saying, leaning across the table toward her and speaking quietly. "The puzzle that is tying my life in knots." He hesitated, then went on as though he'd decided he could trust her with his problems, after all. "How do I get a mother for Katy without having to hire on a wife for myself?"

"Hire?" She raised one eyebrow and stared at him, inexplicably offended by the way he was thinking of this.

He spread his hands out and looked at her candidly. "I don't see it happening any other way."

She studied him for a moment, then decided he wasn't serious. He was just being dramatic because he was so frustrated. "You'll meet someone," she told him confidently. "You'll fall in love."

"Oh, yeah." He gave her a look of pure disgust. "I already caught that movie. And the sequels are never as good as the original."

That stopped her short. She snuck a look at his face, expecting to see a hint of the anguish he must feel from having lost his wife. But his expression was bland. If he was in agony, it didn't show. In fact, she thought there was more of a bitter look to the twist of his mouth than anything else. Strange.

Everyone knew he and Grace had been the perfect couple. Everyone said he'd been heartbroken when she'd gone down in the small plane over the panhandle. Everyone wondered if he would ever love again.

Now Jodie was beginning to wonder if everyone knew what the heck they were talking about.

"You met Grace in college, didn't you?" she asked, knowing she was treading on shaky ground, and ready to retreat at the barest hint that he didn't want to discuss it.

He nodded. "We met in a class on fungi. There was a field trip every other Saturday, so we had a chance to get to know each other." His eyes took on a dreamy look. "She was beautiful. Long, silvery hair down her back, pale blue eyes. She looked like an ice queen." He shook his head, talking more to himself than to her. "I couldn't get enough of her."

Jodie looked away, just this side of embarrassed at the candor of his statement.

"So we got married as soon as I got my degree," he said more briskly. "And we moved to New York City and lived like jet-setters for a while. Then Grace got pregnant and everything changed."

His eyes were stormy now, clouded with some emotion Jodie couldn't quite identify—and wasn't sure she wanted to understand. She waited for him to go on, but suddenly, he looked up as though he'd only just remembered she was there. His eyes cleared and he smiled at her.

"Hey, enough of that. Tell me about your work as a physical therapist. What made you want to go into that, anyway?"

She started off slowly but soon gathered speed, telling him all about how she'd worked two jobs and got her classes in at night, until she qualified for a scholarship and only had to work one job to make enough to live on. They talked for another half hour, and then it was time to take Kurt home so he would be there when Tracy brought Katy back.

"She'll be asleep," he mused, almost to himself, as they drove down the wide street toward his neighborhood. "Tracy will carry her in, and her sweet little face will look so angelic."

Jodie looked at him sideways. It was very appealing, the way he loved his little girl, but it put a sick feeling in the pit of her stomach. There was no way she would ever have a relationship with a man who had children. It just wasn't in the cards for her. And she'd better not forget that fact.

She pulled up in front of his house and he turned to her, smiling in the dark.

"Thanks for rescuing me, Jodie. I really didn't think I would be able to stand another night clumping around in my living room. You gave me a welcome break."

"Anytime," she said breezily, though her attention was all on his luscious mouth, and whether or not he would try to kiss her again.

Stupid, she scolded herself silently. *This isn't a date. There is no reason for him to try to kiss you again.* That one kiss had been just a moment of insanity, never to be repeated again.

But she couldn't convince herself of that. Probably

because she wanted him to kiss her again. She wanted it more than she'd wanted anything for a good, long time.

The night sky was black by now. There was no moon yet, and tiny diamonds twinkled like holes in heaven. It was a Texas sky, big and bold and full of magic. Maybe if she wished on one of those stars…

His face was so close. His hand was in her hair again, his fingers kneading softly. His gaze was soft as velvet. "You know, Jodie…I really, really want to kiss you."

Her heart lurched. "Oh."

His mouth twisted. "I'm not going to kiss you, though."

She gazed at him in horror as he went on with his stupid explanation.

"Doing something like that would go against all my plans, all my principles. I've really tried to take a firm stand against—"

She'd had enough of this gibberish. Principles be damned! She wasn't going to let him go on this way, or even finish his sentence. Instead, she took a firm grip on his head, one hand on either side of his surprised face, pulled him down within range and kissed him.

"There," she said breathlessly when it was over. "Now was that so hard?"

He stared at her for one long second, and then he began to laugh. Reaching out, he gathered her up, pulled her to him, and his mouth came down hard on hers.

Bells were ringing. Stars were shooting in the sky like fireworks. Violins were playing. And her body was responding to the heat of his mouth by going into total meltdown.

When he finally pulled back, she heard a small, plaintive sound, and realized it was hers. She had actually whimpered. But she was too overwhelmed to feel embarrassment. Kurt was a man who surely knew how to kiss. And she wanted him to do it again! And again...

"Good night," he said softly, and then he turned to let himself out of the car.

"'Night," she echoed.

And then he was gone.

Gone, but never forgotten.

Of course, Jodie knew things couldn't go on like this. But she wasn't taking it all that seriously. All she was doing was rekindling a teenage crush she'd once had and almost forgotten about. She would get over it soon, surely.

Still, she was a little worried the next morning as she made her way to Kurt's house. What was going to happen during these many hours they were forced to spend together? Was it going to be possible to ignore the attraction that was simmering between them now?

It had to be done. They couldn't let it get in the way of business. Which was exactly why he'd resisted kissing her the night before. She understood that. And in some ways, she knew she should regret having forced the issue.

But she couldn't. Even if they never kissed again, she

would never forget how wonderful it had felt being in his arms.

Once at Kurt's house, she found she needn't have bothered with all the worrying. It seemed that Kurt's home was about to become a hub of activity, a sort of annex to the Allman Industries building downtown. The day was filled with people coming and going.

Rafe was already there when she arrived.

"Hi, sis," he said, barely looking up from his work. "I'm going over some figures with Kurt. Pull up a chair. If you want to help, start collating these forms."

Paula, the marketing secretary, dropped by to pick up some dictation tapes. A little later, Matt arrived to check out Kurt's leg, and then David showed up at the door with an extralarge pepperoni pizza.

"Well, I heard the whole family was gathering, so I knew you'd all be peckish by now," he said in his South Texas drawl. "Maybe we should give Rita a call and tell her to get over here?"

"Rita took Pop into San Antonio to see the oncologist," Jodie said quickly. "So she's not available."

"How is your father doing with the chemotherapy?" Kurt asked, glancing at Matt first, then Jodie.

She shook her head. "He's a fighter. He's pretty tired most of the time, but he has flashes of his old self, pretty much daily."

"That's good," he said, but he was looking into her eyes, and she knew he wasn't thinking about her father any longer.

"What, no red halter top?" he murmured to her when they both took a trip to the kitchen for a glass of water.

She laughed, leaning against the counter as she poured water from the pitcher. "I guess this boring old outfit is a disappointment, huh?"

Coming up behind her, he dropped a small kiss at the nape of her neck. "Nothing about you is disappointing," he murmured. Then he turned and left the room.

Okay, you can stop hyperventilating now, she told herself firmly.

But it took a few long minutes of calming down before she felt like herself again. When he came back into the kitchen to get something he'd forgotten, she snagged his arm to make him stay for a moment.

"Listen," she said, wishing he didn't look so kissable. "I know this is my fault. But we have to stop it."

She could tell that he knew exactly what she was talking about, but he waited for her to say it.

"We've got to keep things on a business level here," she said earnestly, searching his gaze for his thoughts on the issue. "You were right in the first place. I was wrong to…to force that kiss on you last night."

He grinned and reached out to give her a soft tap on the chin with his fist. "You're such a Jezebel," he said lightly. "I'm putty in your hands."

She started to protest, but he stopped her. "Don't worry, Jodie. I understand. And reluctantly agree. No more making out in the shadows." He touched her cheek, then dropped his hand and shook his head. "But you can't stop me from dreaming."

She took a deep breath as he left the kitchen, closing her eyes and leaning against the counter as though she needed it to hold her up. She had to get out of this, and she knew it. But her rebellious streak was showing up again. She was going to enjoy it while it lasted. Why not?

Meanwhile, her brothers were giving her significant looks, and an occasional snicker could be heard among them. That put her back up enough to make her snap at Rafe at one point, when Kurt was out of the room. "Did you really come over because you had work to do, or did you come to act as a chaperone?"

"Why not both?" he countered with a grin. Then the amusement faded from his face. "Actually, kiddo, the business has got some cash-flow problems right now. I needed to work some things out with Kurt. With Pop out of the picture for the time being, we've hit a few snags."

"Are you serious? I had no idea."

"Not to worry. I'm working on it." He smiled teasingly at her again. "Just enjoy your little oasis while you've got it. Before you know it, you and Kurt will be back in the office and the good times will no longer roll."

She made a face at him, but his words stayed with her. She'd assumed, once the business took off and became a success, that things would just keep getting better and better. Of course, that was silly and naive. Nothing good remained so without a lot of work behind it.

Kurt came back into the room, and Rafe looked up from the computer screen.

"By the way, I saw Manny yesterday. He was all upset about some trespassers. He wanted me to ask you about them."

"Me?" Kurt looked surprised.

"Yeah, he seemed to think you might know something about them. Says he ran them off, but they came back the next night. They're skulking around in the vineyards and he doesn't know why." Rafe shrugged, turning away. "You know Manny. He tends to get riled up pretty easily. He said at first he thought it was like *The X-Files,* and they were government men come to search for extraterrestrials."

"I hope he doesn't try shooting one of them," Jodie said. "He could end up making things really hard for himself."

"And even harder for the guy who gets shot."

"True."

She met Kurt's gaze and knew they were both thinking about that day in the vineyards. He smiled at her and she smiled back. Something flashed between them— some sort of special bond. She looked away quickly, but her heart was beating very fast. This was what it felt like to be a part of a couple. She only wished she had the courage to make it real.

"It seems like you're spending a lot of time out of the office these days," Shelley said, as she noticed Jodie piling up work to take with her.

It had been over a week since she and Kurt had taken the trip out to the vineyards, and they had developed something of a routine. Jodie went into the office in the morning and gathered up work, took it to Kurt's house, and they sat down at his dining room table and did what needed doing. Kurt made some phone calls. She typed up some letters. They broke for lunch, finished up loose ends, and she left to spend the rest of the day at Allman Industries.

That would have been an invitation to intimacy, one would think. But it hadn't worked out that way. Luckily. And not because they were staying true to their decision to cool it, but because other people kept showing up and interrupting what could have been a cozy time together.

And then the weekend had come. She'd never known two days to stretch out so long and lonely. She'd spent the entire time doing nothing but think about him. She liked the guy. She couldn't help it. She *really* liked the guy. And that was so dangerous. So why was she sticking around? Self-hatred? Masochism? Or just plain old weakness?

After all, it was more than just resisting the urge to touch him. Even if he might go for a little cuddling, he'd made it very plain that he wasn't interested in pursuing any sort of long-term relationship. But then, if anyone had asked her a week ago, she would have said she wasn't, either. And now that was all she could think about.

"You going over to Kurt McLaughlin's again?" Shelley added.

"Of course," Jodie told her with something of a wist-ful smile. "The man can't get along without me."

Shelley laughed, but quickly sobered and then began to look concerned. "You're not falling for the guy, are you?" she asked.

Jodie struck a pose. "Shelley, do I look like a woman in love?"

Shelley pretended to gaze deep into her eyes. "I don't know. I see a few hints of insanity deep down there."

"Don't worry. I'm having those removed as soon as possible. Minor surgery."

"Good." Shelley grinned, then looked serious again. "Just be careful, okay? The McLaughlins are notorious as love-'em-and-leave-'em sort of guys. It seems to be something in the gene pool with that family." Looking as though she regretted the note of bitterness that had crept into her tone, she smiled quickly and patted Jodie's arm. "I don't want to see you get hurt, sweetie. You de-serve better than that."

"I won't get hurt, Shelley. Don't worry about me. I've known too many members of that family for too long to be fooled by anything they do."

She knew she sounded a bit defensive. But darn it all, she *was* feeling a little defensive, when you came right down to it. Watching Shelley walk away, she had to wonder if her best friend had really noticed something. Was it that obvious?

She slumped down into her ergonomically correct desk chair and sighed heavily. Kurt could be so darn appealing sometimes. And the truth was, she had a little crush. That was all. It was a very small crush, and no one ever had to know anything about it. And it probably all hinged on the fact that it had been so darn long since she'd had a man in her life.

But it would be a very good thing if she could get a transfer to another department and not have to be alone with Kurt every day. She was beginning to think that was the only thing that was going to save her from making a first-class fool of herself.

Not that anything had happened.

Not that anything was *going* to happen.

She went to his house every day, and he teased her and mocked her and made her furious. And then all of a sudden, her gaze met his and held for just a beat too long—and something stirred inside her, and she was breathing too hard and thinking about hot kisses and shooting stars. It wasn't fair!

At least she'd managed to avoid having to deal with his little girl. The baby had gone to her grandmother's every day by the time Jodie got there, and Jodie left before someone brought her back. Tracy came over in the evening to help him with the child. Jodie was on guard all the time against being asked to help with the baby herself. That was something she wasn't prepared to do. The very thought made her cringe.

But she didn't want Kurt to know that. It was just plain stupid to be so paranoid about Kurt's baby. But she couldn't help it. She would just as soon never have to meet the child.

She glanced at her watch, deciding to stop at the Coffee Cabin to pick up a couple of tall Breakfast Blends and some doughnuts to take over to Kurt's. She'd noticed he seemed to respond well to arrivals bearing gifts of food.

A sleek, and very expensive, blue sedan sat in Kurt's driveway when Jodie drove up. She didn't recognize it, but she had a pretty good idea whose it had to be. Kurt's sister would drive a car like that.

She looked down at the things she'd picked up at the coffeehouse. What now? Oh, well. They could share things if they had to. She hadn't seen Tracy for a long time. It would be nice to see an old friend again.

Ha. Who was she trying to kid? "Friends" was something she and Tracy had never been. Rivals, sure. Competitors. Even enemies. From the first day five-year-old Jodie had hesitantly stepped into the kindergarten classroom, Tracy was always trying to gather the other children into her camp and leave her Allman rival out of things. Every time there was a snake lurking in her desk, her homework papers disappeared or there was a birthday party she didn't get invited to, Jodie knew whom to thank.

But that was then and this was now. And the feud was supposed to be waning, wasn't it? Gathering the sweets and coffee, she got out of the car and started up the walk. She could hear voices coming from the house, but it wasn't until she was up on the front porch that she could understand what was being said.

"Kurt, you can't really expect Mother to go out of her way to take care of your baby when you won't even do what she thinks is right about this Allman business."

Jodie stopped dead. The front door was standing open, and the voice inside, raised high with emotion, had to be Kurt's sister.

"Tracy, you don't understand." The deeper, masculine voice was Kurt's.

"I think I understand only too well."

"When this is all over, you'll see why—"

"When this is all over, I hope I'll be living happily in Dallas, my only contact with Chivaree by e-mail for the rest of my life."

"This will always be your home and you can't change that. And you'll always care. Believe me, I know."

"No. I cared when this town was our oyster. Now that the Allmans have turned everything upside down, I hope the place goes to hell. I'm sure the Allmans will do their best to take it there."

"Tracy, calm down. You'll wake up Katy."

Jodie stood where she was, not sure if she should go on in or head back to her car. The conversation was private, and it was heated. But her family's name had been mentioned. She shifted her weight from one foot to another, undecided.

Tracy spoke again, her voice lower, obviously trying to get control of herself.

"Look, I know you keep trying to convince Mother that you're doing something here that is going to return our family to its former so-called glory. But I don't know why you care about that. This whole town is a dump. It always was and it always will be. If you think you're going to make things better by hanging around with those low-down, thieving Allmans, you just go right ahead and do it. I'm getting out of here. And I'm not coming back."

It was at that moment that Kurt noticed her, as he looked up over his sister's shoulder.

"Jodie."

She was numb. What Tracy had said was skittering around in her head, but she wasn't letting it penetrate. Instead, she started forward as though she'd just arrived on the scene.

"Good morning," Jodie said with forced cheer. "I brought coffee and doughnuts." She waved the bag, walked right in and put everything on the table. Then she turned with a wide smile to greet Tracy.

"Tracy. So good to see you again."

"Well, if it isn't Jodie Allman. You hardly look any different than you did in high school."

Jodie couldn't say the same about Tracy. She'd been such a pretty girl, and now she looked strained and a little hard, wearing too much makeup and too many pieces of flashy jewelry.

Still, she knew very well that Tracy's comment wasn't meant as a compliment, but that only made her smile more broadly.

"And you look just gorgeous. But then, you always were the prettiest girl in town, weren't you?"

"I don't know, Jodie." Tracy's smile gleamed unnaturally. "You were the one who beat me out for homecoming queen, weren't you?"

"A fluke." Jodie waved it away. "I think someone must have stuffed the ballot box."

"Oh, no." Tracy shook her head. "You deserved every one of all those honors you were racking up in those days."

"As I remember it, you did your fair share of blowing away the competition for everything from president of the junior class to queen of the grape festival." Jodie smiled, feeling like a mechanical doll. Looking back, it seemed that she and Tracy had fought it out for every one of those things. Sometimes Tracy won, sometimes Jodie did. Another battlefield in the old family feud. From this vantage point, it all looked a bit pointless.

But she noticed that Kurt was watching their exchange with a look of pure disbelief on his face, and she knew exactly what he was thinking.

Women! How can they act like best buddies when they hate each other? If this were a couple of guys, someone would have a shiner by now.

That made her laugh inside as Tracy prepared to leave. He just didn't get it. Everything she and Tracy were saying to each other was meant to hurt. Just tiny little paper cuts, but they stung. The two of them understood each other perfectly.

Just before Tracy went out the door, she turned back and landed her final bomb.

"Oh, I almost forgot to tell you, Kurt. Mother's hired a housekeeper for you. She'll do your cooking and cleaning and take care of Katy. I just can't do it anymore, and I won't allow you to get Mother more involved." Her teeth flashed in a smug smile. "In fact, I've convinced Mother to come to Dallas with me for the time being. So you'll be on your own."

Chapter Seven

Kurt looked pained as he leaned against the open door.

"A housekeeper?"

"She's very good. Wonderful references." Tracy waved a hand in the air and added, "She's Swedish," as though that explained everything.

"Swedish?" he said, eyes lighting up. "As in, the Swedish Girls Bikini Team?"

Tracy rolled her eyes and looked at Jodie as if to say, *"Men!"* Even though mortal enemies, they were both women, and therefore subject to mutual exasperation about the opposite gender.

"She's a housekeeper," Tracy said, carefully enunciating the word to make sure he understood. "I doubt very much she'll be wearing her bikini to work."

Kurt looked pathetically hopeful. "You never know. Those Swedish girls…"

After flashing him another look of complete irritation, Tracy glanced at her watch. "I do have to fly. She should be here by noon." Giving Jodie an arctic smile, she added, "Nice to have seen you again. We probably won't be having a repeat. I'm moving to Dallas. For good." She waved at the two of them. "Ta ta." And she was off down the walkway in her expensive Italian pumps.

Kurt and Jodie stood watching her go, then Kurt slowly closed the door, his face dreamy. "Swedish," he said softly. One eyebrow rose. "Hmm. This could be interesting."

Jody was feeling just as exasperated as his sister had been. "Or not," she muttered, heading for the table and the coffee.

"Well, you heard what Tracy said." He joined her, lowering himself carefully to the chair, his cast out straight before him. "They've hired a Swedish woman to come and 'do' for me."

She looked up and found his eyes were sparkling. He was teasing, goading her, hoping for a reaction. She supposed she might as well play along for the time being. He was getting such a kick out of this.

"What exactly are you thinking this Swedish woman is going to 'do' for you?"

He shrugged expansively. "Who knows? You know what they say about those Swedes. She may just be the kind of wonderful woman who wants to take care of the 'whole man.'" He sighed happily at the thought. "She may just be anxious to attend to my every little want, need and desire."

Jodie was tempted to roll her eyes, but Tracy had already done that, and she didn't want to be repetitive. Still, she had to do something. She decided to tease him back a little.

"I thought that was what I was here for."

That surprised him. "You!"

"Why not me?"

For a moment, she could have sworn he was tempted to take that further. But only for a moment. He seemed to remember that theirs was supposed to remain a working relationship, sometimes skating on the edge of flirtation, but never risking actual contact. As she watched, he opted for safety, taking a long sip of coffee and reaching for a doughnut.

"Know any words in Swedish?" he asked her as he munched, reverting back to the subject at hand.

Jodie blinked. "I'm sure she speaks English."

"Yes, but if I could welcome her with some words in her mother tongue, who knows? It might make her feel more at home."

Her impulse was to snarl at him. She wasn't sure why, but this was beginning to annoy her. "If she wanted to talk to Swedish people, she would have stayed in Sweden."

He nodded thoughtfully. "Good point."

Despite herself, Jodie started to laugh. This was all so ridiculous. She reached for another doughnut, but

Kurt reached out at the same time and snagged her hand, holding it in his.

"You look good when you laugh," he told her.

The laughter died quickly. His eyes were too serious. She looked down at his hand holding hers. His fingers were long and beautiful. She thought about what they would feel like on her body, and shivered.

"I know you heard what Tracy said about your family," he went on. "I'm sorry. She didn't really mean it. She was just…"

Exasperated, she pulled her hand away from his. "Oh, Kurt! How can you say she didn't really mean it? Of course she meant it. It's you who are not dealing with reality. The Allman-McLaughlin feud is alive and well and we're all a part of it. Face it."

He was shaking his head, rejecting her pessimism. "The only reason feuds like this keep going is because people keep saying things like this to each other. When people are always trying to score points against each other, nothing gets accomplished."

She shook her head slowly. "I don't know if you can say that. After all, the bad feelings come out of some pretty bad actions, not just from talk."

"Yeah? Like what?"

She stared at him. Surely he didn't think the feud was all based in head games and hurt feelings? There was a lot more to it than that.

"Don't tell me you've never heard about how your great-grandfather, Theodore McLaughlin, kidnapped my great-grandfather's wife and locked her up for weeks, only letting her go when Hiram—my ancestor—gathered enough men and weapons to storm the ranch house where he was holding her?"

Obviously, that story was coming back to him now. He looked just a mite pained.

"Okay, so there were some romantic shenanigans back in the Chivaree Stone Age. But our two families were practically the only people living in this valley at the time. Who else were they going to mess around with?"

She went on, her face set. "Then there was your grandfather stealing the lease to my grandfather's land."

He groaned. "Ancient history. And disputed history, at that. Can't we just move on?"

"Move on?" She threw her hands in the air. "Sure, why not. Let's move on to the day that your father and your uncle ganged up on my father and tied him to a post in front of the city hall in his underwear for everyone in town to see and laugh at."

He made a show of looking very bored. "They were teenagers. Are you done yet?"

Something about his manner told her she'd made her point. "Well, there are many more things I could bring up. But I'm done for now."

"Good." He favored her with a dazzling smile. "How about sharing that last doughnut?"

She sighed. He really couldn't handle the details of the feud. He really thought he could just wish it away, and all those old, dirty deeds could be assigned to a family history museum somewhere. Easy for him—his family was the perpetrator of most of the bad stuff. Her family, being the weaker in the old days, had been the victim. It was a little harder to forget when you were the one whose nose was rubbed in the dirt again and again.

Or was she the one being naive? Was there more to it than that? After all, her original suspicions had gone underground, but she hadn't proved them to be wrong in any way. Was all this just a cover-up for his real agenda?

She looked at him sharply, but the misgivings faded a bit once she took in his face. It wasn't just that he was good-looking. There was a sparkle in his eyes that made her want to smile, and a twist to his wide mouth that made her want to tease him. Either he was real good at hiding his true feelings, or she was going to have to admit he was coming across as a really good guy.

But then, she was nuts. What did she know?

"Hold still," he told her. "You've got sugar on your face."

She held still, scrunching just a little as he carefully wiped the sugar away. He was so close, she could feel the heat from his body. An overwhelming urge came over her to lean into his chest and bury her face against him. Her gaze met his, and she could tell he knew exactly what she'd been thinking.

His eyes darkened. He was going to kiss her. She drew her breath in sharply, knowing she should turn away. But she was frozen to the spot, heart beating, head light.

His arms came around her, drawing her into the shelter of his embrace. That was the way it felt, as though he was enclosing her in a magic space away from time and trouble. And beyond all reason, she let herself enter the dream. With a soft sigh, she lifted her own arms and circled his neck, pulling him closer, wanting to feel his body against hers. His mouth was hot and hard and she opened to him eagerly, thrilling to the sense of his obvious desire.

She knew this was crazy, but she didn't care anymore. It felt so right, so good, to be with this man. Was she falling in love? Was she really brave enough to let herself do that?

Drawing back at last, he looked down at her and she tried to read what his gaze was telling her. She could have sworn he looked a little shocked, a little disconcerted. Had her response surprised him? She didn't care. If he kissed her again, she would respond just as intensely.

But he didn't kiss her again. Instead, he asked, "So, you want to see Katy?"

"What?" Alarm shimmered through her veins. She'd forgotten that the baby was still here. "No. I…I mean, shouldn't we let her sleep?"

"Come on." He grabbed her by the wrist, hoisting himself up with one crutch. "I want to show you my pride and joy."

There was no way to avoid this, and it would be silly to try. Bowing to the inevitable, she forced a smile and went along with him into the bedroom at the end of the hall, her heart hammering in her chest. They entered quietly. The drapes were pulled but there was plenty of light. Jodie followed Kurt to the side of the crib and looked down.

Golden curls tumbled over a cheek round as an apple. The little mouth was slightly open. A small fist lay on the pillow. A tiny button nose. Fairy eyebrows. A beautiful, beautiful child.

Something like a sob choked Jodie. This darling, adorable little girl looked so much like the image she had of the baby she'd carried for four and a half months. Those days came flooding back to her. The long nights crying because Jeremy had abandoned her. The way those emotions had changed once she began to feel the presence of another life inside her. The way she'd taken her unborn baby to heart, loved it, vowed that she would do all she could to make sure the child had a happier childhood than she had had. They would be a pair, the two of them, mother and child.

And then, suddenly, that dream was dead, too. It had seemed too much to bear at the time.

She gripped the railing of the crib, trying to hold back the emotion. She was going to cry. Oh, no. This was totally unfair. She wasn't the crying type. At least, she tried hard not to be. And here she was, her eyes filling with tears, her shoulders shaking. She had to get out of here before he noticed.

Too late. He'd already seen it. She turned away but he pulled her back.

"Jodie, what is it?"

She could try to tell him a dismissive lie, but it wouldn't work. When your throat closed up, it was hard to get words through. Shaking her head, she pulled away from him and headed back out into the living room.

He followed her, clumping along with the crutch, but he was slower, and she had time to take a deep breath and wipe her eyes.

"You know," she said brightly, as he came into the room, "I really think I ought to go back to the office. I forgot to bring those new ad sheets you wanted to see. So if you think you can handle things here without me…"

"Sit down," he said, gesturing toward the couch.

"What?"

"Sit down. We need to talk."

"Oh. I don't think so. I'm okay, really, I just—"

"Sit down."

The tone was definitely autocratic and, as a modern woman, she knew she ought to challenge it. But somehow she found herself sitting down.

He sat beside her, grimacing as he stuck his leg out straight. Turning, he looked deep into her eyes.

"Jodie, tell me what happened to your baby."

Her heart lurched. "I…I've never had a baby."

His eyes darkened. "But you were pregnant."

She turned her face away. She couldn't deny that. And she felt like a fool.

"Tell me about it."

She shook her head. "Why? Why do you want to

know?" She shook her head again, harder. "Lots of women lose babies. It's no big deal."

He moved closer and took her by the shoulders, turning her so that she had to face him. "Remember when you told me that you liked me?" he asked.

She nodded, feeling like a child.

He touched her cheek and smiled gently. "Well, Jodie, I like you, too. I care about you. You're hurt, and I want to help you, just like you've helped me with my leg."

She searched his green eyes, looking deep, hunting for clues. Did he really mean it? Could she trust him? Or was it just that she wanted him to mean it?

She'd never told anyone the full story about what had happened ten years before. The man who was supposed to be her worst enemy should be the last person she told. Life was so strange sometimes.

"Kurt, I don't know…"

"Tell me."

She took a shaky breath. And with his hands still on her shoulders, warm and protective, she began.

"I took off right after high school. I had to get out of here." She looked down at her own hands, noting absently that her fingers were tangled together. Deliberately, she relaxed and let go.

"My mother died when I was sixteen, and that devastated me. I did nothing but fight with my father for the next two years. It was awful at home. I was sure anywhere else would be better. So I headed for Dallas as soon as I could scrape together the bus fare."

"It's a common story," he said, pulling her loosely into the circle of his arms. She let him. It felt right and natural, somehow.

"Yes," she said, as she settled against him. "And one that doesn't always have a happy ending."

"What happened?"

"Well. There was a boy."

"There's always a boy."

"Of course." She actually smiled for just a moment. "And I thought I loved him. Worse, I thought he loved me."

His arms tightened around her.

"We were sweethearts in high school. He came to join me in Dallas and we had a great time for a few weeks. But when I told him I…" She took another breath, suddenly having a hard time saying the word. "That I was pregnant, he let me know he had no intention of giving up the good life he'd just begun to sample." She winced, remembering. "He found it very amusing that I was so naive as to think he would marry me. He made it very clear that people like him didn't marry people like me."

Her voice wavered. Should she tell Kurt what he'd really said? Could she repeat it? No. But his words would echo in her ears anyway.

Are you crazy, Jodie? It's a historical fact. McLaughlins sleep with Allman women, but they sure as hell don't marry them.

"I felt as though the earth had opened up and I was falling down through the core. There were times when

I couldn't catch my breath. I didn't know what I was going to do, where I was going to go. I lost my job and then I lived off soup kitchens for a while."

"Jodie…"

"And then I lost the baby." She shivered. "It was pretty messy. I was already in the fifth month, and it was bad." She looked up and met his gaze, and because he looked so sympathetic, she told him another thing she'd never told anyone else. "It's possible I won't ever be able to have children."

"Oh, my God." He pulled her in tightly, burying his face in her hair. "Oh, Jodie."

His comfort felt like heaven, but she knew it was a dangerous sort of paradise and she tried to pull back. "If you hold me like that, I'll start to cry again," she warned.

"Good," he said, smoothing back her hair. "You go ahead and cry."

She wasn't going to. She didn't want to. But his comfort destroyed her defenses, and she did.

But not for long. After all, this was all so stupid. How could she be so weak? Other women lost babies and they squared their shoulders and went on with their lives. They didn't develop phobias about being around children. What was the matter with her?

One thing was undeniable. She couldn't let a poor little defenseless baby bear the brunt of her own neuroses. It was way past time she faced this bit of squeamishness and conquered it. Somehow.

A crash came from the bedroom, and then a wail.

"Katy!" Kurt attempted to jump to his feet, forgetting about the cast, and fell onto the floor.

Jodie jumped up, too, and looked at where he lay, flailing like a turtle on its back. She turned toward the bedroom where the cry was coming from. She could stay here, pull Kurt to his feet and hope he hadn't hurt anything. Or she could skip the delay and go to the baby herself. Split seconds passed, but it felt like huge, long moments were hanging in the air.

And then she was moving. She never thought it out, exactly. She didn't plan it. She didn't even tell herself that it had to be done. But she did it.

She ran for the bedroom. Katy was on the floor, holding one hand to her head and crying as though she'd been abandoned. Huge tears were rolling down her round cheeks. But the minute she caught sight of Jodie, the crying stopped dead and she stared, fascinated.

"Are you okay, honey?" Jodie asked, bending down but not sure if she should touch her. "Did you get hurt?"

"Da da da," the baby said. She gave Jodie a penetrating look and made up her mind. Her little, chubby arms shot up over her head and she waved them at Jodie, begging to be held. "Da da da," she repeated, adding a little sob at the end.

Jodie licked her dry lips and looked back toward the doorway, hoping to see Kurt arriving. "You want to go to your da da... I mean, daddy? He will be here in a second if you just wait—"

"Da da da!" The arms waved more vigorously, and

the baby got the look of a very determined chipmunk about to launch itself into space if someone didn't do something to facilitate travel immediately.

"Okay, okay." Jodie bent down and reached for the child, not sure how this was going to be accomplished. But Katy helped and, in no time at all, she was firmly ensconced in Jodie's arms, and Jodie was breathing hard.

"Oh!"

She was holding a baby and she wasn't throwing up. She wasn't going to faint. She wasn't even going to make faces. Because it wasn't hard at all.

She turned as Kurt entered the room. She couldn't believe how wonderful this little princess felt in her arms. "Look," she told him, her face shining. "Here she is. I think she's okay."

Kurt stopped and looked at them, wearing a crooked smile. "I guess she's taught herself at least part of the way of how to climb out of the crib," he said, his green eyes taking in every nuance. "A new problem to deal with."

But Jodie didn't want to hear about problems anymore. She handed the baby over to Kurt, but she didn't move away. Instead, she stayed close, brushing the curls back off the baby's forehead, taking in the beauty of the child and resonating to it.

So many years of avoiding the issue, and once she confronted her greatest fear head-on, it filled her with a feeling of triumph. Cowardice didn't pay. That was a good lesson to learn.

They spent the next hour with Katy. Though she

would always have an ache in her heart when she thought of the baby she'd lost, she was learning to enjoy watching Kurt interact with the child. And she even enjoyed it a bit herself.

After all, who could resist Katy? She was a laughing, bubbling bundle of pure joy, exploring everything, reacting to all stimuli, so surprised with the tiny details of everyday life. Jodie just couldn't be sad with such a beautiful baby at the center of attention.

All this made Jodie wonder about something else. And as time went by, she worked up the nerve to ask Kurt about it.

They had been sitting around in a sort of circle, rolling a ball to the baby. The ball had stopped in the middle, making Katy laugh and clap her hands. Kurt leaned in and got it rolling again.

"When you look at Katy, does she remind you of Grace?" Jodie asked softly. "Do you miss her an awful lot?"

"No." He looked up from Katy, his eyes clear. "I don't miss Grace at all."

Jodie sat back. She'd had a few hints that maybe his marriage hadn't been as special as people said, but this total aloofness was a surprise.

Kurt shifted his weight so that he could turn toward her more easily.

"In fact, the truth is, if Grace hadn't died, I probably would have divorced her by now."

"Oh, Kurt." She had a guilty twinge. She had to

admit, if he'd teared up and pledged unending love for his late wife, she would have been tortured by such a declaration. So what was she supposed to feel now? Elation? Hardly that. And she hated to think of Kurt being unhappily married. But at the same time, she couldn't help but be glad he wasn't as grief-stricken as some would have said.

"The only thing that was holding me back," Kurt said, "was trying to figure out how I could do it without risking losing Katy."

Jodie shook her head. "Kurt, I'm sorry. I shouldn't have brought it up. It's really none of my business."

His eyes seemed to burn into her as he gazed at her for a long moment. "But it is, Jodie," he said softly.

Chapter Eight

Before he could elaborate, the doorbell rang.

Jodie looked at Kurt and they both said it at the same time.

"The Swedish housekeeper!"

Kurt used his crutch to leverage himself to his feet and went to the door. Just before he opened it, he gave Jodie a significant look and she had to smile, knowing what he was hoping would be on the other side. He opened the door with a flourish. And then took a step backwards.

The woman who stood on the doorstep was at least six feet tall, and looked as though she might choose trying out for an NFL team as her second career. The steely blue eyes that stared out from under a granite brow brooked no nonsense. She carried a small overnight bag and wore a heavy sweater, though the day had turned very warm.

"I am Olga," she said in a thick accent. "I come to take care of the baby."

"What?" Kurt stepped forward again, and it looked like he was considering barring the door. His dream of a nubile Swedish maiden had apparently just gone up in smoke. "I…are you sure?"

"Where the baby?" She took a step toward the door-way and Kurt took a step back again, then glanced at Jodie as if asking for help.

"Uh… Listen, I don't think we've decided yet just what sort of help we're going to need," he said, obvi-ously grasping at straws. "Maybe you could leave your number and we'll call you…."

Olga wasn't one to wait around for an invitation. Pushing Kurt back brusquely, she came striding into the house.

"I know babies, Mister," she said, fixing him with a glare. She dropped her overnight case and looked around the room. "You let me have that baby. I take care of 'em."

Two long strides brought her to where Katy was playing on the floor. Leaning down, she picked the baby up and held her out while she fixed her with a fierce look. "She goin' to be okay."

Katy looked stunned. She glanced at her father, then back at this woman-mountain who had her in its grasp. Her little mouth opened, but she didn't make a sound.

"Which way to baby's room?" Olga demanded. "Needs new diaper."

Jodie pointed silently and the woman thundered off.

Kurt started after them, then turned back to look at Jodie. "Help," he said in a rather small voice.

Jodie laughed and grabbed his arm. "Let the woman do her job," she told him. "Tracy said she has excellent references. And I'm sure your mother wouldn't hire someone unqualified. Relax."

He stood restlessly before her. "You really think she's going to be okay?"

Jodie nodded. "Sure. Give her a chance."

He paced, muttering his doubts, and she hid her smile. Olga returned with Katy slung over her arm, looking shell-shocked and holding her arms out for her father's comfort.

"I'll go see the kitchen," Olga said cheerfully as she handed the child off to Kurt.

"Uh, Olga," Jodie said. "Mr. McLaughlin was wondering what exactly his mother had hired you on for. We assume it includes baby-tending and cooking."

"Oh, yah. Some cleaning, too. And I do massage."

"Massage!"

Olga laughed and gestured toward Kurt. "Come here. I give you a good one."

Jodie caught the look of pure horror on Kurt's face. It was a sight so precious, she would preserve it in her memory forever, bringing it out on cold winter nights to warm her soul.

"No, thanks," Kurt said grimly. "I think the baby care and housekeeping will be enough for now."

Jodie accompanied Olga to the kitchen and gave her a quick tour of the cabinets and appliances. Strangely, she felt an almost proprietary sense of things. She'd only been coming here a week or so, but she felt like it was hers.

Olga seemed fine to her. A bit bossy, perhaps, and a little loud—but competent and basically a good person. Definitely reliable. So she gathered her things and prepared to go back to the office.

"You're not leaving, are you?" Kurt said with alarm.

She had to smile. For a grown man who she'd seen square off against men twice his size, he was acting very skittish about this housekeeper.

"I've got to get going," she said blithely.

Kurt followed her to the door. "You can't leave me here alone with her," he whispered, looking back over his shoulder.

Jodie bit her lip, but then shook her head. "Oh, I can. And I will."

It wasn't pure sadism on her part. She had to go. She needed some time to process the changes she'd gone through today. Any more, and she would have gone into overload mode, and a catatonic state couldn't have been far behind.

"Jodie." He caught her arm and pulled her back, looking down into her eyes. "Come back soon."

Something in the intensity of his voice stayed with

her all the way to the office. Darn it all! She was falling for the guy, big time.

"Oh, happy day," she muttered to herself sarcastically.

"So I hear Tracy McLaughlin is planning on getting married again."

Dinnertime at the Allman house was Rumor Central these days. Jodie glanced up at her older sister and realized that statement had been directed at her. Of course.

"So it seems," she said casually, hoping to head off a larger discussion of the issue. "Pass the salt, please."

"What is this?" Matt commented. "Marriage number three?"

Rita nodded. "Hope she has better luck this time."

"Ha!" Rafe threw in. "McLaughlins never stick with anyone. Look at the parents. Not exactly the role models you would choose."

Rita waved a fork at her brother. "As I remember, you once had a pretty fair-sized likin' for Tracy."

"Me?" His handsome, dark face looked aghast. "No. I never had any feelings like that for a McLaughlin. I'm no traitor."

Jodie's jaw dropped. "Listen, y'all are sitting around bad mouthin' McLaughlins, but you think nothing of having Kurt work at the business. You want to explain that one to me?"

David shrugged as though it weren't even worth trying to explain. "Well, see, Kurt isn't like the others."

"Naw, he never has been," Rafe chimed in. "He and I were lab partners in chemistry in high school, and after the original snarling at each other, we got along fine. I always knew he was a good one."

"Not like those cousins of his. Every one of them is a skunk," David declared.

"I wouldn't turn my back to a single one of them," Matt added.

"No, Kurt's a good guy," Rita agreed. "I said as much when he came back home to Chivaree to raise his kid right. After the way his wife treated him…" She glanced at Jodie and her voice trailed off.

"Yes, go on." Jodie leaned toward her. "After what way his wife treated him?"

Rita sighed. "You didn't know?"

"If I knew, I wouldn't be asking, now would I?" Jodie looked around, realizing everyone seemed to know about this except for her. "From what I heard, she died in the crash of a small private plane. Is there more?"

The others looked at each other as though trying to decide who should be the one to tell her. Rita took over the story, by default.

"Well, from what they say, she was running off. Leaving him and the baby."

"Oh." Her heart lurched with pain for Kurt.

"She was on her way to meet her boyfriend when the plane crashed in the mountains."

"Oh." Jodie went cold. She'd had no idea. No one had said a word, least of all Kurt. Still, he had let her know things hadn't been good with his marriage. So this shouldn't be a big surprise. And it certainly explained that haunted look in his eyes on occasion. And his vow never to love again.

Well, he'd never actually said that. But she knew it was implicit in his attitude toward ever marrying again. It must have been agony for him to have the baby that he loved and wanted so badly, and have the baby's mother betray him just when he needed her most. She had a real surge of empathy for that one.

She couldn't eat any more after hearing this story. Her siblings went on to another subject, but she was silent. She wanted to go to Kurt, wanted to comfort him somehow. But anything along those lines was playing with fire, and she knew it. So what could she do?

They had all barely finished dinner when the phone rang and Kurt was on the line.

"Jodie. Thank God you're there. You have to come over right away."

"Why? What's happened?"

"I'll explain when you get here."

She frowned, her hand tightening on the receiver. He really did sound as though something terrible had happened. "Kurt, where is Olga?"

There was a pause, then Kurt said firmly, "Jodie, you've got to fire her for me."

Jodie's eyes widened. "Where is she?"

"I've…got her in a safe place."

"Kurt! Where?"

She could hear him taking a deep breath before answering. "I locked her in the laundry room."

"Kurt!"

"I had to do it. She was going crazy."

"What did she do?"

"I'll explain once you get here. Come quick."

She couldn't imagine what Olga could have done. Poor Katy! Jodie got angry in her own right. How could an adult do such a thing to a poor, defenseless little child. What exactly that "thing" was, she wasn't sure. But it had to be bad for Kurt to have locked the woman in the laundry room. She hurried over with her heart in her throat.

"Okay, tell me," she said as she burst into the house. "How is Katy? What did Olga do to her?"

"Look." He gestured toward the high chair, standing by the table and covered in a gooey-looking reddish-purple substance. "She was making her eat beets."

He said it as though he were talking about bamboo shoots under fingernails, and henchmen arriving with cat-o'-nine-tails slapping against their steel-protected palms.

"Making her eat beets?" Jodie repeated, thinking she couldn't have heard correctly. Or maybe, because she didn't know much about babies, she didn't realize the significance of this. She turned back to look searchingly at Kurt.

He nodded, outrage burning in his gaze. "Katy hates beets. She always has. She screams when she sees them coming. And that woman was forcing them on her."

Jodie blinked. "Forcing them?"

"She said babies have to be taught they can't get away with not liking certain foods. Poor Katy was crying as though her little heart would break and that…that woman kept stuffing beets into her mouth."

Jodie turned away. She really didn't know what to say. But one thing was certain—Olga wasn't working out. She and Kurt just didn't jibe.

"Okay," she said, her voice choked. "I'll go down and talk to her." She looked at him. "But Kurt, what are you going to do without someone to take care of Katy?"

"I've got that covered," he said simply. "You can stay and help me out."

The nerve of the man!

That phrase kept running through Jodie's mind. Funny, though, that instead of making her angry, it made her laugh. It was awful nervy to expect her to drop anything that might be going on in her life and come take care of his. But he did it with such open innocence, she couldn't take offense.

Besides, he wouldn't be in the predicament if she hadn't caused the accident. So she did owe him some consideration. Still, to casually assume that she would be there if he needed her…it took her breath away.

And that was the point. He needed her. Katy needed her. And—this was a new revelation to her—she loved being needed.

She handled the firing of Olga with skill and tact,

if she did say so herself. She explained to the woman that Kurt was under great stress and not functionally sound at the moment—that he had abandonment issues and certain irrational phobias that made it imperative that she, as a therapist, take over his treatment for the time being. The fact that her therapy training was in the physical, not the mental, realm was something Olga just didn't need to know. Bottom line, she convinced the woman that Kurt just wasn't ready to give up the care of his daughter to a real professional quite yet.

"Oh, yah," Olga said. "He is off his rocker. I could tell that." She made a derisive sound as she pointed a finger at her head. "And he going to spoil that baby rotten. You better watch 'em."

"Oh, I will," she told the woman as she escorted her out the front door, with Kurt nowhere to be seen. "I'll watch him like a hawk. Please send a bill for your services."

"Oh, no. Mrs. McLaughlin, she gave me a nice check already. Give me a call when the man get better, okay? He gonna need a woman like me to take over his life. You betcha."

"I…I'm sure he'll be thinking about you as soon as he's ready to take that step," she said, waving goodbye and sighing as she closed the door. "There you go," she said to Kurt, who came around the corner, holding Katy in his arms. "Got any more dragons you need me to slay?"

"My hero," he said with obvious relief. "Listen, I didn't mind shoving her into the laundry room, it was just talking to her that gave me the willies. She wouldn't listen to a word I said."

"Don't worry," Jodie teased. "She'll be back to take over your life once you are well enough to accept her services."

Kurt talked straight at Katy. "We're moving and leaving no forwarding address, aren't we girl?"

"Da da da," she agreed companionably.

He looked up, his eyes warm. "But we're taking Jodie with us. Okay?"

"Da da da." Katy gave a jump in his arms as emphasis for the last "da," and they all laughed.

"Will you stay?" he asked as they sobered. "I hate to ask you, but I don't have much choice."

She searched his eyes. They were troubled, and she knew he was as reluctant to risk being close to her as she was to him. She bit her lip. She knew what she ought to do. But she also knew what she wanted to do. Desire won out over mature thinking.

"Of course I'll stay," she said. "But just for tonight."

Chapter Nine

Three days later she was still there, and wondering if she would ever get up the gumption to leave. Not only was she madly in love with Kurt, she'd fallen under the spell of his little girl, as well, and she couldn't imagine giving up caring for her to anyone else.

Still, it had to happen. Once Kurt had his cast off and was wearing a knee brace instead, things would go back to normal for him. He and she would both go back to work at the office. And someone would have to be hired to care for Katy.

But she didn't want to think about that. They made a happy little family, the way things were. She slept in the third bedroom. In the mornings, she got up and went straight to Katy, who was usually gurgling happily and playing with her crib toys. After changing her, she carried her into Kurt's room, where he would sleepily accept his little sweetie while Jodie went into the kitchen to start something for breakfast and try to forget how sexy Kurt had looked with sleep in his eyes. By the time breakfast was ready, Kurt would have Katy in her high chair, and begin feeding her. They sat around the table for at least an hour, laughing and playing with the baby. She was such an irresistibly sunny child.

After breakfast, Kurt gave Katy a bath while Jodie cleaned the kitchen and set things up for the workday on the dining room table. Kurt put Katy down for a nap, and they would get in an hour or so of work before Katy woke again and called out for someone to come get her.

The rest of the day, they played it by ear. Work was interspersed with taking care of Katy's needs or playing with her. Other people dropped by, either with business or just to say hi. In the afternoon, they would go for a drive and stop at a park so that Katy could run through the grass and watch slightly older children on the play equipment. In the evening, the adults usually got takeout of one kind or another, while Katy had baby food from jars, and a bottle.

And once she was in bed for the night, Kurt and Jodie were on their own.

Sometimes the night would start with a movie in the DVD player, sometimes with a board game or a crossword puzzle. But no matter how things began, no matter how much Jodie vowed it wouldn't happen, every night she and Kurt ended up in the same position—in each other's arms.

She knew it had to stop. It was going nowhere, and she was asking for trouble. But it felt so good to feel his arms around her and have him whisper scintillating things in her ear. He was everything she'd ever wanted in a man. In fact, he'd turned her around in many ways. If he ever got to the point where he wanted a real relationship...

Oh, who was she kidding? There were just too many things between them for that ever to work. He didn't want to marry again. He'd been betrayed by the woman he'd chosen, and she knew him well enough by now to know that he felt as though he'd taken his shot and that was over.

He liked her. She could tell when a man liked her. And he liked the way she related to Katy. In fact, he told her every day that he'd lucked out having her as an assistant. But as for marriage—well, that was something else again.

She wondered, sometimes, if the feud was part of his reluctance, as well. He claimed he never gave it a thought, but how could you throw away something that had been embedded in you from the day you were born? She knew it still ate at her sometimes. She had moments, even now, when she wondered about Kurt, wondered about his motives in working for the Allmans. His explanation that it was the best job he could get seemed plausible, but just the same...

Tonight, with Katy tucked away in bed, they were snuggling on the couch. Kurt was lying down with his head in her lap, and she played with his thick, curly hair. He'd just been telling her about the Saturday before, when Manny's son Lenny had come over to play with Katy, and the two of them had fought over a toy.

"I guess the social skills don't come naturally at this age," he said, laughing at the scene as he remembered it. "I couldn't believe it when Katy picked up a plastic block and bopped poor Lenny on the head."

"And you thought she was too demure?" Jodie said. "I guess you haven't noticed the banshee shrieks she can give when she thinks she's not going to get her way."

"You're not trying to imply my little angel is spoiled, are you?"

"No. But she's no shrinking violet, either. Just a normal, healthy little girl." She smiled down at him. "You're going to have your hands full with that little darling as she gets older." They had just finished up a game of Scrabble, and she had won, so she was feeling a little cocky. "Girls rule, you know."

"Hey, you're starting to make me feel outnumbered already."

That would only work if she hung around too long. And that wasn't going to happen. Taking a deep breath, she changed the subject.

"Say, did you ever get back to Manny about those trespassers he was so worried about?" she asked, running her fingers through his hair and loving the way it sprung up to her touch.

"There's no problem," he said, reaching up to brush a strand of hair back behind her ear, his fingertips leaving shock waves behind. "I know who they were."

She managed to hold back the gasp his touch brought on, but she still ended up sounding a little squeaky as she said, "Really? Who?'"

"They were from the university." Turning, he pulled up to a sitting position beside her. "The Botany department." His arm slid around her shoulders and his breath tickled her ear. His tongue flickered out and tasted her ear lobe. "They wanted to get more samples, that's all."

"Oh," she said breathlessly. "Okay."

She swallowed hard. This was where she should pull away and tell him the kissing had to stop. But her muscles felt like rubber bands, and her mind was turning to mush.

"Mmm," he purred, as he began to drop tiny kisses down the cord of her neck. "Okay is not the word for this. Magnificent might apply, though."

She was melting. She always melted at his touch. She turned her head to protest. "Kurt…"

His mouth stopped her words in her throat. Closing her eyes, she let his heat fill her, like a shot of brandy on a cold winter's night. The man set her off like nothing she'd ever known before. His kisses were intoxicating, drugging, addictive. She let the sensation flood through her, luxuriating in the magic, wanting to stretch her body out, wanting to feel him against her.

But this wasn't what she'd planned. Slowly, she forced herself to emerge from the spell of it. She had to stop this now or she would be lost in his silken net forever.

"Kurt, stop."

His hand cupped her cheek. "I don't want to stop."

"I don't either, but…Kurt, you have to stop. We can't go on like this."

"But we can, Jodie. And once I get this cast off, we can go even further."

The shock of that thought gave her a surge of strength. "No. Stop."

He pulled back and looked at her, his green eyes unreadable. "What's wrong?"

She rose from the couch, looking down at him in despair. "Kurt, this is crazy. We started out being perfectly honest with each other. Neither one of us was looking for a romance. I don't know quite how this happened…."

"I'll tell you how it happened." Reaching out, he grabbed her hand. "It's an ancient tale, replete with hormones and moonlight. We hung out together and found we're attracted to each other. End of story."

She closed her eyes and shook her head before glaring down at him again. "You see, that's just the problem. That 'end of story' thing you just said. This shouldn't be an end. This should be a beginning. And since it's not, the other stuff is just treading water."

He looked at her quizzically. "The other stuff being…?"

She sighed sadly. "The physical attraction thing."

"Ah. The urge to merge."

"Kurt!" She threw up her hands. "You see? It's no use. We can't even talk frankly about these things without you making a smart-aleck remark. We just don't have a future together, do we?"

She waited, every nerve on edge. If he'd changed his mind, if he really had developed a new opinion, now was the time for him to say so. Her heart beat in her throat and she waited. And waited. But when he finally responded, it wasn't with the words she'd hoped for, and her heart sank.

"I'm sorry," he said calmly. "Really. I didn't realize you were taking this quite so seriously."

She stared at him. So it was all fun and games to him?

"Oh!" Jodie said. Without another word, she turned on her heel and stomped off.

"You know, day after tomorrow Rafe is taking me into San Antonio for a series of X-rays," Kurt told her later as they were having a last-minute cup of tea in the kitchen. "It's likely the doctor will shift me over to the brace."

Then it was almost over. She turned to look at him, a fist-sized ache starting up in her stomach. What he'd said earlier about her taking their relationship too seriously was still echoing in her head. He was right, of course. She'd known from the beginning nothing long-term could come of this. "We'd better make some plans, then," she said, maintaining a cool outward appearance. "We're going to have to find day care of some sort for Katy."

It wasn't until he looked at her with one eyebrow raised that she realized she'd said "we." She flushed. Well, that pretty much gave the charade away, didn't it? She did think of them all as a "we." If only he did.

"Not Olga," he said. "Might as well send Katy off to military school."

"Poor, misunderstood Olga." Jodie shook her head. "Okay, if not Olga, who?"

He frowned. "Don't you know any older women who might do it?"

She shook her head again. "Not really."

"How about your sister?"

"Rita? No, she's got her hands full with Pop right now." She frowned, thinking hard, then remembered something. She turned to look at him. "I was thinking…. Kurt, tell me this. How do you get along with your cousins these days?"

"My cousins?" He looked as though, had she not reminded him he had some, he would have forgotten all about them. "Some of them, great. Some okay. And one doesn't bear talkin' about."

She looked at him sharply but she didn't pursue it. She'd been thinking that someone who was related to Katy would be better than a stranger. So, if any of the cousins were available, that might be an avenue to pursue. "What's happened to all those cousins, anyway? Are any of them still around here?"

"Sure. Josh is managing the ranch, and trying to bring it out of the hole my uncle and my father ran it into. Jason's in San Antonio, running McLaughlin Management. Kenny and Jake are in the Middle East. They're both Special Ops. Jimmy and Bobby are both in college. And Jeremy…"

His voice trailed off. She waited, heart thumping. *What about Jeremy?*

"I guess Jeremy doesn't come home much these days, does he?" she ventured hopefully. *Oh, please, tell me he's on a ten-year safari to the heart of the African jungle,* she thought. *Please tell me not to expect him back here ever again.*

"No, I don't think even Jeremy would have the nerve to come back here," Kurt said, a sudden touch of bitterness lacing his words.

She looked at him quickly. Did he know? But he wasn't looking at her. He was staring off into space, as though he had his own bad memories of Jeremy. Well, that she could believe. Jeremy was bad news all the way around.

Suddenly he turned back, leaned across the table and took her hand, staring deep into her eyes.

"The man who left you high and dry when you were pregnant was my cousin Jeremy, wasn't it?"

He said the words softly, but there was a deadly menace behind them that made her shiver.

"How did you know?" she asked him, feeling very much alone. It was something she hadn't told anyone about, and she wished it were something she could forget.

"Jeremy told me. Well, he didn't actually name you, and didn't give me all the details, but he told me enough for me to guess it had to be you."

The jerk. He couldn't even keep his mouth shut. She nodded. "It was me."

"I'm sorry, Jodie. Jeremy is a regular bastard. I wish there was some way I could make it up to you." He hesitated, then went on, his eyes hooded. "There's just one thing I've got to know. Do you still love him?"

Her head whipped around. "Who? Jeremy? Oh, my gosh, no."

He was gazing at her intently. "Are you sure?"

"I haven't seen him in ten years. And I haven't wanted to see him."

"He hasn't ever contacted you?"

She looked at him and raised her chin. "Not since the night he told me that McLaughlins don't marry Allmans."

Kurt went still as a statue. "He said that?"

She nodded. "Don't worry about it. The sting has pretty much worn off after all this time. And I don't hold it against you, for heaven's sake."

Groaning, he reached out and pulled her into his arms, then into his lap.

"Jodie, Jodie. I wish I could wash away all the bad things that ever happened to you."

She sighed, wishing that, too. But just being held by him went a long way toward fixing everything.

He kissed her, and that made things even better. She

opened to him, savoring the sensation of his lips on hers as she teased his tongue. Then the heat began to build, and she was gasping as the kiss turned passionate. His mouth was everywhere, branding her with his lips, and she shivered with a new delight that she'd never known before. When his hand slid under her shirt and tugged on her bra, she stretched back to give him access, whimpering as he found her nipple and teased it between his fingers. There was a fire within her, a fire that was going to smolder until she had him inside her to quench it. The deep throbbing had begun, and she knew she had to stop things or…

"Okay," he said huskily, his mouth against her neck. "That's enough. For now."

They pulled apart and she looked at him, bleary-eyed and out of breath.

"Oh, boy," she said, for lack of anything more intelligent being able to penetrate her love-wracked brain. "Oh, wow."

He laughed, pulling her close again. "Jodie Allman, you crack me up," he said.

But his eyes said that she did more than that. And she was tingling with the joy of it for hours afterwards.

They took Katy to the park the next day, and someone mistook them for a real family. They pretended no mistake had been made, and it deepened the bond that was developing between them. Jodie put Katy into the protective seat, and Kurt stopped her before she got in the car to drive them home. He dropped a kiss on her lips.

"You know how I once told you that the only way I would ever get a mother for Katy would be to hire one?"

"I do, indeed."

He was smiling, but there was a strange light in his eyes that made her wonder.

"Well, here's the deal. How much would you charge?"

She stared at him, appalled. She knew he had to be joking, but she didn't find it very funny. Was he actually talking about hiring her to be a mother to his child?

"I'm serious," he was saying, the merriment fading from his eyes and a new look taking over, as though what had started as a joke now looked like something to consider. "I know I'll never have another chance to hire anyone who fits the bill like you do."

She gaped at him. "Do you know how insulting that is?"

He looked surprised. "Why? Because I made you a straightforward offer? I suppose you'd rather I asked you to marry me?"

If ever a fellow needed a thumping! "You can ask anything you like, Kurt McLaughlin. I'm not marrying anybody. Not for love, nor money. So keep your silly ideas to yourself." She flung herself into the car.

"I'm not marrying anybody, either," he said grumpily as he got into the passenger seat.

"Then I guess we're even."

"I guess we are."

They glared at each other all the way home.

* * *

The next morning Jodie saw Kurt off to San Antonio, with Rafe driving. She waved as they disappeared, then went back into the house and began picking up things in the living room. The testy mood that had begun the day before was still with her. Today would probably be her last day in this house. Once she and Kurt went back to the office, would their relationship shift back to what it had been originally? Maybe it should.

She'd hardly begun tidying up when the phone rang. It was Manny Cruz.

"Hi, Jodie. You got Rafe's new number? I want to call him about something."

Rafe had just moved into his own apartment. His brothers were teasing him about wanting some privacy to improve his social standing with the dating set. And truth to tell, he didn't deny it.

She gave Rafe's old friend his new number but added, "You won't catch him today. He took Kurt in to San Antonio to see the doctor."

"Oh." Manny sighed deeply. "Maybe I ought to go ahead and tell you," he said.

Her ears perked up. "Sure. Tell me. I'll help you if I can."

"Okay," he said, sounding reluctant at first. "Here goes. I've got this friend who is always on about conspiracy theories, you know? And he got me to thinking. And once I started thinking, well…I just can't get it out of my head."

"What is it, Manny?"

"Suppose…just suppose, there was this company. It's a successful company, but it's going through a bit of a tough time. Stretched a little thin, maybe. The boss is having health problems. It's not in the strongest position it could be in. You know what I mean?"

"This sounds suspiciously like Allman Industries," Jodie said.

"Yeah, well, whatever. Now, there is this guy who wants to buy the company. But the owner won't sell. So he worms his way into the company, gets people to trust him, looks for weakness. And then he gets a bright idea. He thinks he has a way to force the owner to sell by making the company weaker."

She went very still. "And what would that be?"

"Introduce some kind of weird disease into the vineyards, something that no one knows how to deal with."

"Manny…"

"Some kind of thing he can control later on, once he takes over the company. Something only he can handle."

"Manny!"

"The owner's going under, so he has to sell. And at a pretty good price, too. So the guy who wants to buy is sitting in the catbird seat."

Her fingers tightened on the receiver. "Manny, what exactly are you trying to say here?"

"You want it straight? I'm saying, once a McLaughlin, always a McLaughlin. And that's all I got to say about it. You tell Rafe. Okay?"

"But Manny, wait. I know you're talking about Kurt. What makes you think he wants to buy the company?"

"'Cuz he tried to buy it."

That hard, stinging fist was forming in her stomach again. "When?"

"When he first moved back here. That's how he got the job with your dad. He wanted to buy and your father said, 'No, but why don't you take a job with me instead?' So he did."

Jodie frowned. "Are you sure about that?"

"Absolutely. Rafe told me at the time."

Hanging up, she felt numb. This scenario would fit right in with her original suspicions about Kurt. But she'd gotten over those. Hadn't she?

No, this was just crazy. Manny was imagining things. Still, maybe she ought to talk to Rafe when he got back.

She bathed and fed Katy, and put her to bed for her nap. Watching her from the doorway, Jodie thought about her own pregnancy, and the hopes and dreams she'd had for her baby. Funny how knowing Katy had softened the sting of those memories. She hated to think that just loving a new baby would blot out all feeling for the lost one.

Suddenly her eyes filled with tears, and she knew that those old feelings would never completely disappear. There would always be a little piece of her heart that belonged to the baby who had been taken from her. But one did have to live life as one found it.

The phone rang again. She stared at it for a moment

before answering. This seemed to be a bad news day. She had a feeling she wasn't going to like what she found on the other end of the line.

A gruff man asked for Kurt and seemed perturbed when she told him about San Antonio.

"You his secretary? Okay, please take a message. Let him know that the loan is okayed, contingent on a face-to-face. They're an old-fashioned firm, and the paperwork is all okay, but with a major loan like this, they want to check him out personally before signing on the dotted line. They like to get the measure of the man, if you know what I mean. So if he could call and set up a meeting, that would be the ticket."

"I'll give him the message."

She wrote down the man's number and hung up, then sat back, her stomach churning. Kurt was taking out a major loan. Did this somehow fit in with Manny's crazy story?

Things started flooding back to her, things she'd pushed aside and ignored. She remembered what Tracy had said the other day when Jodie had overheard her arguing with Kurt. Something about Kurt restoring the family to its position in the town. And Kurt said something about how his family would understand what he was doing when it was all over. Why hadn't she dealt with what she'd heard before now?

Because she wanted to pretend she hadn't heard it.

She was such a fool. How could she have let herself fall for a McLaughlin—again?

Chapter Ten

It was late afternoon when Rafe dropped Kurt off in front of the house. Jodie was watching for him. The cast had been removed, and his walk was almost normal as he came up the path to the front porch. Watching him, she felt a surge of emotion. She loved this man. But what was she going to do? Should she confront him with her suspicions? Or go to Matt and Rafe? Either way was disloyal—either to her family, or to the man she loved.

She had her things gathered and her keys in her hand by the time he had the front door open. She had to find a place where she could think this through. And she couldn't stay here with Kurt any longer. After all, he wouldn't need her now. Though it broke her heart, she knew she needed to get away from his influence so that she could think.

She'd been right from the beginning. She should have known better than to get involved with Kurt and his baby. But she had known, hadn't she? And she'd tried to stay away. She'd known deep down that it would only lead to heartbreak. And that was exactly what had happened.

Kurt stared after Jodie as she hurried to her car. He had no idea what had upset her.

The expression on her face as she'd left wasn't a look of betrayal. He knew that look. He'd seen it in Grace's eyes often enough. It was seared in his memory.

No, Jodie's gaze had held the look of loss. A look of goodbye.

Not the sort of goodbye that Grace's face had mirrored. Not that sort of sneaky, furtive, I'm-going-to-cheat-on-you goodbye.

No, it was more an I-found-out-something-about-you-that-I-don't-like goodbye. Where had that come from?

Katy was crying. He went to her quickly and picked her up, holding her to his shoulder and murmuring comfort. She was all he had in the world, and he was all she had. But they both needed more. She felt precious in his arms, but she kept crying, sounding as though her heart would break. It wasn't like her to cry this way. She must be missing Jodie already. And maybe she felt the tension. He began to walk with her snuggled against his chest, stroking her back as he went. But his mind was consumed with Jodie, and that look in her eyes.

Funny how Jodie had always seemed to be lurking

somewhere in the back of his mind. From that day in the park as a little girl, when she'd thrown down the ice cream cone he offered her, she'd stuck in his consciousness like a burr. She was a puzzle, a mystery that beguiled him from afar. Then he'd seen her at that rodeo, in the red halter top, and sexual attraction had entered the picture, increasing his fascination. She was too young then, and he'd left her alone. He'd always thought that later, when she was older…

But she'd disappeared from Chivaree and he'd met Grace, and life had gone on. Still, when Jodie had walked into his office just over a month ago, those old feelings had flooded back. There had always been something about her that had captured his fancy, and that something was still going strong.

He was a different person now, of course. He'd experienced love and death and betrayal. He'd thought these things had taught him to keep a wall of protection around his heart. Never again would he let someone else rule his emotions. Even Jodie.

But when he'd seen the look in her eyes as she'd brushed past him this afternoon, his guts had begun to churn. What the hell could it be? What had set her off? He looked around the room, but the only thing he found was a note on the pad of paper by the telephone. Jodie must have taken a call and jotted down a message for him. He scanned it. Gerhard Briggs had called to tell him the loan was probably a go. Great. But that was the least of his worries now.

He stared at the note, at the clear, curved script of Jodie's handwriting. He loved that writing. She was so…so perfect. So perfect for him. Something stirred in his chest.

Had he lost her?

No. Unacceptable. He couldn't let her walk away.

The last few weeks had been the happiest of his life. Katy had brought him overwhelming joy, but Jodie, he knew with sudden conviction, could bring him inner peace. There was no one like her.

But what could he promise *her?*

He'd loved Grace once, too. That was what made him antsy about this whole love thing. Looking back now, he realized they had been strangers to each other long before Katy arrived on the scene and the breach between them became a canyon. The rift had begun years before, and accelerated once another man complicated things.

An old friend of Grace's had shown up on their doorstep a few months before Katy was born. He was checking out New York City and needed a place to stay for a few days, so Kurt offered him a bed in their apartment. A few days stretched into weeks. He was looking for a job, he'd said. He began hanging out with a crowd Kurt didn't like. Kurt had ordered him out.

Grace had been angry with him at the time, but she was on the verge of giving birth, and all wrapped up in the excitement, so he hadn't thought too much about it. Ah, hell. The truth was, he hardly paid any attention to

Grace anymore by then. He was excited about the baby, but Grace and her ups and downs had finally become so annoying, he pretty much tuned her out.

He had a lot to regret about his marriage. He certainly hadn't been a perfect husband, and there was a measure of guilt on his side. He could have worked harder at pleasing Grace, or at least, in understanding what it was that would please her. Somehow the love between them had turned to a sort of poison.

Did he love Jodie? And if he did, would it last longer than his love for Grace had lasted?

Putting Katy, now asleep, down in her crib, he paced his house restlessly. He wanted to go to Jodie. But what could he say? What could he offer her?

Suddenly, he knew. He checked his watch. It was getting late. He had to go out. But there was Katy. He had to find someone to stay with her. Maybe a neighbor...

The doorbell rang. Jodie was back, Kurt thought. His heart surged in his chest and he sprang to the door, ignoring the sharp flash of pain in his knee. Throwing it open, he found Manny Cruz on his doorstep.

"Listen, man," Manny said without preamble, jabbing an extended finger in his face. "I gotta talk to you."

Kurt's initial disappointment faded quickly. "Come on in, Manny," he said, turning back into the house and searching for his wallet. "Thank God you showed up. I need you." Manny could baby-sit. He was a baby expert.

"For what, man?" Manny bounced on his toes, looking loose. "Hey, come on back here. I called over here to fight you."

Kurt barely looked up. "What are you talking about?"

Manny stationed himself where Kurt couldn't ignore him. "I'm not going to let you steal the business from the Allmans, okay?" he said, trying to sound threatening. "I'm not going to let you ruin that great family. I finally figured out your game, and I'm going to be the one to stop you."

Exasperation filled Kurt, and he stopped, looking the shorter man in the face. "Manny, listen. I have no intention of ruining the Allman family, or taking their business away from them."

"Oh, yeah?" Manny's chin stuck out belligerently.

"Yeah."

"Then why are those dudes prowling around in the vineyards?"

"Those are graduate students in botany at the university. They're collecting more samples of the problem with the vines."

Manny's face changed. "Oh."

"I've talked to my old professor," Kurt said, finally finding his wallet and putting it into the back pocket of his jeans. "He thinks they might be able to come up with a diagnosis and some remedies we can try. He's pretty optimistic."

"So…you're not trying to ruin the crop?"

He stared at Manny, incredulous. "Why would I want to ruin the crop?"

"So you could buy the company cheaper."

Kurt blinked, then swore softly. "Manny, I'm not trying to buy the Allmans' company out from under them."

Manny frowned. "But you tried to buy it from the first."

"No, I didn't. I invested a good deal of money in it. That's true. And I'm taking out a loan to help pay for a couple of new bottling machines. I'm fully committed to this company. I think it's going to turn this town into a prosperous place. But it will always belong to the Allmans."

Manny frowned, digesting the news. "Hey, I guess I had you pegged all wrong," he said, his face turning a deep shade of red. "Sorry about that."

"No problem," Kurt said amicably.

Manny cleared his throat. "So you think they found a cure for my vines?"

"It's possible. I'm going to have my professor friend come out and talk to you soon."

Still intent on getting to Jodie as quickly as possible, he picked up his car keys and looked around the room to see if there was anything he was forgetting. "But right now, I've got a problem to take care of."

He stopped suddenly and frowned, turning to look at the other man as an unpleasant thought came to him. "Listen, Manny. Did you tell anyone else you suspected me of trying to take over the company?"

Manny nodded. "I came over here earlier. I was so upset. I only told Jodie, though. Hey, you gotta tell her I was wrong, okay?"

Kurt's face froze and his heart sank. So that was what

Jodie's strange mood was all about. "Sure," he said slowly. "Sure. I'll tell her." But he set his keys back down and changed his mind about asking Manny to watch Katy for him.

They talked for a few minutes and then Manny left. Kurt stayed where he was, staring into the gathering darkness. Had it really been so easy for Jodie to believe the worst of him? Just one rant from Manny and she'd turned against him. He was a McLaughlin, wasn't he? And therefore, not afforded a benefit of the doubt. Still, it was hard to believe she hadn't even thought to give him a chance to give his side of things. It was almost as if she'd jumped at an excuse to sever the ties. Maybe she was actually more like Grace than he'd known.

She was gone. He closed his eyes and faced the truth. Yes, she was gone. He wasn't going to go after her and beg her to come back. He knew from experience that sort of thing didn't work for long. It would only put off the ultimate agony.

And it did hurt. He'd thought he'd protected himself from ever feeling this sort of pain again, but here it was. And along with the pain came a deep, burning anger. How could she have been so ready to believe he was a liar and a cheat?

Maybe it was just as well. And certainly it was better that it happen now, before they'd made any sort of intimate commitment. But the thought that he might never kiss her again, or see her smile at him with that sunny joy in her eyes, cut like a knife.

Swearing softly, he looked out the window into the night. Maybe she'd been right from the beginning, and their relationship had always been doomed by that damned feud.

Jodie looked up and saw Kurt stepping off the elevator with a small group of others. Quickly, she looked back down at her work, but she couldn't stop her heart from beating wildly as it always did when she caught sight of him. He and the others passed by not far from where she sat at her desk, but she pretended to be engrossed in work.

It had been almost a week since she'd last been at Kurt's house and they hadn't had one real conversation. They had worked together every day, but only here at the office, and every word they'd spoken had been concerned with the job. At one point she'd been about to ask him how Katy was, but she'd overheard him telling Shelley that one of his ubiquitous cousins was taking care of the baby temporarily. So her own question was answered.

She hated this. She knew he was angry at the way she'd left. He knew she'd thought he was guilty of something. She also knew that the suspicions Manny had kindled in her that day were false. Matt and Rafe had both set her straight on that score, and she deeply regretted that she'd let herself fall into such a stupid mistake.

But things had gone beyond that now. The way she saw it, Kurt had taken the opportunity to dump her once he no longer needed her. He'd hinted it was coming when he'd told her she was getting too serious. After all, he'd told her from the beginning he wasn't in the market for a committed relationship. She'd gone into the whole thing knowing what she was risking. And she supposed she'd gotten what she deserved.

But that didn't stop her from crying herself to sleep at night. She was in love with the man. What could she do?

And then there was Katy. Sweet, dear little Katy. How she ached to hold that wiggly little body in her arms again! She'd gone from wanting nothing to do with children to loving one completely, in just a few days. Was it possible to change so quickly?

Yes, if fear was faced down.

Hmm. That was something that might bear further thought.

It was only a half hour later when Shelley stopped by her desk.

"Hey, your boss wants to see you in the boardroom."

"Do you mean Kurt?" she asked, looking up in surprise.

Shelley made a face at her. "Isn't he your boss?"

Of course he was, much as she'd tried to change that from the first. Rising, she took a deep breath and made her way to the boardroom. She assumed he had some comment to make on the advertising proposals she'd turned in that morning. They'd worked together so closely for a while, been so in tune with each other, it felt awkward to go back to being a plain old employee again. Still, it had to be done, and she was determined to be as bright and cheerful as possible.

"Good morning," she called out as she pushed open the heavy door to the boardroom and breezed in.

The room had recently been remodeled and it was now her father's pride and joy. One wall was lined with impressively ornate bookcases full of beautifully bound volumes, while the other was paneled in elegant mahogany and decorated with framed awards the company had won. The table was long and heavy and the chairs that lined it were richly upholstered.

Kurt was sitting at one end of the table, his auburn hair slightly longer than usual, as though he hadn't taken time for a haircut lately. There was a sense of expectation in his green eyes as they met hers. And then she noticed he was holding something in his lap. It took her a second or two to realize it was a child.

"Katy!" she cried out before she could stop herself.

The little tousled head turned and Katy squealed with delight.

"Ma ma!" she cried, throwing out her chubby arms toward Jodie. "Ma da ma da!"

Jodie ignored Kurt, ignored the nonsense syllables the baby was crying out, and reached for the little girl she'd so recently grown to love. Kurt didn't prevent her, and in no time at all she had Katy snuggled securely in her arms. She cooed loving sounds to her, kissing her round cheeks and laughing along with the child.

"Did you hear that?" Kurt said casually. "She called you Mama. Does that bother you?"

She turned to look down into his handsome face. His

gaze was unreadable, but something in the air made her heartbeat start to race again.

"Kurt, what are you trying to do to me?" she asked him.

He shrugged and a slight smile twitched at the corners of his mouth.

"I'm just exploring the idea of you being a mother. What do you think? Is there a possibility you could warm to the role?"

She stared at him, forgetting to breathe. "What?" she said, groping for context. "Are you talking about hiring me again?"

Before he could answer, Shelley came in with some papers and Kurt rose, taking Katy from Jodie's arms and handing her to Shelley.

"Can you take her down to the lunchroom and give her an ice cream or something?" he asked.

"Sure." Shelley looked from one to the other of them with a smirk. "We'll have a great time, won't we Katy?"

Jodie's gaze was still locked with Kurt's as Shelley and Katy disappeared.

"Sit down," he said.

She slid carefully into the seat beside his and waited for him to begin.

It took him a moment. He seemed to be collecting his thoughts. And then he turned to her again.

"I've been doing a lot of thinking over the last few days," he said.

She nodded. "Me, too," she admitted softly.

"I've been an idiot."

Looking quickly into his eyes, she tried to read his meaning. Was he regretting their rift? Or was he sorry they'd ever gotten so close? It was hard to tell. But there was one thing she was sure of.

"You're still angry with me."

He hesitated, frowning. "A little," he admitted.

She ran her tongue over her dry lips and pressed on. "Why exactly?"

A look of pain flashed over his face. "Because you didn't trust me. I thought you had gotten to know me pretty well, and still you had no faith in me."

Her heart sank, but she couldn't leave him with that impression. Because suddenly she realized it wasn't really true.

"No," she said earnestly. "That wasn't it. Don't you see? I had no faith in *myself.* I…I was scared, and I needed some time, some space to think things over. When all these signs seemed to point to you betraying the company, I…okay, it did upset me. And I sort of used that as an excuse to run away."

He nodded slowly. "But that still doesn't answer my basic question. You fell for it too easily, Jodie." The color of his eyes seemed to deepen. "Was it me? Or was it that stupid feud?"

She looked down at her hands, gripped tightly in her lap. Then she looked up again. "The feud is still there, still a part of me. I'm going to have to work very hard to get rid of it. But Kurt…" She bit her lip, then went on. "Kurt, I will get rid of it. I'll erase it from my system. I know I can do it."

Reaching out, he took one of her hands in his, lacing their fingers together. "So you don't think I'm trying to cheat your family?"

She closed her eyes for a second. "Oh, Kurt…"

"Because I'm not, you know."

"I know." She winced, looking guilty. "Rafe explained to me how you've been bankrolling things for Pop for months now. That if it hadn't been for you, the company would have gone under by now."

"Well, I don't know about that, but…"

"I just have to say one thing," she said, determined now to get this all out while she still had the courage to do so. She squeezed his fingers tightly. "I just want you to know. I love you, Kurt McLaughlin."

There. She'd said it and she braced herself, not sure what to expect. Would he get that wary look on his face and draw back and start talking about her getting too serious again? She held her breath, waiting.

He looked astonished. Then, slowly, he began to smile. Leaning toward her, he slid his free hand into the hair at the back of her head and began pulling her closer.

"Do you know how much I've missed kissing you?" he said huskily.

"Oh!" She put a hand on his chest to hold him back. "We can't kiss here. It's the boardroom."

"Hey, you forget. I'm the boss. I can conduct this meeting anyway I want to." He grinned at her. "And I say, when love's involved, kissing is mandatory."

She still held him off. "Does that mean…?"

"What? You want me to say the words?"

She nodded hopefully.

"Okay. Here they are. I love you, Jodie Allman. Though I'm planning to change that last name of yours as soon as possible."

She laughed, but not for long. His mouth covered hers and she melted against him, soaking up his tenderness and returning it in kind. Joy shimmered through her. She could hardly believe her dreams could come true this way. Drawing back, she smiled at him, her lips tingling.

"Oh, Kurt, I'm so sorry I put you through all that. You didn't deserve the distrust."

"No. Actually, I didn't." He grinned, touching her cheek, his love shining in his green eyes. "No more feud, okay?"

She held up her hand. "I swear. No more feud."

They smiled into each other's eyes, feeling like lovebirds.

And then Kurt pulled her close again. "Listen, Jodie," he said with sudden urgency. "Are you going to marry me and be the mother of my children or not?"

"I don't know. This is all so sudden."

"The hell it is. I've been looking at you since I could barely shave and you were jailbait. It's time we put some closure to this thing."

Tilting her head back, she searched his eyes and was happy with what she saw there. "You do mean it?"

"Cross my heart."

She sighed. "Oh, I do love you!"

"I love you, too, Jodie."

"Oh." Tears glistened in her eyes.

"So. Will you or won't you? Say yes."

She smiled up at him. "Yes. Oh, yes!"

"Good."

And he kissed her again, just to seal the bargain.

* * * * *

Trading Places with
the Boss

Chapter One

"Here we go," Shelley Sinclair whispered to the co-worker sitting next to her in the plush seats of the auditorium.

Jaye Martinez nodded and gave her a quick grin.

Shelley took a deep breath, closed her eyes for luck, and opened the folded paper she'd been handed.

Allman Industries, Team A
Role exchangers: Rafe Allman and Shelley Sinclair

She stared at the notation in dismay. *No! Not Rafe Allman!*

Jaye glanced at her own paper, then leaned close to see Shelley's. Her eyes widened and she whispered teasingly, "Whatever you do, don't show fear. Men like that can sense it, like dogs, and they'll rip you apart."

Still reeling from the horrifying partner she'd been given in the conference competition, Shelley didn't get it right away.

"What?" she said.

Laughing, Jaye patted her arm. "I'm only kidding. Rafe Allman isn't really that bad. In fact, he's about the hunkiest boss in this part of Texas, so you ought to be able to put up with a little arrogance if that comes with the deal."

"Speak for yourself," Shelley muttered, looking over to see who Jaye had drawn. Then she sighed, completely jealous and careless about showing it. "You got Mr. Tanner. He's such a sweetie—you'll have a great time with him."

Jaye nodded happily. "I'm already planning ways to wrap him around my little finger. I've got four whole days to convince him I'm the only woman in the world made just for him. What kind of odds will you give me?"

Shelley managed a wistful smile, looking at her beautiful friend whose raven tresses were a direct contrast to her own long blond hair.

"He's a goner. No doubt about it."

Jaye put on an innocent look, making Shelley grin. Then she rose, joining the throngs of others leaving the auditorium. Shelley gathered her conference bag and the stack of handouts and followed her. As their crowd emptied into the foyer of the luxury hotel where the confer-

ence was being held, she caught sight of Rafe Allman and
Jim Tanner waiting for them at the bottom of the ramp.

She groaned—partly because she dreaded meeting
up with her assigned partner, and partly because she
hated the way her heart began to pound out a nervous
rhythm at the prospect. Even so, the crush of people was
slowing progress long enough for her to make a studied comparison of the two men.

Jim Tanner was tall and blond with a twinkle in his
eye and a face that looked ready to smile. Rafe Allman
was a different sort entirely. Just as tall, his shoulders
were square and broad giving him a look of strength Jim
Tanner just didn't have. His dark eyes had a searching
look and his face seemed more ready to twist with cynicism than to smile.

And still, he was devastatingly, head-turningly handsome. Countless women would have jumped at the
chance to spend four days in close contact with the man.

Unfortunately she wasn't one of them. Maybe she'd
known him too long—and knew enough to stay away.
She'd always thought there was something wild in Rafe,
like an animal that had been gentled, but never tamed.

His head went back as he spotted the two women. He
gave Jaye a welcoming smile, but that smile dimmed a
bit as he made eye contact with Shelley. She lifted her
chin. That was fine with her. They were going to have
to work together, but that didn't mean she was ready to
let down any safeguards.

Rafe was the de facto head of Allman Industries, a

distribution center for local Texas wineries, even though his father was still the actual president of the company. And Rafe fulfilled the role of the man in charge with cool assurance.

"Like lambs to the slaughter," Jaye said under her breath just before they met the men.

"Who? Us or them?" Shelley was afraid that she and Jaye had a slightly different perspective on the matter.

"You missed the introductory address," Jaye told the men as they met them, her tone accusing but also just this side of flirtatious. "You missed all the information about what we're supposed to do."

"That's what we have you lovely ladies here for," Rafe said with a humorous gleam in his eye. "We're counting on your legendary attention to detail."

"We'll share the burden," Shelley said lightly. "Next meeting, you two can attend, and Jaye and I will play hooky."

Rafe raised one silky dark eyebrow, looking surprised. Did he think she was being a bit presumptuous, considering he was the highest-ranking Allman Industries executive here and she was a lowly administrative assistant? Little did he know that situation was about to make a radical change. Her pulse was racing at the thought.

Her gaze met his and caught for just a beat or two, and suddenly she knew it was more than her attitude he was aware of. He was thinking back to last New Year's Eve when, for just a moment, the possibility of some-

thing romantic had sparked between them. It hadn't
lasted long, and they had both spent the rest of the year
avoiding each other like the plague, despite the fact that
they worked for the same company. But it was always
there between them, every time they met.

"We've got a table in the bar," Jim Tanner was saying. "Come on and fill us in over drinks."

Jaye very happily took his arm and began teasing him
about how surprised he was going to be when he found
out what the theme of the contest was this year. That left
Shelley and Rafe to walk stiffly side by side, each trying to ignore the other.

The bar was noisy and crowded but the table was
being saved by a couple of other employees from Allman
Industries and soon they were all six jammed around it.
Shelley talked and laughed with the others as they ordered drinks, but she noted that Rafe had very carefully
taken a seat as far away from her as he could get.

"Well, I really wish someone would explain to me exactly what we're doing here," Dorie Berger, a pert young
office worker, said plaintively. "Everyone keeps telling
me this is such a privilege to get to attend, but no one
ever bothered to fill me in on what goes on at these
things."

"This is the way it works," Rafe said, giving her a
smile that seemed to Shelley to be mostly about showing his admiration for Dorie's tight-fitting sweater. "The
competition is in a different city each year. Each company is allowed to submit up to three teams made up of

seven of their employees each. They all spend the four days of the conference getting their presentation honed and ready. On the last day, each team does its thing in front of the judges and the winner gets a nice big trophy for the trophy case at work—and the prestige that goes with it in the industry."

"But what's the point?" Dorie asked, still looking bewildered.

"It's supposed to make us think outside of the box and come up with new ideas," Jim Tanner offered. "The point is to encourage us all to strive for excellence in our business dealings."

"Not quite," Rafe said deliberately, and suddenly everyone was quiet, listening to him.

That very fact alone drove Shelley wild. Why did they all act like he was the most marvelous thing since the invention of the wheel? He was just a very handsome, very dynamic, very charismatic—regular guy. That was all.

"The point," he was saying dramatically, "is to give the best damn presentation in the competition. The point is to grind your competitors in the dust. The point…" He raised his glass and looked around the table, his own dark eyes hinting at a steely determination. "The point is to win."

"Hear, hear," said Jaye, and they clinked glasses all around.

Shelley joined them, but her heart wasn't in it. Taking on the leadership role here was going to thrust her into a position she might not like very much. She was going to have to fight Rafe all the way. Was she really ready for this?

Quickly she shoved that thought aside. She would have to think about that later, when she was alone. Right now dealing with being at a table under the direct observation of Rafe's too-knowing gaze was about as much as she could handle.

"Well, what are the competitions like?" Dorie was asking.

"It's different every year," Jim said. "One year you had to pretend your product was a politician and develop an election campaign around it. Campaign signs and speeches."

Shelley smiled, then offered up, "Last year we had to develop a ten-minute musical for our product, with each person on the team singing something for at least one minute."

"Oh, no!"

"Did we win?" Rafe asked, gazing at her levelly.

Shelley hesitated. "I think the A team came in fifth." She saw his look of disapproval and she bristled. "That's not so bad. There were ninety-two teams competing."

His gaze sharpened. "So you came last year? I thought this gig was on a three-year rotation."

Attendance was considered a perk and company policy was that each employee could only do it once every three years so that the spots were shared more equally around the workforce.

"Yes, I came last year," she admitted. "Actually, Harvey Yorgan was supposed to come with you all today, but his wife went into premature labor, so I got volunteered at the last minute."

Actually, she'd volunteered herself, and with an ulterior motive that she couldn't reveal to anyone. But that was something she hoped no one would figure out, most of all, Rafe Allman.

"Well, we're down to the wire," he said, looking at her expectantly. "Let's have it. What is it this year?"

She licked her dry lips. "This year one member of the squad has to change places with the boss."

He stared at her as though he didn't understand what she was saying, so she amplified.

"The highest ranking person on each team has to become just one of the employees," she explained. "And one of the employees becomes the new boss."

The air seemed still between them as he digested this setup. Then he shrugged.

"Great." Rafe gave her a comical grin. "So I don't have to do any work."

Everybody laughed. Everybody but Shelley. He was still staring into her eyes, and she was staring right back. She was not going to let him intimidate her. But her heart was still pounding.

"So who is it?" he asked at last, but surely he already guessed.

"Jaye will be trading with Jim." She smiled at her friend, then glanced at Rafe. "And you and I will be switching," she added, trying not to sound as breathless as she felt.

He cocked an eyebrow. "Interesting."

Something in his voice—and his eyes—sent a shiver slithering down her spine.

"*Don't show fear,*" Jaye had said. She'd been joking, but she'd been closer to the mark than she knew. Shelley had to admit it, if only to herself. The man scared her.

Not in a physical way. She didn't suspect he had an abusive side. But there was a streak of animal magnetism to him that sent her over the moon. Maybe it was just a quirk in her own character. Maybe she had a natural weakness for men with midnight eyes and chiseled chins, like some women had a weakness for wine or chocolate. Whatever—she knew she was drawn to him, and she also knew giving in to that pull would be very bad for her.

"Then what do we do?" he asked at last. "Learn to tap dance to our company theme song?"

Her smile was tight. "We develop a business plan that will enhance the operations of our company in some way."

His gaze became speculative. "You mean besides providing a product along with jobs and benefits for our employees and making a little profit off the top."

"Yes."

"Right." He grinned and leaned back in his chair, taking a sip of his drink. Then he looked at them all with a reassuring smile. "Don't worry. I'll handle this."

That did it! How could she be so attracted to a man

who made her so angry at the same time? The condescending tone did it for her. It conjured up too many memories of times in the past when he'd tormented her in one way or another. Reaching into one of her Quality in Performance and Leadership Conference folders, she pulled out the information sheet and put it in front of him so that he could see the setup for himself.

"Actually, *I'll* be handling it," she told him as calmly as she could manage. "And the first decision I'm making is to have a strategy meeting."

He looked surprised. "What for?"

Oh, he was going to be tough. She could see it right now. He wasn't going to give up the reins of power without a fight. There was no way he was going to submit peacefully. But he was going to have to.

"We need to get going on a project right away," she said quickly. "Five o'clock. My room. Please let the others know, Rafe. The list of our group members is attached." She smiled at him, trying to maintain a professional air despite the fact that she was furious with him. "Your first assignment."

His eyes narrowed. Shelley had a sense of everyone else at the table holding their breath, waiting to see what was going to happen next. She had to make a move before he did.

Grabbing her purse, conference bag and papers, she rose from her chair.

"Oh, and Rafe?" she said, turning back, her heart beating hard in her chest. "For the next four days, why don't you call me Miss Sinclair? That might help you keep our new positions straight."

She smiled sweetly at everyone, noting the stunned faces all around, and then her gaze came back to meet Rafe's. Was that anger she saw? Laughter? Mockery?

She couldn't tell. But there was no time for analysis. If she delayed this dramatic leave-taking any longer, she would spoil the whole thing.

"See you at five," she said, turning to go.

She didn't hear what he said, but she recognized his low voice saying something, and the table erupted with laughter just as she reached the doorway. Had he been making fun of her? No doubt. Her face was suddenly very hot and she knew she must be glowing like a neon sign.

"Darn you, Rafe Allman," she muttered to herself as she went quickly toward the elevator. "Darn you and the horse you rode in on!"

Five o'clock came and Shelley waited nervously, adjusting chairs, turning down the music. What if Rafe defied her and didn't show up? What if he didn't tell the others? What if he did show up and made fun of her all through the meeting?

Think it couldn't happen? Hah!

The thing was, she and Rafe had a track record that went back over twenty years. There were times when her close friendship with his sister Jodie meant that she had practically lived at the Allman house. Growing up, her mother had been busy all the time with the coffee shop she ran, Millie's Café. On hot summer days, Shelley usually found her way to Jodie's and the two of them did all the things young girls frolicked in together.

Even back then she and Rafe had been adversaries. He was always finding some way to embarrass her or make her feel inadequate. He was, after all, the one who pointed out to everyone at the Allman dinner table when she was eleven and wore her first training bra to dinner at their house. Her face still burned when she thought of the looks on all their faces as they stared in surprise and amusement at her youthfully modest chest.

Too bad she didn't find a way to murder him then.

Never mind. She was stuck with him for the weekend so she would just have to make the best of it. She knew he must hate her in the position of being his boss, even if temporarily. And she knew she was going to have to fight him all the way just to keep him from taking over.

If only Rafe's older brother Matt had come instead of Rafe. Matt was older, wiser…nicer. She considered him the ideal big brother she never really had. She would do just about anything for him.

A knock sounded and she jumped. Taking a deep breath, she walked quickly to the door and opened it.

"Good evening, *Miss Sinclair.*" Rafe stood looking down at her, the mockery in his eyes echoing the mockery in his voice.

Behind him was the rest of the group. She did a quick inventory. Candy Yang, a paralegal, would make a great assistant. She'd dealt with her before. Jerry was head of finance, but she also knew he was a home carpenter who loved woodworking and could easily supervise building sets. Pretty little Dorie Berger was an entry-level office worker, a sweet young thing who would do pretty much as she was told. And the two others were people she didn't really know very well, but they seemed agreeable.

"Here we are," Rafe was saying, draping himself across her doorway. "Your loyal minions, awaiting your command."

"Good," she said, standing back. "Come on in. We need to get started right away."

Her gaze met his as he sauntered into the room. Something hard and challenging lurked deep in his eyes, and her mouth went dry as she noted it. The weekend was going to be a rough one. Her challenge had only begun.

Chapter Two

Sometimes that whole damn sex thing just got in the way.

Rafe sat toying with the remains of a sumptuous dessert, moving curled pieces of bitter chocolate from one side of the plate to the other with his silver fork. But his mind was on the woman at the other end of the long table.

Shelley Sinclair. He'd known her just about all his life. And here she was, complicating things for him once again. It would certainly be easier if she didn't have that long, silky hair that fell down into a sensual curl just over the swell of her left breast. If she didn't have those doe-shaped eyes that seemed to hide a secret sorrow. If she didn't have that soft, lush mouth that always made him think of long, hot kisses and the scent of gardenias.

Why gardenias? He had no idea.

And the entire thing disgusted him anyway. Just looking at her now, as she slowly put another forkful of whipped cream in that beautiful mouth, he felt a surge of desire that almost made him groan aloud. He was too old for this sort of thing, dammit! Lusting after anyone would have been a problem, but lusting after Shelley Sinclair was nuts.

It hadn't always been like this. Years ago, when Shelley had hung around the Allman house with his little sister Jodie, and the two of them had spied on him and teased him and made his life miserable, he certainly hadn't thought of her as sexy. In fact, if he thought of her at all, it had been with extreme annoyance—as in, "What a brat!"

But that was then.

Now she was another sort of irritant. And he couldn't let that get in the way of what had to be accomplished here. He hadn't asked for this assignment, but now that it had been thrust on him, he was damn well going to come out of it with a trophy in his hand. Allman Industries had to win this competition and it was up to him to make sure that happened. This whole setup, where he was supposed to switch places with Shelley, was going to work against him having the control he needed. And he was going to have to do something about that.

The strategy meeting had been frustrating. He'd assumed that after a little bit of moderating for window-dressing, she would gracefully sit back and let him take over. After all, that was where he belonged, where he usually was—in charge. It was the natural order of things and everyone knew it.

Everyone but Shelley, who seemed to be on another trajectory entirely. She'd held onto the floor, stubborn as a squirrel with the last fall acorn. She had plans and she laid them out, talking fast, assigning workshops for the next morning, giving out instruction sheets. He'd hardly gotten a word in edgewise.

And just when he'd had enough and he'd stood up to take over the reins by force if he had to, she'd given him a triumphant look and adjourned for dinner. Then they had all trooped down to the restaurant to meet the other Allman Industries employees for a totally choice meal. All twenty-one of them. Made you wonder who was home minding the store.

But that was okay. This competition was important, more important than the others here knew. It wasn't just his competitive nature that was at stake here. A major supply contract hinged on the outcome. That was the way they had built the business, scraping and fighting for every advantage. He'd promised his father he would deliver a win and that was what he was going to do. After all, if he was going to prove to them all that he was the natural pick to take over the company, he had to show that he could be just as ruthless as his father ever was.

The others were rising from the table, preparing to go back to their rooms and get some sleep before attending the workshops in the morning. Rafe rose, too, nodding to Jim but brushing aside a melting look from Tina, the raven-haired, statuesque director of personnel who had been giving him the come-on for weeks now, and he headed straight for Shelley.

She looked up, surprised, when he took her arm and leaned close.

"We need to talk," he said softly near her ear.

Her lovely mouth tilted at the corners. "Talk is cheap," she quipped, gathering her things and looking toward the exit. "Send me an e-mail."

His fingers ringed her upper arm. He wasn't about to let her bolt, despite the way her flesh felt under his hand.

"You want all communications in writing, so you can hold my words as evidence against me?" he responded in kind. "Just a bit too transparent, Shelley. I'm not going to fall for that one."

"Too smart for me, huh?" She gave a significant glance at his hand on her arm. "Or, if brains don't work for you, you're ready to move on to manhandling. Is that it?"

He didn't let go. "Intimidation can come in many forms," he noted dryly. "Some of them just your size."

"Are you accusing me of using my feminine wiles to intimidate you?" she said, looking more amused than anything else.

He opened his mouth to say something that would get him into a lot of trouble, but luckily, he thought better of it in time.

"Shelley, I just want to talk to you. Don't make a federal case out of it."

"Okay." She made a face that made it obvious she was surrendering to the inevitable. "Come on up to my room. I'll give you fifteen minutes."

Rafe drew in a deep breath, looking down at her. Okay, here was the crux of his dilemma. Every part of him yearned toward an evening alone in her room. He could already see the soft light, feel the romantic music coming in over the sound system, taste the way her mouth would yield under his....

No way. Couldn't be done. How about the bar?

The music there would be throbbing with sensual urgency, the atmosphere provocative, the sense of impending possibilities tantalizing, her mouth would be just as tempting—and alcohol would be involved.

No. Too dangerous.

"Let's walk down to the canal," he said quickly, deciding a public walkway filled with tourists would pose the least risk. "Soak up some of the ambience."

A slight frown appeared, but she nodded. "Fine. Let's go."

The evening air was unusually warm. The crowd was thick and in a rollicking mood. Lights from the boutiques and clubs bounced off the water and laughter formed a foundation for the music that filled the night. The scene was celebration.

But Rafe felt edgy. He shoved his hands into the pockets of his jacket to keep from reaching out to help guide Shelley as she walked along beside him. Glancing sideways he saw that she came up above his shoulder. The perfect fit for him. He could already feel how it would be to put an arm around her slender form and curl her up against him.

He swore softly, fed up with the way his mind kept trending.

"You rang?" she said quizzically, glancing upwards in a way that emphasized the almond shape of her big brown eyes, her dark lashes leaving long shadows on her cheeks.

He swallowed hard and looked to the heavens for help. "Sorry," he said shortly. "I just had a thought."

"Quite an unusual experience for you I guess," she said archly. "Do you swear every time you get one of those?"

He stared at her, fighting off the impulse to grab her and either shake her or kiss her. "You know what?" he said instead. "You're as big a brat now as you were when we were kids."

She glared at him. "Why not? You're as big a bully."

The crowd surged around them and someone bumped against Shelley, sending her reeling into his arms.

"Sorry," said a disembodied voice but Rafe's first instinct to go after the perpetrator evaporated as he looked down into her face and felt the fragility of her body against the strength of his.

Time stood still. He couldn't breathe. The background faded into a swirling mist and all he could see were her huge eyes.

Then things went back to normal and they pulled

apart, avoiding each other sternly, walking quickly toward the river. Rafe turned into a viewing bump-out and she settled alongside him as he leaned his elbows on the railing and stared into the inky waters below.

It was too late to pretend he didn't react to her like a bug on a hot skillet. Everything she did, every time she moved, everything she said, triggered a response in him of one kind or another. If he couldn't conquer it, at least he had to learn to hide it. He stood very still, steeling himself. Time to take back the controls, all the way around. Otherwise he was going to turn into a mushy mess. And that couldn't happen.

Shelley was floundering. She had no idea what was going on with Rafe. He was acting so weird. He probably hated her.

And why not? She'd never liked him much.

Of course, there had been that New Year's Eve party when they had both had a little too much to drink. He'd hung around making caustic comments and she'd given as good as she got—but when midnight came, he'd kissed her. The surprise of that kiss had shocked them both and they'd drawn apart unable to look each other in the eye. If it had been anyone else, that kiss might have launched a torrid affair. But since it was the two of them, they hadn't spoken to each other since—until this weekend. The fact was, any sort of civil relationship between them just wasn't meant to be.

Sighing, she looked out at the water, enjoying the bobbing lights reflected there. A slight breeze pressed the lacy fabric of her skirt against her legs.

"I love San Antonio," she murmured, mostly to herself as she drew her shawl closer around her shoulders.

He turned to look at her, then looked away again.

"Funny how it used to seem like this huge city when I was young," he said. "Now it seems more like an overgrown small town."

"That's what I like about it. You can wrap your arms around it and become a part of it so easily."

"I didn't say I didn't like it. I like small towns. In fact, it's cities I hate."

She bit her tongue. If he was going to make everything into an argument, she just wouldn't talk anymore.

The silence stretched between them. She risked a quick look his way. His attention was on the other side of the river, giving her an opportunity to study him for a moment. He had a rugged, masculine appeal, untamed and proud of it. Pure Texas. She remembered he'd always looked so very good riding a horse.

But that was then. And remember, she'd never liked him much. She had to keep that in mind at all times.

Suddenly, as though there had been no pause in their conversation, he spoke softly.

"My mom brought me to San Antonio for a weekend one November when I was a kid, to see the Christmas lights on the river."

That surprised her, and not only because he was talking like a normal person for a change. "Just you? Not any of the others?" There were plenty of Allmans.

He shook his head. "Just me. I was about thirteen and she thought I needed something special. I think she was trying to make up for the fact that Pop was making it pretty plain that he considered Matt his fair-haired child and thought of me as good for nothing much."

He stopped, frowning fiercely. Why the hell was he telling her all this? Of all people, she was the last…

But maybe it was because they'd known each other forever, practically grown up side by side. Too bad he couldn't just think of her as a sister. But the feeling that swelled in him whenever he looked at her had nothing to do with brotherly love. So he had better stop looking.

"You were her favorite," she said softly.

"Me?" That startled him. When he thought of his mother, he remembered a warm smile and a feeling of peace. She was just about perfect in his book. No one could ever touch her. It still hurt to know she was gone. "Nah. She didn't have favorites. She was good to everyone."

Shelley nodded. "She was a wonderful woman and she died much too young." Reminders of that awful time, when Jodie's sweet mother was dying of complications from heart surgery, made her wince. "But believe me, she had a special soft spot for you."

He turned to look at her, frowning. "You were just a kid. You paid attention to things like that?"

She couldn't hold back a smile. "Of course."

His gaze lingered, then he turned away and her smile drooped.

But he'd unlocked a lot of memories. She'd spent so much time at that house, with that family, probably because she didn't have much of a family herself. All she had was her always busy single mother. No one else. Millie avoided any talk about who her father was, so she'd made one up for herself. Tall, handsome, kind and loving, he was ideal—though he tended to evaporate into mist whenever she tried to reach out to him. That was the trouble with fantasy fathers.

So that really didn't fill the lonely hole in her heart. She'd prayed every night for a brother or sister, until she'd finally gotten old enough to begin to understand why that wouldn't ever happen. So she'd attached herself to the Allmans.

"You seem to have grown up okay despite losing your mother," she told Rafe now. "And being left to the untender mercies of your father."

He shrugged. "Pop's okay."

That almost made her angry. It wasn't the way she remembered things.

"He can't hit you anymore, can he?" she said softly. "You're bigger than he is now."

He reacted as though she'd said something crazy.

"What? Ah come on, he never hit me all that much."

He turned to lean with his back against the railing, his arms crossed over his chest. This was something no one would ever understand. His father had always been rough on him. But that only made the times he came through and surprised the old man all the more satisfying.

"Anyway, that was the way his generation dealt with things. Say what you want about Pop, he's a man of his time."

She shook her head, wondering how he could defend the man. Jesse Allman was a character, a legend around their hometown of Chivaree, Texas. A hardscrabble sort of guy, he'd managed to work his much-scorned family out of poverty and up into dizzying success. He was a genius in his own way, and adept at turning his life around and making something of himself. But he hadn't been a gentle father.

"You wouldn't hit a child, would you?"

He gave her a look of weary resignation. "It's called spanking, Shelley. And no, I don't suppose I would do that. How about you?"

She shrugged. "I'm never going to have children."

He stared at her, then shook his head. "Going for that big career in the sky, are you?"

For some reason, she felt like shivering. Was she really considered a career woman now? Oh, well, she supposed that was better than some things she might be called.

"Something like that," she admitted reluctantly.

He turned back to look at the water. "You're doing pretty well. I've heard good things about your work from Clay in Legal."

Clay Branch, her supervisor in the legal division, another bothersome man in her life. "Maybe if I do a good job at this competition, Clay will finally pay some attention to my requests to get management training."

"You want to be a manager?"

"I want to move up in my field. And that's pretty much my only avenue, don't you think?"

"Maybe so." He grinned. "I guess that's why you're jumping at the chance to boss me around, huh?"

"I didn't set up the framework for this competition." She gazed at him challengingly. "But I'm not running from it, either. Do you feel threatened by that, Mr. Boss Man?"

Rafe didn't respond but he moved restlessly, indicating he was ready to walk on, and she obliged. They passed a small club. Pieces of acoustic guitar music floated out into the night. The crowd was thinning out and the lights were not quite so bright in this direction.

"You used to live here in San Antonio, didn't you?"

She nodded, feeling suddenly wary. It was not a period of her life she relished discussing. "Not for long," she murmured, looking away.

"And you worked for Jason McLaughlin during that time, didn't you?"

His question hit her like a slap in the face and she gasped softly. She sneaked a quick look at him. How much did he know?

Back in Chivaree, the McLaughlins were the family who founded and ran the town, and the Allmans were the outcasts. Things had changed over the last decade, and now the Allmans were riding high, running a company that was putting the McLaughlins into the shadows.

But the old legends still hung on. The McLaughlins were considered legitimate. The Allmans were the outlaws. And the two families had always hated each other.

So it was a big deal for Shelley, who had grown up identifying with the Allmans, to have worked for a McLaughlin. In many quarters, that would be considered the move of a traitor. Looking back, she considered it the move of a crazy person, a woman who had temporarily lost her mind and good sense. It certainly wasn't something she bragged about, or wanted to remember fondly.

"That was a long time ago," she said evasively.

"Only a little over a year, isn't it?" He stopped, hands shoved into his pockets and looked at her searchingly. "So I guess this will be a reunion of sorts for you."

Her heart was thumping in her chest and she reached up to finger her gold necklace nervously. "What are you talking about?"

"I just noticed it on the roster. McLaughlin Management is in the competition." His stare was hard and penetrating. "Jason is here. Didn't you know?"

"No, I didn't know." She wanted to reach out for something to lean on but she knew she couldn't allow herself that luxury. This was something she hadn't prepared for. She knew Jason's business was doing very well, but they had never entered the competition before. Why did they have to decide to start now?

"Or is that exactly why you asked to be included in the team even though you had your turn last year?"

She looked into his face, bewildered. Did he really think she wanted a chance to get close to Jason McLaughlin again?

Then he knew—or at least suspected—about her past relationship with the man. That was embarrassing.

Still, a lot of people knew, so why wouldn't he? It wasn't anything she was proud of. And she certainly didn't yearn for a repeat performance, if that was what he was implying. Anger shivered through her.

"Don't worry, Rafe. I won't be taking time off from the competition to dally with our competitors. We'll put up a good fight for your beloved trophy."

She started to stomp off but he grabbed her arm and pulled her back.

"Shelley, don't act like I'm all alone in this. Of all people, you should understand. We both come from dirt-poor backgrounds. We know what it's like to scramble for a little dignity."

She turned her face away, unwilling to join him in this, even rhetorically, as he went on.

"We're not like the McLaughlins, either one of us. No silver spoons for us. We fight for every inch. So I think you understand me when I say we've got to win this thing. And a good part of the satisfaction in that will be beating the McLaughlins."

"Beating the McLaughlins," she echoed softly.

"Sure. They've always got the establishment behind them. We're the little guy. We have to try harder."

That was Rafe to a T—always trying harder. Always trying to show his father that he could be good at things. And the funny thing was, he was very good at just about everything. Too bad Jesse Allman never seemed to notice.

But she didn't want to waste her time feeling empathy for Rafe. He was studying her reaction and she knew it. He wanted to know that she was on the side of Allman Industries, that she wasn't going to defect to the enemy. Rebelliously she refused to give him that comfort.

She looked out at the water again. "I thought maybe, now that Jodie is marrying Kurt McLaughlin, the feud between your two families would begin to fade away."

His mouth hardened. "The feud will begin to fade away when the McLaughlins stop being coldhearted bastards. Except for Kurt, of course. He's always been different from the rest of them."

She nodded. She had to agree on that score. Kurt had started working at Allman Industries some months before, despite a lot of resistance and bitterness from his own family. And when Jodie had come home to work there, too, a romance between the two of them had quickly blossomed.

Shelley loved Jodie and wished her the best, but she had to admit she was a little worried at first about the McLaughlin angle to it all. Her own experience told her that all the years of antagonism between the two families was based on more than pure spite.

She was still thinking about the McLaughlins as they started to walk back toward the hotel. There had been a time when she'd been so in love with Jason McLaughlin she could hardly see straight. And maybe that was why she didn't realize what a jerk he was until it was too late.

No. Wait. That wasn't really fair.

Jason hadn't been so much a jerk as she herself had been blind and hopelessly naive. She hadn't known he was married at first. From what she learned later, the marriage was stormy—with the two of them separated more often than they were together. She had started dating Jason during one of those separations. Still, only a fool would have believed his lies about it being over for good. Anyone with half a brain should have seen where things were headed. Only, she had been too overwhelmed by the chance to be with Jason. She *had* a brain, she just hadn't used it. She still cringed when she remembered the day his wife had returned to find Shelley ensconced in their apartment. The bitter contempt in the woman's eyes had been like a brand on her soul. And she knew she deserved every bit of that scorn.

"So I know you're going to cooperate here. Right?"

He wanted reassurance. Well, too bad. At this point she wasn't sure he deserved it. Looking at him, she made a face.

"Are you still obsessed with being number one all the time, Rafe? Is that all life is to you, always winning?"

"What's wrong with winning? It's better than being a loser." His dark gaze raked over her sardonically. "Or maybe you prefer losers?"

"Not really. I'd say I prefer people of goodwill."

He started to say something, then stopped himself and shook his head. "Goodwill, huh? Hey, I'm dripping with it."

"Really?" The picture that conjured up almost made her laugh. She raised her eyebrows instead, then smiled faintly and made a grand gesture with her hand. "Perhaps I should clarify. I prefer people with a broader scope," she said, purposefully making it sound snooty.

"Oh." She was happy to see amusement begin to bubble in his gaze. "Broad scope, eh? Excuse me while I adjust my cravat."

She gestured again, chin in the air. "You're excused. Carry on."

"Such graciousness. You put me to shame."

She smiled impishly. "Then my work here is done."

A faint grin actually appeared on his face. "Oh, no, honey. I'm going to be more of a challenge than you can imagine."

Her breath caught in a little hiccup in her throat and she blinked to cover it up. "That's a little scary. I can imagine a lot." She flashed him a look. "I'll clarify even further. I prefer men with a little sophistication."

He cocked an eyebrow. "I suppose what you really prefer is Jason McLaughlin."

Her head whipped around and she glared at him. To her complete shock, he actually looked chagrined.

"Sorry," he muttered. "That was a low blow."

"You should know," she said tartly. "You're the king."

"Of low blows?"

"And other assorted indignities."

"Indignities." He mocked the way she'd said the word, humor softening the edges. "Gettin' sorta high falutin with your language there, girl. I knew you way back when we were both prairie rats. You can't fool me."

He was teasing her, but in a gentle way, not the way he used to when they were young. If he didn't watch out, she was going to start to like him.

"Maybe you can't be fooled," she said. "But at the same time, you *can* be persuaded. You're a smart guy. You know there's nothing wrong with reaching for something a little higher."

A boisterous bunch of young people was headed straight for them. Reaching out, he put a hand at the nape of her neck, guiding her with a protective touch as the youngsters passed.

"Just as long as you don't forget where you came from," he murmured.

The feel of his hand on her skin was seductive and she felt a lazy sense of warmth seeping into her system. Taking a quick step to the side, she managed to pull away as she pretended to need the room to turn and face him.

"Well, look at you," she said earnestly. "You were in

a business suit this afternoon. You had on a tie and everything. Your shirt was crisp and white and your slacks had a great crease. You looked wonderful. Your father never looked like that in his life."

His face twisted into a thoughtful frown. "So I'm aiming for a higher place just like you think I oughta, just by wearing a suit?" He gave her a look of pure exasperation. "Listen, Shelley. Nobody ever worked harder to make a 'higher place' in this world than my father did."

"Except maybe my mother," she shot back. "How do you think she managed to run Millie's Café on her own? Nobody handed her anything."

A reluctant grin began to surface again on his handsome face. "Well…my pop can outhustle your mom."

Her chin went out. "Cannot."

His eyes twinkled. "Can, too."

She smiled back, just barely, flashing her eyes at him. "Well…maybe. But he can't cook like she can."

He nodded. "You got me there."

They were back in front of the hotel. Without saying a word, they both paused. Neither seemed anxious to go in. She turned to look at him and he met her gaze.

"So you swear you didn't come to the conference because of McLaughlin?" he demanded.

She hesitated, then held up her hand like a Girl Scout. "I swear to you. I probably wouldn't have come myself if I'd known he was going to be here."

He nodded slowly as though thinking that over. "So

tell me…why did you come? Just what is your ulterior motive?"

She couldn't keep meeting his gaze after that. Because the truth was, "ulterior motive" was a good phrase for her purpose. She had agreed to come at the last minute, knowing it would give her an opportunity she wouldn't otherwise have to do a little detective work that needed to be done. But she couldn't tell Rafe about that. To do so would involve telling a secret that wasn't hers to share.

Taking in a deep breath, she raised her gaze to his again. "You know, there are some things that are just plain private," she said firmly, though her pulse gave a nervous flutter as she noted his reaction. "My reasons have nothing to do with the business," she added. "And anyway, you have no right to ask me."

"You won't tell me." He looked astonished at her defiance.

She shook her head and shrugged, her palms out. "You have no need to know." It was only the truth. Why couldn't he accept it and move on?

His eyes looked very dark in the lamplight. "You realize that means I can't put my suspicions to rest."

She turned her head so fast her long silky hair whipped around her shoulders. He was being impossible. But then, that was his nature, wasn't it? She'd almost forgotten with him seeming so approachable.

"Then you just suspect away all you want, honey," she told him with her thickest Texas drawl. "As long as you do a good job for me tomorrow. Because for the time being, I…am…the…boss." With a look daring him to dispute what she'd said, she whirled and strode for the elevators.

Chapter Three

In the morning, the first person Shelley saw as she stepped off the elevator on the lobby floor was the very man she dreaded seeing—Jason McLaughlin.

"Shelley. It's been a long time." The tall blue-eyed man in the Italian silk suit stepped forward and took both her hands in his, smiling down at her. "You look wonderful."

For a moment she wasn't sure if she was going to be able to speak. Did he know her well enough to see the turmoil her heart was in? Did he notice the tightness around her mouth, the panic in her eyes?

Probably not. After all, there was no real evidence that he had ever known much of anything about her, that he had ever really cared. She'd warmed his bed and kept his apartment picked up. That was all he'd ever really wanted, wasn't it?

On the other hand, she'd spent all of her teenage years watching everything he ever did. She'd even kept a notebook about him, hidden under her mattress and only brought out late at night to write some new secret in. *Saw Jason at the feed store this afternoon. He had holes in his jeans and looked so cool. He turned my way and I almost had a heart attack. But he walked right by. I don't think he saw me.*

He was her one and only teenage crush, and when she moved to San Antonio after college and got a job in his firm, she was in seventh heaven. And then he actually noticed her, picked her out to be his special assistant, and very quickly, his special girl. It was like a dream come true. Until she woke up.

"Jason," she said, finding her voice at last. "I'm surprised to find you here. I would have thought this would be a bit too bourgeois for you."

"Don't be silly," he said, beaming at her. "This conference has become the highlight of the business year in San Antonio. We came to win the competition." He laughed lightly, his white teeth flashing

Sharks have white teeth, too, she thought a bit wildly. *Translation: beware!*

Aloud she said, "Good luck. We're hoping for a good result as well." But she felt as though she were in deep water and in danger of losing her grip on the surface with predators circling.

He still had hold of one of her hands and he tried to tug her a bit closer. Looking down dreamily into her eyes in a way that would once have sent her reeling, he said coaxingly, "Listen, we're both on our way to breakfast, aren't we? Come have it with me. We'll get a booth. We need to catch up on old times."

She opened her mouth to respond, planning to put him in his place with a well-chosen word or two. But she wasn't quick enough, because suddenly Rafe was there, sliding his arm around her shoulders.

"Sorry, McLaughlin," he said coolly. "I've already got her booked up. You're out of luck."

"Rafe." Jason's face changed completely, but only for a moment. Very quickly he had his smooth, cultured mask on again. "I would make a crack about bad pennies, but that would be rude."

"Go ahead and be as rude as you like," Rafe told him evenly. "We're all such old friends. You can be yourself around us if you like."

Jason had a faint smile that didn't warm his eyes at all. "Have a nice day," he said, sarcasm coloring his tone as he turned away.

"We will," Rafe promised, tightening his hold on Shelley's shoulders as he began to lead her toward the breakfast area.

She went willingly enough, but her nerves were jangling and she pushed his arm away. The hostess indicated a table big enough to take the others as they arrived. Shelley turned and faced Rafe as they approached it.

"I could have handled that myself, you know," she said.

"I have no doubt about it," he said smoothly, escorting her into her seat at the table. "If you'd wanted to."

Her eyes widened. He really didn't trust her. She leaned forward, looking at him across the table. "Are you accusing me of something here?" she demanded.

He smiled thinly, then picked up the huge menu and began to peruse it. "I'm not going to tolerate any traitors on our team," he said from behind it. "Just giving you fair warning."

"Rafe Allman...." She clenched her hands into fists on the table. "You...you make me so mad!"

He looked around the menu as though surprised. "No reason for anger, Shelley. Don't you get it?"

He dropped the menu and reached out to grab one of her hands. "The fact that we strike sparks off each other should be a plus for us. It's great for creativity. It produces a tension that can help us create a dynamic that will blow everyone else in this competition away."

She blinked at him. "Either that, or we'll kill each other."

He nodded. "That's always a possibility, of course."

But his eyes were smiling and she couldn't resist smiling back for just a moment. Then she pulled her hand away from his and reached for her own menu.

"Don't bother," he said. "I know what I'm ordering for you."

"What?"

"Dollar-size blueberry pancakes with cherry syrup and sausages."

She stared at him, dumbfounded. He looked up at her, and she almost thought he was half embarrassed.

"Listen, I remember how you used to pack it away on Saturday mornings when Rita would cook a big breakfast for us all."

Rita was the big sister, the oldest daughter in the All-man clan. "She cooked enough for half the neighborhood it seemed sometimes," she murmured, remembering.

He nodded. "Anyway, you always loved those little round pancakes and that thick cherry syrup."

How funny that he remembered that. A wave of nostalgia swept over her and she smiled. "Those were the days before I had to start watching my figure."

"Hey, I'll watch your figure for you. No problem at all. And I'll let you know if I notice anything going wrong with it."

She sighed. "Now you're starting to disappoint me. That is such a lame joke."

"Who's joking?" He said it softly, his eyes burning.

The waitress arrived at their table, pouring them both cups of steaming coffee, and Rafe ordered for them. Shelley was too involved in thinking over what he'd just said and the way he'd looked to remember that she'd planned to stop him from ordering pancakes for her. And then it was too late and she decided to let it go.

She looked at him a bit warily. He looked back. She searched for something to say.

"Well. Ready for the big day?"

He grunted and took a sip of scalding coffee, making a face as it burned his tongue.

"The workshops last until noon," she said, talking quickly to fill the silence. "We'll meet for lunch in the Tapa Grill and then our group will adjourn to my room to decide on our plan. I've got some really interesting ideas."

"Do you?" He looked surprised.

"Yes, I do."

He shrugged. "I've got a few ideas of my own. Some pretty great ideas. I guess it will be the battle of the ideas. We'll see whose ideas come out on top."

She made a face. He was making this sound like some sort of monster truck rally or something. "I think mine are pretty good."

He nodded, his dark gaze searching her face. "'Pretty good'," he echoed mockingly. "You see, there's your problem, Shelley, 'Pretty good' is not going to win this competition. 'Over-the-top pretty damn sensational' might have a chance." He shook his head, stabbing a fork into the air. "This is what worries me. You don't have the killer instinct."

She wrinkled her nose. "I should hope not."

"But don't you get it? The killer instinct is going to be bottom-line imperative to win this."

"Oh, stop being so melodramatic. We're going to do just fine."

He stared at her for a moment, then groaned, throw-

ing his head back. "Shelley, Shelley, Shelley. You've got
to toughen up, girl. You cringe at the sight of blood.
Metaphorically speaking. You can't go for the throat, regardless. You're not ready, willing and able to wage all-
out war on everyone and everything that gets in your
way." His penetrating gaze stung. "And I am." He sat
back, looking infuriatingly pleased with himself. "You'd
better leave this to me."

She had to bite her tongue for a moment, and even
count to ten. She didn't want to start screeching at him.
That would be embarrassing, especially with Jason
McLaughlin sitting across the room, watching every
move they made.

"You go ahead and give advice to the B group," she
said at last. "You *are* the highest ranking officer from
Allman Industries. You have a right to manage us all you
want. But as for our group, for the next four days, I'm
the boss. You're going to do what I say, Rafe Allman."

He looked at her with heavily lidded eyes. "Is this
some kind of payback?"

"Payback!" She rolled her eyes. "You are such an
infuriating man. You really think it's all about you,
don't you?"

"Well, isn't it?"

She stared at him for a long moment. He really
meant it.

"You know, you're right. This is payback." She
leaned forward again, speaking earnestly. "It's payback
for the time you put green food coloring in the sham-

poo while Jodie and I were swimming and we ended up with green hair—and green faces and green hands."

His eyebrows knit together as he recalled the incident. "I must admit, I hadn't thought that through very well when I did it." Still, he grinned. "But you two sure did look funny."

She wasn't going to concede that. She wasn't going to concede anything to him anymore.

"It's also payback for the time I was drinking milk at your house and thought I felt a lump go down and you convinced me you'd put a frog in my glass. I nearly went crazy, sure that I could feel it wiggle around inside me."

"Poor little frog." He actually looked concerned, glancing at what he could see of her tummy area. "He must be in there still."

She gaped at him. "There was no frog!"

He looked doubtful. "You'll never know for sure, will you?"

How many years did you get for murder in Texas these days? Surely jurors would take into account that this was a crime of passion. Passionate anger!

She'd started down a memory lane that didn't seem to have an end. Now that she'd brought it up, she could think of so many times he'd driven her crazy.

"How about when I was just learning to drive and you told me the bump I went over was Jodie's dog Buster. I couldn't find that dog anywhere for hours, crying the whole time, thinking he was in the bushes somewhere, hurt."

He grimaced. "That one might have been a little mean."

"A little!" She shook her head, glaring at him. "I hated you!"

"For what? I was just being a dopey kid. And so were you." He looked at her quizzically. "Remember the time you switched the tuna sandwich in my lunch bag with one made of cat food?"

"I didn't do that." She managed to look innocent. "And anyway, it was Jodie's idea."

He grinned and she couldn't help but smile back, just a little. But there wasn't time for anything else. Jim and Jaye were coming toward their table and some of the others weren't far behind. Shelley sat up a little taller and put on her more public smile. Too much dallying with Rafe Allman was a danger to her peace of mind, and probably to her sanity. The day was going to be very full and it was time to get her head on straight.

An hour later, Shelley was sneaking down the back stairway to the parking garage, hoping no one had noticed her slipping out of the time management workshop. Skipping that and the forum on brainstorming would give her exactly two hours before she had to be back for lunch. Hopefully, she would have some answers to her questions by then.

Her car was waiting and soon she was cruising along the familiar streets of San Antonio, heading for Chuy's Café. She really hoped this top-secret mission she was on for Rafe's older brother, Matt, would be successful.

She'd always looked on Matt as her own older brother as well. He was the sort of guy you could depend on, the sort you wanted only good things to happen to. She'd been in college in Dallas while he was going to med school there and she'd become good friends with his girlfriend at the time, Penny Hagar. She and Penny had even shared an apartment for a while. So her relationship with Matt had only become stronger. And when he'd come to her a few days ago and explained that he needed to find Penny again, Shelley had jumped at the chance to help him out.

Now she was on her way to the coffee shop that served as a hangout of sorts for the group of young people she had socialized with when she'd lived here in San Antonio. Hopefully someone would remember Penny, who had supposedly returned to San Antonio after leaving Dallas three years before.

She knew Penny had a brother named Quinn who was still in the area. In fact, she had hung around with a group of people who knew Quinn when she'd lived here. He was more or less on the periphery of the group, but they'd been friendly acquaintances and had even talked about Penny a time or two. If she could only find Quinn, Penny's whereabouts ought to be easy to locate.

A little over an hour later, she was turning back into the hotel parking area. She'd found a couple of old acquaintances having a late breakfast at Chuy's. They had been very helpful in giving her names and telephone numbers that might serve as leads, but she really hadn't gotten hold of any firm information that would help her search.

Still, she was back in time to stop by her room for a moment to freshen up before she needed to meet the others for lunch. Once again, she took the back way, hoping to avoid anyone she knew. Taking out her card, she slid it quickly into the slot in her door and went inside, sighing with relief that she'd made it without being observed. She switched on the light in the entryway and walked into the semidarkened room when a voice stopped her cold.

"Welcome back, Shelley."

Rafe! She whirled and faced him where he sat in the large armchair by the window. Putting a hand over her heart, she caught her breath. "How did you get in here?" she demanded.

He shrugged, his face in shadows. "What can I say? Maids love me."

"Oh!"

She walked quickly to the drapes and pulled them open, flooding the room with light, then turned to face him again.

"So where've you been?" he asked.

"Out."

"So I noticed." His hard mouth twisted. "Out where?" She turned away and he went on.

"I've been thinking this over. I let you outmaneuver me last night and that's not going to happen again."

Rising, he stood where she couldn't avoid him. "I was under the impression that I was the boss, as it were. *Your* boss, at the very least. And as such, I think I can demand a few answers from you. Don't give me that old excuse about this being none of my business. You're here on company time." His look hardened. "So I'm going to ask you once again. Where have you been?"

She looked up into his dark eyes. "Driving around," she said reluctantly.

"Driving around where?"

She shrugged. "Different areas of San Antonio."

One dark eyebrow rose. "Just seeing the sights?"

She looked away.

"What were you looking for, Shelley?"

Closing her eyes, she bit her lip. If only she could tell him. But she couldn't betray Matt that way. Opening her eyes again, she looked at him beseechingly. "Oh, Rafe, please don't ask. I really can't tell you that."

He stared at her for a long moment, then turned away, looking out the picture window at the blue sky. "You weren't just thinking?" he offered her. "Mulling over your life?"

She knew he was giving her a way out, if she wanted it, and her heart skipped. She wouldn't have expected that from him. Too bad she couldn't make things easier for both of them and accept his offer.

"No," she said softly, shaking her head. "I'm not going to lie to you."

Turning slowly, he faced her again. "It just so happened that Jason McLaughlin was missing from his workshop, too."

"Oh, for heaven's sake, you don't think that I was out meeting with Jason, do you?"

"I don't want to think that."

She threw up her hands and he caught them with his. "No, actually I think you're too smart for that. But you've got to admit, it looks pretty fishy."

It did. She knew that. Suddenly her eyes were misting. Everything seemed so relentlessly difficult. No matter which way she turned she was bound to hurt someone. Maybe even herself. Despite all that, a smile trembled on her lips as she looked up at him. His face softened and he pulled her closer.

"God, Shelley," he said, his voice low and husky. "Why'd you have to turn out so damn beautiful?"

She drew in a shaky breath and smiled almost impishly. "To annoy you, I guess. There doesn't seem to be much else it's good for."

He hesitated, his gaze searching hers, and then he kissed her.

His unexpected embrace sent shock waves through her. She'd been kissed before and by some pretty great guys, but there was nobody like Rafe when it came to kissing. This was just like that New Year's Eve had been, only more so. His mouth was filled with a sort of irresistible heat that made her yearn toward him, hungry for more. His tongue scraping against hers set off a series of small explosions in her nervous system, making her think of naked bodies rolling together on satin sheets. The man had a magic. That couldn't be denied. And when he drew back, swearing softly and shaking his head as though he couldn't believe he'd just done that, she had to fight hard to keep from whimpering for more.

Chapter Four

He should never have kissed her.

Rafe stared at the chart Candy Yang had put up to show them when their presentation was scheduled but his mind was on Shelley's mouth. Here he was in the middle of a business meeting in her hotel room, doing important work, and all he could think about was kissing her again.

Well, Shelley obviously didn't share the sentiment. She couldn't get rid of him fast enough after the deed was done. She'd blown their embrace off as if it had never happened and he had played along to preserve his healthy male pride.

This was stupid and it wasn't like him. He knew how to focus. He knew what was important. Kissing Shelley was not important, dammit!

It was just about time for him to give his proposal for the plan for their entry. It was a winner and he had no doubt they could sweep the competition if they played it right. The strategy had some real meat to it.

Shelley had already given her presentation and he felt a little sorry for her. Her idea involved day care or something. How had she put it?

"A human resources goal of setting up job sharing arrangements for employees who have children to avoid losing some of their best employees."

He wasn't really listening as she gave her talk. For one thing, the subject didn't exactly excite him. For another, he was obsessing on her mouth and the way it formed words rather than the words it was forming.

What did they call that...bee-stung lips? He grimaced. He didn't like that. This had nothing to do with insects, but everything to do with the fact that he wanted to kiss her so badly it was like an undercurrent in his blood.

Anyway, he'd almost wished he'd told her not to bother with presenting her idea. Everyone was asking her questions about it, taking up a lot of time. But he was sure that once they heard his brilliant proposition, hers would be forgotten.

He glanced at his watch. Who knew, maybe they could wrap this up quickly, get rid of the other people in the room, and have a little time together before the afternoon session began. Involuntarily, he glanced at the bed in the standard hotel room model. He had a flash of two bodies intertwined tangling those crisp white sheets and couldn't help but smile slightly.

When he looked up, his gaze met Shelley's. And suddenly he was blushing again. He swore softly. This was getting to be ridiculous. It was as though being around her catapulted him back into his teenage years. Only when he was a teenager, he wouldn't have been caught dead being attracted to Shelley Sinclair.

Maybe that was the secret antidote. Maybe if he cast his mind into rewind and recalled what she was like when he couldn't stand her, he could get his mind straight again.

Squinting, he thought back to that last summer before she went away to college. The picture his mind dredged up was funny at first. He remembered Shelley at the Fourth of July picnic. She'd worn the prettiest little sundress, her hair all curled and nicely coiffed, but then someone pushed her off the dock into the lake and she came up sputtering, looking like a drowned rat.

His mouth tilted in a slight smile as he thought of it. Yeah, everyone had laughed their heads off over that one. He'd laughed right along with them. Only, then, as the water molded that little sundress to her body, he'd begun to see something not quite so laughable. That was the first time he'd really noticed how large and full her breasts had become, the way her waist nipped in, emphasizing the full rounded nature of her hips. Shelley had turned into a very attractively proportioned woman while he was still thinking of her as a snot-nosed brat.

"Rafe?"

"What?" He looked up, getting the guilty feeling familiar from being called on unexpectedly in class.

"Didn't you have a suggestion for the contest?"

"Oh. Yeah, sure."

He rose and turned to the group. He knew them all, most of them pretty darn well, and he was sure they were going to like this one. Standing before them with his hands shoved into his pockets, he launched into his sales pitch.

"I'm counting on your discretion," he told them, looking squarely into each gaze in turn. "This is information I just got today. It won't be announced until Monday. But Quarter Season Ranch is going up for sale."

Mouths dropped all around the room and he watched with quiet satisfaction. Quarter Season Ranch was one of the oldest and largest in their area and no one had thought that old cowboy Jake Quartermain would ever let go of it. The guy had to be in his nineties. Now it seemed his grandchildren had prevailed upon him and he was finally selling out.

"But, what exactly does this mean for us?" Candy asked, bright-eyed.

Rafe smiled, giving a dramatic pause, and then he told them. It meant work. It meant lobbying to make sure the zoning went their way. It meant creating designs for land use. It meant a full court press of Allman Industries to beat their competitors out for that ranch. Just think of the vineyards they would have. The place was perfect in setting and soil composition. All that had ever been on it before were cows.

"You're going to have a fight on your hands," Jerry Perez, the plant manager, said skeptically. "There will be big developers salivating for that land."

"That's why we'll have to move fast and get the ear of a few legislators to make sure the zoning goes our way," Rafe said with satisfaction. "I've already spent a few hours on the phone with some Austin people. But here's the part that's relevant to you at the moment. Putting our heads together and producing the game plan for that fight will be our entry in the contest."

He grinned, shrugging. "Smooth, huh? We have to do this foundational stuff anyway. On Monday morning, when you all show up at work, we'll have it halfway there."

He went on to explain. He was excited about it and he could tell he was communicating that excitement. People were nodding. He had them in the palm of his hand. It was great, really, a stroke of genius.

When he was finished, he looked expectantly at them all.

"What do you think?" he asked confidently.

There was an uncomfortable silence for a long moment.

"It sounds great, Rafe, but…" Candy looked uncertain. "I guess we'd better vote on it."

"Vote?" He shrugged. He supposed that would make it official. "Why not? Everyone who's for my plan, raise your hand."

"Wait!" Candy looked toward Shelley. "Don't you think it ought to be a secret ballot?"

Shelley rose slowly from her seat. Her face was flushed as though she were upset about something and he couldn't imagine what it could be.

"Yes," she said clearly, giving him a look that had a little too much defiance built into it for his taste. "A secret ballot is just the thing."

It was a waste of time, but he sighed and nodded. "Okay. Let's get it over with."

It couldn't be that easy, of course. First someone had to find a pad with enough papers on it, then the right amount of pencils had to be produced and then Shelley insisted on a quick summary of both plans to remind everyone what was involved.

"My plan deals with the problem every parent has as an employee—what to do about child care, especially for the youngest ones, the sick ones, the ones who need after school care. In this scenario, our workplace sets up a child-care area where employees can bring their kids and each person who uses the service donates a certain amount of time as a child-care provider. It's work sharing. The company hires a supervisor to coordinate things and throws in some extra time off for employees who participate."

She then did a quick rundown on Rafe's plan, emphasizing its benefits in a way he couldn't complain about. He was satisfied. But he was looking at his watch by the time they settled down and voted. He wrote out his own plan's name quickly, folded the paper and handed it to Candy. Then he went to sit down in a place that would give him the best view of Shelley's lips.

She looked up and caught him in the act. He smiled at her, determined never again to be disconcerted by letting her see he was attracted to her.

She didn't smile back. Holding up the papers, she said calmly, "Thank you all for participating. My plan has won. I've drawn up a script and made lists for each of you. Pick up your copy on your way out. It is getting late and the afternoon lecture begins in half an hour, so if you have any questions…"

Rafe blinked, incredulous.

"Wait a minute," he said. "What do you mean, your plan won?"

She licked those beautiful lips and met his outraged gaze. "I got more votes, Rafe."

He almost choked. "I don't believe you. Let's see them."

It was her turn to redden. "I got more votes. Leave it at that."

"That can't be." He really thought there had to be some mistake. "My plan's perfect."

The others were shuffling their feet and not meeting his gaze. He began to realize things really weren't going to work out the way he'd thought they should.

"Your plan is a very good one," Shelley conceded. "But my plan won."

He narrowed his eyes. Was that a spark of triumph he saw in her eyes? "What was the vote?" he demanded.

"Rafe, just…"

"I want to know. What was the vote?"

Shelley drew a deep breath. "Six to one," she said softly.

He thought he hadn't heard her correctly for a second or two, then he realized he'd had a pure and simple mutiny on his hands. He looked at the others in the room with an outraged sense of betrayal.

"No," he said shaking his head. "You can't possibly be for hers over mine. That just defies logic."

Candy finally looked up and tried to smile.

"Look, Rafe, there's no question your idea shows potential to appreciate earnings and all that good stuff. And if we were back home and the outcome mattered to our bottom line—we'd have to go with it."

She looked around the room for support and the others nodded.

"But that's not what we're doing here. We were all discussing this earlier, before you came. We're presenting something to judges. Only half of them will be from the actual business world. The rest include a local TV anchor person, a magazine writer and the head of the local garden club."

Candy looked at him earnestly. "These are touchy-feely people. They're not going to care about the bottom line. They want something that plays on the heartstrings. The child care exchange idea will be right up that particular alley."

Rafe looked at them all, then at Shelley. He was angry. He was affronted. He even felt a bit betrayed. And he knew this wouldn't have happened if Shelley hadn't taken over as boss the way she had—taken to it with a vengeance. He wanted to lash out at them all and tell them what he thought of them.

But he wasn't stupid and he knew having a tantrum about it would be foolish. It wouldn't get him anywhere and it would make him look like a sore loser. Was he a sore loser? Hell yes!

But he calmed down. This wasn't the end. After all, there was more than one way to bell a cat. So, exerting all the self-discipline he could muster, he shrugged and smiled at them all.

"Okay," he said. "What do you want me to do?"

Shelley raised a finely sculpted eyebrow and looked at him sideways. She wasn't fooled. She knew he hadn't given up.

"I'm going to ask Candy to take a couple of people with her, along with a video camera, and do a little taping for background footage," she said. "I've already called the director at a private school nearby and they said they would allow it."

"Okay," he said. "But what's my role in all this?"

Before she had a chance to say anything to him, her cell phone rang and she excused herself, retreating to the little table by the window while the rest of them rose, reached for assignment papers and began to talk excitedly among themselves.

Rafe smiled and answered when spoken to, but his attention was absorbed by Shelley and her phone call.

Concentrating hard, he was able to make out a few phrases here and there.

"Thanks so much for the information," he heard just below the buzz of conversation as she prepared to hang up. "I'll get over there as soon as I can."

She turned to look at him as she put the phone away. He held her gaze, but this time he didn't smile.

Shelley knew she ought to be feeling good right now. She ought to be pumping her fist in the air and bowing to the accolades of the crowd. After all, she'd defeated the great Rafe Allman in a vote.

She hadn't been sure how it would go, and actually, she'd been surprised it had gone so decisively her way. Everyone loved her idea. All except Rafe, who hadn't been paying attention when she presented it anyway. But the others voted with her and that gave her a feeling of empowerment like she hadn't had in a long, long time. Maybe she was actually doing something right for a change.

But then there was Rafe—and the feeling of triumph hadn't lasted. She didn't like to see anyone lose when you came right down to it. Even if it was Rafe Allman. She knew he felt as though the rug had been pulled out from under him. And she knew him well enough to know he would have something else up his sleeve. He didn't give up this easily. She was going to have to be careful.

Still, all in all, it had gone really well. She was doing

better than she'd expected in holding her own against his overpowering presence on her team.

Well, except for that slipup earlier when they'd melted into a kiss. But that was a one-time deal. She'd obsess over that later. Right now she had to get away and try an address an old friend had phoned her with. She only had a short time to find Quinn so she had to take every opportunity.

She slipped out of the lecture by the back way, hurrying down the hall, hoping to avoid being seen and feeling like a criminal. But what the heck—these lectures pretty much contained common sense. That was something she had in spades.

She used her cell phone to call for her car to be ready at the front entrance as she made her way around the building. And there it was, right on time. She handed the attendant a bill and slipped into the driver's seat, not realizing she had company until the attendant had firmly closed her door.

"Rafe Allman!" she cried in dismay as she turned toward the man who was filling her passenger's seat. "Get out of this car!"

There he sat, big as life, and he had the gall to look surprised at her reaction. "Why?"

She bit her lip to keep herself from screaming, then raised an imploring hand and waved it at him. "Because you should be at the afternoon session."

He pretended bewilderment at her statement. "If you can miss it, why can't I?"

"Oh!" She closed her eyes for a moment, holding back fury. "I have something I just have to do. I'll be back as quickly as possible. In no time at all." She looked at him and tried to keep from letting her anger get out of hand. "But someone has to be there to make sure they get to work on things. Listen, you go on into the hotel and…"

He grinned. "Nice try, Shell. But it won't wash. You're the boss, remember? It's your idea we're supposed to be working on. You're the indispensable one, not me."

Clenching her jaw, she glared at him. "Is that what this is all about? You're upset because you lost the vote and you're going to take it out on me?"

"No."

He frowned, having second thoughts about his protestation of innocence.

"Well, I *am* upset that I lost. My proposal is a very good one. Something like that doesn't fall into your lap every day. I have the inside track on something that is going to be common knowledge next week and I think we really should take advantage of it."

He cocked an eyebrow her way, sure she must understand that he was right. Any clear-thinking person could see that. Unless their view was clouded by private animosity and petulance.

"Too bad," she said crisply.

"Come on, Shelley. You know my idea would work better. It's based on something solid and substantial, not fluff."

She drew in a deep breath, staring at him. She would not give in to temptation and lunge at his throat. Staying calm would win in the long run.

Think Zen. Think peace.

"And the truth is," he added, "I think the day-care thing is a lousy idea."

"But mysteriously popular," she pointed out carefully, marveling at her own self-control.

He nodded. "Very mysteriously." He made a face, then looked at her sharply. "But that is not the matter at hand."

She blinked. "No?"

"No. The matter at hand is—where the hell are you going?"

Nowhere if she couldn't get rid of him.

She stared at her own hands on the wheel of the car, trying for the stone-faced look. "It's none of your business."

"It may not be any of my business, but I'm not getting out of the car, so I guess I'll find out soon enough."

Turning toward him, she felt suddenly drained. Staying firm wasn't working. Saying mean things wasn't working. Beating him in the vote hadn't even chastened him. What hadn't she tried? Pleading for mercy?

Taking a deep breath, she went into pleading mode. "Oh, Rafe, please…"

That was as far as she got before a horn honked from behind them. Rafe turned to look and waved an acknowledgment to the attendant.

"Well darn it all," he said with a smug glance her way.

"Looks like we're going to have to take off. They want you to move out of the way. You're causing congestion."

"And you're causing *indi*gestion," she quipped through gritted teeth as she started the engine and began edging down the driveway.

"Sorry. That's what happens to people who try to sneak around behind other people's backs and…"

She couldn't stand any more of this. Heading for the main street, she gave up on trying to keep everything from him. It had become an untenable position anyway. But she talked without looking at him.

"Okay, look. I'll tell you basically what I'm doing. If you promise to go back to the hotel."

"No promises, Shelley. I'm here for the duration."

"Oh!"

"Calm down. You're driving. I'm just coming along for the ride." He looked over at her. "But you might as well give me some idea of what you're up to anyway."

She took a deep breath and let it out slowly. There didn't seem to be any point any longer in keeping everything a secret. Maybe she could foster some goodwill on his part if she let him in on some of it. She might as well try. He was probably going to figure out this much for himself anyway.

"Okay," she said reluctantly. "Here's the deal. I'm trying to find a man named Quinn Hagar."

He went very still. "An old boyfriend?" he asked softly.

"Hardly." She rolled her eyes. "It's nothing like that.

I just need…to get some information from him. For someone else."

"Who?"

She glanced at him. "I can't tell you that. We've been over this ground before."

"So it's someone I know." He looked at her sharply. "It has to be, or you would tell me who it was."

She sighed. The man was impossible. Making a turn, she began to head toward the seedy side of town.

Rafe went on speculating. "Okay, you've said it's not McLaughlin."

"It's not him."

"Hmm. Is it—?"

"Don't start this game, Rafe," she cut in firmly. "I'm not going to play."

He nodded. "That's smart of you, actually. I had a long list ready to quiz you on. That would have been somewhat tedious."

She shook her head as she slowed to a stop at a light and looked toward the heavens. "Why are you torturing me?"

"Why not?" He grinned. "Who better to torture than you, my lifelong nemesis."

She looked at him, wondering how they had come to this stage in their relationship. It seemed so strange. She'd known Rafe Allman all her life, and yet she didn't really know this man beside her. Was he a good guy, after all?

He certainly came from a good family. Well, his

mother had been an angel. His father was a bit more problematic. Still, his sister Jodie was a peach and her best friend as well. His brother Matt was another very good friend, and the oldest girl, Rita, was a carbon copy of their mother. David, who was younger, was a scamp, but perfectly decent. All her life it had only been Rafe who had sometimes made things miserable.

"I'm not your lifelong nemesis," she said softly.

His eyes seemed to darken. "You're probably right. That would be overstating it a bit. Still, we were enemies."

"Oh, yes. We *were* that."

The look they exchanged conveyed what neither was willing to vocalize—that the steamy kiss they'd exchanged earlier had redefined their tenuous relationship in ways neither could comprehend. The light changed and she turned her attention back to her driving.

"Given our past history, a little torture seems to be in order, wouldn't you say?" His tone was light, almost teasing.

She actually smiled a little. "That means I have to find a way to torture you back."

He groaned. "You're carrying this women's lib thing a bridge too far, don't you think? You've already done your own small part in ruining my weekend."

"Because I won out over your idea?"

"Yes. I consider it a downright disaster, believe it or not. We've got to win this contest and your idea won't do it."

Was he purposely trying to put her back up again?

Well, she wasn't going to take the bait. Drawing in a deep breath, she went on calmly. "Tell me why it's so important."

He stared at her as though she'd asked him why bread came in loaves. "You can ask that?"

She glanced at him sideways. "It's for your father, isn't it?"

His face darkened. "Look…"

"No, it is, isn't it? You have to come back waving a trophy for your father. Don't you?"

He slumped in his seat. "You don't know what you're talking about."

"Yes. I do. I used to be part of the family, remember?" She sighed. "Rafe, why bother to deny it? You've always had this thing about your father. And your father has always used it to play you off against Matt and…"

"That's enough, Shelley," he said, his voice tight and hard as a diamond.

But inside he wasn't so hard. She was bringing things up into the light that he would rather stayed buried. What good did it do to hash this stuff over endlessly? Things were the way they were and you had to deal with them that way. Yeah, his father could have been more understanding. He could notice how well Rafe could handle the company business once in awhile, instead of always looking to Matt to do everything. But he wasn't like that. So Rafe would go on, fighting and winning and handing his father proof he didn't really want to see. Until someday….

Oh, hell. Why had she brought this all up, anyway? He glanced at her, wanting to be angry with her, but his anger melted right away. She was so damn delicious-looking. And all she'd done was thrust some truths at him. He could handle truth. He could handle anything.

"Sorry," she said, knowing he was looking at her. "I guess I'd better learn to keep my mouth shut, huh?"

He didn't answer and she slowed, knowing they were near the address she was looking for. She fumbled for her purse and he took it from her, plucking out the paper that was sticking from the front pocket and reading out what was written there.

"It's 3457 N. Fardo, apartment 13." He grimaced. "I thought they didn't number things thirteen if they didn't have to."

"I wouldn't have thought you would be superstitious," she noted, turning on Fardo.

"I'm probably a lot of things you never thought of."

"No doubt."

He scanned the addresses. "Here we go. Left side of the street. Big orange building."

Shelley peered out in the direction he indicated and hung a U-turn to park in front of the building. Rafe looked up at it, too.

"So, I take it your friend Quinn is down on his luck?" he said softly.

She squared her shoulders and gathered her things. "Could be," she said shortly. "Now you just wait here and I'll be right back."

"Fat chance," he muttered, getting out on the other side as she got out on hers.

"Rafe…"

"You're not going into that building alone."

There was no use arguing here on the street, so she flashed him a look and let him accompany her into the lobby of the place. The walls were grubby. One of the mailboxes was hanging open. The smell of burned onions filled the air and a baby was crying somewhere close by.

"There it is at the end of the hall," she said, pointing out the door with the metal 13 on it. "You stay right here. I have to do this alone."

He nodded. He apparently knew when to stand back and give her some room.

"Stay in the hall, though," he warned her. "Don't go into the room without me."

She hesitated. That wasn't what she'd envisioned, but when you came right down to it, that was probably good advice.

"Okay," she told him, and started down the hall.

The place was creepy and she felt the hair rise on the back of her neck. She remembered Quinn as a handsome, happy-go-lucky kid with bright eyes and a ready smile. She hadn't known him well, but she would have said he was someone with a future. This place looked too dead end for that.

She knocked on the door. Nothing. After waiting a moment, she knocked again.

"Quinn?" she called.

There was no answer. Someone in another apartment opened their door a crack and looked at her, then closed it again. Taking a paper and pencil from her purse, she jotted down a quick note that included her cell number and pushed it under the door. When she turned back, she had to admit it was a relief to see Rafe still waiting for her by the entrance.

"No luck, huh?" he asked as she reached him.

She shook her head. "He's not home," she said.

They walked slowly back out into the light. Shelley noted that there was a parking area under the building. She thought about going down and seeing if she could get into it to see if a car was parked in #13's spot, but she shrugged the idea away.

"I left my number," she told Rafe as they lingered by the car, looking up and down the street. It wasn't particularly busy, but cars were going by on a regular basis, and somehow she just had a feeling… "Maybe he'll call me when he gets my note."

"Maybe."

Rafe opened her car door and she frowned at him.

"What are you doing?"

"Pretending to be a gentleman," he said with a grin.

"I suppose it's a real effort," she said, but she was smiling, too.

Standing there with the sun in his eyes, his hair so dark, his shoulders so wide, he looked like more than a gentleman. He looked like a hero. For some stupid reason her heart was suddenly pounding in her chest and she looked away from his gaze.

And that was how she noticed a blue car coming out of the underground parking and speeding away.

"Ohmigod!" she cried. "Quick, get in!"

"What?"

"Get in! Get in! That was him."

Rafe got in, barely getting the door closed before she gunned the engine and peeled out into the street.

"Hey," he said, alarmed. "What are you doing?"

"I've got to catch him," she cried, concentrating on her driving and going much too fast. "It could be my only chance."

Chapter Five

Adrenaline was pumping but Shelley felt cool and in control.

"Look, Quinn's turning up ahead," she said, squinting as she tried to cover all the bases at once.

"Shelley, take it easy," Rafe was saying, securing his seat belt and reaching around to get hers locked into place, too. "It's not like he's taking off in a plane. He'll still be there even if you don't catch him right away."

She didn't answer. Something told her she had better catch Quinn now, because he was obviously trying to avoid her and would take care she didn't find him again if she didn't do it this time.

She made the same turn the blue car had, her tires screeching on the asphalt.

"Hey, you took that corner a little fast, didn't you?" Rafe said, sounding a little unsettled.

"You just hush and hold on tight," she ordered, totally concentrated on the blue car disappearing around another corner.

"Shelley!"

"What?"

"Slow down!"

"I can't."

But she had to. Noticing pedestrians, she dropped back down to the limit, then had to stop at a crosswalk. Even catching Quinn wasn't worth risking hurting someone.

"Darn," she muttered, trying mentally to hurry the two men crossing in front of her. Her fingers drummed on the wheel. "Come on, come on."

Rafe started to say something but she wasn't listening. The way had opened up and she took it. Then she was on the highway with clear sailing ahead. The blue car had taken off and she pressed on the gas, racking up speed. She didn't look over but she could tell Rafe was staring at her in amazement. She didn't care. Her heart was racing and she was a good driver.

So there.

Quinn turned off onto a side street and she slowed to take the corner more carefully this time. They barely caught sight of him turning again a few blocks down. Shelley raced to that corner and they turned, but there was no blue car in sight.

"Which way?" she cried in anguish.

"I don't know. Turn right."

She turned right, and suddenly a huge chain-link barrier stood in her way, blocking the street.

"Whoa!" Rafe yelled.

She jammed on the brakes, throwing them both forward, but the seat belts caught them and the car careened to a stop just short of the barrier. Shelley whipped her head around, looking the other way on the street, but there was no blue car to be seen. Turning back, she slumped and they both sat still, staring at the fence and marveling that they were still alive.

Suddenly Rafe was laughing. She turned to look at him and he turned toward her. "That was one wild ride," he said, but his amusement was already fading.

His gaze dropped to her lips and she knew he was going to kiss her again. It seemed only right. Some gesture was needed, something to fit with the way her blood was pounding in her veins, the way his excitement shone in his eyes. Every nerve ending tingled as she waited, lips slightly parted, for it to happen.

He didn't hesitate. He kissed her hard on the mouth and she responded, kissing him back, her body molding into his. She knew she shouldn't be letting this happen, but it was so good. His mouth was hot and moist and delicious, and she wanted as much of him as she could get. And suddenly she wanted too much in a way she never had before. The sensation flared in her and she jerked back away from him, shocked at her own response.

"I can't believe this is happening again," she said breathlessly.

His dark eyes were searching hers. "What do you mean?" he replied, his voice husky.

"You know—kissing." She put both hands on his chest to shove him back into his seat. "You're not supposed to kiss me."

"Why not?" He was still hovering so close, she could feel his breath on her cheek.

"Because…because we hate each other, don't we?" She didn't sound as though she was sure about that.

"I don't know." He touched her chin with his finger, then leaned closer.

"What are you doing?" she asked softly, her hands completely ineffectual as they rested helplessly on his chest.

"I'm going to kiss you again."

She frowned, gathering herself together and firming her resolve. Glaring at him, she shook her head. "No, you're not. Only one kiss per car chase. That's all that's allowed."

He hesitated and to tell the truth, she wasn't sure whether she would rather he defy her or leave her alone. And when he drew back and settled in his seat again, she knew she felt more disappointment than she ought to.

So she turned her mind back to Quinn.

"Darn it all," she said. "We lost him."

"Why was he running?" Rafe asked.

She shook her head, pondering that question herself.

"I have no idea. We never had anything but a cordial relationship. In fact, we were pretty friendly at one time."

She took a deep breath and put the car back in gear, maneuvering for the return trip. Rafe watched as she turned the car around and headed back to the highway.

"Maybe there was something he didn't want to have to tell you," he suggested. "Could that be it?"

She glanced at him. "I don't see how. But I suppose anything is possible."

He grinned at her. "Whooee. That was some little adventure there, girl. I didn't know you were a drag-strip queen."

She couldn't help but smile, secretly pleased with herself.

"After all," he went on. "I was there when you learned how to drive. Remember?" He laughed. "In fact, I probably taught you a few of those moves myself."

Her smile faded. She remembered all right.

"Rafe Allman, you did not teach me anything. Your brother Matt taught me how to drive in that old Ford station wagon. With you sitting in the back seat half the time, taunting me and making me crazy."

He seemed affronted by her attitude and lack of appreciation toward his past efforts on her behalf.

"I was not taunting you. I was giving you pointers. Constructive criticism. Expert advice."

"Taunting is taunting. You were downright rude and you know it."

"Maybe you're just too sensitive. Ever think of that?"

"No. I always knew where the misery came from." She glanced at him sideways. "And it came right from you. You were giving me grief from the get-go. And gosh darn it all if you aren't doing it to this day."

Rafe stared at her for a moment, then his head went back and his laughter rang out, loud and infectious.

Shelley smiled. She hadn't achieved her goal this afternoon but she felt very good inside anyway. And she knew darn well it had everything to do with the man sitting beside her.

"Well, look what the cat dragged in."

Shelley gave Candy an apologetic look as she entered the small partitioned-off conference room that was where they were to develop their campaign. She knew the whole team must have been rudderless while she and Rafe were out chasing Quinn through the San Antonio streets, but they were back now and there was no time for recriminations.

"Sorry, everybody," she said, turning to look at what they'd accomplished so far. "We've still got two hours before dinner. Let's use them to the best advantage we can."

"No problem, Shelley," Rafe said, giving her a wink. "I've got things under control."

She stared at him in surprise. They'd both headed for their respective rooms to freshen up before they rejoined the group—or at least, she'd thought they'd both done that. It seemed Rafe had done an end run around her instead. Here he was with his shirtsleeves rolled up, looking like he'd been working here the whole time.

"Listen," he was saying to Candy. "I want to screen the video you took. Can you rack it up over here on this monitor?"

Shelley stepped over to his side.

"What are you doing?" she asked him, her voice low but insistent.

"Trying to get things moving here." He smiled at her, looking comfortable with the way the situation was developing. Looking like the boss.

"I'm the one who is supposed to be doing that," she told him, glancing around to make sure none of the others could hear.

But even if they couldn't hear what she was saying, they were watching, and she knew right away they were waiting to see how things were going to shake out. Either she was going to be in control, or Rafe was. Taking a deep breath, she tried to gather her strength. It was time she made a stand. But looking at Rafe, so handsome and confident, she had to wonder how she was going to do this.

"Look, Rafe, I'm supposed to be the boss. Remember?"

"Sure. I remember it well." He smiled at her. "No problem, Shelley. We'll work things out just fine."

He looked up as Dorie, the young office worker, came up to him.

"Mr. Allman," she said hesitantly, her blue eyes wide and innocent. "I did that collating you wanted done. Did you want me to go find a copy machine and make copies of the script for you?"

"Why thank you, Dorie," Rafe began, holding out his hand for the collated pages. "And yes, I do want you to go…"

"Hold it."

Shelley could hardly believe that was her voice, but as she looked around at the interested faces, she knew it had been her and that she'd said it loud enough for the entire group to hear. She was going to challenge Rafe and try—very hard—to put him in his place. Were they all going to think she was a witch when she did that? Yes, she supposed they would. But deep down, she knew it had to be done.

"I think we're forgetting what the focus of this com- petition is," she said, feeling a little shaky. "It's called 'Trading Places.' The whole point is for bosses and em- ployees to switch places and bring their own unique out- looks toward solving a problem, and at the same time, begin to see things from the other side for a change. We're reversing the order of things. Getting new ideas from people in the trenches, so to speak."

She paused. The faces were all staring at her blankly. Only Rafe had a spark in his gaze. Was it anger or humor? She couldn't tell.

"We're going to be getting points on how well we do that, not how good our central project idea is," she added, mostly to Rafe. "So let's work hard on follow- ing the theme. Okay?"

Rafe looked at her, one eyebrow raised. "You think the judges aren't going to be swayed by how good the central idea is? You're nuts."

Oh, for heaven's sake! He was still hoping to get his idea used instead of hers. She couldn't believe it. She'd won the vote, but as she looked at the uncertain faces among the team, she wondered if that vote would hold if he pushed it.

"Rafe, your idea was very good, but we've decided to go with mine," she said firmly. Anger had snuffed out all shakiness now.

He shrugged and looked at her blandly. "I know that."

She gritted her teeth. He wasn't going to let this go, was he?

"If you're so crazy about your idea, why don't you give it to the B team?" she suggested. "From what I hear, they're still struggling for something to sink their teeth into."

He reacted with shock. "Give it away? Hell no. It's my idea. I'm holding on to it in case your idea falls apart."

Her jaw dropped and she had to use all her self-discipline not to let herself respond. He was being a jerk, forcing her to get tougher than she wanted to. But she knew if she didn't stand up to him now, he would make her life miserable for the rest of the weekend. And so would all the rest of them.

"Okay, here's the deal," she said, making sure everyone heard what she was saying. "For the purposes of this weekend, I'm the boss. Candy is my assistant. Rafe is Candy's assistant. I'll relay instructions through Candy. You can go to her with your problems and she'll relay them to me."

They were still waiting, standing there like cattle and she wondered if she wasn't being forceful enough. What did she have to do, scream at them all to make them understand?

"Then I guess it's back to the name thing, isn't it?" Rafe said in what she considered a slightly mocking tone. "We should all call you Miss Sinclair."

She looked at him defiantly. "Yes. For the purposes of this contest, I think that would be a good idea." She looked at the others. "If y'all are calling Rafe Mr. Allman and calling me Shelley, that sends a bad message as far as our goals are concerned. You do get that, don't you?"

A couple of them giggled, but they sobered quickly when she looked at them. Good. The aura of command was already taking hold. Either that, or they were getting ready to run for the hills. She wasn't about to let that happen. Looking around, she grabbed the script.

"Let's get going on casting for the skit, shall we? Okay, Candy, you're the mailroom girl with the heart of gold. Dorie, you're the pregnant secretary. Jerry, you're the father of the baby. Rafe, you'll play the part of the skeptical supervisor who doesn't think it's going to work."

He grinned, arms folded across his chest. "That'll be easy enough to do."

She glared at him. "Only in the end, you'll become

convinced that it's the wave of the future and you'll become one of the biggest champions of the program."

He groaned, making a face. "That'll take a little more acting ability."

"Then you'll just have to dig deep, won't you?"

He blinked and looked at her as though he was finally beginning to realize that she wasn't going to back down.

"Wow, give the woman a little power and she turns into a dictator."

He looked at her assessingly, but she couldn't help but think there was a grudging sort of respect growing in his eyes.

"Why do *you* pick and choose who gets what parts?"

She drew herself up as much as she could, though she knew it still seemed puny compared to his six-foot-two frame. Looking around, she raised her arms like a band conductor.

"Because—shall we get everyone to say it in unison?—Shelley Sinclair is the boss!"

They all muttered it with varying degrees of enthusiasm. All except Rafe.

When she looked at him with her eyebrow arched, he looked rebellious. "I won't say it."

She stared at him, hard. "You say it or you're fired."

He stared at her and she held that stare, bound and determined she wasn't going to let him win. If she "fired" him it would just be for this competition, but it would make a mark all the same. Was he going to challenge her? Was he going to force her to go through with it? Her heart was pounding. This would make or break the whole program right here.

He was staring deeply into her eyes and she knew he was trying to decide if she would hold firm. Then something changed in his dark gaze. She wondered if he was remembering the way she'd barreled down the street after Quinn's car. Maybe so, because he seemed to come to a conclusion about what she was willing to do to attain her goal, and his defiance relaxed into a smile of benign amusement.

"Okay." He threw up his hands, turning to the others, and this time he led the rest. "Let's all say it together. Shelley Sinclair is the boss."

She sighed as relief flooded over her. Something told her this was it. Rafe wasn't going to confront her any longer. At least, not about this.

"Now don't you feel better?" she said to them all.

Everyone laughed. They thought it was mainly a joke, and it was. But she wondered if they didn't pick up on the underlying thread of real antagonism between Rafe and her, because it wasn't gone, despite the adventurous afternoon they'd had together. Despite that unforgettable kiss they'd shared, the discord was very much alive. And though they'd gotten past this bump in the road, there would be others. She was going to have to be wary.

They worked on the skit for the rest of the afternoon, going over and over it, improving on it, working like a real team. Shelley was very happy with the way things were going. Rafe treated her with just the right combination of polite deference and jocular companionship. It worked. What a relief.

They adjourned to their rooms and met at the restaurant for dinner and had a rousing time. Everyone was in great spirits. The talk and the laughter ran rampant as they ate, and they lingered longer than they'd planned. Then, as they rose from dessert, Rafe came up to help her with her chair.

"So, where are we going tonight?" he murmured near her ear.

Chapter Six

Shelley turned to look at Rafe. Of course he'd guessed she would be out looking for Quinn again. There was no way to keep it from him.

"Who invited you along?" she asked, gazing at him quizzically.

"I did." He smiled at her, standing a little too close. "I'm sticking to you like glue."

She searched his eyes, wondering about him and his motivations. "Why?"

"Because you're skulking around in neighborhoods where you're going to need someone watching your back." He gave her a grin. "And I'm volunteering for duty."

They were making their way out into the hotel lobby by now. It was teeming with people returning from dinner or just getting ready to find a good late place to eat. The mood was celebratory and a bit noisy, forcing them to walk very close together in order to hear each other.

"Really?" she countered his offer of refuge. "While you're guarding me against street scum, who's going to guard mc against you?"

He put a protective arm around her shoulders, helping to steer her through the crowd.

"What do you think you have to worry about me for?" he said, turning so that his mouth was very near her ear. "What do you think I'm going to do?"

She shivered. His breath touched her skin and made her want things she didn't want to want.

"I don't know," she said, feeling a little careless, a little excited. "Sell me off to the highest bidder, maybe."

He pulled her even closer. "Hey, I wouldn't ever want to get rid of you that way."

"Oh, no?" She looked up into his face. "What way *would* you want to get rid of me?"

He grinned, then pretended to think it over. "Highest bidder, huh? Got to admit, it's definitely something to think about."

"Rafe!" she wailed.

"Hey, it was a joke. You set it up so beautifully, I had to follow along." He guided her down the steps onto the walkway. "I mean, what could I do?"

"What could you do?" she echoed archly. "Say something nice, maybe. Ever think of that?"

They were outside now, the air cool compared to the

heated atmosphere inside the hotel lobby. Lights glittered up and down the street and people were scattered in groups of twos or threes. Music was coming from a dance club across the street.

He was looking down at her. "What do you consider nice?"

"Have you gone so far?" she asked teasingly, pretending great concern about his state of mind and character, "that you don't even know what 'nice' is anymore?"

He stopped and thought for a moment, actually taking her ribbing seriously, pulling her into an enclave sheltered from the general crowd by a clump of desert palms.

"'Nice,'" he said musingly, his face crumpled in concentration. "I think I remember 'nice.'" He looked down at her, a hint of humor in his dark eyes.

"Like kittens? Like the sun coming out after the rain?"

He stroked her face with his forefinger and his voice got husky.

"Like looking at a beautiful woman?"

She stared up at him and her heart did a little flip and she knew she ought to tell him to go back to his hotel room and leave her alone. She tried. She even took a very deep breath and tried very hard. But she couldn't form the words. It was just too delicious being with him this way. She couldn't resist it.

Even though she knew!

Oh, what was wrong with her? She knew this man as well as she knew anyone, didn't she? She'd known him all her life. She'd fought with him and hated him and tricked him and been done dirty by him. She'd seen him being kind to his sisters and seen him being playful with his brothers and seen him being loving to his mother. But she hadn't often seen him being nice. Especially not to her.

So what was she doing here? Where was she going? And why didn't she listen to the alarm bells that were telling her he couldn't possibly mean it when he acted like this?

Because she didn't want to. And that was that.

But somewhere inside she knew she was acting like a fool. She'd been there before, hadn't she? She'd listened to Jason McLaughlin's lies and pretended to believe them. In her urgent need to find love, she'd let herself become something she despised. How could she risk doing something like that again? Was she really so weak?

It seemed to be the case.

"You need more, huh?" He seemed to take her silence as a rebuff. "Okay, here goes. I'll show you nice."

He bent closer, his gaze skimming over her features as though he were evaluating each one, and his hands slipped up from her shoulders to cup her head lightly, as though holding a precious treasure.

"You've somehow developed the most kissable lips I've ever seen before in my life," he said softly.

Her heart skipped a beat but she had to pretend it hadn't. Every muscle went limp, every instinct yearned for him. But she couldn't let him know, now could she? So she took a deep breath and pretended to be unimpressed.

"Are you implying you think I got injections or something?" she grumbled. "Because I didn't. These are my lips, love 'em or leave 'em. They haven't changed at all since…since…"

"I'll take 'love 'em,'" he said evenly, still holding her there.

She blinked at him uncomprehendingly. "What?" she said, only the word came out like a whisper and she winced, knowing she needed an emergency implant of spine at this very moment and not sure help was on the way.

He shrugged his wide, wide shoulders. "You gave me a choice. I choose 'love 'em.'"

"Oh."

She wanted him to kiss her and she knew she couldn't let that happen. Reaching deep, she conjured up her last scrap of will and forced herself to shake off the misty sensuality that was sapping her strength. Pulling away from his touch, she tried to force a sense of exasperation where there was nothing but warm fuzziness instead.

"You're impossible to talk to," she said, gratified to hear a note of firmness in her voice she was nowhere near feeling in her heart. She turned from him. "Did you know that? You turn everything into a game. You're driving me crazy."

He gripped her arm and pulled her back to face him, leaning close. "Crazy with untamed desire?" he asked hopefully.

She sighed with relief. The aching sensuality in his eyes had been replaced by something closer to playfulness, as though he also realized they had been coming too close to the edge. If they both worked at it, maybe they could keep from falling over.

"No," she said firmly, planting two hands flat against his chest to keep him from leaning any closer. "More like unbridled annoyance. Or maybe plain old aggravation."

He stared down into her eyes as though unsure of which way he really wanted to go. She tried hard to make a stand and convince him she meant it. And to her surprise, he seemed to see that in her for the moment.

"Okay," he said, almost carelessly. And then he let her go, pulling back and shifting gears so quickly, she was dizzy.

"So why don't you let me in on the agenda," he said, looking at her expectantly, making her wonder if she'd dreamed the last few exchanges they'd had.

"O...okay." She shook her head a little, just to clear it. "It's nothing particularly exciting. I'm planning to make a visit to the Blue Basement Club."

"Sounds like a good old low-down dive."

"It's not really that bad. It's where a lot of the people I knew hung out when I first came to San Antonio after college."

He nodded thoughtfully. "You're hoping to catch Quinn there, I take it?"

She nodded. "Either that or somebody I used to know who might be able to get a message to him."

He shrugged. "Let's go."

As they walked the three short blocks to where the club she remembered was located, she bantered back and forth with him as though they were old friends instead of old enemies. As though they might be lovers. And, she had to admit, she cherished every moment of it.

They'd both changed for dinner and were dressed for the evening—Rafe in a suit cut to set off his elegantly lean body, Shelley in a little filmy dress that swirled around her knees as she walked. She knew they looked good together; she could tell by the way people looked at them.

She was falling in love with the evening, but she was hoping she could keep her head where Rafe was concerned. She was going to try very hard. After all, she had a very bad track record with men. Experience was everything in a relationship like this. Once burned, twice shy.

There was a crowd outside the club, waiting to go in. But the doorman took one look at them and let them go to the head of the line.

"Why us?" she whispered to Rafe, looking back at the envious frowns.

"Maybe he thinks we're celebrities," he said back with a laugh. His arm was around her shoulders again and he looked down. "Or maybe he thinks we're in love."

Just his saying that was electric, and not just to her. She saw it in his eyes. He couldn't believe he'd actually said such a thing. They stared at each other for a long moment, both a bit horrified, both a bit intrigued. And then the door opened and they were in the cavelike room.

The atmosphere was dark and hazy and they had to be very careful to keep from stumbling over other people as they made their way to the tiny table along the side of the room. The stage was the size of a postage stamp. A tall, lanky singer in a silky gown came out and crooned a few obscure songs in French while draping herself all over the piano, then disappeared again to a smattering of applause. The piano player filled some time with an atonal composition that seemed to be searching fruitlessly for a melody. Then a young man came out with an acoustic guitar and played some wonderful Spanish-flavored numbers.

"It's quite a mixed bag here, isn't it?" Rafe noted dryly. "From the sublime to the ridiculous and back again."

"It used to be more like a straightforward jazz club when I used to come here," she told him. "But most came to see and be seen. I'd say it's probably the same today."

"No doubt." He glanced around the room, peering into the mist at the few people he could actually see. "Any sign of anyone you know?"

"No." She did some peering as well, but nothing triggered any recognition. Returning her attention to closer at hand, she found Rafe gazing seductively at her face again.

"What are you doing?"

"Studying your features."

"What for?"

He put his hand against his chest in a pledge position and put a solemn look on his face, though his eyes were sparkling with something that could only be humor.

"I'm going to hold your image in my heart as my standard for beauty from now on. And when I meet a woman, and feel attracted, I'm going to call up the memory of your face and see if she meets the standard."

She was half embarrassed, half flattered, and she didn't know if he was doing this to throw her off guard or to "be nice."

"Rafe. If you don't stop mocking me, I'm going to get up and walk out of here."

He looked shocked that she would take it this way. "What makes you think I'm mocking you?"

"Aren't you?"

"Good Lord, no."

And the funny thing was, for a moment, she almost believed him.

"Let's dance," he said.

She frowned, holding on to her drink as though it was going to save her from something she didn't want to experience. "I don't know. It's awful crowded up there."

"That's okay." He took her free hand in his and kissed her fingers. "All the better to hold you close, my dear."

She smiled into his eyes and let him help her to her feet.

"Now you sound like the big bad wolf," she noted. "This is not reassuring."

His arms came around her and he began to sway with the music. "'Bad' has nothing to do with it. I'm a very good wolf."

No doubt about it. She closed her eyes and let the sensation of his hard warm body holding hers wash over her. She could get used to this real fast. How wonderful it would be to fall in love with a man like this and give yourself up to the emotion of it. For just a moment she let herself dream.

But then she pulled herself back with a jerk. If she was going to stay strong and resist all temptation to do some really stupid things, she was going to have to forgo the dreaming. Stick to business. Eschew all sentiment. Resist the urge to let her heart take over and plunge her into danger.

But how was she going to keep her head above water? Conversation. Think of something to talk about. For a few moments, she could only come up with things about Rafe and the way it felt to be in his arms. But gradually, her mind cleared and she remembered that this moment in time didn't exist in a vacuum. There was actually something going on back at the hotel and they were both inherently involved in it.

She looked up at him.

"I feel kind of guilty doing this while the rest of our group is slaving away making posters and editing videotape," she said, wishing her voice didn't come out quite so husky.

"You're ignoring one of the first rules of management," he told her. "Never let the underlings make you squirm."

She gave him a look. "Oh. Is that one of the axioms you live by?"

He grimaced. "Not really. But maybe you ought to adopt it for the night."

"Adopt being an overbearing arrogant boss?"

He shrugged. "Why not? It won't make you popular, but it gets results."

She would have quizzed him about his philosophy of management styles, but she caught sight of someone she recognized sitting at a table along the other side of the room and stopped short.

"Ohmigosh. There's Lindy. And I remember those two guys with her, but I don't remember their names. This is exactly what I was hoping for."

"Good." He looked toward where she was staring. "Let's go over and say hi."

They made their way across the room, threading through the tiny tables, and he didn't release her hand. For some reason, that warmed her as much as anything else he'd done that evening.

Reaching the table, she smiled at the heavyset girl with the black bobbed hair and the two young men, both sporting long ponytails and beards.

"Hey y'all. Remember me? Shelley Sinclair."

"Shelley!" Lindy leaped up and gave her a big hug.

"It's been ages!" She indicated the two men. "You remember Henry and Greg, don't you?"

"Sure." She nodded to them. "This is my friend, Rafe Allman. Mind if we join you for a minute?"

Lindy seemed happy enough to accept them, but the two men had obviously been drinking a bit too much and didn't make an effort to seem very pleased. Rafe pulled over a chair from another table for Shelley and found another one for himself. They sat and smiled. Only Lindy smiled back.

"So, you all were friends when Shelley used to live here in San Antonio," Rafe said as an ice breaker.

"Oh, yeah," Greg said, holding his glass of amber liquid high and staring at the lights coming through it. "We were great friends. We used to hang out all the time. Remember, Shelley?"

Shelley opened her mouth to agree, but he went on without waiting for her response.

"Until she hooked up with her hoity-toity friends and decided she was too good for us, that is." He put down the glass and adopted a sneer. "Suddenly she was riding around in limousines and such. Waving at us from the window like the Queen of England or something."

"Yeah," Henry agreed, looking as though the memory saddened him. "Who was that man you were living with over in that swanky high-rise?" he asked her. "Wasn't he your boss or something?"

Shelley was glad the gloom didn't allow anyone to see her redden at his words.

"Never mind that," Lindy said, kicking him under the table. "We're just glad to see you again, Shelley. How've you been?"

They chatted for a few minutes, then Shelley broached the subject of her visit.

"Do any of you still keep in touch with Quinn Hagar?" she asked.

Was it her imagination, or did a cold draft suddenly seem to be wafting about the table?

"I see him every once in awhile," Lindy admitted at last. "Why?"

"I'm looking for him. I wanted to ask him some questions about his sister, Penny. She and I were friends and roommates in college and I wanted to find out how I could get in touch with her."

The silence at the table was eerie. Looking at their faces, she was sure they were holding out on her for some reason.

"So if any of you see Quinn in the next day or so, please let him know I really want to talk to him. Okay?" She told them where she was staying, giving them the room number.

No response, although Lindy looked embarrassed and Shelley was sure she knew something. Should she play this close to the vest, or lay her cards out on the table? Considering the time element, she didn't have much choice.

"Did any of you know Penny?" she asked.

Henry frowned down into his drink and Greg stared

into space. Lindy looked at them furtively, then turned to Shelley.

"Actually, I met her a couple of times," she said. "She seemed like a nice person."

Shelley nodded. "She's great. We had a lot of fun when we were roomies."

"So…you're trying to find her again?"

"Yes. Do you have any idea where she is these days?"

Lindy licked her lips nervously but shook her head. "Not really," she said evasively.

"Too bad. Well, I heard she'd had a baby. Do you know anything about that?"

Lindy looked up, surprised. "No. I never heard that."

Shelley nodded. Lindy's candid reaction to the last question was believable but made her other answers all the more questionable. It was pretty clear that everyone here knew more than they were saying.

"I saw Rickie Mason yesterday," Shelley offered. "At Chuy's Café, where we always used to meet for breakfast on Saturdays. Remember? She found Quinn's address for me. I went over there today, but he took off when he saw me." Shelley shook her head. "We were friends once. I couldn't believe it when he ran off. Do you have any idea why he would have done that?"

She looked from one face to another, and finally they seemed to be beginning to squirm a little.

At last, Greg shrugged and glanced briefly into her face. "Maybe he thinks you're trying to get some money from him."

She made a face. "Why would he think I was trying to get money from him?"

Henry finally met her gaze. "Because everyone is always trying to get money from him. He's been in some…" He paused, obviously making a great effort on the next few words to overcome the handicap of being too tipsy to speak easily. "Fi-nan-cial diff-i-culties lately." He looked pleased that he'd come through okay. "Played a little fast and loose with the loan sharks and some big boys are after him, from what I hear," he added wisely.

"In that case," Rafe interjected mildly, "tell him there will be some money in it for him if he shows up and tells Shelley what she wants to know."

"I'd really appreciate it if you could relay that message for me," she said, throwing Rafe a grateful look.

Lindy knew something. She was avoiding Shelley's gaze and that was a sure sign of it. They lingered a few moments longer with Shelley hoping Lindy would decide to go ahead and tell what she knew. But that didn't happen and finally they excused themselves and went back to their own table. Rafe ordered another pair of drinks and they sat without speaking for a few minutes.

Finally Rafe grabbed her hand and held it tightly. "Look. So you lived with Jason McLaughlin for a while. It's no big deal."

She looked up with a smile a shade too bright. "What makes you think that's what's bothering me?" she asked him.

"Because I saw your face when that guy mentioned it. Shelley, it's really no big deal."

She drew air deep into her lungs and let it out slowly. "You're wrong. It's a very big deal." She looked at him, wondering if she could make him understand. "Because it's emblematic of all the bad choices I've made in my life."

"You're not exactly the Lone Ranger in making bad choices." His smile was gentle and completely sympathetic. "That's what growing up is all about, learning from mistakes."

She winced. "Yeah, well, mine are doozies."

He was silent for another moment, then leaned closer.

"Listen, Shelley, you didn't exactly have the ideal home and family life, as I remember. Your mother was busy trying to run that restaurant almost by herself. That didn't leave her much time to pay any attention to you and your little girl needs."

"I know," she said, feeling suddenly a little weepy. "My poor mother."

He played with her fingers. "You don't harbor secret resentments?"

She looked at him in surprise. "Toward my mother? Good grief, no. She is the hardest working woman I know. It wasn't her fault that my father abandoned us."

He nodded.

"Not only that," she went on, giving in to the impulse to unburden herself of pain from the past. "I kind of broke her heart by taking up with you people."

His smile disappeared. "What do you mean?"

She shrugged, almost wishing she hadn't mentioned it. What was the point, after all?

"She...well, she sort of felt like I'd chosen you over her. There was one time I remember when I was in high school—we were talking late at night and she just sat there and cried. She thought I'd pretty much given her up as a mother and attached myself to the Allmans, turning to your family for my nurturing. And I couldn't really deny it." Her voice shook slightly and she closed her eyes for a moment. "I know that hurt her deeply. But it was the truth."

"You *were* always underfoot in those days," he agreed. "I remember asking my father once—when I was particularly annoyed with you for some reason— if we'd adopted you yet."

She looked at him and smiled, though her eyes were brimming with unshed tears. "*You* were annoyed with *me?* I can't imagine that happening. I was such an angel."

"Really? Then I must have you confused with some other Shelley Sinclair who practically lived at my house."

"Must be."

He smiled into her eyes and she melted a little. There was something about his smile that seemed to wrap itself around her and warm her in a way no one else's smile ever had.

"Did that change things with your mother?" he asked. "Getting it out in the open, I mean."

She nodded. "In a way. I know I tried harder to let her know how much she meant to me." Her smile was rueful. "But I still got out of Chivaree as fast as I could."

He laced his fingers with hers. "How about now?"

"Now?"

"You're living with her, aren't you?"

"Yes. And I'm also helping out at the restaurant every chance I get." She sighed. "I'm trying to give her a little bit of breathing room. I'd like to make enough money so that I could get her to sell out and take life easy. I could take care of her for a change."

His fingers tightened on hers. "You're a good daughter."

"Am I? I'm not so sure of that."

They danced again and Shelley noticed Lindy and her friends were gone. Scanning the crowd, she didn't see anyone else she knew.

They left soon afterward. The crowds had thinned by the time they wandered their way back to the hotel. The air was soft and warm. A fresh breeze was coming off the desert. They didn't want to let the evening end. Lingering outside under the trees, they talked softly about inconsequential things, and then Rafe got serious for a moment.

"Okay, you want to tell me what this is about—a baby?"

She looked up, startled. "Oh. Yes. It seems Penny had a baby."

"I see." He was quiet for a moment, but when she didn't go on, he added, "So this is what you're really chasing after, isn't it?"

"Yes."

He waited a moment, and when she didn't add anything to the one word answer, he looked at her in exasperation.

"Do I have to drag every detail out of you? Come on, Shelley. You can trust me with the truth."

She sighed. There didn't seem to be much point in holding out any longer. And he was right. Though she wouldn't have been able to say that a day or so ago. But now that they'd spent some time together, she did trust him.

"Okay, I'll tell you the whole thing."

Except for one little detail, and that was something she was not at liberty to divulge. She couldn't tell him that the person she was doing all this for was his own brother.

"My friend—the one who started all this—just found out recently that his old girlfriend, Penny Hagar, had a baby shortly after they broke up. He'd never known she was pregnant. He assumes this must be his child and he wants to know what happened to it. Knowing the child exists is torturing him. He feels a huge sense of responsibility and wants to do what he can for the child, especially if Penny needs any help or whatever."

He was silent for a moment, nodding slowly as he digested the information.

"Okay," he said at last. "Now that there's more form to this search, maybe I can help a little more directly. So…tell me who this man is."

She shook her head, wishing he wouldn't ask. "I can't do that."

He grimaced. "Okay, tell me this. When it comes out—and you know it's eventually going to come out—who you're talking about, how am I going to feel about it?"

She started to answer and then stopped herself, glaring at him.

"Oh, no, you don't. You're trying to trick me. You're trying to get me to talk about it and then you're going to start pulling facts together to try to figure out who it is, aren't you?" She turned away. "No. I'm not going to say another word about it."

"Shelley, Shelley, you're so suspicious of my motives. I'm just trying to help you."

She stared off into the night, looking stubborn.

"So what's your game plan about finding Quinn?"

She sighed. "I hope the promise of money will bring him out of the woodwork," she said. "That was a good idea you had there."

"I'm full of good ideas."

"No doubt."

He grinned down at her and she couldn't help but smile back.

Taking her by the shoulders, he gazed down into her eyes. "I really, really want to kiss you," he said.

Her breath caught in her throat but she kept her cool, flipping her hair back pertly. "You already did."

He frowned, looking a bit puzzled. "A kiss is not usually a once-in-a-lifetime thing, like climbing Mt. Everest or parachute jumping. Just because I've done it once doesn't mean my quota is filled for all time."

She looked away. "I don't think we need to revisit that territory."

His eyes narrowed. "I see." He thought for a moment, then went on philosophically. "So you're looking at it as a goal to be attained, after which one would sit back and rest on his laurels."

He slid his fingers into her hair, tilting her face up toward his, and went on in a lower voice. "Whereas I see it more as a carefully achieved milepost toward bigger and better things."

She looked up into the laughter that she knew she was going to find in his eyes, but she noticed something else there, too, something that made her pulse race a little faster and made her think of how good his body would feel against hers.

"That's the crux of the disagreement right there," she said quickly, pulling away from him, wanting to forestall any further move on his part. "And that's why we'd better consider this evening over."

Turning, she started toward the entrance to the hotel and he followed her. He caught up with her and held the door.

"Would that be so terrible?" he asked softly as she passed him.

She took a deep breath and turned to face him as they reached the elevators.

"Terrible isn't the word I would use," she said, glancing around to make sure there was no one else in earshot. "Inappropriate would fit a bit better, I think."

He frowned. "Why?"

"I'm the boss. I can't take advantage of you that way."

He threw his head back and laughed and when she met his gaze again, she could see a certain respect for her that made her heart sing.

Why was it so important that he respect her as a person even while he was attracted to her as a woman? She wasn't sure, but she knew it was one of the most important things of all. And to feel that she had that, at least a little bit, made sure that all the rest of it wouldn't be devalued in the end.

"So what does that mean?" he was asking her as they got into the elevator car. "I have to wait until Monday before I can attempt any sort of intimacy with you, no matter how innocent?"

"Hmm." She pretended to think about it, then frowned. They reached their floor and got off and she started toward her room. "No. Sorry. That won't work, either."

Reaching into her pocket, she produced her plastic room card and pushed it into the slot. "On Monday the inappropriateness turns in the other direction and it would be *you* taking advantage of *me*."

Her door opened and she turned to smile impishly at him.

His answering grin was endearingly lopsided as he leaned with one arm against her doorway.

"You know what? This inappropriateness thing is a dodge. You're trying to avoid being kissed."

She laughed right up into his face, backing into her room and beginning to close the door.

"And tell me, kind sir," she said through the narrowing opening, "what gave you your first clue?"

Chapter Seven

Rafe tilted his chair back on two legs and watched the others going through the paces of their part of the skit. He had to admit it was getting more coherent each time they ran through it. He still thought his idea would have been much better, but he'd just about resigned himself to the fact that Shelley's idea was pretty good, too.

Now he just had to come to terms with the fact that he was enjoying everything about Shelley. Everything.

Watching her now as she directed the skit, he had to grin. She was a natural leader. It was probably a good thing that this competition had given her the chance to show how good she was at organizing and motivating people working for her. How long would it have taken for the management at Allman Industries—or even he himself—to recognize the leadership qualities she possessed if she'd never gotten this opportunity to showcase them? He was definitely going to find her a more effective position when they got back on Monday.

"Hey, kiddo," he called to her softly as she passed his way, heading for some items she planned to try out as background props. "I've got something to tell you."

She turned back, her eyes bright, but then pretended to look very stern. "If this is about that kissable lips thing again I don't want to hear it," she claimed.

He grinned. "Naw—I'm saving that sort of talk for later, when I get you alone."

"Rafe!"

"Nothing that exciting, actually. I just wanted to let you know that Matt called on my cell a few minutes ago. Pop's on a tear. He's getting all het up about this competition and he's sending Matt to help out. He'll be here tomorrow."

"Oh." She sank into the chair beside his. "Oh, Rafe, I'm sorry."

He looked at her blankly, not sure why she was suddenly brimming with sympathy.

"You don't have to be sorry. It's okay. Matt can't be on the team, but he might be able to give us some pointers. He'll have a fresh outlook."

She sat back. "Okay," she said carefully. "Then you're happy about this?"

"Why shouldn't I be? Matt can be a big help." He

studied her curiously. "I thought you and he were such good friends."

"We are," she said quickly. "It's just…well, your father is always trying to shove him into the limelight. I just thought…"

So that was it. He allowed himself a silent groan. He should have known. Shelley's theory again—that everything he did was driven by his reaction to his father's preference for his older brother.

And he had to admit, there was a sting involved. Did he ever let it interfere with his relationship with Matt? He let the question linger for a moment, but he didn't want to deal with it. Wincing, he pushed it away.

"Shelley, I'm not jealous of my big brother," he said with more bravado than conviction.

She stared at him. "Are you sure?"

He laughed a bit awkwardly. "Yeah. I took a poll. Every part of me agreed." Reaching out he took her hand. "Hey, I appreciate the concern. But it's not necessary. Matt and I are cool. We always have been. Don't worry about it."

He could see that she wanted to explore the issue further. Women! They always wanted to probe for motives and reasons why. He was going to have to train her to live a little more for the moment. Take things lightly. Go with the flow. Just as soon as he learned how to do that himself.

"What time is he coming?" she asked, obviously swallowing other things she would like to have said.

"Early in the morning, from what he said."

She made a face, thinking out loud. "Oh, darn. I haven't talked to Quinn yet."

He blinked at her, not making the connection. "What does that have to do with Matt coming?"

She looked startled, then evasive. "N...nothing. Nothing at all. I was just saying...you know, my day is pretty full."

Her face changed and she rose from her chair.

"Hey, lazy. Come on. I plan to get a lot more work out of you before lunch. I really need that tape of the school children to be edited down a little."

Going back to her original objective, to bring out more props, she set a large mirror up on an easel and stood back to see how it looked.

"The tape is full of some really cute stuff but it's too long for the segment I want to use it in. We have to stay within seven minutes for the entire program. So many things are going to have to go."

Looking up, she threw him a quick smile, then looked back at the mirror, adjusted it and checked to see how it looked from the audience level.

"That's the hard part. We're going to be cutting things ruthlessly." She narrowed her eyes, looking at the mirror placement from another angle.

"Well, hold on just a minute here, boss," he drawled, following her. "I don't think tape editing is in my job description. I haven't had the proper training for it. I'm not so sure I should be doing it."

She turned to look at him, exasperation flickering in her eyes. Putting her head to the side, she tapped his shoulder with her pencil.

"Edit tape," she said crisply, "or turn in your resignation. Either way. Your choice."

He scowled at her, his arms folded across his chest. "Killjoy," he muttered.

She grinned, then stifled it and became the boss again. "Okay, here's the tape. The editing equipment is in the audiovisual center. Let's go. Time's a-wastin'."

He lingered another moment. She'd warmed to him, hadn't she? She was feeling loose. It might be worth a try to see if she would reconsider his idea. It was such a great idea and he knew it would blow away the competition. That need to win was hanging over his head. This was probably his last chance to bring it up and hope for any sort of favorable reaction.

"You know, it's not really too late to think about using my proposal for the competition," he told her. "It wouldn't take many props and I've pretty much worked out the…"

Shelley's eyes flashed pure fire.

"Why can't you just adjust to reality and get behind this one hundred percent?" she said earnestly. "We're doing my idea. And if it's really so important to you to win this competition, you'd better get busy and make sure we do."

Turning, she grabbed a pair of scissors and began cutting up construction paper, getting ready to work on a set piece and making sure he knew she was ignoring him.

He stared at his own reflection in the glass of the large mirror on the easel.

She's right, you know, the reflection told him wisely.

He growled at the image staring at him. Of course she was right. He knew that. He took the tape, gave her one last long lascivious look that she purposefully ignored, and headed off to work on the editing. Even he could tell when the boss had just about had enough of his fooling around.

They were working very hard and Shelley was getting very nervous. When this had all begun, she hadn't cared very much about winning the competition. She certainly cared about doing a decent job, and not embarrassing herself or her company, but winning? It seemed a bit pointless.

But that was before she realized how much winning meant to Rafe. She knew it had more to do with proving something to his father than anything else, but that was important to him. And now, things that were important to him were important to her. She'd seen the way his father had ignored him time and time again when they were kids. It was always Matt he looked to in the past. It was Matt he wanted to take over the company, not Rafe, who was so much better for the job. And the irony was that Matt didn't want any part of the company.

So now she cared whether or not they won. In fact, they had to win—for Rafe, at the very least. She wanted first to prove to him that her idea would work out, and second—well, she just wanted him to be happy.

But she was worried. The few hours they had left didn't seem enough to do the work a really good job would require. Some of the set pieces she'd wanted were going to be impossible to get done in time. And the special shirts they were supposed to wear in the competition as part of the Allman team hadn't arrived yet.

Each team entry had its own style and color of shirt, advertising their company. It was all part of the theme. Without the shirts, she was afraid they wouldn't even place in the contest. Still, the gang was working really hard and she was pleased with the effort they were making.

It was a bit disturbing to find monitors from the conference committee peering over her shoulder every now and then. They were watching how well each team dealt with the boss-employee switch, which was the theme and the main competition point, so they had to be tolerated. But it made things awkward now and then.

Still, the weekend had turned out to be more fun than she'd expected. The way she'd dreaded having to work with Rafe seemed almost quaint now. They still had issues between them, but he was becoming a presence in her life in a way she had never dreamed he would.

She hadn't gotten in touch with Quinn yet, though she'd spent a long half-hour that morning calling every number she could think of that might give her a lead. Luckily she'd been able to avoid coming face-to-face with Jason McLaughlin again. In fact, most of the time she didn't even remember that he was there. That sure was a change from the old days when he'd been her major obsession.

And working on this project had given her a lift she'd never expected either. She was actually finding out she was pretty good at organizing people and getting things done, and the team seemed to turn to her naturally now, as though they sensed she knew what she was doing. If only that were completely true! There were so many loose ends to tie up at all times.

The team was working out well, though she'd found out that a few of them took off and went out clubbing with some members of team B and even some of the other teams the night before. It seemed little Dorie had been quite the party girl, if the snippets of conversation she'd overheard this morning were true. She didn't know exactly what the girl had been up to, because people tended to stop talking about it when they noticed she was near. Still, she couldn't really say much since she'd been out at a club last night as well. And everyone had shown up for work bright and early so there didn't seem to be any harm done.

All in all, things seemed to be going well. But she had enough experience to know that a crisis was likely lurking on the horizon.

Rafe hadn't returned yet with the newly edited tape when Candy answered a phone call and pumped her fist into the air, hung up and crowed, "The shirts are here! Someone has to go up to the main lobby and pick them up right away."

"Oh, thank heavens," Shelley said. Maybe it was a sign that things were going to be okay after all.

"Oh, I can hardly wait to see them!" Dorie said happily.

Shelley grinned, peeling off the plastic gloves she'd been using while gluing a sign together. "I'll go get them. I'll be right back and we can all try them on."

The conference rooms were on the lower level, so she had to take the elevator up to get to the main lobby. She was heading for the concierge desk when she heard someone call her name and she turned to see who it was.

"Jason!"

He snagged her arm before she could get her bearings and pulled her into a side alcove.

"Shelley, Shelley," he said seductively, his eyelids drooping over a gaze that was completely suggestive. "I've been looking for a chance to get you alone. We really need to have a good long talk, you and me."

Shelley glared at him. Deep inside, her system was shivering with revulsion.

"I'm busy, Jason. Our shirts were sent to the wrong hotel or something and they've finally arrived, so I'm picking them up and…"

"Come on, Shelley baby." His hand was rubbing up and down her arm. "We need to escape this rat race for a little while and talk over old times. Dredge up some old memories." He raised an eyebrow significantly. "Try out some old moves."

She stared at him. He was still an attractive man, but the sleaziness was beginning to show through the veneer of playboy good looks. Especially in the eyes. How blind had she been not to notice that before? His eyes were cold, mean, humorless. She thought of Rafe's warm gaze and Jason's absolutely repulsed her.

"Doing anything with you is the last item on my agenda, Jason. We've said all we need to say to each other and we did it long ago."

She tried to pull away from him, but his grip on her arm only tightened.

"You know there's still a spark between us. Can't you feel it tugging on you?"

This couldn't be the technique that had stunned her into blind adoration over the years—could it? She must have been crazy. And very, very dumb.

"Sparks don't do much tugging," she told him tartly, taking him literally just to annoy him, "not having the arms that would require."

"What?" He stared at her blankly, not getting it.

She sighed impatiently. "No, Jason. That's not a spark you think you see. It's a smoldering fire—a fire of resentment at what you put me through that summer."

He looked shocked at her reaction, as though no one had ever rejected his advances before. "Hey, listen honey, that wasn't really my fault. If you had just waited a few weeks, I could've gotten rid of Frances and…"

He was talking about getting rid of his wife in order to take up with his mistress again. The man was scum. And what was she for having fallen for this stuff in the old days? It made her feel like she needed a long, hot shower and a lot of lather from some gritty soap.

"Let go of me, Jason," she said evenly.

His grip was so tight it was starting to be painful. She glanced around, wondering where all the people were. She might have to start yelling if this didn't stop soon.

"This isn't amusing."

"No, Shelley," he said, his voice still smooth but his touch getting rough. "You're not being reasonable. You have to give me a chance to explain."

She tried to twist away but his sinewy strength was too much for her. "Jason, this is going to get ugly if you don't…"

Another hand reached in and took hold of Jason's wrist in a move that was obviously meant to inflict pain, and his grip on her arm came loose right away.

"Hey!" Jason cried out, jerking back.

"Touch her again and I'll break your neck."

Shelley was breathless. It had happened so fast. Rafe was there and Jason was backing away.

"You know," he was saying spitefully, rubbing his wrist, "you Allmans really should learn how to act in civilized society."

"If you McLaughlins are the product of civilized society," Rafe retorted, "I'll stick to my low-life ways. And I don't need you giving me etiquette lessons." He slid his arm around her. "And neither does Shelley."

"Oh," Jason said sarcastically. "You speak for her now?"

"Yes," Shelley said loud and clear. "He can speak for me any time he wants to."

Jason looked resentful and shrugged as though it was all the same to him. "We'll see how you feel about that tomorrow," he said. "After the competition." His grin was mean and humorless. Turning, he disappeared around the corner.

Rafe looked down at her. "What did he mean by that?"

She shook her head. "Who knows." Looking up, she smiled and without hesitation, threw her arms around his neck and hugged him tight. "I'm so glad you showed up. Thank you, thank you, thank you!"

"Anytime," he said, but the way he hugged her in return didn't seem as enthusiastic as she would have expected. "What happened, anyway?"

She pulled away. "I was coming down to get the shirts and Jason waylaid me. That's all."

His dark gaze was searching hers, studying her face, looking for answers.

"So what's the deal?" he said softly. "Do you still have feelings for this guy?"

"No, Rafe," she said earnestly. "I swear I don't. Not in the least."

He wanted to believe her but he felt a wariness he didn't even understand himself. "Then what's up with the reaction I see in you?" he asked carefully.

Reaction? For a moment she wasn't sure what he was referring to. How could her reaction look like anything but revulsion? But maybe it wasn't the current reaction he was talking about. Maybe it was what he'd noticed in her over the years.

"It's just…" She licked her lips, wanting to get this right. "It's impossible to erase all the feelings the years build up in you. Don't you think?"

He stared at her, waiting for her to explain.

"Jason was a big part of my life at one time. I can't pretend otherwise. You wouldn't believe the huge crush I had on him in high school. It was major. So when I came to San Antonio and got a job in his company, I was on cloud nine." She stopped herself, wishing she hadn't gone that far.

He waited, not sure he wanted to hear this but knowing he had to. Her words were like daggers in his soul.

He'd had old girlfriends, too. So she'd had a crush that turned into a lover. So what? Most of the women he'd ever been with had experienced much the same and it had never bothered him before. Looking back, he hardly remembered much about any of them. Not many stood out or meant anything to him now. In fact, over the years he'd begun to wonder if falling in love was just something he wasn't set up to do. It didn't happen. And now…now this. Now Shelley.

What was different about her? Why was she able to reach inside him and take hold of his heart, twist his emotions in a way no other woman ever had? He didn't know. But he listened as she finished her explanation, even though it was the last thing he felt like doing.

"So I spent some time with Jason," she said, talking quickly, wanting to get this over with. "And I wish I never had. But I did. And it didn't take long to realize that was all wrong. But it took a little longer to realize *he* was all wrong. That he wasn't worth the effort. That he's a jerk. Far from having warm feelings for him, I really can't stand the man. I hope I never have to have any dealings with him again."

He nodded, but his gaze was clouded. "Okay. Thanks for being honest with me, Shelley. I appreciate it." He gave her half a smile. "Hey, I came down to help you with the shirts. Let's go get them."

She took his arm and they started toward the concierge desk. But something fluttered uneasily down inside her. Something about the way Rafe had taken her explanation hadn't quite jelled. He wasn't completely convinced. What could she do to prove it to him?

The shirts were a big hit. Soft blue and made of a great grade of cotton, they had the Allman logo over the pocket and a picture of a winery on the back. Surprisingly everyone had the right fit. They paraded in front of a long mirror and admired themselves. They looked like a real team.

Shelley looked at her watch. "Oh, gosh. Now we have to take out an hour for lunch. We can't afford to do that!"

"Don't worry," Rafe told her. "I made an executive decision and ordered in pizza. We won't have to leave the room."

"Oh, you're a lifesaver. That is the perfect solution. We'll have pizza but keep right on working." She smiled at him. "I knew it would pay off having you around."

"I exist but to serve."

She was happy to see the humor back in his eyes.

"Okay, everybody," she called out when the pizza arrived. "Have some lunch but we can't slack off. The schedule for dress rehearsals has been posted and we've got the 6:00 p.m. slot. We've got to be ready by then."

There were groans all around.

"We'll work right up to five and then I want all of you to go to your rooms and get a nice hour's rest. Okay?"

"Hey," Rafe said about an hour later, motioning with a nod of his head, "It looks like you've got a visitor."

Looking up from the background poster she was painting, she saw Lindy smiling from the hallway.

"Hi!" she called, waving a paintbrush. "Just a second."

Rafe took the paintbrush from her and she wiped her hands on a towel, then went out to join her old friend in the hall.

"I'm so glad to see you."

Lindy looked around a little nervously. "I wanted to talk to you for a minute. Can we take a walk around the courtyard?"

"Sure."

Shelley glanced back at Rafe. He nodded, knowing she was silently asking him to take over and keep things moving. Amazing how they had gone from animosity to silent communications in a matter of days.

She and Lindy went out into the courtyard. Landscaped to remind guests of a tropical island, it was filled with lush greenery and palms, with an aviary full of chattering birds along one side and a sculptured swimming pool down the middle of the area. Small waterfalls fed into the pool and the sounds of the tropics came from loudspeakers hidden in the bushes. Shelley took Lindy's arm and they began to make their way through the jungle.

"I had to come and see you," Lindy began, pushing her shiny dark bangs aside and smiling at Shelley. "I'm sorry I was so remote last night, but I couldn't really talk in front of Henry and Greg," she said apologetically. "They and all of that group have this whole us-against-them mentality. You must remember how they are."

"Oh, yes." Shelley stopped just short of rolling her eyes.

"They consider you a traitor of sorts, you know. Because you dumped us and went off with your boss like you did. They think you sold out."

"I know that's how they feel. And I don't blame them for being annoyed about that. I'm annoyed at myself for doing it." She looked at the dark-haired woman, wondering about her and about her life. "How about you? Do you feel that way, too?"

"Of course not. I always liked you, Shelley."

Shelley smiled at her. "So when are you going to move on, Lindy?" she said.

Lindy shrugged. "I've had my ups and downs. I won't be hanging around here forever."

"I hope not." She squeezed her arm affectionately. "You've got a lot of potential. But I'm sure you hear that all the time and I don't want to lecture you. So, what did you come over here to tell me? Have you talked to Quinn?"

"No." She shook her head. "I tried but he's not answering his phone. I think it's disconnected. But I can tell you something about Penny."

She licked her lips, giving Shelley a worried look, then looked around and spotted a bench. "You'd better sit down. This isn't going to be easy."

"What?" Shelley didn't sit down, but she grabbed Lindy's arm again, a quiver of alarm racing through her system. "What is it?"

Lindy took a deep breath. "Penny died over a year ago."

"What?" Shelley gasped and did slide down onto the bench after all. "Oh, no. What happened?"

Lindy dropped down to sit beside her.

"Pancreatic cancer. It came on very suddenly and she was gone in a couple of weeks."

"Oh, that's terrible." Shelley put her hands over her face and rocked back and forth. "Poor Penny. Poor Quinn." Dropping her hands, she looked at Lindy. "And the baby?"

Lindy shook her head. "Honestly, Shelley, I never heard of any baby. If Penny had a baby, she didn't talk about it. And Quinn never said a word."

Shelley stared at her. "Then where could the baby be?"

Lindy shrugged. "Are you sure there really was a baby?"

Slowly shaking her head, Shelley sighed. "I'm not sure about anything, to tell you the truth."

"I take it you know the father."

"Maybe. If there *is* a baby."

They were both silent for a moment, awed by the forces of life that seemed so overpowering and unpredictable. Lindy looked at Shelley.

"You still need Quinn to find out more, I guess."

Shelley winced. "And Quinn doesn't want to be found."

"No." Lindy gave her a quick, mischievous smile. "But you seem to have found a new man to make your life more interesting. I've gotta say, I approve. I was so jealous last night. You both look like you're so in love."

"In love?" Shelley's world rocked for just a moment. "Rafe and I?"

Lindy shrugged. "That's the way it looked. I watched you when you were dancing." Her mouth turned down at the corners. "So it's not a romance? Too bad. He's a hottie."

A romance—with Rafe? The thought boggled the mind, and yet it sent out tentacles of interesting emotions at the same time. A romance with Rafe. Why not?

Oh, for Pete's sake—there were a thousand reasons!

Chapter Eight

He's a hottie.

The words kept running through Shelley's mind and she couldn't shake them. Every time Rafe was near, she didn't have to look up to see him, she could feel his presence. And in her mind the words came again. *He's a hottie.*

That was fine for hotties, of course, but tough luck for dumb fools who fell for them.

It was almost an hour later, long after Lindy had gone, that she managed to get Rafe off to the side and tell him what she'd learned. He was almost as stunned as she was, which warmed her. After all, he didn't even know Penny. They mulled it over for a short time, talking softly, knowing they had to get back to work but lingering together for a few moments more. He reached up and brushed her cheek with the palm of his hand, his dark eyes filled with sympathy.

Oh, he's much more than a hottie, she thought to herself.

And then he noticed something at the other end of the hall and his eyebrows went up. "Look. Matt's here. I guess he decided to come on down instead of waiting for morning."

"What?" Shelley whirled and searched the hall, spotting him right away. "Oh, no!" Turning back, she grabbed Rafe's lapels in anguish. "Oh, Rafe, how am I going to tell him?"

He frowned down at her. "Tell him what?"

She pulled back, her face mirroring her realization of the mistake she'd made, and his own face cleared with sudden comprehension.

"Oh, man. Do you mean to tell me Matt is this friend you've been talking about? Matt and Penny…?"

She shook her head, eyes closed, sick at heart. It was all too much. "You're not supposed to know this," she mumbled miserably.

But it was too late. And Matt was approaching fast.

"Hey there, bro, good to see you," Rafe said. Matt gave him a hug and smiled down at Shelley.

"Do I get a hug from my favorite girl?" he asked.

She felt close to tears but she hid it and threw her arms around his neck, hugging tightly. "Oh, Matt!" she wailed.

"Hey, what is it?" He pulled back and looked at her stricken face. "Did your team get disqualified from the competition or something?"

She shook her head. "Much worse than that," she said, taking his hand and looking up into his dark eyes, so like his brother's. "I've got some terrible news."

Rafe gestured to them both to follow him and he led the way out into the courtyard. Luckily it was empty and they could talk privately.

Quickly and precisely, Shelley gave Matt the details, watching as he turned an ashen color. She explained how she knew about Penny's death and related the fruitless search for Quinn.

When she was finished, Matt merely said, "The baby?"

She explained that they didn't know much and what they had heard was merely speculative. "We really need to find Quinn so we can get the whole story," she said.

She exchanged a glance with Rafe. Matt didn't seem perturbed at all that his brother had been let in on this secret without his permission. That was a relief. The two brothers really seemed to be closer than some people realized. There were dozens of reasons why the two of them might resent each other—especially on Rafe's side. And yet, she never saw any evidence of it. She hoped it was true and that Rafe wasn't just hiding it well.

Matt was obviously shaken. Rafe gave him a half hug and he tried to smile, but he couldn't quite manage it yet. Nodding slowly, he thought over all the implications of what he'd just heard.

"Take me to that apartment."

She glanced at Rafe again. They were in the middle of preparing for the dress rehearsal. How could they possibly leave the others to fend for themselves? "Right now?"

"Yes." Matt had a way of making his judgments seem eminently strong and sure. "If the three of us go, maybe we can catch him."

Rafe shrugged and said, "What do you think, boss?"

Boss. She heard the word with a start. She'd forgotten she was the boss and had to make the decision. And she could hardly believe that Rafe was voluntarily deferring to her. Bosses got to make the hard calls, but they had to take the responsibility if things went wrong, too. Did she dare chance this? She looked at her watch and took a deep breath.

"Okay. I'll tell Candy. But we have to be back by four at the latest."

Matt's car was still parked in front of the lobby and they piled in. He drove quickly but with quiet skill, following Shelley's directions without saying anything himself. Shelley's heart was fluttering in her chest. She wasn't sure what he was planning. Things were changing too fast for her.

He pulled the car over to park half a block from Quinn's apartment building. They all got out and started toward the entrance.

"I'll go down into the parking garage and find his car," Rafe said. "So he can't get out that way this time."

Matt nodded. "Got your cell on?" he asked his brother. "I'll call you when I know what's happening."

Nodding, Rafe headed for the parking garage. Shelley followed Matt into the building, pointing out Quinn's apartment. They approached it gingerly and Matt stood back away from the viewing lens's range while Shelley knocked on the door.

"Quinn?" she called when he didn't answer right away. "It's Shelley Sinclair. Please let me talk to you for a minute."

No answer.

Matt moved closer along the wall and pressed his ear to the door. Jerking upright, he pulled out his cell phone. "He's going out the window," he told Shelley. "Rafe, he's coming your way," he barked into the phone. "We'll be right behind him."

Adrenaline raced through her as they hurried back outside, running to the back of the building. As they came around the corner, they found Rafe struggling with Quinn at the entrance to the garage. Matt joined in and they had the younger man pinned to the wall in no time. Rafe got control of his arm and pulled him out to face the others.

Matt stared at him and he stared back defiantly.

"Well, Quinn," Matt said. "It's been a long time."

Quinn didn't respond. A tall, thin man in his midtwenties, Quinn looked undernourished and overly hostile. A mop of dark blond hair that hadn't been cut for much too long crowned his head. He wore a white

T-shirt, dirty jeans and even dirtier sneakers. The total effect was less than pleasant.

"Hey, that's not very polite," Matt told him. "You should answer when you're spoken to. Need a lesson in etiquette, do you?"

Rafe jerked the arm he held behind Quinn's back and Quinn yelped in pain.

"Hey," he said. "Cut it out. There's no need for any rough stuff."

"Of course not," Matt said smoothly. "Because you're going to tell me what I want to know, aren't you?"

Quinn's head went back and his eyes narrowed, but he started muttering. "Everything's cool. I remember you, Matt. I'll talk to you."

Matt looked at Rafe. They gave each other an imperceptible nod, the sort of wordless communication brothers have with each other.

"Okay," Matt said, standing with his legs wide apart. "Why don't you start with why you keep running away from Shelley?"

The kid glanced at her and gave her a brusque nod. "Sorry, Shelley," he said gruffly. "You gotta be careful around here."

He looked back at Matt, beginning to lose the resentful pose and becoming a real person again.

"Look. I've been running for a while now. I've changed apartments three times in the last month. I don't know how you even found me."

"What are you hiding from?"

He shrugged. "Loan sharks. I got in too deep and I'd like to get out without having my legs broken."

Matt nodded slowly, studying Quinn hard. "Sounds like a worthy goal. How much do you owe them?"

Quinn hesitated, then said a figure that made Shelley's eyes widen.

Matt hesitated, then took out a pen. "Give me their names."

Quinn looked confused. "What for?"

Matt's gaze was calm and sure. "I'll take care of it."

Quinn's jaw dropped. "You'll take care of it?" he repeated incredulously.

"Yeah. It's the least I can do for Penny's brother." He gestured to Rafe to let Quinn loose, then stood poised, pen ready. "But you've got to do something in exchange."

Quinn rubbed his arm and gave Rafe a look, but he didn't seem damaged. "What is it?"

Matt glanced around at the shoddy surroundings. "Get out of this place, away from the people that keep you mired in this lifestyle. Move out of here and come to Chivaree. I'll get you a job. Maybe even at Allman Industries."

"Chivaree?" The kid was aghast. "The place is a dump. It's nowhere."

"Sure. That's what you need, a nowhere town. The kind of place where people look out for each other and put you straight when they can see you're taking a wrong road. It's somewhere you can heal and get better and become a worthwhile human being again." His gaze hardened. "You going to do it or not?"

Quinn moved restlessly, rubbing the back of his neck with one hand. "You'll pay off the loan sharks?" He looked at Matt as though he couldn't really believe it.

"I will."

There was something about the way the man said it that left no room for doubt.

Quinn moved restlessly, looking at Rafe, then at Shelley. Finally he looked back at Matt. "Okay," he said, somewhat reluctantly. "I guess I could give it a try."

Shelley watched, her heart aching. It was funny, but watching Matt be brave and compassionate and magnanimous made her like Rafe all the more. She already knew Matt was all those things. Now she was pretty sure Rafe was, too. In fact, at the moment, she was pretty crazy about the whole darn Allman family…all except for the father. Him, she could do without.

"We just heard about Penny's death today," Matt was saying to Quinn. "I'm really sorry. She didn't deserve that."

Quinn nodded, suddenly unable or unwilling to make a statement and ducking his head.

"Now," Matt said, "tell me what happened to her baby."

Quinn's head rose sharply. "Baby?" he said, looking from one to the other of them with a shifty glance.

"She did have a baby, didn't she?"

He relaxed as though he'd realized it was too late to lie about that. "Okay. You're right. Penny had a baby."

"When?"

He thought for a moment, then named a date that had Matt nodding.

"That would be about six months after we broke up," he said solemnly.

"Yeah." Quinn looked up at him and almost smiled. "She told me you were the father."

The emotion that flashed across Matt's face was indefinable, but deep and obviously painful. "Where's the baby now?" he asked, his voice rough.

Quinn shook his head and looked apologetic. "I don't have the slightest idea." He shrugged. "She gave it to someone else."

Matt looked thunderstruck. "She put it up for adoption?"

"I guess."

"What was the name of the agency?"

Quinn hesitated, scrunching up his face. "I don't know if she did anything official. She was pretty much running below the radar, if you know what I mean."

Matt was having a hard time keeping his temper now. "No, I don't know what you mean. Where the hell did she take that baby?"

"Listen, I don't know." Quinn took a step back to get out of Matt's immediate reach. "She had the kid and then she didn't have it. I never even saw it."

"There was nothing in her papers when she died?"

"Nothing I saw. I threw away most of that stuff." He looked at each of the three of them in turn. "You can look through what I kept if you want. She didn't really have much." He cleared his throat. "She didn't ever get much of a life, poor girl."

They were all silent for a long moment, paying a tribute of sorts to the woman who died too young.

But Matt had one more question. "Was the baby a boy or a girl?" he asked softly.

Quinn shook his head, his eyes luminous in the afternoon sunlight. "Sorry, Matt. I really don't know."

Shelley coughed. She had to. She'd been agonizing for the last few minutes. It was getting late and there was a competition that had to be won.

"I hate to do this," she said at last, "but we've got to get back for the dress rehearsal."

Matt turned and looked at her as though he'd forgotten she was there. "Go ahead," he said, pulling out his car keys and tossing them to Rafe. "You two go on. I've still got to get those names. Quinn can take me back to the hotel. Right?"

Quinn shrugged. "Sure."

Rafe frowned, looking as though he didn't want to leave his brother behind in this neighborhood. But if Matt was going to stay, they really had no choice. He pulled his brother aside for a moment of private conversation, then joined Shelley. They started for the street. When she looked up at his face, she found him grinning.

"What's so funny?" she asked him.

"Life," he said. "Damn." He stretched. "Matt shows

up and things start popping." He shook his head in admiration. "It's always been like that. What a guy."

She stared at him, bewildered. There truly didn't seem to be any envy in him and she found that hard to understand. It was true that Matt always came across as the winner, the best guy, the natural leader. But she'd come to realize that Rafe wasn't much different.

Still, he seldom got that kind of recognition. Especially from their father. So why didn't he resent it more?

"He's always been your hero, hasn't he?" she said softly.

He nodded. "Sure."

That was only natural on one level. Most boys idolized their big brothers. But Rafe was a man now and life had given him so many reasons to go against that trend.

"And I'll bet David looks up to you the same way," she offered.

He looked surprised. "I doubt it."

"Why?"

His mouth quirked at the corner, a sure sign he was getting annoyed with the topic.

"You deserve it," she added staunchly.

He groaned. "You've got a rosy view of life, don't you, Shelley? Haven't you figured out yet that you don't usually get what you deserve? That most things are going to flake out on you?" He shook his head, looking out at traffic. "You've only got yourself, you know. Don't go counting on anything or anyone else. There's no guarantee they'll be there for you when it counts."

She sat very still and didn't answer. There it was, the little kernel of truth that she realized she'd been searching and probing for. There *was* a resentment buried deep inside him. Much as he tried to pretend otherwise, he was only human, after all.

The dress rehearsal was a disaster. Lines that had flowed from the tongue a few hours before were completely lost. Background set pieces fell over. The VCR wouldn't work, and when it finally did, the tracking was all off. Candy walked up to the microphone for her speech, tripped and fell to the ground, sliding under the chairs and knocking them over. In flailing around to catch herself, she grabbed the corner of the tablecloth, pulling down the entire display. Dorie leaped forward to save the display and fell flat on her face as well.

"They're going down like bowling pins," Rafe said, shaking his head in resignation. "Maybe we should call for a paramedic van to be placed on call tomorrow, just in case."

Shelley closed her eyes. "A bad rehearsal means a great performance. Doesn't it?"

"And the Easter bunny lays chocolate eggs," Rafe said skeptically. "Yeah. Well, we'll see, won't we?"

Everyone was pretty gloomy at dinner. Matt didn't join them. He didn't feel much like eating and Shelley couldn't really blame him. She didn't feel much like it, either, but she felt, as the "boss," she had to be with her team. What little conversation there was seemed strained and no one ate very much.

Dinner over, the team repaired to the conference room to work on all the snags they'd come across during the dress rehearsal. It was almost ten o'clock when they finally gave up and headed for their respective rooms. Shelley rode up in the elevator with Rafe. She looked at him bleakly.

"So what do you think?" she said. "Is there any hope?"

Gazing at her steadily, he didn't answer. She closed her eyes and began to laugh. "I am so tired. I feel like the last two days have lasted about seven years."

"I know what you mean."

"This being the boss stuff isn't all it's cracked up to be, is it?"

"It has its pluses and minuses. All in all, I'd rather be in charge than being told what to do."

She opened her eyes and looked at him, not sure if she felt the same. They reached their floor and got off the elevator. He walked her slowly toward her room.

"I know you still think we should have used your idea," she told him. "And who knows? Maybe you're right. If this doesn't pan out tomorrow, I'll owe you a big apology."

He frowned at her. "Don't be ridiculous. I'm as committed to your idea as anyone now. We're going to make it work. It's got a great theme. As long as we can keep Candy from destroying the scenery, we've got a chance."

She laughed. They'd reached her door. Turning, she prepared to say good-night. "I'll meet you early," she told him. "I'm going in now and going to bed."

His eyes seemed black as coal. "Can I come with you?" he asked simply.

He'd surprised her. "Rafe…"

"Look." He touched her chin with his forefinger. "I just want to be with you for a while. No strings attached. I just want to talk and sort of get some things straight in my head. Do you mind?"

Looking up into those dark eyes she knew she couldn't deny him anything. But it might be wise to try.

"We're old friends, remember?" he said.

"Old enemies," she reminded him.

He shrugged. "Old friend, old enemies. They pretty much blend together after a while."

"You think?" She surrendered to the inevitable and opened the door wide.

He came inside her room and she felt her heartbeat quicken. He was so impossibly handsome and so completely male. A very dangerous combination. She could probably fall in love with him if she let herself. But she knew better. Didn't she?

"Would you like a drink from the little refrigerator?" she asked, pointing to the guest bar in the corner. "Or would you like a cup of mint tea?"

"Mint tea?"

"I brought my own setup. I just plug in my little jug and in a couple of minutes, boiling water for tea."

"That would be great."

She chattered on about nothing while she brewed the tea and poured it out into two mugs. Then she looked around her room and realized there weren't many places to sit that didn't bring on thoughts of intimacy.

"Let's go out on the balcony," she suggested.

"Why not?" he replied obligingly.

She turned to look into his face as they made their way out into the night air. He looked calm, pleasant and everything he was saying was so agreeable. Was this really the same Rafe Allman she'd known all her life? Even two days before, he'd countered everything she said with some sort of smart-aleck remark. Now he was like a great big kitty cat, ready to please and purr.

It was a little cool on the balcony, but she had on a long-sleeved cotton sweater and he wore a loose shirt of heavy jersey. They sat on wooden chairs with a small table between them and listened to the sounds from the street below. A mariachi band was playing somewhere, the sound of the horns sailing up through the palm trees. A piece of the river was visible if you knew where to look, and the lights of San Antonio twinkled all around. Hard as they'd worked, this had been a good weekend, an oasis from real life that was going to end in another twenty hours or so.

"So what happens when we go back to Chivaree on Monday?" she asked him softly.

"What happens? Life goes on." He shrugged, sipping

his tea. "If we win, we'll go back in triumph. And Pop will be happy."

"And if we lose?"

He was quiet for a moment, then said calmly, "We won't be triumphant. We'll tell everyone to wait until next year, just like the baseball teams do."

She was glad to hear he wasn't considering slitting his wrists over it. But that didn't really take the pressure off.

She moaned. "I'll probably get fired."

He looked at her in surprise. "Why would you be fired?"

"Because I'm the boss. If we don't win, it's my fault. Isn't that the way it works?"

He chuckled. "Don't worry. I'm not going to let anybody fire you."

She pulled her legs into the chair under her, getting comfortable. "It might not be up to you."

He grinned. "Let me tell you a little secret, lady. Most of what goes on at Allman Industries is up to me."

She knew that, but she wasn't going to admit it to him. "Maybe so. But your father is still the president of the company."

He turned and looked at her. "And you think he's still trying to get Matt to take over for him," he said dryly. "This is quite a little hobby horse you've taken on for yourself."

She twitched nervously. That wasn't what she'd been thinking, but now that he mentioned it, that was pretty much common knowledge around Chivaree. Everyone knew Jesse Allman wanted his oldest son to take over the company. And everyone knew that Matt had avoided the issue by going off to medical school and staying away for years. Meanwhile, Rafe was always there, doing what had to be done.

"Isn't he still pressuring Matt?" she asked simply.

Rafe growled at her. "Matt has never wanted to take over the business. And I've always wanted to."

"And your father has always made it very clear he thinks Matt should be the one."

He hesitated before he answered her. "Yeah. I guess it's not a secret."

She sneaked a peek at his face. "You can't tell me that doesn't bother you."

He waited a long moment before answering.

"I don't think *bothers* is the right word." He ran a hand through his thick hair, standing parts of it on end. "Sure, I wish my father would be more realistic. But it would also be nice if he didn't swear so much and stopped drinking whiskey. He's not going to change. And we all have learned over the years to work around his idiosyncrasies."

She looked over at him. His eyes looked huge and dark in the shadows. She felt an overwhelming empathy for him. It came over her in a wave and she went on with the subject, even though she knew he wanted her to drop it. Somehow she just couldn't right now. These were wounds and feelings she'd witnessed since childhood and once she'd begun to release them, it was hard to shut off the flow.

"Don't you also wish he gave you a little more credit for the great job you do running the company, instead of always trying to get Matt interested?"

"Shelley…"

"Because I do," she said, her inner anger finally showing through. "It makes me crazy to see him overlooking all that you do. I want to shake the man."

His white teeth flashed. "Don't do that. He's falling apart as it is."

She winced. The man deserved sympathy for his struggle with cancer, but that didn't give him carte blanche to treat his family cruelly. "Rafe, don't you see that you crave your father's approval as a way to make up for all this other stuff? Don't you see how it's affected your life ever since you were a child?"

"Oh, please," he said dismissively. "I'd like his approval, sure. But it's not keeping me up at night."

"Isn't it?" She just didn't believe that. "Then why this drive to win the competition? Doesn't it have at least something to do with your need to prove something to him?"

He stopped and thought, then looked up at her candidly. "Sure. There's probably some of that in there."

She nodded.

"But so what? It's all part of life. I can deal with it."

"But it bothers you."

"Okay, okay—yes, it bothers me."

He was getting annoyed with her and she didn't blame him.

"Okay, I admitted it," he said. "Are you happy now?"

She sighed. "Yes," she said, though she wasn't sure it was true.

It still didn't change anything and she wasn't sure what she'd thought she was accomplishing here. But somehow, something had to be done. Rafe deserved it.

She didn't dare bring up the other element she was sure was a part of the way he protected his heart and his feelings from too much close contact with anyone else. The pain he'd gone through over the death of his mother had to be behind a lot of the cool exterior he presented to the world. His mother had been his main cheerleader and once she was gone, he had to struggle with his father unprotected. That hadn't made it easy on him, growing up in the competitive Allman family.

"It's much better to get these things out in the open," she offered tentatively.

He groaned. "Spare me the psychology, Ms. Freud."

He stretched his legs out, looking comfortable even though she was pushing a theme he didn't want to deal with. She felt a rush of affection for him. Why had she always considered him so ill-tempered? She knew better now.

He was looking out at the lights of the city. "I suppose you're going to tie all this in with the fact that I haven't found a woman to marry," he mused softly.

"Well…" Actually, that was a bit of a touchy subject for her to be getting into.

"And you're going to tell me I can't connect with

women because my father doesn't respect my work enough."

"Well…"

"And I'm going to tell you that it's all horse manure. Because, you know what? I haven't found a woman to marry because I've been too busy running a business. End of story." He turned on her challengingly. "So what's your excuse?"

She blinked. "Pardon me?"

"Why aren't *you* married? Why can't *you* find someone to connect to?"

"I…well, I…"

"See? Not so easy when you're the one being attacked."

He was right. And she deserved what he was saying. But she didn't buy that the two of them were in the same boat. After all, she'd had a few relationships in her time. The story on Rafe was that he just didn't do that. He'd dated enough. Girls fell for him like leaves in a breeze, but as far as she knew, he'd never had one woman, one girl, to call his own. And that had to be entirely through his own choice.

"Have you ever been in love?" she asked him.

He seemed to find that a hard one. Looking out into the night, he swallowed a couple of times before he answered. "You got me there. I never have been." Turning, he fixed her with his dark stare. "How about you?"

"Me? Yes, actually. At least I thought I was in love."

"Oh. Of course. Jason McLaughlin."

He was still staring at her, and suddenly it felt as

though his gaze was boring holes in her soul. But she knew it was her own fault. After all, she was the one who had insisted on going down this road to instant personality analysis. Live by the sword, die by the sword.

"So what was that like?" he asked, his tone just this side of sarcasm. "A good experience? Did you grow as a person? Did love turn you into a more compassionate human being? Or did it turn you against romance altogether?"

She took a deep breath. She really didn't want to talk about this right now. So maybe she should have laid off him a little, too. Was that his point? Because she had to admit, he was probably right.

"You win," she said, looking up at him. "I'm sorry I pried so much. And you know what? I would really appreciate it if we didn't talk about Jason."

He grimaced, looking away. "You see, it's the way you react whenever McLaughlin comes up that makes me wonder…"

"Don't," she said shortly, stifling the fluttering in her heart. Didn't he know that it was guilt that haunted her, not affection? "There's nothing to wonder about. I can't stand the man. Now can we drop this?"

He looked at her for a long moment, then looked away.

"I guess I'd better get going. Tomorrow is the big day."

"Already?" Despite everything, she felt a sense of disappointment she hadn't been expecting.

He nodded, pushing himself to his feet and looking out at the velvet night. She rose and stood beside him.

"Whatever happens tomorrow," she said softly, "I'm really glad…"

He looked down at her and smiled, touching her cheek with the palm of his warm hand. "What? What are you glad about?"

She hesitated, wanting to keep his hand there as long as possible. "I'm glad we got to know each other better," she said softly. "I mean, I never realized…"

She looked up at him, at his dark eyes, his hard mouth, his rumpled dark hair, and she wanted his kiss more than she'd ever wanted anything in her life.

He saw the longing in her eyes but he hesitated. Kissing Shelley like this wasn't going to be a casual thing. If he took this step…if he took her trust and her heart in his hands he knew instinctively that it would mean something. Exactly what, he didn't know. But it would be a commitment of sorts.

Commitment was something he'd avoided for almost thirty years. Why would he want to give in to it now? No, it wasn't worth it. Shelley was very appealing, but she was like a human trap, lying in wait for him to take one step too far and then the string would snap and the rope would yank and he'd be hung out to dry, twisting slowly in the wind. He was too wary and aware. He wasn't going to let that happen to him.

"Better get some sleep," he said gruffly, turning away and starting into the room. "I'll see you in the morning."

She didn't answer. She was following him and just before he reached the door, he felt her touch his arm.

"Rafe?" she said softly.

He turned back, though he knew before he started to move that it was a mistake.

"Rafe?" she said again, her gaze misty, like smoke from a smoldering fire.

It was something in the sound of her voice that got him. For one second, then two, he was afraid. It shivered through him, a brief regret, a sigh, a sense of saying farewell to a part of him that was leaving now. Because once he looked back down into her eyes he was lost and he knew it. But he did it anyway. And the fear evaporated like summer rain on concrete and he abandoned himself to the inevitable.

It was bound to happen. It had been in the cards from the moment their gazes had met that first day of the conference. He had to experience her, to touch her, hold her, kiss her. And once he did that, he would know the trap was sprung.

"Shelley," he murmured, one last lingering hope of saving himself that disappeared before it was even fully formed as she reached up to touch his face with her hand.

It was such a relief to give in. She curled into his embrace as though she'd been born to please him, surrendering her warm, sweet mouth to his exploration. He took her, held her, drank from her as though he were dying of thirst. She felt so good. Every rounded part of her fit so well against every angular part of him and he pulled her closer, wanting to feel her everywhere. Each sigh, each moan, aroused him more, until he was throbbing, aching with need for her, blind and deaf to anything else but that pure building desire.

His hands slipped under her shirt, sliding up her smooth back. She felt like fine silk and tasted like an exotic wine. When he cupped her breast, feeling the nipple harden in his hand, she cried out and her whole body shuddered, as though some new force was invading it. Her responsiveness was the most provocative thing he'd ever had under his control and the sensation nearly drove him mad.

The bed was right there and they both knew it. It was a destination, a place where their need for each other could be played out in full. He was fully aware of it the whole time, and Shelley was only vaguely aware.

Still, Shelley knew what she was doing, tempting fate, tempting danger. But she'd decided she didn't care anymore. She was all feeling and she didn't want thought to intrude. She pressed her body to his and joy sang in her veins as she felt his response.

You've been here before, something inside was warning. *Don't you remember Jason? Don't you remember the agony when you realized he didn't really love you? Don't you remember the shame when you saw his wife?*

She did remember, but the memory of those things was being blotted out by the heat Rafe conjured up in her, the feel of his hands on her skin, the feel of his hard body against hers, the smell and the taste of him.

I'm in love with Rafe Allman.

What?

Yes. In love with Rafe. Forever and for all time.

The shock of that discovery jolted her and she pulled away, wiping her mouth with the back of her hand and looking at him with a sort of horror.

"What?" he asked her between labored breaths, still reaching to bring her back into his embrace. He was clearly oblivious to anything but the urgent need for her.

She stared at him in wonder. Another moment and they would have gone over the edge and into a whole new level of relationship. She wasn't ready for that. She couldn't risk it. Not yet.

"I think you'd better go now," she said, backing away.

Catching himself, he took a deep breath. His blood slowed and his brain reengaged.

"Shelley, I'm sorry," he said quickly. "I promised you this wouldn't happen."

She shook her head. "No, no, it's my fault. But I just didn't realize…"

"What?"

"How important it would be," she said softly, willing him to understand.

He frowned, puzzled, but slowly his face cleared. He got it. He'd been thinking something very close to what she was saying, hadn't he? That was when he realized she was as scared of this as he was.

Looking at her, he gave her his most crooked smile. "Shelley," he said, touching her hair with his hand, letting his affection for her show in his dark eyes. "Shelley, you're very special to me."

She nodded. "You, too," she whispered. Taking his hand, she pressed a kiss into the palm, closing her eyes.

"I'd better go," he said, reluctant but determined to do the right thing for once. "Sleep tight."

"If I can sleep at all," she said.

He grinned, because he knew it was going to be a problem for him, too. "'Night." He dropped a kiss on her lips, then turned to leave.

"'Night," she echoed, watching him go.

And then the door closed.

Sighing, she fell on the bed. She was in love with Rafe. It was all over but the screaming. Softly, she laughed at herself, at him, at the world. Oh, what was she going to do?

Chapter Nine

It was nail-biting time, but Rafe wasn't thinking about that. He'd really wanted to win the competition, but recently he'd discovered he wanted something more. He wanted Shelley.

The feeling was growing inside of him and he couldn't stop thinking about it. He liked women. He liked dating. He liked flirting and having other intimacies. But he'd never wanted a woman for his own, to be with him for the rest of his life—never, that is, until now.

Actually, she'd been around most of his life. She'd been a part of his life almost from the beginning. And now he wanted to make sure she stayed there, permanently and firmly. He wanted guarantees, because for some reason, he suddenly couldn't imagine life without her.

This morning he found himself walking in the gentle radiance of that new realization, smiling at everyone he met. He was feeling good. *Like I'm drunk on love,* he thought to himself. It sounded stupid—but it sounded right.

At breakfast, Shelley sat across the table from him and he couldn't concentrate on anything but her. The sunlight streaming in from the tall windows behind them turned her hair to gold. Her slow smile and almond-shaped eyes made his blood dance in his veins. She was so familiar, and yet, so new. And he wanted her more than he'd ever wanted anything else in his life.

It looked to be a long morning. After breakfast the team congregated in the conference room—going over last minute details, running through the items again and again and trying not to get too nervous. They were scheduled to be one of the last teams to perform. In the meantime, they had to sit and wonder how the others were doing. They were allowed to go and watch some of the other teams put on their submissions if they wanted to.

"I can't even imagine doing that," Candy said dramatically. "I'm sure everything I saw would make me feel like we were doing it all wrong, and then by the time our turn came I'd be a wreck."

Rafe had to agree with that to some extent, but he was feeling so restless, he had to get out and move.

"I'm going to take a walk," he said to the group, though everyone immediately understood whom he was talking to. "Anyone want to come?"

Shelley looked up and he caught the warmth in her eyes as they met his. He knew she felt the same way about him that he felt about her. Unless he was crazy. Unless he was misreading everything. If he could work up the courage to follow through—if he could work up the nerve—this was going to be a good thing.

"I can't go right now," she said regretfully. "I promised Dorie I would go over her lines with her one more time. You go ahead. Maybe I can meet you later."

He strolled out into the main hall, luxuriating in the glow of this new feeling. It was so new he still marveled at it. He'd never thought he would have anything like this. He'd never understood how men he knew suddenly felt they wanted to have one woman only for the rest of their lives. But now he knew. He had that feeling, too. And he knew that was what had been missing from his life.

He passed near one of the halls where the competition was going on and he paused, looking in. There was Jason McLaughlin on the stage. This had to be the McLaughlin Management entry. He shook his head. This ought to be good. Silently he slipped into the hall and took a seat near the back.

It only took a few moments for him to realize they were doing his idea. There it was, right on the stage. Jason was playing the part he should have been playing, directing the others in preparing to lobby hard for circumstances conducive for a winning bid on the Quarter Season Ranch.

At first, he couldn't believe it. His mind kept trying

to find reasons this couldn't be true. But he finally had to admit it to himself. They had stolen his idea. How could that be? Turned to stone, Rafe sat perfectly still, staring at the stage and unable to look away.

Shelley took a short turn out into the lobby, hoping she would catch a glimpse of Rafe somewhere, but he was nowhere to be seen. Instead she found Quinn coming her way. His hair was combed off his face and his clothes looked clean and pressed. Funny how little things like that could make such a difference in a man. Today, he looked like someone worth knowing.

"Quinn!" she said. "Good to see you again. How are you?"

"I'm okay, I guess." He stopped to grin at her, his hands shoved down into the pockets of his jeans.

"Did you come to watch the competition?"

"Yeah. Matt told me to come and right now, I'm doing whatever Matt tells me to."

"Good thinking." She smiled at him. "Listen, weren't you in a band in the old days? How's the band going?"

He gave her a quizzical look. "The band broke up over a year ago. I've been getting a few gigs on my own. Now and then." He shrugged, looking away. "Things are a bit tight in the music world right now."

"Oh. Well. Have you thought about trying something else?"

"No." He frowned at her as if she just didn't get it. "How can I do something else? Music is my life."

She offered him a smile. "If your life keeps trying to starve you to death, it might be time to start thinking about dumping it for a new life."

She could tell by the look on his face that he didn't much care for her advice.

"Well, right now my life is going to change anyway." He grimaced. "I'm going to get stuck in that little podunk town, Chivaree."

"Hey, I'll have you know Chivaree isn't so bad." She almost laughed aloud to think that she was the one saying such a thing. Defending Chivaree, imagine that. "It's grown a lot lately. We've even got a new TidyMart."

"Hey, that's exciting."

"And some big box stores, and the latest in fast food cuisine drive-thrus."

"I can tell I'm going to feel right at home."

She made a face at him. "Your sarcasm is uncalled for, Quinn. I think you're really going to be surprised at how much you like it in Chivaree."

"Yeah, maybe." His eyes brightened. "Hey, Shelley. Sorry about ditching you the other day." He grinned at her suddenly. "That was some driving you did. I thought you were going to catch me for a moment, there."

"I still don't get why you were avoiding me that way."

"Listen, you never know. Those gangsters I was running from are smart. They could send you or someone like you in to trap me. I couldn't take the chance. I've been ditching everyone for weeks."

"Well, they haven't caught you yet. You've still got your legs."

"Yup, still got 'em. With Matt helping me, I might be able to keep 'em."

She laughed and let him go on in to look for Matt. Surveying the room, and then the hallway, she still didn't see Rafe. Frowning, she went back to join the others.

The McLaughlin presentation was over. People were leaving, and Rafe still sat where he was, thunderstruck. He could hardly believe what he had just witnessed. How could this have happened?

The ranch sale prospect had been leaked to him in confidence by a very close friend who was involved in the proceedings and had authorized him to use it if he wanted to. Therefore he knew no one else knew about it except those on the Allman A team. And now, it seemed, someone on the McLaughlin team.

Jason had spotted him and was coming his way. Then he was standing in front of him, smirking with obnoxious triumph.

"How did you like it?" he asked, looking malicious. "Did you think I did your idea justice?"

Rafe just stared up at him and didn't answer for a long moment. "Who told you?" he asked at last, his voice hoarse. "Who gave you that plan?"

Jason's grin got wider. "I can't really tell you that. I wouldn't want to get her into trouble. But I think you know who I'm talking about, don't you?" He shook his head. "I've always had a special bond with this woman. There's just something between the two of us that won't be denied. She tries, of course. But when I ask her for something I need, she gives. She's all about giving, isn't she?" His eyes gleamed maliciously.

Rafe still couldn't believe it. It couldn't be true. And whether it was true or not, he wanted to kill Jason anyway. So he started up, ready to go after him, but someone grabbed his arms from behind.

"Hey," Matt said, appearing just in time to stop him from doing something very stupid. "I don't think that would be a good way to earn any points for the team, do you?"

Rafe turned on him. For once in his life he was furious with his brother.

"Leave me alone," he ordered, shaking off Matt's restraining hands.

When he turned back, Jason was gone. Glaring at Matt, he left the room as well, heading out into the street. He had to get some fresh air and get this dead feeling out of his system.

It was time to go on stage. Shelley's knees were knocking but she forced herself to ignore that. She was going to do a good job of this if it killed her.

"Where's Rafe?" she said urgently. He hadn't come back from his walk and that had been over an hour ago.

Candy shrugged.

Shelley went to the door and looked out into the

larger hall, only to find Rafe's sister Jodie and her fiancé, Kurt McLaughlin, coming toward the conference room.

"Jodie!" she cried, glad to see the woman who had been her best friend since early childhood.

Laughing, they hugged and looked at each other as though they hadn't seen each other in ages instead of just a few days.

"I can't believe you came for this!"

"Well, Kurt and I were sitting there at your mom's café having breakfast and wondering how things were going here and, all of a sudden, Kurt said, 'Why don't we just go and see for ourselves?' So we took the kid over to stay with Rita and here we are."

"I'm so glad you came. I just hope we don't make you sorry."

"Don't even think that way. You guys are going to do great."

That was the hope, but things were so nerve-racking now that Shelley couldn't really think straight. All she knew was, it was time to present. Looking around she saw with relief that Rafe had finally showed up. Then, moments later, they were marching into the hall, ready to take the stage.

All in all, the team was pretty happy with the way things went. The skit went off great. Candy didn't fall down and nobody knocked over any scenery. The VCR worked fine and the piece of videotape went over well.

As the moderator, Shelley started the presentation off. She stood to the side as the invisible narrator, explaining what was going on, interspersing a few jokes, which actually elicited a few laughs. Candy was great as the program coordinator and Rafe was convincing as the traditional skeptic who was won over in the end.

They wrapped it up and the judges left. And they hugged each other in relief and happiness that the ordeal was mostly over. Shelley looked around for Rafe and, when she found him, she threw her arms around his neck and gave him a hug as well. Even with all the talk and laughter around them, she noticed that his reaction wasn't all she could have hoped for.

But there was no time to ask him about it. They were due in the auditorium for the awards ceremony and they had to hurry over. The teams had been assigned to seating areas and they were all given pompoms with their team's colors on the way in. As leader of her team, Shelley had to direct the cheers. Even those were a part of the competition, and she did her part with suitable enthusiasm. When she returned to her seat, she found herself sitting between Jaye and Candy. Rafe was sitting two rows back with his brother and sister, and when she looked back, he didn't seem to notice her.

She was getting a bad feeling and it was growing. Something was wrong and there was no way to get him alone to find out what. The first speaker was funny and the second told a touching story of faith and hope, but Shelley didn't hear much of either. All she could think about was Rafe and his sudden coolness. Was it just because the weekend was ending and he wanted to get back to normal? She couldn't believe that. Not after the way they had connected last night.

Finally it was time for the awards. They sat on tenterhooks as the moderators started with tenth place and slowly worked their way toward the top. Jason's company won fifth place. But when second was called and it still wasn't Allman Industries, the tension was so taut it almost killed them all. They held their breath.

"And first place, for the best exploration of the theme of trading places with the boss, goes to…Allman Industries!"

They went crazy then, jumping up and down, whooping and hollering. They were actually going to take that huge trophy back to Chivaree with them. It was a wonderful moment. Shelley and Rafe went up together to accept the top prize, and they each made a short statement. And for those few moments, they were both grinning from ear to ear.

They had already reserved a banquet room in the hotel dining room for their end-of-competition party and all started heading that way, pushing their way through the crowd to get there. Shelley took a detour to her room to freshen up a bit, then took the elevator back down and started for the dining area. And there, standing at the checkout desk with his bags in tow, was Rafe.

She headed right toward him.

"Where are you going?" she asked him in amazement. "We won! Don't you want to celebrate?"

He turned to look at her, his dark eyes remote. "I've got some thinking to do," he told her.

She went very cold inside. "What do you mean?"

He shook his head. "Don't worry, Shelley. It's just me. I've got to think some things over. Get my head straight. It's a long drive back to Chivaree. I'll have a lot of time to do it." He gave her a fleeting smile, picking up his bags and turning toward the entry. "Talk to you tomorrow," he said.

And he was gone.

Shelley stood staring after him. Something had happened. But what?

Hurrying to the dining room, she sought out Matt, who was talking to Jodie.

"Rafe has gone home," she told them. "What's wrong?"

Matt looked surprised, then swore softly. "Oh, that idiot. He shouldn't let it get to him like that."

Shelley shook her head, still puzzled. "Let what get to him?"

"You haven't heard? Jason McLaughlin's team did what I guess was the idea Rafe wanted to do with your team. He sat there in the audience and watched them do it. He seemed pretty upset."

She frowned, shaking her head. "I still don't get it."

"The plan about preparing a frontal assault on getting hold of Quarter Season Ranch?" Jodie explained. "It seems Jason's people put it on pretty much the way Rafe had meant to do it. It was obvious to him that someone gave them the plan."

"Oh, no!" Shelley gasped, knowing that would infuriate Rafe. She wished she could go to him. Why hadn't he told her? "Oh, my gosh. No wonder he's upset."

"If it had been anyone but Jason McLaughlin..." Matt said, shaking his head.

"But they didn't win," Shelley pointed out. "They didn't come anywhere near winning. We won." She thought for a moment, frowning worriedly. "Well, I can understand why Rafe was angry. But why do I get the impression that he's blaming me?"

Matt shrugged, hesitated, then told her point blank. "From what I gathered of the conversation I heard, Jason implied he'd obtained the whole plan for the presentation...from you."

She froze. "From me?"

"He didn't?" Jodie said quickly.

"No." She shook her head, frowning with bewilderment. "I never breathed a word of it to anyone."

Jodie shrugged, though she looked relieved. "Well, let him go stew for a while. He'll come back to his senses soon enough."

Shelley was torn. Part of her wanted to go after him—but that was pretty silly. She wouldn't find him until she got back to Chivaree. Besides, she couldn't leave. She was still the boss until the end of the conference and she had the other teammates to think about. So she joined the others in celebrating and tried not to think about Rafe.

Of course, that was impossible. But the more she thought about him, the more she got a little angry herself. He didn't really think she would betray him that way, did he? If he did, he had no faith in her at all. That didn't sit well. In fact, she was getting downright furious about it.

Still, she was determined not to let Rafe's actions dull the pleasure she took in the win. After all, this was a credit to her to some extent. And she was proud of it. She'd proved that she could do things that she hadn't thought she could do. She was sure that her life was going to take a turn for the better after this. Unless...

Unless Rafe decided he couldn't stand her after all and never wanted to speak to her again. A queasy feeling swept through her at the thought, but she pushed it away. She just couldn't believe that could happen. They'd been so good together!

She wasn't going to let anything destroy this day. Pasting a smile on her face, she joined in the general hilarity and tried to have a good time. She would think about Rafe later. She wasn't going to be a victim of circumstances this time. She would think of something.

Chapter Ten

Rafe had a sick feeling in the pit of his stomach as he turned his car onto the highway. He hated that horrible empty feeling. It reminded him of something but he didn't know what. He frowned, trying to place it. Whatever it was, he didn't want to go there.

Suddenly he had a flashback to the way the house felt, the way his stomach felt, the day of his mother's funeral. That was it. A swell of nausea hit him and he cursed, fighting it back. He wasn't going to let himself feel this way. There was no reason for it. This was nothing like losing his mother. Nothing else had ever hurt so much and nothing ever would.

Still, he knew now what it came from: trusting, caring, believing and having all those things thrown back

in your face. In other words, betrayal. Loving and losing. Or something like that. Where was little Miss Analyze Everything to dig the truth of this out of him?

Maybe he'd been right to hold off the way he always
had, to protect himself. If this was what you got when
you opened yourself up, he wasn't sure it was worth it.
Suddenly the words of wisdom he'd heard years before
from a friend echoed in his ears.

"If you don't want your heart broken, don't fall in love."

Words to live by.

Good thing that hadn't happened yet. Good thing
he'd been forced to come face-to-face with the reality
that Shelley might not ever be able to love him the way
he would need her to—if he did fall for her.

He didn't want to think about Shelley. And yet, he
knew she was all he was going to think about all the way
back into town. Pressing down on the accelerator, he
headed for home.

"Ah, forget him," Candy advised with a wave of her
hand as they stood in line at the hotel checkout, ready
to pack up their cars and turn toward Chivaree. "Men
are all the same. Don't take any one of them seriously.
Two-timing louses."

Shelley stopped. Something inside her was rebelling.
Candy sounded very much like the things she used to say
herself. But this wasn't like that. Rafe wasn't like that.

Oh, stop it! You've been wrong before, haven't you?
What makes you think you could be right this time?

Yes, she had been wrong before. But she'd learned something here this weekend. She'd been put in the position where she had to try to do something she didn't think she could do. And she'd done a pretty darn good job of it. If she hadn't tried it, she wouldn't know it was possible. She wouldn't know how far she could go.

She'd chickened out before. She'd turned and walked away when things got tough. How would she ever face herself again if she did that now? No. She had to reach out. She wasn't going to give up on him, not this easily. If she truly loved Rafe, she had to go after him. Even if she was risking everything to do it.

She said goodbye to Matt before departing. "I hope this works out, you bringing Quinn to Chivaree," she said. "I hope he doesn't disappoint you."

Matt shrugged. "That's really not the point," he said. "I just want to do what I can to help him. And in the meantime, he might be able to help me more than he knows in finding my baby."

"So you're seriously looking?"

Matt nodded. "I've got to. That baby is out there somewhere and I have to make sure it's being cared for."

She understood that and thought all the better of Matt for it. But she was afraid his search was going to be long and lonely.

"And Shelley," he said, turning back and smiling at her warmly, then giving her another bear hug. "I don't think I've thanked you for finding Quinn and doing all you could to help me. I want you to know how much I appreciate it."

"No problem," she said, her eyes misting. "I wish you all the luck in the world."

She drove back to Chivaree with Jaye Martinez riding along. The B team hadn't placed, but they'd had a lot of fun and Jaye gave her all the details all the way home. She was talking so much she didn't seem to notice that Shelley barely said a word.

Her mind was racing, thinking over all the angles. It was all very well to make plans to go after Rafe—but if he hated her now for something she hadn't done, maybe he wasn't worth pursuing. But she refused to believe that.

When you got right down to it, there might be more than met the eye. There was her past, after all. Maybe he'd finally digested what she'd done, how she'd been with Jason when it was so wrong. Maybe he'd come face-to-face with the whole picture and he just couldn't accept it. Maybe he'd decided she wasn't worth the effort or the emotional currency.

Maybe—if she didn't want to risk being cut to the quick by finding out what he really thought of her— maybe she ought to leave well enough alone and just accept things as they were.

But she couldn't.

She ached to see the light of pure affection in his gaze again. She loved the man. And she wanted him to love her.

But she wasn't desperate. No, sir. She'd learned a lot this weekend. She'd done a good job and she was darn proud of it. She'd proven her worth to herself. Never again would she feel the need to find some man to hang her life on, the way she'd tried to with Jason.

She certainly wasn't looking for another Jason to undermine her self-confidence.

Oh, yeah? a little voice in her head said mockingly. *Then why'd you go ahead and fall in love with Rafe Allman?*

"Because he's different," she muttered aloud. "He's worth fighting for." Then her mouth tilted in a tiny smile, because she knew she was right.

Monday morning in Chivaree usually meant a cup of steaming coffee at Millie's Café, and that was where Rafe ended up.

Millie greeted him with her usual friendly smile as he took a stool at the long counter. Most seats were filled and the place buzzed with casual conversation. The smell of coffee and bacon filled the warm air. Millie took his order from the other side of the counter and he leaned close as she wrote down his request for a bagel and a cup of black coffee.

"Hey, Millie," he said as she started to move away. "Did you know I spent the weekend with your daughter?"

"You did *what?*" she demanded, swinging back to face him, her still-pretty face registering astonishment.

He gave her his slow grin. "We were both at the conference in San Antonio," he said.

"Ah." She relaxed. "I didn't think it could have been

anything more romantic," she admitted. "You two have been at each other's throats all your lives. I can't count the number of times she came home when she was a kid, yelling about 'that darn Rafe Allman' and whatever you'd done now."

"'That darn Rafe Allman.'" He nodded, smiling ruefully. "Yup, that's me."

Millie obviously needed to get to other customers, but she lingered, looking at Rafe as though she could read the edginess in him. "What's the matter, honey?" she said. "Somethin' got you spooked?"

He smiled at her, but instead of answering, he asked, "You knew my mother pretty well, didn't you?"

She reached out and touched his arm with a soft hand that managed to convey understanding along with sympathy. "The two of us didn't see much of each other in those last few years, but there was a time when we were real good friends."

Rafe stared at her. Why had he brought this up? He wasn't sure. But she seemed to find it a natural enough question.

"I always thought her going so soon affected you the most," she said musingly. "You were her special one, you know. And when we lost her, you seemed to pull back into a shell for the longest time." She shrugged and smiled at him. "I'm so glad you finally found your way. From what I hear, you're doing real well at that business of your father's."

She ruffled his hair as though he were still that little boy.

"I know your mother is looking down right now and she's real proud of you," she said, a slight catch in her voice. With a quick smile, she turned to get him his coffee.

He watched as she drifted on to serve coffee to someone else. She moved with sure and steady charm, topping off one customer's cup, stopping to say a word to another. What exactly had he wanted from her? Sympathy? She'd given that. She always had. Despite the animosity that sometimes simmered between him and Shelley, he'd often looked to Millie for a little mothering in the old days. Funny how easily you forgot those things as you grew up and left childhood behind. He hadn't thought about that for years.

He shook his head ruefully. Millie was a nice lady but her daughter was messing with his mind right now. He should find a means of forgetting about her. There had to be a way.

"You look like a man who could use a piece of pie."

He looked up, startled, and found a new young waitress with the name "Annie" on her label pin standing over him, waving the aforementioned pie. It was cherry and she'd added a little mound of vanilla ice cream for good measure.

"Uh, no, thanks," he said, shaking his head. "I didn't order pie."

"I know that, but honestly, this one's left over," she said, plopping it down in front of him. "It won't fit in the display case. I thought you might like it."

He gazed at her quizzically. Her dark hair curled out about her pretty, friendly face and her protruding stomach showed that she was about six months pregnant. "I can afford to buy my own pie, you know. If I should want some."

She made a face. "Boy, talk about looking a gift horse in the mouth. You're not very good at accepting favors, are you?"

Her smile was infectious, but he was resisting. He was, after all, in the middle of his great dilemma. Was he or was he not going to try to have a relationship with Shelley? "I've got thinking to do here."

"Thinking goes better with a piece of pie." She pushed the plate more solidly in front of him. "What I know from experience is this—a man who looks so sad while he's thinking could use a piece of pie." She nodded knowingly. "And I also know that he's probably thinking about things he said to his woman, and how to get back into her good graces without losing too much of his dignity." She shrugged and leaned toward him over the counter. "I've got one word for you, mister," she said confidentially. "Red roses."

She was persistent. He had to give her that. He wasn't sure if it was an endearing quality—or just plain annoying.

"That's two words."

"But one concept."

"True." He gave her a twisted grin. "How do you know I was the one in the wrong?"

"Are you kidding?" She turned to go. "Does it matter?"

"What do you mean? Of course it matters."

She looked back at him, hesitated, then gave him one more piece of advice. "This isn't likely to be a situation where logic and justice apply. The only thing you need to think about is—how are you gonna make her smile?" She shrugged. "Red roses."

With one last arch look, she was gone. But Rafe hardly noticed. He was having an epiphany.

He was an idiot.

Of course, that wasn't news, but in the current situation he hadn't realized just how stupid he was. Here he'd been angry because Jason stole his idea and put it on at the conference, and he'd been resentful of old ties Shelley had with Jason. All that had him all tied up in jealous knots. And he thought that was his problem.

But that wasn't it at all. He knew damn well that Shelley hadn't given his idea to Jason. And she'd proved to him again and again that she didn't want anything to do with the man. So what was his problem now? He was just acting like a big baby, wanting the whole world to shower him with some sort of sympathy. Wasn't he?

And why was he letting himself devolve into this infantile state? Fear. Pure fear. And an excuse to set himself up to be left behind again. He glanced up toward the heavens. Millie was sure his mother was up there, looking down. What the hell—maybe she was. Just to be safe, he smiled for a second. And felt a flood of warmth and well-being.

"Hi, Mom," he mouthed. Then he picked up a fork and started in on the cherry pie.

It was almost an hour later when Rafe strode confidently into the lobby of Allman Industries and met his sister Jodie coming out of the personnel office.

"Hey, where've you been?" she said. "Pop's here and he's been holding court up in the boardroom, congratulating the team and gloating over the trophy. He's happy as a pig in a new load of Galveston mud. You ought to go on up there and join in on the general festivities."

He grimaced. "If I must," he told her.

But he did want to. He took the ancient elevator up and got off at the top floor, then met most of the team going the other way.

"Hey. Is it all over?"

"Pretty much," Candy said, grinning at him. "But Shelley's still in there with your old man. Where were you?"

"I got delayed."

"You gotta get in there and see how good that trophy looks in the middle of that table. *Hoo-eee!*"

"It's going to look even better in the trophy case," he told her.

She frowned. "What trophy case?"

"The one we're going to build."

Her face cleared. "Oh. Right." She grinned as he went on toward the boardroom.

He pushed open the door. His father was sitting at the

head of the table. Gaunt and gray-haired, Jesse Allman still had the look of a force to be reckoned with.

"Hey, Pop," Rafe said, sliding into a chair to his right. "I hear you're pretty partial to this old tin can we brought back for you."

He glanced at Shelley, hoping to read in her eyes what she was thinking, surprised at the way his heart was thumping at the sight of her. She was standing, holding a stack of folders to her chest, as though she was about to go. But her eyes were shaded and he couldn't see a thing there. He looked away, heart sinking, and hardly heard his father at first.

"Yeah, that's one beautiful trophy y'all won," Jesse Allman was saying, nodding at Shelley approvingly. "I'm a happy man today, I can tell you." He grinned, his gold tooth flashing. "Good thing I got Matt to go down and help y'all out. That was the smartest thing I ever did. You can always count on Matt to come through."

Shelley stiffened, glancing quickly at Rafe, then away again. Should she say something? No, it really wasn't her place. But if Rafe was just going to let this go...

"Hold on just a darn minute, Pop," Rafe said to her surprise. His expression was casual, benevolent, but she had a feeling there was something less benign going on under the radar. "Where'd you get the idea that Matt had anything to do with this?"

"I sent him down there, didn't I?"

"Sure," Rafe said slowly, his gaze meeting hers for only a second, then moving on. "And having him show up was a morale boost, no doubt about it." He hesitated, then charged on. "But he was taking care of some private business and he wasn't even there until he came at the end to watch us put on the performance. The rest was all up to one person." Rafe turned and looked at Shelley. "And you're lookin' at her right now."

Jesse looked annoyed. "Well, I know she did a real good job. I thanked her plenty and I told her she's gettin' a bonus, just like all a' them."

Rafe shook his head, his jaw set, his gaze holding hers. "Not good enough."

Jesse frowned at his son. He wasn't used to being contradicted by anyone, much less one of his children. "What the hell you talkin' about, boy?"

Rafe wasn't going to be intimidated by his father's usual temper. "I'm talking about the fact that Shelley Sinclair took charge, fought me off, brought in a killer idea and pulled off a show-stopper of a submission to the competition. She showed every characteristic of a damn good manager."

He was still holding her gaze and she was breathless.

"She's getting more than a bonus," he went on confidently, "she's getting a promotion. And we're darn lucky to have her working for us."

Shelley was tingling with the praise. Having her hard work recognized would be wonderful. But somehow bittersweet. And suddenly she realized that she would rather have one warm and loving smile from Rafe than all the bonuses and promotions in the world.

"Well, okay," Jesse was saying reluctantly, his brows knit. "That's good. I'll talk to Matt and see if he knows somewhere we can use her."

"No," Rafe said, his voice low but strong. "I'll take care of it."

Jesse reared back. "Now you just hold on. I'm the president of this company…"

"And I'm basically the CEO." He finally tore his gaze from hers and looked at his father. "And I'm making a command decision. I want Shelley in charge of research and development planning."

"What? She's not qualified for that!"

"Pop, it's my decision." He rose and stood beside Shelley. "We're going to go now and talk it over. I'll present our offer to her and see if she accepts it." He put a hand on the small of her back and began to escort her out of the boardroom. "I'll let you know if she takes the position. See you, Pop."

Jesse was muttering something malevolent but they didn't stop to hear what it was. Shelley's head was spinning. She was glad Rafe had finally let his father know he wasn't going to take his browbeating with a shrug and a smile any longer. That was a very good thing. And she was gratified that he was thinking of new positions for her. She'd been working toward that for a long time. But that still didn't resolve things between the two of them, and when she looked at his face, she couldn't see anything there that reassured her. She knew now that he wanted her promoted, but did he still want her in his arms?

They took the elevator down to the floor where her desk was, along with five other women in the section. Rafe talked quickly, outlining what her new position would require and sketching in the duties and new pay schedule. Shelley nodded but she only half heard what he was saying. It was a fabulous offer, of course. Better than she'd ever dreamed of. Better than her ambitions had allowed her to think of. And she was going to turn it all down.

The elevator came to her floor and they stepped out, pausing in the empty lobby.

"Well?" he was saying. "What do you think? Does it sound like something you would be interested in?"

She looked up and searched his face. He really did think this was going to make up for everything, didn't he? He would hold out this reward, this wonderful chance, and she would take it. They would be even. He wouldn't have to worry about her anymore. He could go on as though nothing had happened between them this weekend. He wouldn't have to open up his heart and commit to anything. No risks.

She knew about that. She'd lived a lot of her own life the same way. But it was no good.

"It's a fantastic opportunity," she told him. "But I can't take it."

"What are you talking about?"

"I can't work here with you."

He frowned, running a hand through his dark hair. "Shelley, I thought we'd worked through all that old garbage…"

"We did. This is new garbage."

She tried to smile but it was a weak effort. Here it was. Did she have the courage to do this? Was she going to reach out and take her chance, or let it slip away?

Taking a very deep breath, she squared her shoulders and held her chin high, meeting his dark gaze with her own clear eyes and praying that her voice wouldn't break.

"You see, Rafe, I'm…I'm in love with you."

His handsome face registered shock, crushing her. He hadn't expected this, had he? And if he loved her, even a little bit, would it have been such a surprise?

"I think you can understand that it would be impossible to work here with you under the circumstances. I mean, since you don't love me."

He took her by the shoulders, staring down into her face. "Who says I don't love you?" he demanded, his voice strangely hoarse.

"Well, I thought…"

"You've got to cut me some slack, Shelley," he said. "I've never been in love before. I'm just feeling my way here."

A delicious sense of hope shivered through her, but she held it back, still too wary to let herself believe in it. He'd only said he wasn't sure—hadn't he?

"So, you're thinking that maybe…?"

He frowned down at her, troubled but strangely elated at the same time. There was no getting around it. He could try as hard as he might, but he couldn't stop himself from loving her. He knew it had to be love because it felt so ridiculous—and there didn't seem to be anything he could do to stop it.

"No, I'm not saying 'maybe.' Shelley, I can't think about anything but you. I dream about you at night. You fill my head and my heart like no woman ever has before. All I want is to be near you. All I think about is how to make you happy. I've got to think that it's love."

She was laughing softly, shaking her head. "Either that or a bad case of the flu," she said lovingly. Her heart was singing. "But I'm ready to risk calling it love if you are."

His large hands cupped her face. "I don't have any choice," he admitted, feeling helpless, looking helpless. "Shelley, I love you."

With a cry of joy, she threw her arms around his neck and he held her tightly, raining soft kisses on her pretty face. Then his mouth found hers and their kiss deepened, growing as their love ignited the passion that was lurking between them.

The elevator doors opened and suddenly Jesse Allman was there, glaring at them as he began to make his way into the lobby, his cane tapping.

"I said it was okay to promote her," he grumbled. "You're taking this a little far, aren't you?"

They pulled apart and Rafe grinned at his father. "I'm taking it all the way, Pop. I'm going to marry her, or die trying."

Jesse harrumphed and went on his way. "Better check with Matt before you get yourself into anything you can't get out of," he said back over his shoulder.

Shelley gasped and looked at Rafe, but he was laughing, so she joined him. She was just too happy to let anything mar the feeling right now.

"Come on," he said, pulling her back into his arms. "Let's go someplace where we can explore this new love thing and all its ramifications without being interrupted."

"Okay, boss," she said, touching his face with her fingertips. "You lead the way."

"Oh, wait," he said, reaching into the pocket of his suit coat. "I forgot to give you this." He pulled out a bedraggled red rosebud with a rather crushed and broken stem and handed it to her. "It was the only one I could find in this whole darn town."

She took it gingerly. "Where did you get it?" she asked.

He looked a bit embarrassed. "Remember Mrs. Curt, the fifth-grade teacher? Her yard. And I had to fight her aged bloodhound to get back out of that place alive."

Shelley laughed. It looked a bit the worse for having been banged around in his pocket, but it was still a beautiful shade of red.

"Why?" she asked him, shaking her head.

"I was told it was required," he said innocently. "Don't you like it?"

She looked down, biting her lip. "I love it," she said, her voice breaking. She knew she would preserve it forever as a token of this wonderful day. Looking up, she gave him a radiant smile, her eyes misting with unshed tears.

He nodded, satisfied. "I guess it works after all," he said. "It's supposed to symbolize something." He realized exactly what as he was talking. "My heart," he said as the thought occurred to him. "It's yours."

She held it close, smiling lovingly at him. "Thanks," she said. "Now that's an offer I really can't refuse."

* * * * *

The Boss's
Special Delivery

Chapter One

Annie Torres was going to faint. The signs were all there. Staring hard at her order pad, she tried to fight the feeling.

Just give me one more minute, she begged silently. *Just let me get into the break room.*

"Oh, wait," her customer was saying. "I think I want a side of fries with that. And can I get a serving of blue cheese dressing to go with the fries?"

The room was starting to turn, very slowly, but it was turning. She felt clammy. It was only a matter of seconds. Flipping her book closed, she started to step away, desperate to get to the break room.

"Miss? Wait a minute. I forgot about dessert. Do you have any of that great fresh peach pie today?"

It sounded like the woman was talking to her from the end of a tunnel. The words were echoing in her head and something was pounding in her ears. She had to get out of there. She tried to turn back, but it was too late. She was wilting like a rose in the hot summer sun. It was all over.

"Hey."

She opened her eyes. There were faces all around, staring down at her. Something in her wanted to laugh. They looked so funny. Then she realized she was lying on the floor of Millie's Café and it didn't seem so funny any longer.

Each face had a mouth and each mouth was moving but she couldn't tell what they were saying. She closed her eyes, wishing they would all go away and leave her alone. Her head was throbbing.

"I'll handle this."

Finally a deep, masculine voice stood out from the babble and she felt cool, strong hands probing for injuries and testing her reactions.

"Does anything hurt?" he asked her.

She shook her head and regretted it, because her head hurt like crazy. But it wasn't from hitting the floor, it was just a headache.

"Sorry," she muttered, trying to get up. "I'd better get back to work."

"Not likely." Suddenly she was being swung up into the arms of what had to be a fairly strong man.

"Hey," she said weakly, pushing back and trying to look up into his face.

"Just relax, honey," he said in a soothing voice. "I've got you."

"But I don't need getting," she protested, pushing ineffectively against his shoulder with her hands.

"Don't try to talk," he told her as he carried her through the crowded café. "You're obviously delirious."

He said it with a touch of humor, so she didn't take it seriously. He was probably trying to put her at ease about the situation. That wasn't necessary, because she didn't need his help. Much.

Though she had to admit, it felt so good to have such strong arms holding her. They were protective. Safe. And from what she could feel of him, pretty darn sexy. Which was exactly why she had to resist. If he would just put her down and let her get oriented...

But at least he knew where to take her. In just seconds she was in the break room and he was lowering her to the couch.

"Thank you, ladies," he said as someone handed him a damp cloth and a cup of water. "Just give us some room, please. Let me give her a quick examination. She'll be good as new in no time."

Bossy guy. As far as she was concerned, he could take that take-charge attitude and—

"Okay, Doctor," someone was saying.

Actually, it might have been Millie. Annie's eyes were closed and it was just too hard right now to open them and take a look. But if Millie was giving him permission to handle this, maybe she could relax a little. Millie was her boss, the owner of the café, and a thoroughly decent woman. Annie had come to realize lately that thoroughly decent people were hard to find and worth their weight in gold once discovered.

And he was a doctor, anyway. She relaxed a little more. She was more disposed to trust a doctor than she was to trust most men. After all, there was that Hippo-cratic oath thing.

"Just give a holler if you need anything," Millie added.

"Will do."

Annie finally got her eyes back open in time to see Millie leaving, and the very large man staying. As he continued to hover over her, he murmured something that made the others melt away. She appreciated that he'd dismissed the audience, because she'd had about enough of being the center of attention for a while.

Still, that meant she was alone with this man. Need-ing to reassert a little control of the situation, she pulled up to sit rather than staying down where he'd put her.

He didn't object. Instead, he put the cool cloth to her forehead, gave her a sip of water and then began taking her pulse. And finally her head cleared enough so that she could see straight again.

She looked him over, still groggy, head aching. Not bad, actually. He was handsome in a rugged, outdoorsy way—his thick hair dark and windblown looking, as though he'd just come in from chopping wood or chas-ing bears or something, and his eyes incredibly blue against his tanned skin. He looked familiar. She'd seen him in here at Millie's before. And she was pretty sure she'd seen him in years past. But it had only been a month since she'd come back to the Texas town of Chiv-aree and her ten or so years away had dimmed a lot of memories.

"How are you feeling?" he asked, studying her in a detached, clinical sort of way.

"Woozy."

He nodded and his eyes narrowed a bit. "Do you do this often?"

She struggled for normalcy. "Meet men by swooning into their arms?" she asked as impudently as she could manage. "No, as a matter of fact, you're my first."

He gave her an assessing look. "You're pregnant."

He said it calmly, but to her it sounded like an accusation, and she bristled. As an unwed mother-to-be, she bristled a lot lately.

"Really?" she responded quickly, straightening her shoulders as though she had to get ready for battle. "What was your first clue?"

He looked up and really met her dark gaze for the first time, really seemed to look into her eyes and see who she was. She had to stifle a shiver. She didn't think she'd ever seen bluer eyes.

But there was more. Something about him made her feel uncertain and a little self-conscious. He had the look of a man who did and said whatever occurred to him, without much worrying about what was appropriate to the occasion. If he saw something about her he liked…or didn't like…he was likely to be quite frank about it. And he proved she'd read him right with his next statement.

"You're also a smart aleck," he said dryly.

Still defensive, Annie stared right back at him. She had to make sure men like this knew she couldn't be intimidated. She'd had a lot of experience at this sort of thing lately. Learning how to protect herself by being a bit caustic hadn't come naturally, but she was learning.

"If I want character analysis, I'll go see a psychologist."

The corners of his mouth twitched. She wasn't sure if it was with humor or a quick irritation. Either way was okay with her—just so long as he realized she wasn't going to put up with any baloney from him—or any other man.

"Why pay for that when I'm prepared to analyze for free?" he said. Putting his head to the side, he pretended to study her. "Let's see if I've got a proper fix on you. You're headstrong, stubborn, sure you're usually right… and a hard worker."

His casual assumptions—as well as his cynical tone—were really annoying her, and she said the first thing that came to mind.

"So's your old man," she shot back.

His sudden grin was a stunner, white teeth flashing, eyes crinkling, and real humor lit up his face. "I didn't know you knew him."

Okay, there it was—the main thing she had to watch out for. Everything in her wanted to like him. He looked…well, nice. And that was even more dangerous than his undeniable sex appeal—the macho way he took charge so naturally; the breathtaking chest muscles that seemed to swell under his light polo shirt; the way he was poised, down on one knee before her, like a knight asking a lady for her scarf to wear into battle.

She blinked quickly and shook her head, furious at herself for letting her imagination run wild on that last one. What was she doing, sinking back into childhood? She'd spent a good part of her youth blocking out reality by creating a dream world in which she was a lost princess. She couldn't go back to that. Too much fantasy could corrupt her reasoning powers and that would be a gateway straight to the danger zone. She was a grown woman with a baby on the way and she couldn't indulge herself like this anymore. Life was tough—she had to be hard to survive it.

Still, that was difficult to do when the man she faced was so incredibly good-looking and dressed so well. Besides the blue polo shirt, he wore clean fashionable denim slacks that fit like a glove and a soft suede jacket that clung to him in all the right places. What a contrast to her slightly silly green waitress uniform. And also, what a clear picture of their different stations in life. He looked like he shopped at Neiman-Marcus. She looked like she hadn't shopped in years. Hardly princess material.

She looked away quickly, aware more than ever that they were alone. This was not a place she wanted to be. Besides, it was time she got back to work. Millie was shorthanded today and Annie didn't want to risk bad feelings at this job. She needed it badly, and there weren't many who would hire a woman almost seven months pregnant.

"May I go now?" she said, needing to ask as he was blocking her way.

He gazed at her levelly. "No, you may not. You're still pale and I don't like your pulse rate."

She flashed a quick glare his way. "There are things I don't like about you, but I've got the manners not to list them."

He made a comical face. "Impossible."

She frowned a little nervously. "What's impossible?"

"That there's something about me not to like." He

was grinning again. She really wished he wouldn't. "I'm a terrific guy. Everyone says so."

Great. That was all she needed. Not only was he incredibly handsome and a great dresser, he was popular, too. At least, if you asked him. Reaching up, she pushed her thick dark wavy hair back behind her ear.

"That's what happens when you depend on selective polling," she said coolly. Even if she looked like a waitress, she could act as snooty as any Dallas cattle heiress if she tried hard enough. "All the votes aren't in yet, mister."

One sleek dark eyebrow rose with just a touch of surprise. "Doctor," he corrected smoothly.

She blinked. "Doctor who?"

"No, that was the TV show. Just plain old Dr. Allman. Or better yet, Matt Allman."

She shook her head. Now he was being plain old annoying and he had to know it was bugging her. Was he doing it to put her down? Somehow she didn't really think so. It seemed more like teasing, like he thought he was being playful. Like he was attracted to her and—

No. Now that was going too far. Why would a man like this be attracted to a woman in ugly green who was carrying someone else's baby? That was just her fantasy side coming out again. She was going to have to learn to turn that little talent off.

"I should have known you were an Allman. I guess that explains it."

"Explains what?"

She flushed, not sure what to say. The Allmans had been one of the founding families of the town, but their reputation hadn't been good when she'd been here in the past. She always had the idea the Allmans were "this close" to being outlaws. Of course, that might have been pure gossip at the time, but something about the family always seemed to signal danger of one sort or another.

"That explains why you look as much like a rebel without a cause as you do a doctor," she said a bit lamely, knowing he was waiting for an answer.

"A rebel." He savored the word, eyes narrowing as though he saw himself from a distance. "I kind of like that."

"Of course you do. You're an Allman."

He thought for a moment, his penetrating gaze clearly taking stock of her. She stared right back at him, not giving an inch. But inside, she quivered, wondering what he saw. A mouthy waitress who ought to be more grateful for what he'd done to tend to her? A pain in the neck? A pitiful ragamuffin, her dark hair a tangled mess?

None of those things were good and she wished, suddenly, that she knew a way to act that wouldn't put her at odds with him. Sometimes it seemed she only had two speeds, mad attraction or complete hostility. And since she'd vowed she would never let herself get fooled by an attraction again, the tough-girl pose was just about all she had left.

But maybe that was okay. It gave her armor against falling for the sort of charm that had left her pregnant and alone. It helped let a man like this doctor know his handsome face and hunky physique weren't going to bowl her over any time soon. If she had to be hard and caustic to make that plain, so be it. Better he know right up front. Better they all know. And better that she keep in mind the consequences of letting silly romantic notions creep into her thinking.

"So I'm an Allman," he was saying, looking quizzical. "What exactly does that mean to you?"

She drew herself up a bit. "Do you really want to know?"

"Yes."

She sighed. "Okay. To me, growing up around here, the Allmans were cowboys, trending toward the wrong side of the law. The Allmans always seemed to be starting fights or causing trouble. Especially for the McLaughlins."

He laughed, and she flushed, not sure what he found so funny. He couldn't possibly know her relationship to the McLaughlins. No one knew. So that couldn't be it. Frowning, she went on.

"Now I come back to town and find the Allmans are the movers and shakers of the place. What happened?"

It was a remarkable transformation from what she'd seen. Those low-life Allmans now had a thriving company and the high-and-mighty McLaughlins had hit hard times. That had to be difficult for everyone concerned.

She'd been thirteen when her mother had finally told her that her father had been William McLaughlin, from the family she'd worked for years ago. And because that family was so important in Chivaree, she'd held the secret close and been proud of it. Watching McLaughlins whenever she came to town, she'd felt an identification with them that she couldn't communicate—and they had fascinated her.

Now, all alone with a baby coming, she'd come back instinctively to the place where her "family" lived, to find out a few things. First, was it true? Did she really have blood ties to these people? And second, would they accept her? Or would they want to deny that she had any right to their attention at all?

So far she hadn't decided exactly what she was going to do—which McLaughlin she would approach and what she would say when she did so. The man she'd been told was her father had died a few years before, so that bit of closure would be forever denied to her. But he'd had other children, three sons. What would they say when she showed up on their doorsteps?

Soon after she'd arrived in town, she'd found a way to insert herself into the McLaughlin consciousness. She'd seen a wanted notice for a once-a-week housekeeper at the McLaughlin Ranch, and she'd applied for the job right away. Since she was only working part-time here at Millie's, she had plenty of time for it, and the housekeeping job gave her a sort of foot in the door. The fact that she was working in a position very like what her mother had once had with the family was a little troubling. But she couldn't be choosy at this point. She needed to get the lay of the land. Time was moving on and a baby was coming. And she knew she was going to have to do something about that very soon.

"What's your name?" he was asking.

"Annie Torres." The first name was pinned to her uniform, but she wondered if he would recognize the last name. Probably not. After all, why would he remember the name of the McLaughlin housekeeper from so many years ago? The McLaughlins themselves hadn't.

"Nice to meet you, Annie," he said casually. "In time I hope you'll come to see that Allmans aren't so bad."

"But that doesn't mean you're now the good guys," she said hastily. "Just because you're rich and all."

"Oh? Why not?"

She shrugged, turning her palms up. "Leopards and zebras."

He looked as though he wasn't sure he'd heard correctly. "What?"

"Spots and stripes don't change that easily."

"Ah." He nodded wisely. "Wolves in sheep's clothing."

"Exactly right." She gave him a skeptical look. "For all we know, you could be playing possum."

He groaned. "Are you always this glib with the animal aphorisms?"

A small spark of satisfaction flared in her chest. She finally felt as though one of her barbs had hit home. "Not always. I'm as game for a good sports metaphor as the next girl."

"Good." He rose and held out a hand to her. "Because you're being traded."

"What?" For some reason, maybe because she was still trying to figure out what he was talking about, she meekly let him take her hand and pull her to her feet.

"How do you feel?" he asked, studying her eyes.

She took a deep breath. He hadn't let go of her hand, but maybe that was to help her steady herself. Frowning, she pulled her hand out of his and rubbed it against her skirt, trying to erase the delicious feeling his touch had given her.

"I'm fine," she said crisply. "I need to get back to work."

He shook his head. "Negative. I'm taking you in to my clinic. You need a thorough checkup."

"I *need* not to lose my job," she told him, trying to maneuver around him toward the door and failing to make any headway.

"You're quitting this job," he told her, looking intently into her eyes for a moment. "Doctor's orders."

This was crazy. It was all very well to tell her not to work too hard, to get plenty of rest and keep her feet up and so forth. But the fact remained that she had to make a living somehow. Lifting her chin, she glared at him defiantly.

"Doctors can throw their weight around all they want, but patients have still got to eat."

She turned toward the door but he moved to block her progress and she looked up, a little startled by how big he was, how wide his shoulders seemed. And how knowing his gaze seemed to be. Did this man ever have any doubts about anything?

"You'll eat," he said. "I've got another job for you. One that won't keep you on your feet all day."

She wondered why he so casually assumed she would trust him enough to hand over life's little decisions to him.

"And that would be…?"

"Office work. My office assistant abandoned me. She's gone back East to help her fiancé pass the New York state bar exam. I need someone to fill in until she gets back."

Office work. Air-conditioning. A soft, plush seat. Regular hours. It sounded heavenly. But it never paid as much as waiting tables and getting tips.

"How long will that be?" she asked anyway, tempted against her better judgment.

"At least three months." His grin had become endearingly crooked. "That fiancé of hers needs a lot of work and she's the determined type."

She looked at him curiously. "What makes you think I'd be good at doing the sort of office work you need done?"

He shrugged. "I've seen you working here with Millie over the last few weeks. Competence just radiates from you. Don't you know that?"

It was a nice compliment, but she hesitated, then shook her head.

"I can't quit here," she said, putting a hand on her rounded belly. "I'm totally dependent on what I make and I need to save for my recovery period after the baby comes."

His blue eyes darkened. "No husband handy?"

He asked it quietly, no moral judgment implied, and she felt a small twinge of gratitude for that. She'd spent too much emotional energy lately in resenting the looks and comments made by people once they realized her situation. No one could be more contemptuous of her idiocy in landing in this fix than she was. She didn't need to hear it from others. Lifting her head, she met his gaze with a steady look.

"No. I'm not married."

If anything, his gaze grew warmer. "No family of any sort?"

She shook her head. "My mother died about a year ago."

"And your father?"

"I don't have one."

He frowned. "Everyone has a father."

"Only in the biological sense," she said.

She could tell he didn't like that answer, but he let it go.

"How much do you make?"

She told him. It wasn't like it was a secret. Everyone knew how much this job took in. She didn't add the amount she made at her second job, but he didn't need to know that.

"You'll do better working for me." He told her a figure that got her attention. "And you'll get benefits, too. You'll need that for when you have the baby."

She shook her head. "My delivery fees will be covered." She hesitated only a second or two, then went on. "I'm considering giving my baby up for adoption. The lawyer will take care of everything."

The very air seemed to go still. And at the same time, something flashed across his face. He looked as though her statement had stunned him. His face was like stone but his eyes were blazing.

"What?" he said softly.

She licked her dry lips. She had expected surprise, maybe bemusement, but nothing like this.

"I think you heard me. Why the shock and amazement? I'm not married."

She hated having to explain. The pain of having to make this decision bled freshly every time. She threw up her hands, half a gesture of exasperation, half a plea for understanding.

"I want what's best for my baby. Adoption can be a

wonderful thing. A nice couple who can't have a child of their own would be a lot better for this child than anything I can promise."

She hated that she sounded defensive, but there it was.

The muscle at his jaw worked for a moment as his gaze seemed to cut through to her bones. Was it the fact that she was considering putting her baby up for adoption that was bothering him so much? She didn't know what else it could be. Something was sure going on inside him. Some emotional chord had been yanked with a vengeance. She watched curiously, wondering what he was thinking as his gaze dropped to study her rounded belly. But his eyes were cool and impenetrable and his face was giving nothing away.

"Let's go," he said shortly, putting a hand in the center of her back to help lead her out the door.

She balked. That hand felt too good—and too controlling at the same time. "Wait a minute. I'm feeling a bit bulldozed here."

He nodded. "You want some time to think it over?"

"Yes. That would be helpful."

His smile was humorless. "You'll have plenty of time in the car on the way to the clinic."

"But—"

"Am I going to have to pick you up and carry you again?"

She drew in her breath sharply. "No." Biting her lip, she let him lead her. After all, what choice did she have?

Chapter Two

"I hope you don't think I'm taking any clothes off."

The first thing Annie noticed when she and Matt arrived at the clinic was that the place was empty. It was getting late. Obviously, the staff had all gone home for the night. Still, it made her feel a bit awkward. Not to mention suspicious.

That was actually somewhat new for her, but she was learning. *Don't trust anyone, especially studly-looking men with flattering words and a roving eye.* She tugged her light sweater tightly around her shoulders and glared at Matt as though he were the archetypal representative of that very group.

"Because any test that needs me naked isn't going to happen," she added, just for emphasis.

To her surprise, instead of getting annoyed, he laughed out loud as he turned to look at her.

"No need for to strip down for this," he assured her.

Ushering her into the room where various types of medical examination machines stood around like alert soldiers, he glanced at the way she was hugging her clothes around herself.

"But tell me—do you usually bundle up as though expecting snow when you're preparing to be examined by a doctor?"

"Not with my *real* doctor," she said archly.

"What do you think I am?" he asked as he motioned for her to take a seat on the end of the table. "A phony doctor?"

"That remains to be seen."

Sliding the blood pressure cuff up her arm, he gave her a sardonic look. "So who is your *real* doctor?" he asked.

"Dr. Marin."

He nodded, adjusting the tester and inflating the cuff, then listening as he watched it count down.

"Ah yes, Raul Marin," he said as he released her again. "His son was a friend of mine in high school." He jotted down her blood pressure reading and turned to get the fetal monitor set up. "Well, if you prefer, I can take you over to his office. It's after office hours, but—"

"But that's just the point. I don't need a doctor. I need to go home."

She frowned. How had she let him talk her into coming here, anyway? What she said was true. She needed to go home, get into bed, pull the covers up…and wait for all this to end.

But her argument didn't seem to be swaying him at all.

"I think we can get a few tests in right now. Enough to reassure me that you and this baby are doing okay."

"Oh, well, as long as *you're* reassured, the world can rest easy tonight."

Her sarcasm fell on deaf ears. He jotted down some figures on a chart, then turned and motioned for her to lie back on the table.

"Let's see how that little guy is," he said.

"Little guy." She liked that. She'd purposefully avoided finding out the gender of her baby, and resisted the temptation to name the child. If she was going to give the baby up for adoption, becoming too close and intimate would just make things that much harder. But when he said "little guy," her heart skipped a beat and she felt a sudden surge of warmth that almost brought tears to her eyes. He was obviously ready to feel an easy affection for this new life she was carrying. She had to blink hard to keep from letting him see how that touched her.

"Okay, Doctor."

He glanced into her eyes. "Call me Matt."

She bit her lip. "How about Mr. Allman?"

A muscle twitched at his jaw. She was finally needling him just a little too much, and when he responded, there was a thread of annoyance in his tone.

"Whatever, Annie. Call me Dumbo if that makes you feel safer." He moved closer, freeing some cords that had become tangled. "Now just relax and we'll get this over with."

She put a hand over her belly, automatically protective. The baby was doing just fine. She was sure of it—as sure as she could be. She was taking all the right vitamins and appearing regularly for her checkups, even though it was difficult to pay for them. She might be seriously considering giving her baby up to someone else to raise, but that was because of how much she loved him…or her. She'd never felt so close to anything in her life as she felt to this baby.

"How much do you charge?" she asked warily as she watched him prepare the monitor. She had some money saved and she didn't want him to think she was expecting a handout.

He waved the question away. "First exams are freebies."

For some reason, that irritated her. She wasn't a charity case. She could pay her own way, even if it was hard sometimes.

"If you're giving people freebies all over the place," she said crisply, "I don't see how you're going to make enough to keep any sort of staff for long."

He looked up after strapping her up to the monitor and laughed aloud. "My God, I'm hiring someone who actually understands how things work. Keep this up and I'll have to make you office manager."

It was humiliating how those half-mocking words of praise made her glow with satisfaction. She had to cover that up quickly.

"You can't *make* me into anything."

He didn't bother to respond. He'd caught on long ago to the fact that most of her words didn't mean a thing and were just a way to keep him at arm's length. That was okay. Although he understood her need to protect herself, he just wanted to make sure that she didn't lose sight of what was important—the welfare of this baby she was carrying.

He'd noticed her over the last few weeks, whenever he'd stopped by Millie's for a quick bite. He'd been keeping an eye on the evidence of her baby's progress, though he'd never said anything to her until she'd dropped into a faint at his feet. She had a bright, intelligent look to her that he'd liked and he'd wondered about her. He'd noticed that there was no wedding ring and it reminded him of his own unsettling situation....

It had only been a few weeks since an old friend passing through the area had called and innocently asked him what had ever happened to Penny Hagar, a young woman Matt had dated in Dallas a couple of years before. And then he'd asked about the baby.

"Baby?" Matt had responded, startled. "What baby?"

That was the first hint he'd ever had that Penny had become pregnant during their relationship. Since that day, searching for Penny and her baby had begun to consume more and more of his time and energy. He'd hired a private investigator once his own efforts had come up dry. So far, even the professional wasn't having any luck. But the whole affair had made him much more aware of the babies around him. The world seemed to be full of them. Including the one Annie was carrying. And considering giving away.

"So what kind of staff do you have, anyway?" Annie asked, assuming she would be working right alongside them soon.

"Here in this office? There are two of us family practice physicians. We've got a combination receptionist-bookkeeper, a practical nurse and an RN. We're thinking of hiring a physician's assistant, too."

She blinked, taking all that in. "So where exactly will I fit in?"

Turning, he looked at her. "I guess I didn't make myself clear. You won't be working here. I've also got an office at Allman Industries. That's where I'm going to need you."

"Allman Industries." She said the words slowly, thinking it over. There had been no such thing as Allman Industries when she'd lived here off and on as a child, but she'd heard it mentioned since she'd come back. As she remembered, it was housed in a big old building just off Main Street, one of those structures with gargoyles at the corners, looking like something that came from times gone by.

"Does that meet with your approval?" he asked her, getting a little sarcastic himself.

"I don't know," she said pertly. "We'll have to see."

He nodded. "I'll be awaiting your judgment with bated breath," he said. "What I need at the office is someone to keep track of what the hell I'm doing. I'm basically the company medical staff at Allman's, but I keep getting drafted into business meetings as well. My father is doing his best to lure me away from medicine. What he'd really like is for me to take over the company. It gets a little difficult to know where I am or what I'm supposed to be doing sometimes."

She couldn't imagine him having trouble telling anyone what he wanted or what he thought they should be doing. The man exuded confidence.

"Why don't you just tell him you don't have time for the meetings?"

He stared at her for a long moment before responding. Then he grinned. "Why indeed? That will be your first assignment. Tell everyone who calls that I'm too busy to accommodate them. You don't know how that would simplify my life."

She shrugged. "That seems easy enough."

A series of expressions moved across his face. She didn't know if he was amused or incredulous.

"You just wait," he said, shaking his head and laughing softly.

"And I can assist you with some of the medical stuff, too," she said, suddenly feeling she needed to explain that she had certain skills that deserved recognition.

"I don't think so," he said. "You don't have any nursing training."

"But I do."

That got his attention. He straightened and stared at her. "What?"

"I was in my second year at Houston Medical School in the nursing program when I got pregnant and had to drop out."

He made a whistling sound. "Wow. That will be very helpful."

She shrugged. "I don't have certification."

"No. And of course, you won't be expected to take over any nursing duties. But just to know you're experienced will be a big help. In a town like this, every little bit of knowledge counts."

He favored her with a lopsided grin that hinted at a new respect for her. That curled her toes for some unknown reason.

"So you see, you were always meant for this job," he said. "Kismet."

Kismet. She shivered. She knew the word just meant *fate,* but she didn't like it. There was something romantic about it and romance was something she was dead set against.

And that reminded her of something. Millie's beautiful daughter Shelley was set to marry Matt's brother Rafe. Everyone at the café had been buzzing about nothing else for days. Annie liked Shelley a lot, and she'd been just as interested as anyone in the progress toward the ceremony. Now she wondered about Matt. She knew he wasn't married, but she couldn't help but speculate about why that was. He was successful and attractive and wasn't getting any younger. Men like him were usually spoken for by now.

"Okay, Doc," she said, forcing a stern frown. Craning her neck, she looked at the monitor screen. "What's the verdict?"

"You and the baby seem fine."

The sense of relief she felt surprised her. She hadn't realized she might be more than a little concerned.

"You see? All that worrying for nothing."

"No." He shook his head. "It's never for nothing."

He had that one right. The longer she hung around this man, the more attractive he was looking. Reason enough to worry. Reason enough to be very, very careful.

And time to escape from this situation.

"You going to let me out of this thing?" she asked.

"Sure. Hold on."

He was turning off switches on the fetal monitor and

she watched, starting to feel pretty darn pleased with herself. She'd been in close proximity to this very appealing man—he'd even had his hands on various parts of her body and had leaned very close a few times, so close that she could feel his body heat and catch a hint of some sort of clean and soapy scent—and had been assaulted with all sorts of tempting male virility. Yet she'd remained completely unmoved by it. She was doing okay. She wasn't even hyperventilating.

Hooray for me, she thought silently, giving herself a little smile.

And then, as he removed the strap, his hand brushed her breast. She froze and her gaze jerked up to meet his. Intentions were everything and she needed to see his, right now. What she saw didn't make her feel any better.

There was no hint of any intention to mess with her, or even to take the chance at a little touching. But there was something else that was even worse. Something in his eyes held hers for a beat too long and while it did, she felt a jolt, a sudden connection, a new sensual awareness that snapped between them and made her gasp.

His eyes changed. He knew exactly what she was thinking.

"Sorry," he murmured, turning to put away the equipment.

But she was breathless and desperate not to let him know, slowly pulling air into her lungs and forcing back the panicky feeling in her chest.

"If you want to get your things together, I'll drive you home," he said, still working with the equipment.

If only it was that easy. If only she could zing back

a one-liner that would singe his hair. If only she could tell him to take a hike, that she could just darn well take care of that herself. But she didn't have her car and she didn't have any friends she could call. So unless she wanted to walk across town as night set in, she would have to let Matt drive her home.

She closed her eyes for a moment, making a silent promise. As soon as she could, she was going to get out of this mess. And once she was back on her feet, she was never, ever going to put herself in this kind of dependency again. One way or another, she was going to take control of her life.

Cruising slowly down the side street and turning on Main, Matt glanced at Annie. Somehow she managed to look as if she were perched on the edge of her seat despite the seat belt that had her securely strapped in. A casual observer would have thought she was being abducted. She looked ready to wrench the door handle open and leap from the car once she got the chance.

Shaking his head, he stifled the impulse to let her know how annoying it was to be treated as if he were conducting a shanghaiing operation. But he was pretty sure complaining would only make things worse. He couldn't yell at someone to stop being so scared of everything. That didn't ever work.

He wasn't sure how he'd ended up taking care of her anyway. He was too busy for this. He'd only gone into Millie's to grab piece of pie and a cup of coffee that was supposed to keep him awake while he worked late at his office at Allman Industries, and the next thing he knew, he was volunteering to take charge of another stray being.

That was what she reminded him of: an injured animal. As a boy he'd been famous for bringing home lost things—puppies, kittens, a garter snake, a baby skunk. He remembered a wounded bird he'd once found. He'd carried the poor thing around in a shoe box, doing everything a ten-year-old kid could think of to help it heal. He'd lavished all sorts of attention on it, trying to get it to eat and drink, and it had learned to stay still in his hands. But the look in its bright black eyes was always wary, as though it was sure, despite all his kindness, that he was probably going to hurt it in the end. And that was the look he saw in her eyes as well.

He felt a quick stab of anger at whoever had done this to her. A woman just didn't get this skittish without cause. He wanted to soothe her, tell her not to worry, but he knew that anything he said might just make things worse.

"So tell me, what made you head back to Chivaree?" he asked, hoping he sounded casual.

She glanced at him sideways. "I told you. I lived here when I was a kid."

"Did you go to Chivaree schools?"

"Off and on."

This was like pulling teeth. She'd dropped the smart-aleck attitude, but now she was being so stingy with her answers, he almost wished she'd come back with another good insult.

"How about your baby. Boy or girl?" he asked.

"I don't know. I haven't asked."

He looked over at her, puzzled. "You don't want to know?"

"I'll know soon enough."

He grimaced, his eyes back on the road. "You're keeping your distance, aren't you? Trying not to get attached."

She turned away. She wasn't going to get into this with him, especially knowing how he felt about it.

"How about you?" she asked instead. "Have any children?"

He didn't answer right away and she looked at him, surprised.

"I've never been married," he said at last.

She shrugged. "Neither have I."

Turning the car off Main Street, he headed toward the side of town she'd told him to aim for. Chivaree had changed a lot over the last few years. Used to be the place had a lonely, wind-swept look that wouldn't have seemed out of place in an old-fashioned Western. But lately the population had surged and new subdivisions were going up on the hills around the town. Chain stores and restaurants were opening up near the highway. Growth was good but it carried with it the inevitable costs.

"Turn left at the next stop sign," she told him.

He nodded, then frowned as he made the turn. He didn't much like the look of the neighborhood. He hadn't been on this seedy side of town for a while. Things had gotten worse in this crime-infested area.

"You living with somebody?" he asked hopefully. He didn't want to face the possibility that she hung around here alone.

"No."

"You're all on your own?"

"Yes."

"You should have someone else with you."

She gave him what sounded almost like a snort. "That's a nice theory. But the fact is, I don't have anybody. I'm fine on my own."

Fine on her own, huh? Then why did she sound so defensive?

She glanced at him sideways. He couldn't help admiring that flash of her dark eyes and the way her thick, chocolate-colored hair swirled around her face.

"Here it is. Pull over behind that red car."

He pulled over and turned off the engine, grimacing as he looked at the grungy building she had indicated.

"Thanks for everything," she said with a breezy tone he knew she was forcing. "I'll see you at Allman Industries in the morning."

"Wait a second. I'll walk you to the door."

She flinched as though that startled her.

"No," she said quickly, that wary look on her pretty face again. "Don't."

He frowned at her. "Why not?"

She ran her tongue across her lower lip nervously. "The neighbors will see you."

"The neighbors?" He stared at her incredulously. "So what?"

"They'll talk."

"They'll talk? Just because I act like a gentleman and—"

"They don't know from gentlemen around here." She pulled her things together and released her seat belt, ready to fly. "The men they see around here are no gentlemen."

His eyes narrowed. "Are you telling me—?"

She glanced at him. "Yes. They'll think—" She shrugged and looked away. "Just let me go alone. I don't need to be fodder for gossip."

He bit down on his tongue. Anger was threatening to take over if he didn't smother it fast. Taking a deep breath, he turned and challenged her.

"Annie, what the hell are you doing living in this kind of neighborhood?"

She lifted her chin defiantly. "The rent's cheap."

"Sometimes cheap is the most expensive of all."

"Listen, Matt. I don't come from money. I was raised by a single mother who did what she could, but couldn't do much. I've lived in places like this lots of times in my life. I can handle it."

Giving him a reassuring look, she slipped out of the car and walked quickly toward the entrance to her building.

He sat where he was, staring after her. He didn't like it. This was no kind of neighborhood to bring a newborn baby back to. He shrugged away the fact that she was considering putting her baby up for adoption.

Assuming, for the sake of this argument, she would be bringing a baby home from the hospital, how was she going to cope in a place like this?

Well, maybe she had some friends.

No. She'd only been in town a month, so she couldn't possibly have built up the sort of friendships that went with providing for a baby's needs.

He thought of her, of her pretty face and those dark,

beautiful eyes. She didn't belong here. He wanted to throw caution to the wind and stomp in after her, grab her and—

Yeah, then what? He didn't know anything about housing here in Chivaree. For all he knew, she was right and this was all that was available. On the other hand, once he got her installed at his office in the Allman building, once he started paying her a decent wage, maybe she would be able to afford a better place. He knew that was a better course. If he tried to go in and force her into doing things the way he thought they should be done, he was going to put her back up permanently.

He almost grinned, thinking of how fierce her pretty face would get, how her perfect little chin would jut out as she defied him. She was a charmer in her own way. Funny how hard she tried to resist that.

Still, the more he thought about it, the more he knew this was just an unacceptable place for her to live. No employee of his should live like this.

He grimaced. Who was he trying to kid? Annie wasn't going to be just any employee. That baby she was carrying was taking on larger than life proportions in his mind—and it was no mystery to him why that was.

It had only been a few weeks since he'd found out he had a child himself. Out there in the world some- where was a baby he'd never known about. That was a completely mind-blowing concept and he still wasn't used to it. So many questions remained unanswered.

It made him sick to think that Penny, the ex-girlfriend who'd had his child and never told him, might have had to live in places like this dump where Annie was staying. But from what he'd learned so far, she'd been on her own when she was getting ready to go through delivery…and preparing to put the baby up for adoption, just as Annie was thinking of doing. So chances were, she'd had to take what she could get at the time.

It was hard thinking that while he was casually going on with his life, laughing, dating, getting a residency in family practice in Dallas, Penny had been taking on all the responsibilities he should have been sharing with her. And that she had made the solo decision to give up her baby—*his baby*—to someone else.

He should have been there.

Maybe he thought helping Annie would make amends to a certain degree. Could that be part of his interest in Annie and what was to become of her? Sure, he knew it was nuts to get involved. And maybe he *was* crazy. But babies had to be protected. Absolutely. A no-brainer. And if he had to take on the mantle of guardian angel, he would.

He switched the engine on and started slowly down the street, but his mind was still back at the grungy apartment building with Annie.

Chapter Three

Annie's eyes shot open. She stared into the dark, wondering what had jolted her awake this way. Had it been a scream? A gunshot? She'd heard plenty of both those things since she'd moved into this dank, dark room.

There was a thump and someone began yelling in the hallway. She tried to relax. *Them* again. It was just the couple next door. The woman was always throwing her partner's things out the window and then he would storm up the stairs, yelling and pounding on the door she'd locked against him. The yelling would go on, back and forth, for what seemed like hours. Finally she would let him back in the apartment and then dishes would crash into walls and he would yell and she would scream. The ridiculous thing was, once they made up, the lovemaking was just as noisy as the fighting had been.

Meanwhile, the people in the apartment on the other

side of her had turned on some strange foreign music, very loud. She knew they were doing it to drown out the fighting, but it was almost worse. Pulling her pillow up over her head she groaned. How was she going to start a new job in the morning with no sleep at all?

Something hit the wall hard and she jerked in response, adrenaline surging. This was impossible. But more than that, it was scary. One of these days she had a feeling something worse than her peace being disturbed would happen. Matt had been right. She had to find another place to live. But how? With no money beyond just enough to feed herself and pay for this place, life was tough.

The woman screamed again and Annie winced. This was just too awful. And the worst was not knowing whether she should call the police again or not. Was the screaming for real? Or just a weapon the woman used against her boyfriend? Annie didn't know how much more of this she could stand.

Suddenly there was a new voice and she raised her head, listening intently. The yelling was more hysterical and the thumps sounded more like a real fight. And then, there was nothing. Silence.

She sat up, frowning. What the heck was going on? The fights were never over this quickly.

Someone banged on her door. She jumped a foot into the air and cried out softly.

Her heart was thumping so hard it felt like it might burst. She closed her eyes for half a second to catch herself, then slipped from the bed and ran softly to the door, just listening, trying to figure out what kind of monster might be on the other side. Was it the man who had been yelling? The woman looking for refuge? The new voice she'd heard?

"Annie? Are you in there? Are you okay?"

It took her a moment to realize it was Matt Allman, and once she did, joy burst inside her.

"Matt?" She tugged on the multiple locks, sliding each back in turn and opening the door. "What are you doing here?"

He looked very good standing there—all tall and dark and strong and male. Just what she needed right now. Relief swept through her and she did something completely unexpected and totally ridiculous. She threw herself into his arms.

It only lasted for seconds, and she jumped back away from him again so quickly, he might have thought he'd imagined the whole thing. But for those few seconds, his warm arms had felt so good against her almost-naked body, her head was spinning.

"Where did you come from?" she asked, backing into her apartment again. A strange fuzzy place in her sleepy mind seemed to think he might have appeared in a puff of smoke. But the strong, protective arms around her had been so real, she might never get that short but sweet memory out of her head.

"I came to get you," he responded calmly. "Get your things together. Let's go."

She stared at him blankly. "I—I can't go. It's after midnight," she added irrationally.

"It'll only get later the longer you procrastinate," he told her gruffly. He glanced down the hall, then looked back at her, his gaze taking in the lacy nightgown and her slender body showing through it. "Let me in. I'll help you get your things ready to go."

She knew she was probably crazy for letting him into her lonely apartment in the middle of the night. After all, the way he'd looked at her had reminded her of just how nearly transparent her nightgown was in the light from the hallway. Not good. Even a pregnant woman might look enticing in flimsy lace in the middle of the night.

"Oh," she said, looking down. Maybe she could ask him to wait in the hall until—

But he wasn't waiting any longer. And suddenly there he was, inside her apartment, closing her door.

"Come on. I'm getting you out of here."

She shook her head, then glanced around for her robe. "No. Where would I go?" she said, lifting it off a chair and slipping it on, hugging it close to her chest. "This is where I live, I—"

He grabbed her arm. She looked up at him, startled. He obviously meant business.

"Look, if you want me to get all caveman on you, I will. Bottom line, I'm not going to let you sleep here one more night."

"But—"

"Annie, be reasonable. It was like World War Three in your hallway when I got here. I had to kick some butt to get them to quiet down. There's no way you can live with this stuff going on." He glared at her. "Don't you ever call the cops on these people?"

She nodded. "I've tried that. They came once, but they don't like to come over here to this neighborhood."

He groaned. "Annie, I mean it. You're coming with me. You have no other option."

Looking in his eyes, she knew there was no point arguing. Turning, she looked at her closet. "Okay. Let me change and—"

"No time for that. Grab your toothbrush and let's get out of here. We can get the rest of your things tomorrow."

Matt took charge. In no time at all she was sitting in the passenger seat of his car, cruising through the dark streets. She was wearing her robe over her nightgown, but her hair was billowing wildly around her head and her feet were in thongs. She did have her toothbrush clutched firmly in her hand. At least there was that.

"I don't know why I'm letting you do this," she said, shaking her head at her own folly.

He glanced at her and a half smile softened the hard edges of his face. "I don't know why either. But it's probably because you know I'm right."

She sighed. "I'll bet you're right a lot of the time, aren't you?" she said.

He shrugged. "Pretty much all the time if you want to know the truth."

She was quiet for a moment, thinking about what might be coming next. She supposed he was taking her back to his place. Where else was he going to take her in the middle of the night? She had to be out of her mind for going along with this. After all, she might have to listen to fights at her place, but at least she was just a spectator, so far. At Matt's apartment she would probably be one of the main combatants. Because if he thought her gratitude for his concern was going to get him anything, he could think again!

She bristled, ready to hate him. Men were all alike, weren't they? A pregnant woman with no man around seemed to act like catnip on the average male. She'd better get ready to let him know just what she thought of lechers. Bracing herself, she waited for him to turn down the street where all the new apartment buildings stood.

But he didn't turn there. He just kept going and she looked at him in surprise.

"Where are you taking me?" she asked.

"Home," he said shortly, not taking his gaze off the road.

She frowned, looking out at the simple frame houses they were passing.

"Whose home?" she countered.

"We're here," Matt said instead of answering her question. He pulled the car up a driveway to stop in front of a house that had obviously once been just like all the other simple frame houses on the block, but had since morphed into something much more grandiose.

"The Allman homestead," he said, squinting as he looked through the windshield at it.

She leaned forward to stare at it, too. The place looked huge, three stories tall, with gables and a round tower, as though someone had taken a liking to the Queen Anne style somewhere along the way. To Annie it looked like a fairy-tale house, with windows for princesses to lean out of and dark recesses for villains to hide in.

"The reason it looks sort of odd is that Pop keeps putting on additions," Matt said. "If he had his way, every Allman would marry and keep his family right here, so there's got to be plenty of room."

"That seems very…" She was about to say *generous,* but she had second thoughts. *Controlling* was probably a better word. "Wait a minute. You live here with your family?"

"Sure."

She looked at the house with alarm. "Are you going to tell me this place is full of Allmans of all shapes and sizes?"

"Yup."

She swallowed hard. She was a McLaughlin, even if he didn't know it. The Allmans and the McLaughlins were like the Hatfields and the McCoys. They didn't mix, didn't speak, didn't tolerate each other at all. And here she was being ushered into the belly of the beast. Yikes! Was this really a good idea?

She was stalling for time and he made an impatient gesture.

"Come on, Annie," he said, sliding out of the driver's seat and coming around to help her out. "Keep it kind of quiet, though. Everyone's in bed."

"So who all's here right now?" she asked, looking nervously up at the second-floor windows.

"Let's see." Leading her across the lawn, he started counting on his fingers. "Pop, two sisters, Rita and Jodie, my brother David…and me."

She came to a dead stop, horrified, as the magnitude of it all rose up in front of her. "I can't go in there."

He frowned at her. "Why not?"

"Because…what is your family going to think?"

He groaned. "You care too much what other people think. Don't worry about them. I'll explain it all to them in the morning." She still didn't move and he added, "Look, where else are you going to go?"

Well, that was it, wasn't it? She had no choice. How the heck had she let this happen to her again? He was right. She looked at him, feeling frustrated and a bit angry. She hated being in this position. But she knew she was going to have to give in to the inevitable. Unless she wanted to sleep in the car.

"Listen, don't worry about it," he said, still trying to convince her. "We've got a lot of extra rooms."

She blinked. "There will be a room just for me?" she asked incredulously.

"Sure."

Touching his arm, she looked up at him searchingly. "So—let me get this straight. You're not trying to smuggle me into your bedroom?"

He opened his mouth to say something, closed it again, then half laughed. "Annie-girl," he said in his best Texas drawl, "you're nervous as a cat in a dog pound. Don't you ever drop the suspicions? You'd think you'd never met a stranger who didn't turn out to be a horse thief."

She shrugged. "The good ones are rare as hen's teeth," she muttered, turning to look at the house again. "But I've still got hopes for you."

He grinned. "You and me both." He tugged on her arm to make her face him and looked down earnestly.

"Annie, I'm interested in two things. Number one, getting a good employee. And number two, making sure your baby is okay. Got that?"

"My baby is fine," she said, knowing the words sounded defensive. Again.

"Good," he said. "Let's keep it that way."

She stood where she was, frowning at him. His handsome face was contorted by the harsh light from the porch, but his determination was clear. This was something more than his professionalism as a physician.

She didn't get it. And because she didn't get it, she was suspicious. What was his angle, anyway?

"You do understand that I'm probably putting this baby up for adoption," she reminded him.

A flash of something that looked close to pain came and went across his face so quickly, she wasn't sure if she'd imagined it.

"So you say."

She shook her head, trying to puzzle him out and failing at it. "Why does this bother you so much?"

"Who said it bothered me?" He started to turn away, then slowly turned back as though he'd thought better of it. "It's just that…well, I want to make sure you think this through."

She fought back a wave of weariness. Did he really think she'd come up with this idea on the fly? It had been the hardest, most heart-breaking dilemma she'd ever faced. How could it be anything else?

"Believe me, I've done plenty of thinking about it."

"A lot of people don't. A lot of people just let things happen without looking ahead to the consequences."

He stared at her as though he expected her to take his words to heart—and maybe do something as a result. "And later, they regret it."

She was tempted to resent his words, but she had a sudden insight that changed her attitude. He was regretting something himself, she could tell. It was written all over him.

She couldn't ask him what it was. They just didn't know each other well enough for that. But she could ask him to explain something else she'd been wondering about.

"Matt," she said, studying his face. "What made you come over to my place tonight the way you did? Were you planning to get me to leave with you even before you saw what was going on in the hallway?"

"Sure," he said candidly, his eyes dark as night in the midnight-blue shadows. "I couldn't sleep thinking about you and that baby staying in that hellhole."

She drew herself up. "So you came on over to manage my life for me?"

Exasperation filled his face.

"Annie, you can go ahead and be outraged if you want to. I don't care. I only did what I had to do. Sue me." And he turned on his heel, striding toward the porch steps.

"I just might," she muttered, coming behind him, clutching her robe in close. It was a weak threat at best. And she really wasn't outraged, or even angry.

In fact, deep inside, she felt a warm sense of relief in having someone to lean on, even if for a very short period of time. Being pregnant and alone was the pits. And now, for better or for worse, she had a friend. Even if he was an Allman.

They moved quietly through the darkened house and up the wide stairway. Matt led her down a long hallway, then stopped and pushed open a door.

"Here you go."

He held the door open and she looked inside. The room was small but nicely furnished with a dresser sporting a huge mirror, a small desk with a chair, and a storybook bed with a fluffy canopy.

"Oh," she said, alarmed. This was too nice. "Are you sure this isn't somebody's room?"

"It's yours for the time being," he said. "But you're going to have to share the bathroom." He gestured toward it. "Girls' is on the south end of the hall, guys' on the north."

She wasn't even listening. She was still turning slowly, enchanted by the room. There was a framed sampler on one wall, a turn-of-the-century picture of farm life on another. The curtains and the bedspread matched the canopy. It was the sort of room she'd dreamed of having when she was a teenager, especially during those awful periods when she and her mother had been living in their car when they couldn't find a relative to stay with.

"Wow," she said, shaking her head. "Do I really deserve all this?"

He frowned, watching her pleasure in the room and not sure why it disturbed him. But it did.

But then, a lot about her disturbed him—like the way her body had felt against his when she'd leaped into his arms at her apartment. Like the way her breasts looked when the robe fell open. Like the way her dark eyes seemed to see into his soul in a way that made him wonder if his secrets were hidden well enough.

"What does *deserving* have to do with anything?" he said gruffly. "This is what's available. That's all."

"That's all," she echoed, spinning around and ending up right in front of him. "This is so great. Thank you, Matt!" And, seized with impulsive gratitude, she threw her arms around his neck and kissed his cheek.

Startled, he turned toward her. They jostled. Her body was there again, so soft and firm at the same time, sending his senses out the window and his judgment around the bend. Then his mouth found her lips and he realized it was pointless to fight the inevitable—a kiss was going to happen no matter what.

There was no doubt he'd been thinking about her. He couldn't get her off his mind. She'd filled every thought he'd had since he'd seen her crumple to the floor of Millie's. She'd been the reason he'd sprawled on his bed and stared at the ceiling for two hours before he finally decided to get up and do something about it. But he thought he'd been thinking about her as a very pretty, very attractive baby transportation device. It had all been about the baby in his mind.

Or maybe not. It seemed there was something else going on, some dark, urgent undercurrent he'd been trying to ignore. But it was there. And now he knew.

The taste of her soft mouth as it yielded to his, the feel of her high, firm breasts against his chest, the fresh scent of her skin, was all so good, so intoxicating—and arousing.

Oh, hell. He was getting turned on by a pregnant woman. What was he, crazy?

He pulled back at the same time she did, but if his reaction was regret, hers was outrage.

"Omigod, I should have known better!" Hands balled into fists and eyebrows knit together in anger, she looked around for her toothbrush. "I'm getting out of here."

"No, no." He grabbed her by the shoulders and forced her to look into his face. "Look Annie, I don't know how that happened. That just got away from me. Really. It's late and I'm tired and…" He shrugged, knowing his excuses were lame ones. "That's the sort of thing I never do. Never."

After she'd calmed a bit, he felt secure in releasing her shoulders. And when he did, she stood still instead of bolting.

"You'll be safe. You can stay here. Look there's a lock on the inside of the door. You can just lock yourself in and never come out. I can't get to you without an ax."

"You swear?" She searched his eyes uncertainly. "Because I didn't come here with you for this."

He groaned. "I know that. I didn't mean to do it. You're just—" He shrugged again, embarrassed. "You're just too damn appealing. It was a natural, automatic reaction." Well, here he was in a hole and he just couldn't stop digging, could he? "Look, I didn't grab *you*. You grabbed *me*. And I couldn't resist quickly enough."

Her eyes widened. "Oh, so now you're saying I threw myself at you?"

He hesitated, trying to evaluate just how much of her reaction was real anger, and how much plain nervousness with the entire situation. He thought he saw more of the latter and his wide mouth tilted into a slight grin, betting on her being receptive to a teasing response at this point. "Yeah. More or less."

"Out!" She pointed the way to the door, only now her fury was pretty obviously mostly playacting.

He looked down at her and shook his head, half laughing. "Okay, Annie. I think you've got everything you're going to need. I'll see you in the morning."

"If I'm still here."

"Right."

At the door he stopped and turned back. She stood looking at him. The anger in her face had melted away and she looked incredibly young and endearing, standing there in her nightgown and robe, her dark hair flying about her in an unruly cloud. He wanted to go back and gather her up in his arms and cradle her through the night.

Wincing, he pushed back the impulse, but he couldn't stop staring at her, wondering where this need to nurture had come from. He'd never had it before. He was good at doctoring, conscientious and talented. But he'd never had the deep sense of commitment to humanity he saw in some of his colleagues. He loved medicine, but it was a job, a career, an identity, not a mission. This was something new and he couldn't help but think it might be something dangerous.

Had it been a mistake to bring her here? No doubt. He was stuck with her now, like the old adage that said once you'd saved someone's life you were responsible for them from then on. He'd taken over her problems and he was now going to have to do something about fixing them. Maybe he should have minded his own business.

Too late for second thoughts. She was here and he was afraid he'd changed his destiny because of it.

"Sleep tight," he said.

"You too," she said so softly it was almost a whisper.

But it was the look in her eyes that he carried away with him.

"Matt? Is that you?"

His older sister Rita opened the door to her bedroom and peered out at him sleepily.

"What are you doing?"

"Nothing. Go back to bed. I'll talk to you in the morning."

She yawned. "Oh. Okay," she said dutifully, closing her door again.

He smiled as he went on toward his own bedroom down the hall. It was funny, but he almost resented that he had to share Annie with the rest of his family. He wasn't quite ready for that. She was a treasure, something he'd found that he wanted all to himself for now. Or maybe it was just that he didn't want to have to explain to everyone just exactly what it was that he was doing with her—why he wanted her in his office, why he couldn't stand to have her in that awful place she was living.

Because he wasn't too sure of that himself.

Chapter Four

Annie's eyes opened and she smiled dreamily. What a pleasure to wake up between these soft sheets in a room that looked as though it belonged to someone who was loved. That someone wasn't her—but it almost felt as though it could be.

She heard a door slam and her smile faded. Memories of Matt and his unexpected kiss flooded her. Challenges like that tended to leap out at the most unlikely moments. This was no time to let herself drift with the tide. She was actually in enemy territory of sorts and she was going to need to be on her toes.

She slipped out of the bed, reached for her robe and opened the door to the hall—just a crack at first to make sure no one else was in sight, then wide enough to let her glide down the carpeted walkway to the bathroom. Luckily, it was unoccupied and she let herself inside, closing the door firmly and looking in vain for a way to lock it. There was some sort of brass thingy but she couldn't figure out how to work it.

Oh, well. She shouldn't be in here long. Turning, she took a look at the place, taking in the bright shiny aqua tile, the huge Roman-style bathtub, the skylighted atrium, the three-sided mirror. And the space. The bathroom was about the size of her apartment.

"Very nice," she murmured with a sigh. She could get used to this sort of living. It was even going to be a pleasure brushing her teeth in this atmosphere. She only wished she had about three spare hours to make use of that great bathtub.

Sadly, there was only time to brush her teeth and she went to the marble pedestal sink, turning on the water from the golden faucet. It poured out like liquid silver and she loved watching it spill over her toothbrush. It also made quite a bit of noise and that was probably why she didn't hear the knock on the door. She was just energetically lathering up when the door opened and a bright young blond woman in a cherry red bathrobe came rushing in.

"Sorry Rita, I've got to—"

The young woman stopped dead, staring at Annie.

Annie tried to smile, but it felt a little silly considering she was foaming at the mouth like a mad dog.

"Oh," she said lamely, her voice coming out a bit muffled. "Hi."

"Oops," the blond girl said. "I'm sorry. I thought my sister was in here." She started to retreat, then her face changed and she came back in. "Uh, who are you exactly?"

"I'm Annie." Grabbing a washcloth, she quickly wiped most of the bubbles from her face. "Matt sort of—"

"Ah." She looked even more surprised, but raised a hand and started to back out again. "Say no more."

Annie took a step toward her. "No, really, I'd like to explain—"

The woman shook her head. "No need." She hesitated, a spark of humor appearing in her gaze. "I'm Jodie, by the way."

Annie smiled uncertainly. "Hi, Jodie. I'm Annie."

"Hi." Jodie looked to be in her late twenties, just about Annie's age, with shoulder-length blond hair and warm brown eyes. She had a friendly manner, but she was obviously still a little skeptical about this stranger in her bathroom. Her gaze dropped to take in the lacy nightgown and the obvious evidence of pregnancy. Her eyes widened. "I'll just leave you to…whatever."

"I'm just brushing my teeth." She waved the toothbrush in the air as proof positive.

"Uh-huh." Jodie's smile was tentative. "Where's Matt?"

Annie thought for a second, then shook her head. "I'm not sure."

"Oh." A slight frown was deepening between Jodie's eyebrows. "I'll just go look for him." She turned to go, but Annie stopped her.

"Wait!"

Jodie turned back with a questioning look.

"First of all, how do you use this lock?"

Jodie laughed. "I guess that would be good to know," she admitted, then showed her the trick to it.

"Great. Now…see, the thing is, I've got a problem." There was no way to soften the embarrassment, so she charged ahead frankly. "You see, I don't have any clothes."

Jodie blinked and swallowed. "Is that right?" she said in a shaky voice.

"Yes. If I could just borrow a few things…"

Jodie opened her mouth, then closed it again. She shook her head and when she spoke again, her voice was higher. "No problem. Uh…"

"Hey, Jodie?" called a male voice from the hallway.

Jodie looked torn. "It's David," she said worriedly.

"The younger brother." Annie remembered about him.

"Yes."

Annie smiled. Despite her own embarrassment, she couldn't help but have some empathy for Matt's little sister. She was obviously trying hard not to slight anyone here.

"Better answer him," she suggested.

Jodie nodded and a determined look came over her pretty face. "I guess so. I'll be right back." Turning, she slipped out the door.

Annie listened as she tried to explain to her brother what was going on.

"*Matt* brought her?" David said loud enough for her to hear. "Matt hasn't had a girlfriend for so long, I was starting to think he'd forgotten how this man-woman thing worked. I've got to see this."

"Shh," Jodie hissed at him. "You're not seeing anything. Get Rita."

"Rita?"

"Yes. Get her. Quick."

Jodie came back into the room, smiling brightly as she closed the door behind her. "Sorry about that. Now about those clothes you need…"

"Yes. Thanks, I really appreciate it. I could use a shirt and—" She looked down at her belly. "Maybe some stretchy pants. Something I can wear to work."

"Of course." She hesitated. "Where do you work?"

Annie laughed, resigning herself to the fact that everything she said was going to make this situation look crazier and crazier to any sane observer. "I know you'll find this hard to believe, but I'm supposed to start a new job at Allman Industries today. As your brother's assistant, actually."

"No kidding?"

Jodie laughed, too, obviously on the same wavelength, and Annie had a sudden intuition that they were going to be friends. As long as nothing came along to change the way Jodie felt about her.

"Jodie?" A new voice sounded outside the door, along with a light knock.

"That'll be Rita," Jodie said. "Mind if I…?" She gestured questioningly toward the door

Annie held up both hands. "Be my guest," she said with a touch of irony.

Jodie grinned and turned to let her sister into the bathroom. Annie noted wryly that it was a good thing the place was as large as the average living room. At this rate, it was filling fast.

"Rita, this is Annie. Matt brought her here."

The two of them exchanged significant glances.

"So David has been telling me."

Rita stuck out her hand and Annie shook it. She saw more of Matt in this sister. Just as blond, she was older than Jodie, not quite as slender, nor as pretty, with her hair pulled back in a got-no-time-for-nonsense ponytail. She had a calm, competent look about her. What she didn't look was pleased.

"So you're a friend of Matt's?"

This one wasn't going to be an automatic friend. Annie felt like an interloper again—like a child caught with her hand in the cookie jar and vamping hard to think of an excuse that would cover it.

"Sort of. Actually, we only got to know each other well yesterday. But he's been awfully kind and…uh…"

Enough already, she was telling herself. Stop. Don't let your nervousness make you say stupid things.

"Ah." Both sisters said it at the same time and both gazes dropped to glance at Annie's rounded belly at the same time as well. They were wondering about exactly how long she and Matt had been acquainted, even if not "really well."

Annie sighed. Obviously she was going to have to try to nip this suspicion in the bud. "Look…I think you people are getting the wrong idea about this," she began.

"Oh, we're not getting any ideas," Jodie denied brightly, shaking her head.

Rita waved a hand in the air but managed to sound just a bit sarcastic when she added, "Haven't had an idea since last Wednesday and I'm not likely to get new ones in the morning, anyway."

Annie appreciated their attempt to reassure her, but there was no point to it. She knew very well what they were thinking.

"I mean…Matt and I aren't…you know…"

"Yes?" They both waited expectantly.

Annie searched for the right word. "Together."

"Oh."

To her surprise, though Rita looked unconvinced, Jodie actually looked a little deflated, as though she'd been hoping there was a budding romance revealing itself. Why on earth, she thought, would she want her brother to be interested in a pregnant stranger he'd picked up off a café floor? Of course, they didn't know about that. But still…

"Hey."

All three of them jumped inches into the air, because this time it was Matt's voice outside the door.

"What's going on?" he called, sounding authoritative. They weren't going to be able to send him away the way they had David.

They looked at each other. Jodie was the first to move.

"Oh, what the heck," she said, surrendering to the inevitable. "Why don't you come on in, Matt? We're having a party in here."

"Is Annie in there with you?"

"Yes, I am," she called back fighting back a bubble of slightly hysterical laughter that was threatening to come up her throat. "Come on in. The more the merrier."

It seemed a simple thing to invite him in, but the moment he appeared in the doorway, a sense of her own vulnerability swept over her. She was so naked beneath the nightgown. Funny how that hadn't bothered her much the night before. Now, it did.

She pulled her robe in closer and she knew both women noticed the move. He stepped in, scowling at each one in turn as they gaped back at him, and the room seemed to shrink in size.

"What are you two looking at?" he growled at his sisters.

"Nothing," Rita said a bit defensively.

"Not a thing," Jodie echoed more innocently, her brown eyes wide.

He didn't buy it but he let it go. "I guess you've met Annie?"

"I guess we have," Jodie said, throwing a quick smile Annie's way. "We've gotten real close in a very short time. In fact, I'm planning on loaning her some clothes."

"Clothes?" Rita asked, startled.

"Yes. It seems Matt brought her here in her nightgown."

"What?" Rita's face registered horror.

Annie wanted to give the background but no one was listening to her. Jodie had a mischievous grin on her face and Rita was demanding an explanation from Matt, which he obviously resented.

"I'll talk to you about it later," he told his older sister sternly. "Right now, do you mind giving us a moment of privacy? I'm sure you have something else to do somewhere else in the house. Like the kitchen," he added pointedly.

"Sexist, ain't he?" Jodie gave Annie a look of pure exasperation. "Take that under advisement, my dear."

But Rita was frowning. "Matt, I don't know if that would be proper. I mean—"

"I know what you mean and I reject it." He jerked his head toward the door.

Annie watched, fascinated. Matt was so sure of himself, so certain of being obeyed by his sisters, that it was a sight to behold. She wondered how he'd trained them so well.

Jodie grabbed Rita's hand. "Come on, sis. Let's get out of here. I'm sure Matt knows what he's doing."

Rita didn't look convinced of that, but she allowed herself to be led out. Jodie called back over her shoulder, "I'll be back with those clothes in a few minutes."

"Thanks," Annie called after her as the door closed.

She looked up at Matt and wished he wasn't so darn handsome that it almost took her breath away every time she really let herself look at him. The dark hair was unruly at the moment, and his white shirt was left open at the neck revealing an impressive view of hard, tanned muscles. For some reason this brought up visions of tangled sheets on a wide bed and memories of his potent kiss. Before she could stifle it, her pulse was soaring.

There was no use trying to pretend otherwise—the man was a danger to her peace of mind. It was too early in the morning for this. Her defenses weren't up to speed. She swallowed hard and faced him.

"We've scandalized your sisters," she pointed out.

He shrugged, looking down at her with a wariness that seemed to be a part of him. "I didn't know that was possible. You learn something new every day."

She bit her lip, considering. "You may think it's a joke, but actually, I don't want to scandalize them."

"It's too late now. The deed's been done."

"No." She shook her head firmly, coming to a decision. "I agree with Rita. This is no time or place for this."

He looked perplexed. "I just want to go over some things with you. First of all, how do you feel? Any problems during the night?" He looked at her rounded belly peeking out from the robe and his face softened.

She was torn. On the one hand, she'd noticed that look on his face and it touched her. On the other, she had to stick to her guns here. There was no way she was going to start following orders the way his sisters did. Hesitating for only a split second, she made her decision.

Lifting her chin, she pointed to the door. "Out."

He stared at her, at a loss. "What are you talking about?"

She drew in her breath and looked up at him. Risky as it might be, she was opting for complete honesty. "I'm standing here practically naked and you're standing very close and we're alone. It's no good."

He shook his head, astounded at her attitude. "This is nuts. What do you think I'm going to do? Grab you and drag you off into the tub?"

"That's not the point."

He blinked at her stubbornness. "Well, you're the one who's 'practically naked,' as you put it. I'm fully clothed." One eyebrow rose. "So I guess you'd have to say the impropriety is all on your side."

She shook her head. She was not going to get sidelined by his attempts at humor. She'd been going along with most of what Matt wanted ever since she met him and it was time she began establishing a set of standards for their relationship. He had to know that she meant what she said when she said it. Otherwise, it would be too easy to let herself fall completely under his control. And that would be disastrous.

"You don't see that your sisters might find a private meeting in the bathroom a little strange?"

"Who cares what they think?"

"*I* care." She pointed at her own chest. "Me. This person right here."

"Annie…" He grabbed her hand and pulled her closer. "Listen."

He'd meant to use logic. A good argument was always useful. Words. Lots of words. But for some reason, words deserted him the moment he felt her warm hand in his and looked down into her dark-brown eyes. He'd had a case to make when he'd started, but it was gone now. He couldn't remember what he'd been talking about.

It was magic. He didn't speak and neither did she, but there was no urge to move along. He could have stayed there for days, just drowning in her gaze—no need for air or food or anything but her. It was very strange. He'd never felt this way with a woman before—as though he wanted to breathe her in until she was a part of his existence.

She broke out of the spell first. Pulling away, she drew in a sharp breath and pointed to the door.

"Out. You can talk to me after I'm done here. When I'm dressed."

For just a second or two, he was disoriented, not sure what was going on. And then he was outside the bathroom and she was locking the door. He stood there for a moment, digesting the situation, and slowly his equilibrium came back to him. But not his peace of mind. What the hell was going on? Was he losing his reason?

Walking down the hallway to his own bedroom, he rubbed the back of his neck with his hand and wondered what he'd gotten himself into. He hadn't bargained for a situation that involved his emotions this way. Every step he was taking seemed to be drawing Annie into his life more and more. It was all very well to keep insisting to himself that he was in this to protect her baby. The trouble was, Annie came along with it. And there he had to keep his distance.

Just as he reached his door, Rita called to him from her room across the hall.

"Hey there, brother. We need to talk."

Turning, he took in the flare of some sort of disquiet in her eyes and he indulged in a silent groan. "What is it?" he asked reluctantly.

She came out to meet him half way. "Look, Matt," she said firmly. "I'm really happy if you've found someone. We've all been really worried about you lately, not having a woman in your life and all." She glanced down the hall toward the bathroom and lowered her voice. "But to bring her here like this is just a bit much."

Matt bit his tongue and told himself to hold back the resentful words he was tempted to use. Rita was the oldest and since their mother had died years earlier, she had been the one who had raised them all. He loved her dearly and was grateful for all the work she'd put in over the years. But sometimes her inflexible manner was a pain in the neck. And this was one of those times.

"Rita, she's my patient," he said once he'd tamed his first impulse to snap at her. "If I feel the need to put a patient of mine up for a few days, I'm going to do it. I do apologize for not consulting the rest of you first, but it was one of those things. There was no time."

"Oh, please." She rolled her eyes, obviously not buying it. "Matt, really! It's only obvious that she is much more than a patient to you."

"Rita, what are you talking about? I'm Annie's doctor. I wanted her here so that I could keep a closer eye on her."

"Sure," she said, not buying a word of it. "I'll believe that when I see you carting old Mrs. Winterhalter over the threshold and into the bedroom beside yours next time she's got the gout. Just to keep an eye on her."

"Rita…"

"Oh, Matt, she's a very attractive woman and you're a very lonely man at the moment. Nothing could be more natural than for you to be interested in her. It's so obvious."

His frown deepened. "It may be obvious to you, but it hasn't sunk in for me yet," he protested evenly. "There is nothing serious going on between Annie Torres and me."

Rita blinked at him, then looked truly distressed. "Matt! You wouldn't bring a one night stand into your own home…"

No force in the world could keep the anger out of his voice now.

"No, of course not. Rita, be serious. Annie isn't my lover in any way, shape or form. Or maybe you didn't you notice? She just happens to be over six months pregnant."

She stared at him for a long moment, biting her lip. The apology he'd been expecting didn't materialize. Then she turned and headed for the stairs.

Matt swore softly to himself, annoyed but controlling it. Just barely. And then he followed her, determined to get her to see how wrong she was. Despite all appearances, he really did care what his family thought of him.

"Listen, Rita," he said as he found her in the kitchen, pulling a carton of eggs out of the refrigerator. "This is what you don't understand. Annie is…" He tried to think of a good comparison. "Think of her as a waif, a little match girl I found shivering in the snow."

Rita choked. "Matt, it's going to be ninety degrees today."

He fixed her with a steely gaze. "I'm using metaphors, Rita."

"Yes. And overblown ones at that." She cracked an egg into a bowl and reached for another. "So you're telling me you found her wallowing around in the snow in that nightgown? With no backup gear?"

"Actually, she dropped into a dead faint at my feet in the middle of Millie's Café."

"Oh. I see."

But of course, she didn't see at all. "What I mean is she was in trouble and she needs a place to stay."

She put down the whisk and stared at the eggs for a

moment, then turned and faced him. "I hope I can assume that you were in no way responsible for the 'trouble' she's in?"

His head went back. He felt as though she'd slapped him. His eyes narrowed. "Why is it impossible to talk to you today?"

"Maybe because I just walked into my bathroom and found a strange pregnant woman in a nightgown brushing her teeth in my sink."

"Rita, her being pregnant has nothing to do with me."

She looked at him steadily. "I hope that's true, Matt," she said softly. "But before we found out about that baby of yours, I would have bet my life against you being involved in anything like that. It does undermine my sense of being able to judge things as they really are."

His heart went cold. So that was it. Now that the whole family knew about his relationship with Penny Hagar they saw him in a new light. The realization hit him like a thunderbolt. He'd always been the oldest brother, the one everyone turned to for wise counsel. He was the role model, the one his father trusted most, the one everyone admired. Was that really all gone now?

He turned from his sister. What more was there to say? If she didn't trust him now, what was the point of making excuses and pleading for understanding? He felt like an outsider in his own home. The only person he wanted to see right now was Annie. And that was just plain wrong.

His cell phone rang. Pulling it out, he glanced at the number in the window, knowing it would be Dan Kramer, the private investigator searching for his baby.

"Any news?" he said without preamble.

Dan talked quickly, but his words rang hollow. There was nothing new. Every lead seemed to peter out.

"Keep trying," he told the man as he signed off.

Keep trying. That advice could apply to every part of his life right now.

Annie drew in her breath and held it for a few seconds, then glanced at Matt sitting beside her in the driver's seat of his car. They were turning into the parking lot at Millie's Café and for some reason she was nervous.

"You'll enjoy it," Matt told her gruffly. "Relax. You'll have someone serving *you* breakfast for a change."

That was hardly the point. She felt odd, as though she were playacting in a scene for which she didn't know the lines. She'd just begun to feel comfortable about being in the Allman house when Matt had whisked her away.

Jodie had brought her a stack of clothes to pick from and she'd chosen dark-blue slacks with a soft and stretchy elastic waistband and a long white overshirt that was a little snug around her swollen breasts, but basically did the job she needed done. Matt assured her he would have someone clean out her apartment and bring everything over to the Allman house by that evening, so she would have her own clothes again. She wasn't sure she was crazy about that idea, but she had to admit she really didn't want to go back to her own place again if she didn't have to. Still, what would his sisters think?

Jodie was friendly and seemed welcoming enough. It was Rita who worried her. But when she'd come downstairs, Matt's oldest sister had smiled at her and begun to show her some of the many projects they were working on in preparation for Matt's brother Rafe's wedding to Shelly Sinclair. She'd been intrigued by the wide variety of supplies including yards and yards of white lace and chiffon, vats of seed pearls and spools of satin ribbon that littered the dining room table. She loved artsy-craftsy things.

But the next thing she knew, Matt was hurrying her out the door as though he didn't want her to spend another moment with his family. Which was too bad. She'd liked his sisters and she'd been ready to get to know them both better.

But he'd reminded her that they needed to pick up her car in the parking lot of the café, and she needed to tell Millie she wouldn't be working there any longer. So, reluctantly, she'd come along to have breakfast in the place where she used to work.

She wasn't sure exactly why she was dreading this, but it came clear to her pretty quickly when two women she knew casually came out of the café just as she and Matt were entering. She nodded with a quick smile and they each murmured greetings, then took in her escort, eyes widening. Identical looks came into both their faces and they glanced at each other meaningfully.

Annie could read their minds.

Aha. How do you like this? So Annie caught herself a live one, did she? Good for her.

Good for her, indeed! She hated seeming to be dependent on anyone other than herself. She wanted to tell them, *No! This is not what it looks like.*

But maybe she was wrong. Maybe it was exactly that.

Nails digging into her palms, she lifted her chin and walked into the café. Matt held the door for her, scanning the place for a sign of Millie. Nina Jeffords, one of Annie's favorites, was the hostess for the morning shift. She looked startled to see her co-worker coming in with Matt Allman, but she resisted the sort of cat-that-ate-the-canary expression Annie abhorred and showed them to a booth along the side.

"Millie's in her office," she told them. "Going over accounts. I would stay away if I were you," she added with a grin. "At least until she's got the books balanced."

"I'm afraid I'm going to have to risk having my head bitten off," Matt said with answering humor. "I've got some things I need to talk to her about." He helped Annie into her seat and turned. "Just coffee and scrambled eggs for me, Nina." He glanced down at Annie. "I'll go knock on Millie's door. You hold down the fort. Okay?"

Annie nodded. If he wanted to explain to Millie that she was losing one of her employees on such short notice, he might as well be her guest. She would have to explain herself soon enough and she wasn't looking forward to it. Maybe he would soften the way for her.

She watched him walk across the room, greeting various other customers as he went. And why not? Everyone in town knew the Allmans. Was that what made him look like small-town royalty? Maybe. Whatever. All she knew was, it made her shiver, and that was darn annoying.

Just before he reached the door to the hallway that led to Millie's office, he turned and found her watching him. She gasped softly as his piercing gaze caught hers and held for another beat. Then he turned again and was gone.

She sank back into her seat, breathing again and shaking her head. This was no good. She couldn't let this sort of thing happen. He was going to get the wrong idea.

"Annie." A hand fell on her shoulder. "I was hoping I'd find you here."

Chapter Five

Annie looked up with a start. Josh McLaughlin stood smiling down at her, his eighteen-month-old baby in his arms. She glanced back at where Matt had disappeared, glad he was out of sight. A meeting between McLaughlins and Allmans could turn into another shootout at the OK Corral. Then she turned the full force of her smile on Josh and reached to take his baby from him.

"Hey there, puddin'," she cooed. The adorable little girl had a pudgy body just made for cuddling and a head full of auburn curls that tumbled around her sunny face. "I've been missing you all week."

Josh laughed and little Emily McLaughlin gurgled happily and reached out a little hand to try to grab Annie's nose.

"You're not working today?" Josh asked her.

She looked up, assessing the man who she was pretty

sure was her half brother, but didn't know it. Tall and
slender as a long-distance runner, his dark-blond hair
looked like he'd lost his comb in a windstorm. It always
looked that way, no matter how much Cathy, his wife,
coaxed and pleaded.

"I'm a rancher," he'd say, dropping a kiss on his
wife's comically distressed face. "Just be glad there's
no hay sticking out of my ears."

Annie loved watching the two of them together.
Cathy was the perfect foil for him with her short, sty-
lish cap of strawberry-blond hair and her impeccable
taste in clothing, despite spending most of her time
working out in the open alongside her husband. She was
an excellent horsewoman and raising Arabians was becoming the specialty at the McLaughlin Ranch these
days. They made a good team, but more than that, they
made a good family. Their relationship went a long way
toward restoring Annie's faith that real love wasn't an
illusion, that it could last, if carefully nourished. And
Emily, the baby, fit into the circle of their devotion perfectly. It was a joy to work for them.

She'd been so nervous driving out to the ranch on the
day she'd answered their ad. Landmarks sparked memories, making it even worse. In some ways, she had been
going home. But it was a home that might not want her.
And she hadn't been sure what she was going to do once
she got there. Would she announce straight out to Josh
that they shared a father? Or would she go ahead with
her plan to apply for the job and see what happened?
Would he take one look at her and know the truth?

Oh, hardly. If it had been that obvious, someone else

would have noticed by now and no one had come close. But what if they hadn't liked her, or she couldn't stand them? They could have ordered her off the premises.

Her knees had been shaking as she'd knocked on the door. She held her breath as she heard footsteps coming closer. And then the door had opened and Josh looked out at her. He hadn't exactly recognized her or seen the signs of siblinghood, but there definitely had been an instant connection—though not in the romantic sense. He'd grinned and thrown the door wide and she knew before he said anything that she was hired on the spot.

Now she wondered if he ever noticed the similarities between them. She detected new ones all the time. Like the way his mouth twisted to one side when he grinned. She did that, too. Didn't he see it? Did he ever look into her eyes and wonder…?

No, that was silly. He had no reason to suspect anything at all. No reason in the world. And what was he going to think once she told him the truth? She shied away from speculating about it. Their relationship was so good right now, she didn't want to do anything to risk ruining it. Not yet.

"Actually, I'm not going to be working here at all anymore," she told Josh, cuddling Emily close. "I may be starting a new job."

He raised an eyebrow. "Are you still going to be able to work for us on Thursdays?" he asked, looking concerned.

"Absolutely," she said, though she hadn't brought it up to Matt yet and didn't know what was going to happen once he realized it was Josh she was working for.

"Great," he said, looking relieved as he reached to take his baby back. "I just dropped by on our way to the feed store, hoping to catch you here, because Cathy wanted me to ask if you could come an hour early this week. She's hoping you'll be able to help her take Emily to Groban's Studios for a portrait sitting."

"That sounds like fun."

"Oh, yeah." He grimaced. "Better you than me."

Annie laughed. "Emily will come alive in front of the camera. Won't you punkin'?"

Emily gurgled happily and Josh made her wave goodbye.

"See you Thursday," he said back over his shoulder as he headed for the door.

"Bye."

With impeccable timing, Matt appeared at the table, but his gaze was on Josh's back.

"Isn't that Josh McLaughlin?" he asked gruffly.

She nodded.

"I didn't know you knew him." He frowned, looking just the way she would expect an Allman to look when a McLaughlin was around. And vice versa. "What did he want?"

Luckily Nina arrived with coffee and scrambled eggs for two and Annie was saved from having to answer that. It was a question that needed answering, but she wasn't ready just yet. The baby was kicking, leaving her a little breathless, and she put a hand over where the little leg seemed to be jutting out, hoping to quiet it.

"Did you talk to Millie?" she asked, changing the

subject as he slid onto the seat across from her and they settled down to eat.

"Yes. I told her. She was sorry to lose you, of course, but she understood, especially after what happened yesterday. And she wishes you well." He buttered his golden-brown slice of toast. "She'd like you to stop in and see her at some point today."

"Of course. I planned to do that."

"Just don't let her try to talk you into anything."

Annie looked up at him. Conflicting emotions were tugging her in all directions. She liked the man. But she was so wary of letting herself depend on him.

She wished she knew why he was being so nice to her. With any other man she would have been suspicious. And in fact, she had her moments last night when he'd carted her off into the dark. But now—despite the kiss they'd shared the night before, she was pretty sure it wasn't anything like that.

Was he just superdoc, concerned with her baby and determined to make sure she ate right and did what she could to start the child off well in the world? Maybe there was a little of that. But there was something else going on, something deeper, something that struck an emotional chord with him. And she thought it might have something to do with what she'd told him about considering adoption for her baby. That seemed to give him fits every time she brought it up. Was he going to try to talk her out of it?

That was just the problem. She couldn't let herself get into a position of doing what other people thought she ought to do, just because she felt grateful to them.

She was going to stay true to herself, even if that meant turning away from Matt and rejecting his help.

"You know, Matt," she started carefully. "I appreciate all you're doing for me. But I'll be the one to decide what I'm going to do. I'm coming in with you to see how this job you're offering me looks. But I'm not making any promises. I may decide not to take it. I may just have to look for something else."

He stared back at her, reining in his impulse to snarl with displeasure. Didn't she understand that everything he was doing was for her own good? And the good of her baby? Did she really question his motives?

But no. Once he'd calmed down enough to really see what was going on in her dark gaze, he began to realize the truth. She was wary. Scared, even. She'd been hurt in the past and she didn't want to risk trusting anyone right now. Yelling at her wasn't going to change that much. In fact, it would probably just make things worse.

Looking at her, he made himself relax. There was something in her that really touched him. She seemed so small and vulnerable, and that was exactly what she was. Pregnant and all alone. But so brave, so firmly standing up for what she thought she ought to. It reached in to his heart and made him smile. And it made him think about Penny.

"Annie." He reached across the table and took her hand, surprising her as much as he surprised himself by the move. "Tell me about your baby's father. What happened?"

She stared at him and suddenly, her eyes filled with tears.

"Oh, damn!" she said, grabbing a napkin with her free hand to sop up the moisture. "I don't ever do this. I never, ever cry."

"Cry all you want," he told her, his fingers curling around hers. "We're in a corner booth. You're not that visible. And if you need to cry…"

"No," she said, jerking her hand away from his and glaring at him soggily. "Don't give me any sympathy, darn it all. Don't you see? That's exactly what's making me cry."

Leaning back, he laughed softly. "Okay. No more sympathy from me. I promise."

Taking a deep, shaky breath, she looked up at him. "Good. Just watch your step." She cleared her throat, blinking rapidly, trying to smile.

He looked down at his food to keep from grinning at her too broadly. "Listen, Annie. Forget I asked. If you can't talk about it—"

"I can talk about it," she said stoutly. "Just give me a moment." She took a sip of coffee and settled back, looking up at him defiantly. "Okay. Here goes. I was in nursing school when I met Rick. We bumped into each other in the cafeteria. Literally. My lemon gelatin dessert went all over the tiled floor."

He nodded as she paused. She had the look of someone going back into time, waiting to see if it still felt the same. He liked the fact that she was doing this right, not just shrugging it off with a caustic word or two as he might have expected. He realized with a jolt that he had an insatiable desire to get to know her better—her background, where she came from, why she did the things she did.

Why was that? He wasn't sure, but he was very much afraid it had a lot to do with the fact that he couldn't get the memory of what her mouth had tasted like the night before out of his mind. Wincing, he shook the thought away and listened as she went on.

"Rick helped me clean up the mess and we laughed about it. Then he insisted on taking me out to a real meal in a nice restaurant to make up for it." A slight smile played at her lips as the memories came to her. "He was so different from any man I'd ever known before. I fell for him the way a brainless teenager falls for the first boy that kisses her." Sighing, she gave him a plaintive glance. "Looking back now, I see how pathetic it was."

"Falling in love is a natural thing to do."

"Sure. But one should try to avoid falling for jerks. And I should have seen the signs." Her eyes took on a faraway look again as she remembered. "He was so handsome. I'd seen him around before. I knew about him. The girls in the nursing program were always being warned to watch out for the male med students. Which only made them seem more appealing, of course."

"Of course."

Picking up her coffee cup, she cradled it in her hands and took a long sip before going on.

"He was so interesting. His conversation was full of talk of European trips and yachts and famous people. It was another world, a world I'd never known before. I was mesmerized by it. I couldn't believe that someone like him was paying attention to someone like me." Her lips took on a faint smile again. "He had a way of leaning close and studying your face as he talked to you. It made you feel as though you were the only person he cared about in all the world." Her short laugh was humorless. "And actually, I'm sure his mind was a million miles away."

Matt nodded, feeling sympathetic, but a little annoyed at the same time. The guy sounded like a con man to him. He would have thought a smart woman like Annie would have seen through his act quickly enough to protect herself.

"There are politicians like that," he said gruffly.

"So I've heard. I've probably voted for some of them. Because I sure fell for Rick's act."

He waited for a moment. She was silent, staring down at her hands on the vinyl tabletop. "Were you in love with him?" he asked at last, wondering if she noticed the gritty sound to his voice as he said it.

She hesitated and suddenly his heart was beating harder. *What the hell? Did he really care this much? What was wrong with him?*

"I thought I was," she said at last. "I really did." She looked up at him, her gaze open and completely candid. "But you know, it's funny. As soon as he looked at me with that cold hardness in his eyes and told me to get rid of the baby or he wasn't interested in seeing me again, it was like this whole fantasy exterior melted away and I saw him as he really was. I saw the real Rick." She made a face. "And that was someone I didn't even like. And when he said to me that his family would hire private detectives who could prove that he wasn't the only one I'd been with…" Her voice choked off and the tears threatened again. Tears of anger.

Matt's mouth tightened. "What a bastard," he said with icy calm. "Maybe I should pay him a little visit and—"

"No! No, that would be crazy."

She stared at him, startled by how quickly he came to her defense. He shouldn't do that. They didn't have that sort of a bargain here.

"And anyway, what makes you so sure he wasn't right about that?" she asked softly, searching his face for her answer.

He didn't hesitate. The answer was right on the surface of his thinking. "Because I know you," he said simply.

She shook her head slowly, feeling a sense of wonder threaded with a hint of apprehension. "No, you don't."

Staring right back, he didn't retreat. "Yes, I do."

For some reason, that choked her up again. She fumbled for a napkin and Matt threw some cash down on the table.

"Come on," he said gruffly, "let's go."

"Oh, I need to go back and see Millie."

"We can do that later."

Later sounded good. She really didn't want to have to make happy talk with someone else right now. She let him lead her out of the café and into the parking lot. She didn't have much resistance left at the moment. Unburdening herself of her story had exhausted her.

"We'll come back for lunch," he suggested as he led her toward the cars. "You can see Millie then."

She glanced at him sideways. He kept saying "we." She had to conjure up enough energy to nip this in the bud at least.

He'd parked his low-slung sports car next to her beat-up old economy sedan. As they approached the cars, she couldn't help but notice the symbolism there. He waited while she unlocked the door to her car, then turned and faced him.

"We're not a *we,*" she said, forcing herself to confront him.

He looked at her, startled. "What?"

"We're not a *we.* In fact, we're not even a *you and me.* I'm Annie Torres and you're Matt Allman, and I'm me and you are you. Two separate people. Not *we.*"

"Oh." His face cleared as he got it. "I agree with you. Absolutely. That's the way it's got to be."

She nodded and he looked a bit sheepish.

"Sorry. I'll try not to let my language get that sloppy again."

"Okay. That'll be fine, then." She got into the driver's seat, wishing he weren't standing there watching. It was an awkward thing to do with this huge baby in the way.

"See you in the parking lot at Allman Industries," she said out the window she'd opened as she pulled on her seat belt and put her key into the ignition. To her relief, the engine roared to life. It didn't always cooperate that easily. She put the car into Reverse. He was still standing there, watching her. "Last one there is a rotten egg," she said, and then added, "Bye loser," before heading out.

She saw his frown of consternation as she drove out of the lot before he even got his car door open. "Don't worry," she murmured as though to the man who couldn't possibly hear her. "I'm not going to drive too fast. I'm going to take very good care of this baby. You just wait and see."

The inside of the Allman Industries building was as musty and old-fashioned as the outside looked but it was buzzing with activity. The energy of success was in the air.

And there was something else. Annie could feel it. It took some time for her to realize what it was, but when she did, it made a lot of other things fall into place for her. The simple truth was that the spirit of Jesse Allman, Matt's father, was baked into the bones of the place. She hadn't seen him here and she hadn't seen him at the house back on Alamo Road, but his presence was a constant in both places. You might almost say he haunted the buildings. She'd heard about him all her life and she remembered seeing him when she was a girl. He'd loomed large, even then.

He was, after all, the enemy of her father, William McLaughlin. She'd never been sure if she was supposed to align herself with Jesse out of anger toward her father for ignoring her, or against him because of solidarity with her family. Different years she felt differently. Now she thought she could stand back and look at it all more objectively, and she'd decided they both were a couple of jerks from a generation where men who did big things thought they could be kings.

But Matt wasn't like that. Or, if he was, he was hiding it. She felt a sudden gratitude and thought she'd better express it before it passed away.

"Matt," she said, slipping a hand into the crook of his arm as they entered the building. "I know I'm sort of…well, prickly sometimes, and I just wanted you to know that I really appreciate what you're doing for me."

He smiled and shrugged. "I should thank *you*."

She blinked. "What for?"

"You woke me up to thinking about someone other than myself for a change. We're both going to do anything we can for that baby in there," he said, nodding toward her belly. "But in the meantime—" he glanced around the lobby "—what exactly can you do?"

She looked around, too. "I told you. I was training to be a nurse."

He grimaced. "How about typing?"

"Minimal."

"That's okay. The hunt and peck style will do for now. There's not that much typing to be done." He nodded and smiled at the main lobby receptionist. "What I mainly need is schedule organization. And a lot of fielding of phone calls. Setting up meetings. Coordinating with my other office staff."

"I think I can handle that."

"Good."

Matt gave her a quick tour of the building, introducing her to a few people along the way, and ended up in his own offices which were on the first floor toward the back in an out-of-the way corridor. The accommodations were plain but newly refurbished and modern. She would have a large desk which sat in the front room. His own setup was in another office that opened off the room where she would be working. It took no time at all for her to familiarize herself with the computer, printers, copying machine and the phone system. Then a call came in and Matt was needed in another area of the plant.

"You'll be okay?" he asked her.

"Of course," she told him, relieved to get some time alone. "Go to your meeting."

She could tell he was leaving reluctantly and she sighed. If their plans were going to work out, he was going to have to get over this right away. Funny, but she didn't worry as much about herself. She'd been through the fires before and she'd learned her lesson. Shaking herself, she rose and went to the file cabinet. There was no quicker way to learn what went on in an office than to try to straighten out the files.

She was still at it almost an hour later when a pretty young woman with sleek blond hair peeked in.

"Annie!"

She looked up and saw Millie's daughter in the doorway. She'd met her a number of times at the café and knew she was the one about to marry Matt's younger brother, Rafe.

"Shelley! Come on in."

Shelley stepped in, looking around the office. "I heard about you working here now. This will be great. We'll have to do lunch one of these days."

"Definitely."

Shelley turned and smiled at her and it seemed to Annie that she was radiating joy. Being engaged seemed to agree with her.

"I know my mother will miss you at the café," she said. "She's always talking about what a good waitress you are. Nothing but compliments."

"I love your mother. She's wonderful to work for. But with the baby getting closer…"

"Oh, yes, an office job is much better for you at this point. No doubt about it." There was a sound out in the hallway and her smile broadened. "Want to meet Rafe?" she said in a loud whisper. "My fiancé."

Annie laughed. From the eager manner in which she asked the question, there was no way to turn her down. She knew Rafe was acting as CEO of the company during his father's illness—despite the fact that Matt was the oldest and their father's choice for the top job. And she had heard that Shelley had recently been promoted right out of the administrative assistant pool into a management job as head of research and development planning. This was, by all rights, a high-powered couple. Impressive.

"Sure," she said in answer to Shelley's offer to meet her fiancé. "I'd love to."

Shelley went to the door and called to him. "Come on in and meet Annie Torres."

The man who entered the office didn't look much like Matt. There was a dark and untamed quality to him that startled Annie a little. But his knowing smile as they shook hands dispelled her unease right away.

"So you're the little lady who's creating such a sensation around the Allman house," he said, raising an eyebrow. "You've got the place in a dither. I've been getting phone calls all morning."

She was blushing. This was crazy! She never blushed. But then, she didn't cry, either. This had been a day for firsts.

"I think you're overstating it a little," she protested.

"Oh, believe me, I've heard all about you and Matt."

That put her back up right away. "There is no 'me and Matt.' Everyone is getting the wrong idea about this. His interest in me is purely—" she patted her rounded belly for emphasis "—professional. In the medical sense."

"Oh," Rafe said with a crooked grin. "Sure it is." He and Shelley exchanged a glance. "Well, it's nice to meet you, Annie Torres. I'm sure we'll be seeing more of you. Shelley is over at the house all the time, getting ready for the wedding."

"And Rafe is over at the house all the time, just because he wants to be," Shelley added in a teasing voice. "Makes you wonder why he bothered getting an apartment since he never seems to use it."

"Oh, it has its uses," he teased right back, sliding an arm around her waist and pulling her close before dropping a kiss at her temple.

She giggled and they started toward the door.

"We'll let you get back to work," Shelley said over her shoulder. "But we'll be seeing a lot of each other, I'm sure."

Annie waved goodbye and turned back to the files, but she heard another comment as they left the room.

"Get a load of those dimples," Rafe said sotto voce to Shelley. "Matt always did go for girls with dimples."

"Shh," Shelley said back.

And then they were gone.

Annie stood frozen to the spot. She was beginning to feel like a winded fish swimming against the tide. What was wrong with everyone?

Don't let it get to you, a voice inside warned. *They're not serious. They're giddy. That's what people are like when they're madly in love. And they want everyone else to be just as demented as they are.*

Madly in love. How would that be? Even when she'd thought she loved Rick, it wasn't quite like that. She was more in awe of him, impressed by him, flattered that he was interested in her. But love? No, it was never really love and she'd been a fool to give in to having a physical relationship with a man she didn't really love.

When you came right down to it, she'd never been in love. To love was to lay yourself open to a lot of risk. Even not being in love, she'd done that. She'd only come close, just touched the edges of what love could be, and even so, she'd paid the price. She'd been slapped in the face. No, it was best to keep things at the level of respect. Love was for people who could afford it. And she'd never been one to squander what little she had on the frivolous.

The baby kicked and she relaxed, whispering sweet nothings as she patted the spot. Work. That was what she needed. Back to the files. She couldn't let herself dwell on Matt or on the expectations of others.

Actually, the job turned out to be fairly interesting. Annie liked bringing order to chaotic situations, so she enjoyed setting up a new filing system for incoming messages and reorganizing the office so that traffic flow was smoother. Immersing herself in her work, Annie had lost track of time when Matt returned from his meeting.

"Hello there. Anything happening?"

She looked up to see Matt smiling down at her. She smiled brightly in return, determined to keep things on a businesslike level.

"Well, let's see. You've had three calls. And you've got a meeting with the hospital board at three o'clock. Oh, and Rita wants you to call your father as soon as possible. He's worried about the Nunez contract."

He groaned. "He thinks if he can get me involved in negotiating that contract, I'll be tied up here for the rest of my natural life," he said. Glancing around the office, he looked surprised. "This place already looks different. What did you do?"

"Nothing much. Just a little dusting. A little straightening up. I moved a chair here, some files there."

He nodded approvingly. "Whatever it is, keep notes. You'll have to give pointers to Maureen for when she gets back."

Annie laughed. "Oh, right. That's just what she'll want—the temp worker to give her pointers on how to do her job better."

"If the shoe fits," he said, heading for his own office to leave his briefcase. "Listen, it's past time for lunch. You ready to go?"

She hesitated. This was exactly one of those places where she should be carefully pointing out to him that they weren't a couple. "You know, I can get myself over to Millie's," she noted.

He stopped, turning back. "You don't want to go to lunch with me?"

His eyes were huge as though it was going to hurt his feelings if she turned him down.

She stared, then threw her hands out. "Matt, don't do this to me."

"Don't do what?"

"Don't put me in this position. We can't be doing things together all the time." She shook her head, at a loss. "People…people will…"

"People will say we're in love?" he teased her.

"Hardly." He was making her laugh again and that was always fatal. "But Matt, you're my boss, not my boyfriend. We should act accordingly."

He sat looking down at her, all tough-guy and stubborn. "And as your boss, I'd like to take you to lunch to celebrate your first day at work."

"Matt—"

"In fact, I insist."

She shook her head, more in surrender than anything else. And deep down she knew it was more because she wanted to please him than because she felt pressured. Red lights should have been flashing. Alarms should have been going off. She was giving in to temptation.

"I swear I won't make you go to lunch again any time this whole week," he promised extravagantly.

"What about next week?" she muttered, still clinging to a modicum of rebellion. "That is, if there is a next week."

He raised an eyebrow. "Expecting Armageddon?" he teased.

She tossed her hair and looked up at him a touch of hostility in her eyes. "Who knows? You might fire me by then."

"I wouldn't risk any money on that," he advised, his eyes crinkling at the corners. "And in the meantime, let's go eat. Okay?"

She made him wait a moment longer, but finally she relented and reached for her purse. "Oh, okay. But really, Matt. We have to be more careful about how we come across to others."

He threw her an exasperated look. "Why do you care so much what others think?"

Raising her chin, she looked steadily into his eyes. "I have to. I've spent a lifetime fighting what other people think about me. It matters. It can make a big difference."

Something changed in his gaze and he reached for her. "Annie—"

"And one more thing," she said, deftly pushing his hand aside and evading his touch. "About my decision."

"Your decision?"

"Yes. About whether or not I'm going to work for you."

"Ah, that decision."

"I've decided I'd like to take the job. But I have to have Thursday afternoons off."

"Thursdays? What for?"

"That's the day…" She took a deep breath and pressed on. It was time to come clean about this. He deserved it. "That's the day I work out at the McLaughlin Ranch."

Chapter Six

The room turned deadly silent for a long moment while Matt digested what Annie had said. When he spoke again, his voice had an edge to it.

"What are you talking about?"

"I told you. I work as a housekeeper one day a week."

"Yeah, but you didn't tell me it was with the McLaughlins."

"Well, it is."

He rose from the desk and began pacing the floor. Stopping to stare out the window at one point, he raked his fingers into his thick hair, making it stand up on end. Then he turned back to challenge her.

"Are you telling me you think you can work for me and the McLaughlins at the same time?"

"Of course I can."

She was going to have to go on the offensive. If she

hung back and waited for him to be logical, she was going to lose the advantage and end up apologizing—or worse, agreeing not to go out to Josh and Cathy's anymore. And she had to maintain her contact with the McLaughlins at all costs. But of course, she couldn't tell Matt why. And without her reasoning, she knew this was going to be hard for him to understand.

"I can and I will."

He looked tortured. "But—"

"But what? You think I'm a spy?" She glared at him. "I thought you could see right down into my soul and knew what sort of person I was." She sighed. "Ah, but now you're wondering, can I really trust her?"

"Trust has nothing to do with it."

"So it mainly boils down to irrational hatred?"

He groaned, shaking his head. "You don't know what you're talking about, Annie. When we have some time to spare, I'll tell you things that will change your mind."

She rose, purse in hand. "No need. I've made my decision. If you can't handle me working for the McLaughlins, I'll have to look for another job. Or go back to Millie's."

He shook his head as he joined her, and there was no sign of any softening in his face.

"We'll talk. Over lunch. Let's go."

They did talk over lunch, but not about the McLaughlins. Annie saw Millie and they had a tearful embrace. And for the rest of the hour, patrons came by their table to wish her well and tell her how much they were going to miss her.

"I'm not actually going anyplace, you know," she said at last. "I'll be right here in town, working at All-man Industries. Anyone who wants to can easily give me a call."

"But it won't be the same as finding you here every day when I stop by for my usual patty melt," Katy Brewster complained. "I swear, your smile just lights up my day."

Annie was pleased and gratified—and very surprised that she seemed to make a difference in so many lives. After all, she hadn't been around all that long. But she enjoyed the compliments, and even more, she enjoyed the look in Matt's eyes as he watched all this.

"Quite the belle of the ball, aren't you?" he murmured to her as they were rising to leave and people were calling from across the restaurant to say goodbye. "Maybe we ought to run you for mayor."

He was being careful not to touch her or stand too close or in any way give off the sense that they had any-thing going on between the two of them. She appreciated his efforts. Still, she knew very well that people would make up their own minds about what was going on, even if she and Matt tried not to give them overt reason.

He helped her into the car and she waved at the last well-wishers, and then was relieved when they hit the highway and she could relax.

"Let's swing out by the new plant," Matt suggested when they reached the crossroads. "Have you ever been out there?"

"No. Actually, I haven't been out in that direction at all." Her heart started thumping. There was a reason she didn't go to that side of town and he was obviously about to suggest they go there. But if he stuck to the highway, they would bypass Coyote Park, the site of her childhood summers. She knew she was being a ninny avoiding it anyway. There was no reason for it.

Who's afraid of Coyote Park?

The taunt was silly enough to make her smile.

"Want to see the new building?" he asked, as she'd known he would.

She hardly hesitated. "Sure."

She'd heard a lot about the new site. Everyone said it was going to be a spectacular new setting for Allman Industries, and from what she saw as Matt slowly drove her around the construction area, they were right. The perimeters had been blocked off and the foundations laid. Very soon a tall building of steel and tinted glass would stand in the middle of what had always been a barren field. The Allmans were moving forward, grabbing the future and making it theirs. She was impressed.

"Stick with us and you'll be working out here by this time next year," Matt said. His deep voice sounded a bit cynical and she looked at him quickly, wondering why. But his eyes were crinkling at the corners and she might have mistaken humor for something more sarcastic.

"How about you?" she asked, curious now. "Will you still be with the company?"

The humor faded from his face. "That all depends," he said evasively, staring out at the structure.

"Depends on what?" she pursued.

She knew Matt had gone away to school partly to get away from his father. Everyone knew that. And he'd taken on the awesome effort of becoming a fully qualified physician. From what she'd heard, he'd only come home and gone to work at Allman's a few months before because of his father's illness. He'd made a point of opening a medical office as well, just to emphasize the fact that he wasn't giving up on practicing medicine. But he'd said himself that his father was working hard to get him to take over the company instead.

"You never know what fate has in store for you," he said, giving her a quick smile. "Look at the way you fell into my life."

"*Fell* is the operative word," she noted. "No conscious effort on my part. Nothing I can claim credit for."

"You mean to tell me that fainting at my feet wasn't a nefarious plan concocted by you from the beginning? You weren't out to steal my heart by playing with my sympathies?"

She looked at him sharply just to make sure he was only joking. If he really thought anything like that, she would have even more reason to get out of his life immediately. But the humor flashing in his eyes told her he was teasing and she relaxed.

"If only I were smart enough to come up with such a plan," she said with mock wistfulness. "You are such a patsy."

"Am I?"

Of course the answer to that was no, but she wasn't going to give him the satisfaction of saying it out loud. Besides, the teasing was getting them too warm and cozy and she purposefully turned away. He got the message and turned the car back out onto the driveway, driving slowly up to a different vantage point.

"Matt," she said, frowning slightly. "Here's what I don't understand. If you don't want to work in business, and you do want to practice medicine, why can't you just tell your father what the facts are? Why waste all this time pretending?"

He laughed softly. "You make it sound so simple," he said. "So simple and so easy. And I suppose it would be for many people. But they don't have Jesse Allman for a father."

"Is he really that autocratic?"

"Oh, he's autocratic all right. But that's not how he gets you. It's the emotional blackmail. The guilt."

"Guilt? What do you have to be guilty about?"

"Life. You know how it is. Sometimes you feel guilty for things you've done, sometimes for things you haven't done—sometimes for loving too much, sometimes for loving too little. You know?"

She shook her head. She really didn't think she did know. After all, she'd never had a father to make her life miserable. She'd never had a father at all. So it was hard for her to sympathize. But it didn't matter. He'd started the car moving again.

"Let's take the old road back," he suggested.

The old road went right past the park. She bit her lip. *What the heck. It would be good to see the old place.*

She didn't have to wait long. They passed a couple of farms and then there it was: Coyote Park. It looked dusty and windswept, with a few stands of stragglylooking cottonwoods and junipers here and there, just as she remembered it. But one thing was different. She didn't see any people.

"Stop," she said suddenly. "Just for a minute. Please stop."

He pulled over, looking at her curiously. She got out of the car and looked around. She didn't dread this place. What had she been thinking? All sorts of childhood memories flooded back.

"Do you have a little time? Mind if I just go down there?" She pointed toward a rickety wooden bridge that still stood guard over the old rocky creek.

"No problem," he said.

Turning, she began to walk toward the bridge. Getting out of the car as well, he followed a few feet behind her.

"What is it, Annie?" he asked as she stepped onto the bridge and turned slowly, taking in everything.

She looked at him, knowing that to tell him her story would be to lower her respect quotient. But what the heck. It was only the truth. And somehow she realized she trusted Matt not to despise her for it as some might.

"This is where we camped sometimes in the summer when I was a kid," she told him candidly. "And not as in 'summer vacation.' This was where we lived. In the years when we had a little money, or a friend, we'd be in a trailer. Other times, it was a tent."

His faint smile was largely quizzical, as though he couldn't imagine such a thing. "I remember when people used to camp here. It's not allowed anymore. They have to go down by the railroad tracks, to the government campground." He paused, looking at her closely. "I remember the old crowd. But I thought they were mostly gypsies."

She smiled, nodding. "Some were. I knew a lot of gypsies in those days."

He frowned. "You're not a gypsy."

"No. My mother was Hispanic and my father…" Her voice trailed off without finishing the sentence.

"Yes?"

Pushing back the dark hair that the breeze was tossing into her face, she shook her head. "Never mind my father. He never did figure into anything anyway."

A shadow of something that looked close to outrage crept across his face and she stopped, wondering what she'd said that had affected him so strongly and in seconds, the look was gone. He didn't say anything but he came up to join her on the bridge and together they leaned on the railing, looking down into the small, babbling stream.

"Too bad the water doesn't last too well into the summer," he said. "This is actually a pretty little river in the spring."

She nodded. "I remember. Some years the water would last. Flood years, I guess."

Looking around, she tried to remember exactly where she and her mother had pitched their tent that last time when she was thirteen. There was the little stucco bathroom and the meeting room attached. Sometimes the county put on summer craft classes in the meeting room. She'd loved those. For just a moment she heard those childish voices echoing through the trees. It had been fun, like a campout that lasted all summer. Everyone was poor. They were all in the same boat. And there had been so many children, there was always someone to do something with.

"You're smiling," Matt said. "Good memories?"

"Some good, some bad." She looked up at him. "The good ones were mostly when I was young. As I got into the teenage years, the shame of living here began to overwhelm everything else. Then it really wasn't fun anymore."

"What did you come here for?" he asked, turning in order to see her better and hooking his elbows over the railing. "And what did you do the rest of the year?"

She looked up at him. His blue eyes were earnest. He was really interested. Something inside her sang and she smiled.

"Let me tell you this way," she said, suddenly eager to unburden herself of this story. If he really wanted to know who she was, she was going to tell him. "My mother's name was Marina Torres. She was very beautiful when she was young. Her parents were sharecroppers and she wanted to break away from that. She wanted to do things, go places, make something of herself. And her first step was to work as a housekeeper at the ranch of a rich family. It was her big opportunity. They paid well and treated her very well and she thought she was on her way. She was saving her money, planning to go to Dallas and get an education."

"Good for her."

"Yes. Unfortunately there was a handsome young man in the family who was often around. She fell in love." She shrugged grandly, palms out. "And ended up with no job, no lover, no future—only me."

He almost seemed shocked by that. "What happened? Couldn't she get any help from the father?"

She turned to look over the rolling hills of the park. "You know, I'm not even sure if she ever tried. If she did, she never told me about it. She quit her job and went away to hide from the world and to have me. And then she had a young baby to drag around with her everywhere so it was pretty hard to get a good job. From then on, it seemed her life was in a downward spiral. She got odd jobs here and there, a little housekeeping, a little waitressing, and then we'd move on. Once she worked as a dog walker and we lived in a room behind a veterinarians' clinic. I liked that one. All those dogs! But nothing ever lasted very long. We were always moving. Still, most summers, we came back to Chivaree."

"And why was that?"

She hesitated. How was she going to explain that without giving away her secret? "It was largely a community thing, I think," she said at last, and it was mostly true, though it ignored the biggest pull that had started the tradition—her father's presence in the town. "The same people came back here every summer. It was like coming home. Our only safe place in a pretty scary world."

"So coming to Coyote Park is like visiting the scenes of your childhood."

She waved an arm. "It's more than that," she said with sudden bitter insight. "It's déjà vu all over again."

He gazed at her questioningly and she knew she should say something bright and chipper and go back to the car. But she was being honest with Matt. Painfully honest. Why stop now?

"I hated growing up the way I did. I always swore I'd never end up like my mother. I'd do better." Her laugh was hollow. "And look at me now. What a joke. I've ended up just like she did."

Matt moved as though her words exasperated him. Taking her by the shoulders, he forced her to face him. "You haven't ended up as anything," he said evenly. "You're young. You're only just beginning. This is very different from what your mother went through."

There was fire in his eyes that startled her. It seemed odd that he would care so much about this.

"How is it different? I'm doing exactly the same things, making the same mistakes. It almost seems as if I'm fated to relive history." She looked at him, trying to make him understand. "Don't you see? That's why I think it might be best to give this baby to a good couple. I have to do something to break the chain."

"No. You're not going to relive history." He sounded so sure of himself. "You've got someone to help you stay away from that."

She looked up at him, wide eyed. "Who?"

"Me."

She'd known he was going to say that, but she still didn't believe him. "But Matt, who am I to you, really? Why would you do this?"

He stared down at her for a long moment, either unable or unwilling to give her a credible explanation.

"I have my own reasons," he said at last, and then he turned and started walking back toward the car.

She started after him, intent on insisting on a better

answer to her question, but her shoe snagged on a loose board, throwing her off balance, and suddenly she was catapulting forward. Matt turned just in time and caught her.

"Oh!" she cried, looking up at him.

His arms were around her, holding her close, closer than necessary, and she was forced to feel the thick muscles of his arms and his chest.

"You again?" he said with a half smile, looking down at her and shaking his head. "You just can't stop falling for me, can you?"

And then his gaze changed. His eyes clouded with an emotion that made her catch her breath. She was suddenly very much aware of her swollen breasts pressing against him and she knew he was, too. He was going to kiss her. She was sure of it. She should be pushing him away, making sure that didn't happen. But she was frozen right where she was, unable to move. Realization swept through her. She *wanted* him to kiss her.

It was more than craving his protection, more than appreciating his help. There was something between them that sparked and sizzled. There was an excitement, a mystery. And the whole thing needed a kiss to seal it. She lifted her face toward his, her lips slightly parted. She saw the answering flare in his gaze. He wanted her. Despite everything, he wanted her. She could hardly breathe.

And then…it didn't happen. Slowly, he drew back and disentangled her from his embrace. Ostentatiously, he glanced at his watch.

"You know, I've got a meeting to get to," he said,

turning back toward where the car was parked and motioning to indicate that he would follow her.

She moved automatically, walking stiffly. He was saying something the whole time, chatting in a friendly manner, but she didn't hear a word he said. Her face was flushing, her blood was racing. He wasn't going to kiss her after all. She'd laid herself out there like a tray of fine chocolates and he'd turned up his nose. She knew she should be grateful that he'd saved them both from something they'd both vowed to avoid, but she couldn't quite go that far. In fact, deep down, she was furious.

The rest of the afternoon at work dragged slowly. It was pretty hard getting her mind back on filing systems when all she wanted to do was demand an explanation from Matt.

Just tell me why! she kept thinking, but she couldn't say the words out loud.

And deep down, she knew that what she really wanted was much more than an explanation. She wanted that kiss, darn it all!

His meeting didn't last long and he was in his office for the next couple of hours. Every time she looked up, there he was and her heart would give a little lurch. Just because she was upset with him, she quickly reminded herself. Not for anything more serious than that. It was just that her back went up. It had nothing to do with falling for the guy. She wasn't about to do that. No man was going to take control of her destiny again. She was in charge. No one was going to tell her what to do.

Not that he was doing anything overt at the moment. His attitude was completely professional. In fact, it was so cool and distant, she half expected him to start calling her Miss Torres at any moment.

Good. That was just the way it should be. She should be perfectly happy. But there was something about looking into those blue eyes that made her heart do that little stutter thing. She hated that.

She really should go and she knew it. This was all too tempting. At any moment she might find herself giving in to the urge to lean on Matt just a little too much. He offered a safe haven. But she knew that was just the cheese on the trigger to the trap. One touch, and she would be caught for good.

Quitting time finally came and she left him still working at his desk. That gave her the chance to get back to the Allman house before he did, much to her relief. *Anything* to begin to negate the picture of the two of them being a couple. Still, she was a little nervous going in to brave the other Allmans on her own. She wasn't sure what her reception would be.

She parked her car on the street, then took the front walk and knocked on the door. Rita flung it open almost immediately.

"You don't need to knock," she told her as she let her in. "You live here now. Make yourself at home." Turning, she led the way through the front room. "We're all out in the kitchen fixing dinner." She glanced down at the evidence of Annie's pregnancy. "But you must be tired. Why don't you go lie down? We'll call you when it's time to eat."

"I'm not all that tired," Annie protested, wondering just how ragged she must look. She felt as though she'd been running marathons. "I'd like to come out to the kitchen and help."

Rita hesitated. "Oh, okay," she said. "Come on, then."

Jodie was at the counter mixing together a butter-and-garlic concoction to smear on slices of thick sourdough bread she had laid out in a flat pan. Shelley was unpacking a large tray that looked familiar to Annie. They both greeted her warmly.

"I don't know if you've met our little brother David," Rita said, pointing out an extremely handsome, athletic-looking young man draped across a tall bar stool and smiling at her. "As you can see, he was born to be a surfer, but somehow got misplaced in the middle of Texas, far from the ocean."

"Ah, cruel fate," he agreed, coming off the stool to shake hands with Annie. "But I've got my board waxed down just in case there's a good rainstorm."

They all laughed. Annie could tell he was lovable, just by the way the others reacted to him.

"Welcome to the madhouse," he told her. "It's wedding central around here. Don't even try to bring up a topic that doesn't have something to do with matrimony."

"I'm afraid he's got a point," Rita said ruefully. "We're planning a huge wedding, plus a major family prewedding party the week before, and we're all working our fingers to the bone trying to get ready for it all. Half the town is invited to the actual event."

"Well, the Allman half, anyway," Jodie put in. "The McLaughlin half—that's another story."

Shelley, looking a bit stricken, turned to Jodie and took her hand. "I wish it wasn't like that, Jodie. If things were different, we could make it a double wedding."

Jodie nodded, looking wistful, her eyes misting. Impulsively, she hugged her future sister-in-law.

"I would love that, Shelley. But it wouldn't really be fair to Kurt to ask him to have a ceremony that left his family out. And you know no McLaughlins are going to come to a wedding in our yard."

"And we wouldn't go to a wedding in theirs," David reminded them.

"True enough."

Annie felt a pang for all of them. This stupid feud. Then she realized that Jodie's intended was Kurt McLaughlin. His father was Richard McLaughlin, her own father's brother. So that meant Kurt was her cousin.

"Is Kurt coming to dinner?" she asked Jodie, then hoped she hadn't sounded too eager. What would the woman be thinking of her?

"Oh, you haven't met him, have you? Yes, he is coming. You'll love him right away. Everybody does."

David groaned and Jodie swatted at him with a dish towel.

"That'll be another wedding to suffer through," he teased her. "Why do you all scorn the good old-fashioned tradition of eloping? So much easier for everyone."

"I take it you're not married," Annie said, smiling at his tone.

"Nope. I've been spared so far. But it's hardly my turn. After all, Rafe and Jodie just finally committed.

And Matt isn't anywhere near doing the same. So I've got miles to go before I can be pressured about it."

"Why, David," Jodie teased, "you've already about gone through all the women in town. What are you going to do when your supply runs out? Going to move to a new town and start all over?"

He shrugged, leaning back with an attractive devil-may-care attitude. "I'm going to find somebody. It's bound to happen any time now. I'm sort of hankering toward settlin' down, ya know."

Jodie rolled her eyes. "I'll believe that when I see it."

They all laughed and Annie helped Shelley pull the foil off the tray of food she'd brought with her. "Mom sent over this pan of lasagna," Shelley said. "She makes the best in town, doesn't she?"

"Oh, yes," Annie agreed. "One of my favorites." If there was one thing Millie knew how to do it was to cook up some great food.

She looked around for something else to help with. Jodie was working on the garlic bread, Shelley on the lasagna and Rita was cutting up greens for salad.

"Shall I set the table?" Annie asked.

"Sure, if you want to." Rita wiped her hands and reached into a cupboard. "Here are the mats and some plastic cutlery. I think we'll eat outside on the picnic table so we don't have to move all the wedding supplies on the dining room table."

Annie took the utensils and mats and headed out the back door and into the backyard. The area included a small vegetable garden alongside the house and a large green lawn that led down into a canyon rimmed with pine and cottonwood. A couple of gardeners were busy clearing sections along the perimeter and planting beds of annuals, probably in preparation for the wedding. In a few weeks, the yard would be crowded with people celebrating an Allman marriage.

Annie smiled despite the pang she felt. Would she ever have her own wedding? Did she even want one? She put a hand on her belly and felt a sudden connection to the baby within, a connection stronger than she'd ever felt before. And along with it came a feeling of well-being that calmed her.

"We're going to be okay," she whispered, as much to herself as to the baby. "Whatever happens, we'll make it."

Turning back to the task at hand, she set the long wooden picnic table, making tents of the napkins at each place. She was just standing back to admire her own handiwork when she heard footsteps coming her way. Whirling, she found Matt bearing down on her, looking incredibly handsome with his shirt open at the neck.

"Hi," he said simply.

"Hi yourself," she said back.

For just a moment, there didn't seem to be anything else to say. They stared at each other, both acutely aware of what had happened at the park. Then Annie cleared her throat and spoke.

"I've been thinking things over." She turned from him and looked out on the kitchen garden. "You know, I do appreciate so much you giving me this job and I really do want it. But as far as living here in your house..." She took a deep breath and tried again. "I just don't think I'd better stay."

Chapter Seven

Matt's gaze went hard as flint and almost as cold. "What are you talking about?"

"I can't be here." Shaking her head, she turned to look at him, as though her eyes might be able to convey her meaning if her words couldn't. "Don't you see? It's already the talk of the town. And your family is looking at me cross-eyed. Everyone I see is giving me that 'uh-huh' look as though they think they know what's *really* going on. And I just can't take it."

He was still looking at her darkly, but he nodded slowly at the same time. He knew what she was talking about and, reluctantly, he was acknowledging it. "You think it would be best if we weren't together quite so much," he noted. "And I've got to admit, you're probably right."

Their eyes met. He didn't have to say anything further. They both knew that the pull between them was getting stronger by the minute. If they didn't do something to head it off, fireworks were on the horizon.

She'd been embarrassed at first for having let him see so clearly that she wanted his kiss on the bridge that afternoon, and then not getting it. But her embarrassment had faded. She could tell that he understood. He knew she'd had a weak moment. Luckily he'd had a strong moment at the same time. They could depend on that, or they could stay away from each other as much as possible. And if that didn't work, maybe she would just head on back to Houston. She had friends there. It wouldn't be the end of the world.

"Don't worry," he said. "I've got the solution."

She sighed and looked up at him sadly. "So do I. I think I'd better move out."

"No, not you," he said calmly. "Me. I'm moving out."

She blinked, not sure for a second if she'd heard him right. "What?"

"It's not a big deal. I'll go stay at Rafe's apartment with him. He's got plenty of room."

Her jaw dropped. "Oh, that's crazy."

"No, it'll be much better for everyone." Now that he'd come to the decision, he seemed almost cheery about it. "All you women can take over the house and dedicate it to wedding preparations and we men will stay out of the way."

"I agree."

Annie whirled to find Rita on the back porch starting down the steps toward them with a tray full of drinks. She seemed to have heard most of their conversation.

"Matt's absolutely right. It would be for the best. We could really use you here as an extra pair of hands, Annie. You have no idea how many table favors and paper roses we're going to be putting together."

"I'll help any way I can," she assured Rita. "But I don't have to stay here to do that."

The older woman put down her tray on the table, took up Annie's hands and held them tightly as she smiled into her eyes.

"Please stay. We do want you to. I'm sorry I overreacted this morning. It was just such a surprise." She flashed a quick look at her brother, a look that seemed to have an apology in it, then refocused on Annie. "The more we get to know you, the more we're glad to have you here."

Annie hesitated. When it came right down to it, she didn't have a lot of good options. And the way the invitation was being presented, she could hardly turn it down.

"Well, I suppose we could try it for a while," she said.

Matt nodded, looking perfectly satisfied with the plans as they stood. "By the way, most of the things from your apartment are here. I had the men put all your clothes in your room. The other items are in a storeroom out behind the garage."

"Oh. Thanks so much." It was a relief not to have to go back to that place. Matt did have a way of taking care of things before she even realized that something needed to be done.

She smiled at him. "I guess that settles it. I'll have to stay for the time being."

"Good." He reached up and began to unbutton his shirt as he turned away. "And now that our living plans are taken care of, I'm going to go change into something more comfortable and get ready for dinner."

Funny how just watching him begin to undress caused a strange little flutter in her chest and made her mouth go dry. She smiled at Rita nervously, hoping it wasn't obvious, and began to help her put out the drinks at the places she'd set. It looked like she was going to stay, but she couldn't keep a sense of disquiet completely hidden inside. It would be better if she was on her own, away from the temptations Matt offered and the trap of depending on others. She knew from experience that help like that could evaporate on you just when you needed it most. She was going to have to stay strong. No doubt about it.

Dinner was lively and fun. Everyone talked and Annie hardly got a word in but she felt as if she got to know them all very quickly. Meeting Kurt was a highlight. Tall and handsome, he had a friendly smile and an easy way about him.

And…he was her cousin! It was so amazing to have all these relatives, even if the relationship was one-sided. And she could tell she was going to like Kurt as much as she liked Josh. She watched as his gaze followed Jodie whenever she moved more than a few feet away from him. He was totally in love with her. And he was obviously such a good guy. Didn't that show the rest of them that McLaughlins might be human, too?

Turning, she found Matt's gaze trained on her just as firmly and she flushed. She wanted to tell him to cut it out, that the others would notice. But she had to admit, it warmed a little hidden place in her heart.

"I'm going to run up to see Jesse," Kurt said as they began to clear the dishes away. "I've got some things to report to him."

Annie grimaced. She hadn't seen Jesse Allman yet. He wasn't well and seemed to spend all his time in bed up in his room at the top of the house. It was a little scary thinking of him up there, like a spider weaving plots. She shivered, not sure why she'd conjured up that picture. It was probably based on her childhood fear of the man and was totally unfair. Maybe.

A half hour later the dishes were done and the others were getting out a board game to play, but Annie had noticed Matt slip away some time before and he hadn't come back yet. She found herself making excuses and following him upstairs. They did have a few more things that needed to be dealt with. Maybe he would have time for a little talk.

Matt heard someone coming down the hall and he wondered if it would be Annie. He'd left his door ajar and was making enough noise while packing his suitcase to lead anyone toward his location. Had he done that on purpose, to make sure she would find her way to him? What the hell? Why not?

And then, there she was, looking in on him, her mass of curly dark hair flying around her face, one strand falling over her eyes in a deliciously seductive way that made his gut churn.

"What are you doing?" she asked, looking as though she were stricken with guilt.

"I'm packing." He threw a couple of socks in, then

glanced at her again, but kept on working. And he couldn't help but notice how her arrival seemed to brighten the room.

That was just the problem. She'd changed his life. Yes, ridiculous as it was, a woman he barely knew had thrown his sense of comfortable stability for a loop. In fact, she'd taken over his mind. When she'd fallen into his life, he'd been preoccupied with finding his baby, wandering around like a man possessed, calling the private detective he'd hired five times a day to check on progress. Now he was preoccupied with Annie as well. All this preoccupation was crowding out anything close to a normal life. In other words, he couldn't get her out of his head. And didn't really want to.

"I feel so bad about kicking you out of your own house," she was saying, standing at a distance, but close enough for him to feel the effect of her presence acutely.

"You're not kicking me out of anything. I'm glad to escape from this pressurized atmosphere."

"The wedding madness?"

"Exactly." And a lot more.

Annie, Annie, if you only knew how you put a guy on edge just hearing your voice. And catching your scent in the air. And getting a glimpse of your pretty face, looking so concerned.

His body was responding. This was crazy. He felt as if he were on something. Overcaffeinated. Overstimulated. Over the top.

Oh, hell. I've got to get out of here.

She sat down on the bed and gave a bounce. It was a good bed, firm but with a nice spring to it. She bounced again, looking delighted, like a child on a carnival ride. He almost groaned aloud. Not only was she outrageously adorable, the bouncing was bringing to mind how good she would feel in his arms, how they would move together, how the mattress would give, then harden under them... Oh, lord, the woman had no mercy.

But then, hopefully she didn't understand how crazy he was getting to be about her. What on earth had caused him to fall for a woman who was about to have a baby that wasn't his? Penny—wasn't that it? And his guilt over not being there for her when she needed him? That was how it started, but this was going way too far. He kept telling himself it was just a passing thing, a momentary madness, and that it would fade away very soon. His sanity would return to him. Someday he would look back on these days with mild amusement, wondering what had caused him to go nuts for a while.

Oh, yeah. Dream on.

"Is this the same room you've had since you were a little boy?" she asked him.

"Nope. This part of the house was added when I was in high school. But I've had this room ever since then. It's been my base, my anchor. I went away to college and came back to this room. Same with medical school."

She nodded, looking about at the photographs of his mother and various friends, the baseball trophies, the books and magazines. He felt a twinge of remorse for talking about how important his room was to him as he remembered what she'd told him at the park, about how she'd grown up without a place to call her own. Along with everything else, he had a strong protective urge toward her. He didn't want anything hurting her. But he knew in his heart that he himself was the most likely to do that.

Yes, moving out was the best answer to the problem.

Sliding off the bed, she started surveying the titles in his bookcase. "I thought maybe we ought to go over a few things," she said without looking around. "I'd better warn you that I'm going to have to take an hour off next Friday morning. I've got a checkup with Dr. Marin."

Raising his head, he looked at her speculatively. "You know, I could—"

"No, you couldn't." Glancing over her shoulder at him, she shuddered delicately. "What do you think— that you're going to come in and deliver the baby when the time comes?"

His grin was lopsided. The prospect actually charmed him. "I could if I had to."

"No way."

She was right, of course. He was getting too close to her to be objective. Dr. Marin was a good doctor, he supposed. He was going to have to trust him with her.

"And, of course, there's Thursdays. I need those afternoons off."

"Yes, I know. You said that before."

That again. He'd been hoping she would get over her sense that she needed to keep that extra job. He was going to control his annoyance. That much he had promised himself. But she had to understand how impossible it was for her to work for the McLaughlins.

"We need to talk about that."

She turned and gazed right at him. "There's nothing

to talk about. I work at the McLaughlin Ranch on Thursday afternoons."

Anger Management 101 said to count to ten before speaking. He only got to five. "Well, you're going to have to stop that," he said firmly.

"No," she replied just as firmly if not more so. Her eyes flashed. "That's one thing I won't stop."

Her tone and manner brought him up short. She really meant it. He found it hard to believe that she would throw away everything just to keep a part-time job out at McLaughlin Ranch.

"I really don't want you to do this," he said as calmly as he could.

She didn't waver. "I'm sorry about that. But I'm going to do it. Nothing you say will stop me."

He shook his head, mystified. "What's so special about this job?"

"It's not the job. It's Josh and Cathy McLaughlin. I enjoy working for them."

"Okay, then what's so special about them?"

She caught her breath, hesitating, then said, "They need me. And I like them."

It was more than that. He knew instinctively that something was going on here. But he also knew that she wasn't likely to come clean about it if he pushed her too hard. So he tried a little sideways action. Sitting down on the edge of the bed, he leaned back against the headboard, watching her through narrowed eyes.

"What exactly do you do there?" he asked her.

She looked at him, then gingerly sat down at the foot of the bed herself.

"Well, I call it housekeeping, but it's actually more like baby-sitting with a little cleaning and food preparation thrown in." She looked to see if he was listening. "I go every Thursday afternoon for four hours. That gives Cathy some time to go shopping by herself or to meet some friends for lunch or go to the dentist. She really needs that time off. She spends most of every day working on that ranch with the baby practically strapped to her back."

He frowned thoughtfully. "From what I've heard, Josh is actually doing a pretty good job of bringing the ranch back to being a going concern after his father darn near ran it into the ground. But I'm sure it's a big project."

Annie stole a look at his face. What he was saying was what she'd surmised but hadn't heard put quite that clearly before.

"How did you get to know them?" he asked.

"I saw the job advertised and I applied for it."

"You didn't know them before?"

"No."

He was quiet for a moment, and she waited, letting him absorb the information.

"You do know about the feud, don't you?" he asked her at last.

"Of course. No one can grow up in Chivaree, even part-time, and not know about the feud. It started about the time the town was founded, didn't it?"

He nodded.

"That's a long time." She raised an eyebrow archly. "Don't you think it's about time to end it?"

"End it?" The concept was a surprise to him, as though she'd suggested breathing water instead of air. "You can't end something that old."

She rolled her eyes. "You know, this silly feud may be important to the Allmans and it may be important to the McLaughlins, but to the rest of us, outside your paranoid little world, it means absolutely nothing. I think you should all grow up and get over it."

"Easy for you to say," he muttered, but his mind had moved on to something else. She'd mentioned her checkup with Dr. Marin and now he remembered she'd said something about his being involved in her adoption plans. "Is Dr. Marin your liaison with the adoption lawyer?" he asked.

She turned to look at him, wary surprise in her eyes. "Yes."

He grimaced, raking his fingers through his hair. "You know, you've got other options. We should talk about—"

"It's a good option," she said evenly. She didn't wait to hear what his ideas might be. "Adoptions can work. There are many wonderful instances of adoption going so well. Just look at—" She was about to say Josh and Cathy, but she stopped in time. He didn't want to hear about McLaughlin adoptions, she was sure.

"I know that," he responded with a touch of impatience. "I just want you to be sure you know what you're doing, that you've looked at every alternative."

He could tell she was biting her tongue to keep from snapping at him. "Matt, do you really think I'm going into this on a whim? Of course I've thought about it, long and hard."

He frowned, then shook his head. "Annie, just because your mother's experience was not so hot doesn't mean that you will have the same life. Things have loosened up a lot since then. You're smart, you're educated, you'll have opportunities she couldn't have dreamed of."

"You don't know anything about it. I lived it. I have to think of the future for this baby. A child does best in a two-parent home." She looked at him defiantly. "You don't think a child needs both a mother and a father?" she challenged.

"Oh, absolutely. If possible. That's why…" His words trailed off and he took a deep breath.

His tone drew her attention and when she looked into his eyes, they were stormy in a way that sent up warning signals all through her system.

"I've got something I should tell you about, Annie," he said softly. "I should have told you about this before, but it's a hard thing to tell. It isn't going to make you think any better of me."

"Why? What is it?"

The sound of laughter filled the air. A few of the others were coming up the stairs. Matt grabbed her hand.

"We can't really talk here. I'll go out and head them off, then you go down the back way to the backyard. I'll meet you out there."

She rose from the bed, looking at him with a worried frown between her beautiful eyebrows, and then she stood back to let him go. But just as he passed her, she reached out and touched his arm, as though to comfort him. As though she could read his mind and knew what was bothering him. He paused, looking down into her pretty face for a moment, then moved on toward the others. But that simple gesture spoke volumes. How could he keep from falling for this woman when she kept doing things like that?

Annie waited in the shadows of an old pecan tree that stood like a sentinel along the margins of the backyard. There was a light on in the window at the top of the house and she knew that had to be where Jesse Allman was. A place where she didn't want to go.

Matt came out the back door and she moved forward to meet him. She had no idea what he was going to tell her but she assumed it probably had something to do with the pained, brooding look that often came over his face. She hadn't known what to attribute it to. Now, maybe she would find out.

"Hi," she said, as though they hadn't just parted company moments earlier.

"Thanks for coming out here," he told her. "Let's walk down by the edge of the canyon."

"Okay."

There were lights strung up in the trees around the yard but the lighting wasn't perfect and he took her hand to steady her as they walked across the grass. His touch was warm. She tried to ignore it. Their steps slowed as they reached the edge of the dark canyon and he dropped her hand. The sound of water rushing over rocks at the bottom of the canyon made a background of sound. The evening air was cool. Annie turned to look at Matt, but she had a hard time making out his features in the dim light.

"This isn't a big secret," he told her, as though he were afraid she might have taken the wrong idea from his earlier words. "Everyone else in the house already knows about it. It's just that I hadn't told you yet, and I thought you ought to know."

She smiled at him encouragingly. "Then I guess you'd better tell me."

He took a deep breath and began. "You know the part your father played in your life? The thing you seem to despise him for?" He shoved his hands into the pockets of his slacks. "Well, I've done the same thing he did. I've got a baby out there that I don't know."

A shock ran through her. "Oh, Matt."

He looked out over the canyon. "I only found out about it a couple of months ago."

Even in the dark, she could see his tortured expression. Reaching out, she put a hand on his upper arm. "What happened?" she asked softly.

He hesitated, looking down at her. "Okay, let me start from the beginning. I went to medical school in Dallas, then did my internship and residency there, too. For a period of a few months I had a relationship with a woman named Penny. She was a lot of fun and we had a great time together." He looked away again. "Eventually, we had a physical relationship. Then things began to come between us and we had a falling out. She left town and I never heard from her again."

Annie nodded. She understood that sort of thing. Happened every day and seemed so harmless at the time. But the ramifications were often huge, like the pebble in the pond. "Were you in love?"

"Love?" He looked surprised that she would even bring it up. "It was a very casual relationship. We were both young and I don't think either of us considered it true love."

She nodded again, yet she couldn't help but wonder if Penny had felt the same way Matt had. After all, it was different if you were the one who was going to carry the baby—a fact she knew only too well.

"Anyway, a few weeks ago I got a call from an old friend who had known us both and in the course of conversation, he asked how Penny was. I told him I didn't know and he asked what had ever happened to our baby." He winced even now, thinking of that conversation and how it had hit him. "I was stunned."

"You had no idea."

"No."

"Have you tried to find Penny?"

"Yes. It was Shelley, actually, who found Penny's brother living in San Antonio. I brought him here to Chivaree and got him a job at Allman Industries." He paused and grimaced before he went on. "But tragically, Penny had died. And no one knows whatever happened to the baby."

"Oh, my gosh!" Her hands went to her mouth. That was a twist she hadn't expected.

Turning, he reached out to lean against a low tree limb. "I've hired a private investigator, but so far, no leads."

"Oh, Matt, I'm so sorry."

Leaning his back against the tree, he looked at her. "So you see, that gives me a different perspective on your situation and your plan to give your baby up for adoption. I'm afraid my baby was adopted. I may never find him…or her."

That put a lump in her throat. She felt sorry for him, sorry for Penny, sorry for the baby who was who-knew-where. She moved closer. "But Matt, I think it's a credit to you that you are trying."

He snorted softly. "A little late."

"My father never tried at all," she mused, more to herself than to him. "Of course, I'm not sure he even knew about me. It's possible he didn't."

He looked away. "I keep wondering if she tried to tell me, if I was just insensitive and ignored the signs. I'm a medical professional for God's sake. I should have seen the evidence."

She put her hand on his arm again, wishing she knew what she could do to comfort him. "Matt, don't do that to yourself. For all you know, *she* didn't know until after she left you."

He looked down at her face upturned toward his with such an earnest look and his own relaxed into a faint smile. "Annie…" He touched her cheek with his forefinger. "Do you despise me now?"

"Oh, Matt! I could never, never…" Words weren't enough. Somehow she had to show him.

When she threw her arms around his neck and pressed herself to him, she hadn't really meant for it to end in a kiss. At least, she didn't think that was what she'd meant to do. Still, it happened. One second she was murmuring reassurance and comfort and the next, she was spellbound.

That was the only way she could describe it when she thought about it later—and she thought about it a lot. It wasn't as though she was a novice in the kissing department. She'd had boyfriends over the years, and of course, there had been Rick. Even as a teenager, there had been experiments during stolen moments at Coyote Park, among other places. She liked kissing. With the right sort of men.

And Matt was all wrong. She knew that, had hoped to hold back what that did to her. When he'd kissed her the night before, it had been fleeting, casual, almost friendly, and he'd pulled back and apologized. But this was different. No apologies were going to cancel out this kiss.

His mouth was hot on hers, hot and hungry, and she responded immediately, just as urgently, her tongue sliding against his, her body arching to feel as much of him against her as she could get. His hands slid up under her shirt, fingers just rough enough to tantalize her smooth skin. And the spell took hold.

She'd stepped off the edge of reality and was spinning in a new place where her mind shut down and her senses took over. Small things took on a huge new importance—the minty scent of his aftershave, the sultry taste of his skin, the sweet torture of the touch of his palm as it cupped her breast. She moaned with pleasure, grinding against him, and his kisses traveled down the chord of her neck, almost biting, but not quite, sending her into a special sort of ecstasy. She wanted him in a way she'd never wanted a man before. How could that be? It was all wrong. And yet, it had never felt so right.

When she finally found the strength to pull back, she was gasping for breath, and his breathing was just as ragged. Looking down at her, he framed her face with his hands, his intense gaze searching her eyes, and he half laughed.

"Oh, Annie, I can't believe how much I want you." He spoke softly but his words tore out of him as though it was agony for him to admit it.

"Which is exactly why we can't do this again," she noted breathlessly. But she said it so sadly, he laughed again, pulling her close and holding her for a moment, her head against his chest.

"Okay," he said, releasing her at last with obvious regret. "We'll be good."

"We'll be good," she echoed ruefully. "Or die trying."

They strolled back toward the house, talking quietly, her hand in his. But he'd dropped it by the time they reached the others, and he rather gruffly said his goodbyes, grabbed his suitcase and left. Afterward, Annie went to her own room to give herself some time to savor that kiss. Savor it, and vow it wouldn't happen again.

Thursday afternoon found Annie at the photographer's, helping Cathy get portraits made of baby Emily. She watched Cathy making faces at her child, trying to get her to smile for the camera. And it worked. Suddenly Emily gurgled with baby laughter and the photographer began clicking away.

"Oh, those are going to be so good," Annie said.

"They better be," Cathy responded, sprawling in the

chair beside her, exhausted. "I feel like I've just broken a bronco here. That was hard work!"

By now, Emily's laughter had dissolved into tears and Annie sprang up to get her. She comforted the child while Cathy dealt with the desk, and soon they were back in Cathy's SUV, bouncing along the rutted road to the McLaughlin Ranch.

Annie felt almost as tired as Cathy did. The last few days had been rewarding but they surely had tried her stamina. Working at Allman Industries was turning out well. She had no qualms about the job, only the fact that she had to do it within twenty feet of Matt. It was very hard keeping her mind on her work when the man who made her dizzy was just steps away. So close she could almost hear him breathing.

He'd been acting the perfect gentleman, she had to say. There had been no more kisses. He hadn't even come over to the house since that night. And at the office he'd treated her with a dignified reserve. But that didn't do anything to stifle the way her heart raced whenever she looked at him.

And it was crazy. She knew that very well. Once burned, twice shy, they said. *Hah. Just tell that to my traitorous heart.*

Luckily, she had a reminder to them both. The baby she carried was getting bigger every day. Every time she was tempted to forget all common sense and throw herself at Matt's handsome head, the baby kicked or moved in that adorable way it had, and she remembered. Next week she would see Dr. Marin and he would want to know if she planned to go the adoption route or not. A hard decision, one she would just as soon put off for a while longer.

She looked back at Emily, now sound asleep in her car seat. Matt's words on the subject of adoption came back to her. She couldn't deny that his arguments had shaken some of her own opinions on whether or not she should go through with it. Glancing at Cathy in the driver's seat, she had a thought. Maybe she could use some input from the other side of the equation.

"Cathy, tell me about Emily. How you adopted her."

Cathy threw her a quick smile. "We found her in San Antonio. It was a private adoption, through a lawyer. Someone who had worked for the McLaughlins for years."

"You were lucky."

"Yes."

"I've heard adoptions are much more difficult nowadays."

"Sometimes they are. It depends on the circumstances." Cathy gave her a sideways look. "Actually, we ended up having the paperwork handled over the border in order to avoid a few rules that might have held us up for months. The lawyer is a real expert in these things and he took care of everything."

"Do you know much about her birth mother?"

Cathy shook her head. "Not a thing. We have some medical information in case it ever becomes necessary. But that's all." She glanced back and smiled at her darling child. "Actually, when we adopted her, the lawyer said that Emily's birth mother requested someone from Chivaree. Something about it all coming full circle.

Which makes me think she must have been from Chivaree herself. I didn't question anything at the time. Once I took one look at her, I just wanted my baby in my arms. But I sometimes look around at girls walking by when I'm downtown and wonder, could it be her?"

"I guess you'll never know."

"And I hope she doesn't know anything about us. You read about these nightmare situations where birth parents try to get their babies back years later. Every time I think of such a thing, my heart stops. It's kind of a strange position to be in and yet, it doesn't really matter. Emily is so ours. She couldn't be more my baby if I'd had twelve hours of screaming labor to get her."

Annie smiled. "I know. I've seen it."

If only Matt could see how this little family created such a warm, loving circle she was sure it would change his mind about adoption. Cathy and Josh had made no bones from the beginning about the fact that Emily was adopted. But just looking in from the outside, no one could have guessed it. The bond among them all couldn't have been stronger.

She loved coming to their house and seeing them interact. Sometimes she felt guilty for taking money for being there. She would have gladly come without that. In no time at all, Cathy and Josh had become among the very closest friends she'd ever had. Her heart ached to think that the relationship they had might be shattered when the facts came out. There was no easy way to break it to Josh that his father was her father, too.

Maybe she should have been truthful right from the start. But if she had, would they have let her into their lives this way? Would she have experienced this? Unfortunately there were no easy answers. All she knew for sure was that she didn't want to hurt anyone unnecessarily. And maybe, in order to do that, she should withdraw without telling them anything at all…

Cathy pulled the car to a stop at a red light and turned to look at her. "Why all these questions, Annie? Are you thinking about putting your baby up for adoption?"

Annie hesitated. She wasn't as brave about it anymore. "I don't know. It's an option I'm considering."

"It's a heartbreaking decision to make, I know," Cathy said. "And no one can make it but you." Reaching out, she took Annie's hand. "Please know Josh and I will be there for you whatever you decide."

Annie felt tears threatening. What the heck was this? She was turning into a waterfall. It had to be the pregnancy. Hormones. Whatever, it was darn annoying.

But she also felt tremendous gratitude to Cathy. She knew things might be very different once the truth was out. All promises would be off by then. Still, it was nice to know they felt this way for the moment.

Josh was in the kitchen as they came into the house. He rose without his usual smile as he faced them.

"Annie," he said, looking troubled. "What's this about you living with the Allmans?"

Chapter Eight

Annie gasped softly, then hoped Josh hadn't noticed. She should have told him and Cathy about this when she first arrived today. It was too late to remedy that now, but she would do her best to smooth that over with a few facts. She explained quickly about what had happened, about the fainting at Millie's, about Matt's concern for her pregnancy and him showing up at her apartment in the middle of the night when chaos was happening next door.

"So he just sort of took you in?" Cathy asked, looking intrigued.

She nodded.

"Well, that seems mighty neighborly of him." Josh's voice was edgy with sarcasm, causing Cathy to give him a reproving glance.

"It was because of my pregnancy I think. He…has reasons to feel especially interested in new babies right now." She hesitated and then decided not to explain how he felt about adoption.

"So is he the first Allman you've ever met?" Josh asked her, scooping Emily up in his arms and looking a little more relaxed as his baby girl laughed and tried to grab his ears.

Annie grinned at him as he fended Emily off. "He was my first. Now I know tons of them."

"We'd better introduce you to some of our McLaughlin relatives fast to provide a sort of antidote," Josh said, only half teasing as he set Emily down again, watching as she ran off to play in her own room. "Too much time with the Allmans has been known to drive the innocent to madness."

"I guess I'm not all that innocent," Annie retorted.

His gaze sharpened. "You do know about the feud between our two families?"

"Oh, yes. I've heard about it for years." Walking toward the pantry, Annie began putting away some of the groceries they had picked up at the store on the way home. "It's pretty much ancient history, though, wouldn't you say? Isn't it time to bury the hatchet?"

He followed her, thumbs hooked in the belt loops of his jeans. "Funny thing about a feud like that. It becomes part of the air you breathe. It becomes ingrained in your heritage. It's a part of you, even though most of us don't remember what started it all."

"What do you suppose did start it?" Cathy asked. She wasn't originally from Chivaree so much of this story was new to her, too, Annie noted.

"Well, the two families were the founders of the

town. That often sets up an adversarial relationship just on the face of it. And I think there was a lot of rustlin' of horses and stealing of each other's women and things like that going on in the old days. That was generations ago, of course."

"So why is the feud still going on now?" Annie asked, folding the brown paper bag.

"I don't know. Growing up it just becomes a part of you. And then you go to school and everyone expects you to stick to your own side and they egg you on. It just continues. The teenaged years are the worst, I guess. We McLaughlins were always pitted against the Allmans at everything. Especially the years where the rodeo thing was big. We were always trying to outride or outbust one or another of them. That's just the way it is."

"How does Kurt avoid it?" she asked.

"So you've met Kurt?" A smile lit his eyes for a moment. "Good old Kurt. Funny, I used to like him best out of all my cousins, and now he's turned traitor and gone and joined up with other side."

She turned on him, frowning. "See, when you put it that way, it sounds bad. But maybe Kurt could be a bridge."

"A bridge?" He made a face. "Who needs a bridge? Who wants a bridge between the Allmans and the McLaughlins?"

But she sort of liked the idea. "Maybe *I* could be a bridge," she murmured, and then looked up quickly when she realized she'd said it out loud.

He was looking at her curiously, obviously wondering why she would say such a thing. She flushed and realized it was time to be getting home.

But she wavered. Here it was, her big opportunity. The conversation had set it up perfectly. The time was ripe. She could tell them right now. Right this minute. She bit her lip, trying to make herself do it.

But she realized that she didn't have the nerve. Not yet, anyway.

"So tell me," she said instead, facing Josh. "I'm going to be living with the Allmans for another few weeks at least. Is this going to be a problem?"

He looked at her for a long moment, then he smiled. "No, of course not," he said.

Cathy breathed a sigh of relief. "Thank goodness. My husband is sane after all."

Annie smiled but she thought she understood Josh a little better than Cathy did. The feud would always be there. Bridge or no bridge, it wasn't going away. There was just no getting around that one.

If Annie had thought the tension would relax when Matt moved in with his brother and wasn't around to provoke her all the time at the house, she might as well have saved herself the trouble. That theory was proved wrong right away. Even in the office, there was electricity between the two of them that she couldn't deny.

That doesn't mean you have to act on it, she kept telling herself incessantly. *In fact, you can't. And you won't. And he won't, either.*

She would be working on a knotty problem, her face twisted with the intensity of her concentration, and then something would compel her to look up and across the office—and there he was at his own desk, staring at her with a look on his face that she couldn't quite interpret. And some little devil of delicious shivering would start up inside her.

Other times it was just the sense of his presence in the room. She could feel him even when she didn't turn and look at him. It wasn't that he was staring at her or anything like that. He was just there. And something about him filled her consciousness with pleasure at the oddest times.

She was getting the office arranged in ways that seemed to amaze him. Maybe it was her nursing experience that helped her know how medical matters should be systematized. Maybe it was the natural inborn ability to organize. At any rate, the office was running more smoothly than it ever had.

Matt was already involved in operating a vaccination clinic for employees and she made the calls and set up appointments so that the whole plant was up-to-date by the end of her second week. Then she arranged a lecture series on workplace accidents and contacted a San Antonio firm that would come to give a talk in the future on identity codes for employees' children, including fingerprinting and imbedded microchips.

In the meantime, Matt saw any workplace injuries or illnesses there in his office and also spent part of every day at his private practice—giving Annie a sometimes welcome break from the intensity of his presence. And of course, there was the business of Allman Industries to run. Rafe was the acting executive officer, though everyone made sure she knew Jesse Allman wanted Matt to take over the job and clearly he felt pressured to do as his

father asked. She would have thought that would make
things awkward between him and his brother, but it didn't
seem to. Perhaps that was because Matt made no secret
of the fact that he wanted to pursue medicine, so there was
really little reason for Rafe to feel threatened.

The days went by quickly, so full of work for both
of them that there wasn't much time to dwell on the way
they felt about each other. When Annie wasn't at work,
she was at the Allman house, working on wedding in-
vitations or favors or finger food. It was only late at
night that she lay in the soft, heavenly bed and thought
about Matt.

Why Matt? She had a sort of crush on the man, she
supposed. He had a knack for setting off certain reactions in her, different from any man she'd ever known
before. And he'd been more than decent to her. She
owed him for that. But once the baby was born and she
was on her own two feet again… Yes, then what?

If things were only different, then she would have
more scope for dreaming. If she weren't pregnant with
another man's baby…if she weren't a McLaughlin…if
he weren't an Allman. And then again, if he hadn't just
found out about his own baby, he probably wouldn't
have given her a second look that day at Millie's. He'd
never made that a secret. His interest in her came from
the baby she carried. Once that was over, for all she
knew, he might not have time for her anymore. Never
again was she going to take a man's interest as evidence
of deep feeling. Things just didn't work that way.

And dreaming was for people who had the time and
luxury for it. She'd had dreams before and look what

had come of them. She had other things to think about—like what she was going to do about this baby.

On the day of her appointment with Dr. Marin, she left the office before lunch and waved goodbye to Matt, who scowled at her instead of waving back. The regular checkup didn't take long, but as the doctor was setting up the monitoring equipment, she blurted out something she hadn't even known she was going to say.

"Can you tell me the gender of my baby today?" she asked.

"Of course," he answered. "I'll show you the latest ultrasound I had the technician take last time you were here."

Her heart beat hard with excitement as she realized what she'd requested. She was going to see a picture of her baby. This pregnancy was finally becoming real to her. She wasn't sure that was a good thing.

"You've got a bouncing baby boy in there," Dr. Marin told her with a grin. "All the signs point to the fact that he looks darn healthy, too."

"Oh." She couldn't think of a thing to say. She closed her eyes for a moment of silent prayer, then opened them and felt as though happiness was flowing in her veins.

His grin faded and a small frown took its place. "Have you been thinking about our talk?" he asked. "Was there anything else you wanted to know about the adoption process?"

"No," she said, losing some of the excitement and avoiding his gaze. "I—I still have to think about it."

"No problem," he told her. "But it would be best to

make sure you're in the proper mind-set if you're going to go through with it."

"I'll let you know," she said quickly. "Later."

"Of course."

She left soon after and headed back to work feeling a little shaky. Her baby was due in less than two months. When she'd planned out her trip to Chivaree, she'd told herself to keep her distance from the life growing inside her. She would do her best for the child with proper nutrition and checkup and everything a baby needed to come into the world whole and healthy. But she wouldn't ask to know the gender. She wouldn't let them show her the pictures. She wouldn't think of names. And now she'd taken two steps she hadn't planned to take. If she thought of a name for her baby, she would be taking a third.

"Three strikes and you're out," she whispered to herself as she drove into the parking lot. "No thinking about a name!"

But she knew she was grasping at straws. Patting her rounded belly, she smiled. Her baby was in there, doing great. What could be more wonderful?

Matt didn't ask her how the appointment had gone and was obviously in a foul mood. Glowering and gloomy, he almost bit her head off for the smallest infractions and left for his private practice as soon as he could get away. She breathed a sigh of relief as he went out the door.

To her surprise, he showed up at the house for dinner that night, for the first time since he'd moved out. Still grumpy, he didn't say much. But the others were so full of good spirits, his brooding went largely unnoticed. Kurt had brought along Katy, his year-old child from his first marriage and she was charming everyone. Watching her play to the audience, Annie wondered what her own baby would be like. Would she get to know?

Suddenly she knew she wanted to—very badly. Glancing at Matt, she noted that he was paying no attention. His mind was on something else and he barely noticed the others at all.

But once the dishes had been cleared, he caught Annie alone and stopped her from going back to the dining room where Rita and Jodie were working on decorations.

"Want to go for a walk?" he asked her.

"Where?" she responded, surprised.

"Down the path along the canyon." He indicated the direction with a jerk of his head.

She hesitated, the blood beginning to beat a rhythm in her veins. "Why?"

He gave her a look she could only categorize as exasperation and took her hand, tugging her toward the door. "Come on," he said gruffly.

She let him lead her outside. It was already getting dark and lights twinkled in the trees. They walked toward the canyon but she was getting more and more nervous about this.

"Did you have something you wanted to say to me?" she asked, hoping to speed things up so that they could go back more quickly.

He swung around so that he could look at her, jamming his hands into his pockets. "I'm sorry I've been so annoying to be around today," he told her. "I heard from Dan Kramer, the private investigator looking for my baby this morning."

"Oh! Bad news?"

He hesitated. "Well, not good news. He's about exhausted the leads on records here in Texas. He's afraid the adoption paperwork might have been filed out of state, in which case, it's going to take a small miracle to find it."

"Oh, Matt, I'm sorry." She reached out to touch his arm. "That's rotten. But you shouldn't lose hope. I'm sure he'll find something."

"Maybe. Maybe not. It depends on how accurate the names used in the filing were." He put his hand over hers. "But that's not your problem."

She felt a jolt as his fingers wrapped around hers. His shoulders seemed wide as the horizon and she felt an odd impulse to curl herself into his embrace. She had to fight off that sort of thing. "Sure it is," she said a bit breathlessly. "I care about you."

"Do you?" He looked completely unconvinced. Then he sighed and shook his head as though he was fed up with himself as well as everything else. "Oh, hell, Annie. I just want to be with you. I want to talk to you and look at you and hear your voice."

The deep emotion in his tone touched a chord inside her and that scared her almost more than his words. "Matt…"

He took her face in his hands and looked down into her eyes. "I just want to touch your hair and look at you in the moonlight," he said huskily, his gaze moving over her as though searching for something he couldn't name but needed badly.

She closed her eyes. His hands felt like heaven on her skin. This was so dangerous. What if she let herself fall in love with this man? Would she regret it forever?

"Matt, why are you doing this?" Sincerely troubled, she looked up at him.

He leaned over her, his gaze on her mouth. "I don't know, Annie. I'm telling myself not to, even now. But there is something pulling me back to you every time I try to break away."

"Matt…"

He kissed her softly. It wasn't like it had been before when they'd fallen under the passion spell. His kiss was soft, as though he cherished her, and she felt a glow from it. After they drew apart, he gave her a long, slow smile, tucked her hand into the crook of his arm, and they continued their walk along the brush-covered edge. She felt strangely light, as though she could dance out over the canyon if she wanted to.

They talked about general things—the preparations for the wedding, the weather, a new store opening downtown. And all the while she felt the glow, and finally she realized what it might be. Happiness. He'd made it clear that he needed her to help him heal the pain of the day. And that aroused warm feelings inside her. There was no way to guard against something like that.

"I found out what gender my baby is today," she told him as they turned back toward the house.

He smiled at her, clearly glad she'd finally done that. "Good. About time. So tell me, what is it?"

"He's a boy."

He nodded, squeezing her hand. "Great. What are you going to name him?"

"I don't know," she said evasively. "I'm avoiding that at the moment."

No name. That was a given. Once this baby had a name, she would never be able to hand him over to another mother.

Did kissing Matt do the same thing—cross a bridge that was hard to retreat from? If she kissed him too often would she fall in love? And if she was in love, would she be able to walk away?

That was just it. She had to give herself that freedom. She knew instinctively that she could depend on him for a lot of things, and that he would never leave her in the lurch the way Rick had. But she also knew that those bare essentials weren't enough. She might be making Matt happy right now, just being with him, but she knew that his feelings for her were based on her pregnancy. And that wasn't enough for her to let down her guard. She wanted it all. She wanted true love. And without it, she would never give up her freedom again.

It was a hot, windy Saturday afternoon and everyone was gone but Annie. Rita and Jodie had driven down to San Antonio to look for dresses for the wedding and David was off playing tennis with friends. Annie was restless.

Her baby was jumping around like a kid on a trampoline, making her laugh. She looked down the corridor. There was Matt's room. Something about it drew her in that direction.

Padding silently down the hall, she tried the knob. The door came open easily. Silently, she slipped into the room.

Just looking around at the pictures, books and personal items made her miss him. He hadn't been back again since the night he'd been so tortured and had seemed to need her to help lift his spirits. At work he was cool and professional. She couldn't tell what he was thinking. After the night they'd walked by the canyon, she'd thought he would be more affectionate in everyday life. But if anything, he was less so. To say she was confused would be to put it mildly.

But that was okay. Being confused was better than being in love.

Nothing had moved in this room since the night he'd packed up and left, just to make her feel more comfortable staying in his house. She picked up an old baseball lying on his shelf. It had an autograph of someone she didn't recognize. She was squinting at it when she thought she heard a board creak. Holding her breath, she listened. Nothing. She relaxed. This was an old house with numerous additions. It was going to creak.

Putting down the baseball, she looked at the picture of Matt's mother. She'd had a pretty face, calm with a sense of fun in her eyes. Losing your mother was always tough. It hadn't exactly been a bed of roses for her, and she'd been a grown woman. But to be a youngster and have your mother die had to be something you never did completely get over.

She sighed. Why was it that every time she thought

about Matt she either found something to sympathize with or something to admire? She had to stop this. Maybe she ought to ask his sisters to itemize some of his bad qualities, just to give her something to use to resist liking him too much.

Turning, she looked at the bed.

That bouncy bed. She smiled. Throwing her arms out, she let herself fall on it, giggling as it bounced. Then she lay still on her back, her hands on her belly, and closed her eyes, trying to catch Matt's scent in his bed. If only…

"So, what do you think you're doin' here, missy?"

The voice went through her like a jagged knife and she shot up to a sitting position. Jesse Allman stood in the doorway. That was who it had to be. Old and sick, he still had the power to scare her.

"N-n-nothing," she stammered.

"Do you know who I am?"

She nodded. "Yes, Mr. Allman. I think I do."

He glowered and pointed at her belly. "Did Matt do that?" he demanded.

She gasped. He certainly did come right to the point. "No, he did not," she told him, managing to sound as indignant as she felt.

"Good." He nodded. "There's been too much of that sort of thing going on around here."

She blinked at him. "There has?"

"Sure. Why I remember, back in the summer of '75…" He caught himself short and looked at her, then cleared his throat. "Well, never mind that." He looked at the evidence of her pregnancy again and shook his head disapprovingly. "I suppose you're not married."

"No, sir, I'm not." She raised her chin, just to let him know she wasn't as ashamed of that as he seemed to think she should be.

"And I suppose you're going to end up marrying Matt, aren't you?"

Her jaw dropped on that one. "No! There's no reason in the world I would marry Matt."

He gave her a scornful laugh. "Sure there is. I saw you a-lyin' there on his bed looking all dreamy and such."

She stood as though the bed had suddenly turned into a hot potato. No force on earth could have compelled her back to that bed now. "I was just…just…"

He waved her to silence. "Honey, I've been around for a long time. I've seen a lot of things. When you're young, you try to pretend you can overcome human nature. I'm here to tell you, your fight will be in vain. When you fall in love, that's all that matters to you and you'll knock over your best friend's mother to get to what you need."

Now she really was offended. "Oh, that's ridiculous."

"You mark my words, sweetie. I've been there. I've done wrong in my life. And I'm paying for it now. This old body has turned on me big time."

He stared at her, narrowing his eyes and squinting as he looked her over. "What did you say your name was?"

She hadn't, but she didn't want to be rude. "Annie Torres."

"Annie Torres, eh?" His mouth twisted in a grin that looked too cynical to be humorous. "Any relation to a little gal named Marina Torres? The one that used to be the housekeeper out at the McLaughlin place?"

She was so used to seeing no recognition in the faces around her she'd forgotten there was always the chance that someone would recognize who she was. Her heart sank and she thought fast. She could lie. But there really was no point, was there?

"She was my mother," she admitted at last.

He nodded, head cocked to the side. "She was a pretty little thing, just like you. How's she doin'?"

"She died last year."

"Oh. Well, I'm real sorry to hear that." He went back to studying her face. "So you're Marina's little girl."

She shivered, sure that he saw everything there was to see inside her, like an X ray.

"Yeah, okay. I see the resemblance."

The way he said it made her wonder what resemblance he was talking about. After all, he'd known both her parents—even if she hadn't. She looked at him sharply but his dark glittering eyes weren't revealing anything at all. Only moments later, his words said it all.

"You know who your daddy was?"

She couldn't help but react defensively. "Why? Do you?"

"Well, I can't say as I know it for sure, but your mother, Marina, she said it was William McLaughlin at the time. And we all figured she knew what she was talking about."

Annie nodded slowly. It took her breath away to have it confirmed like this. "That's what she told me, too."

"Them two McLaughlin boys, William and Richard, neither one of 'em was good for much." Obviously tiring, he looked around for support and pulled out the desk chair, sitting in it heavily. "Tell you one thing," he said. "We Allmans may have had the reputation for being the prairie scum of the town patriarchs, but I wasn't ever unfaithful to my Marie, not one time. Not in word, thought or deed. She was the light of my life. When I lost her, I thought I wanted to die, too. Instead, I built myself a business. Funny, isn't it? I guess a man's got to put his passion somewhere."

"I'm sure she would be proud of you," Annie said, then wondered why she had automatically wanted to comfort him. Strange.

"Sure," he said. "I was always prouder than a peacock of her. She was an angel. Did you know she probably saved your mother on her last night in town when the McLaughlins kicked her out?"

Annie's chest suddenly felt very tight. Reaching out, she sat back down on the bed. "What are you talking about?"

"My Marie found your mother shivering in Coyote Park in the dead of winter, pregnant and crying, with nowhere to go. She brought her home, fed her, made her up a bed on the couch. I remember how small and miserable she looked lying there. And the next day, Marie drove her all the way to San Antone to her brother's place."

"My uncle Jorge."

"That's the one. I guess he put her up until you were born."

"Yes."

"Well, she brought you by a couple of times over the years, when you were just a toddler. You wouldn't remember that. But then we didn't see any more of you and your mother. Marie used to wonder how you were doing. And now you're back here in the very same house where your mother was. Life is peculiar, no doubt about it."

He pulled himself out of the chair and left without another word. Annie stared after him, stunned by what she'd heard. She'd had no idea.

And then she realized she had to do something about this and do it fast.

Chapter Nine

Matt was sitting in a corner booth at the café, contemplating a meal of Millie's deluxe version of huevos rancheros with red salsa and black beans. He'd been out running at the high school track and this was the reward he gave himself for being so virtuous in the exercise department.

"Doesn't the meal kind of cancel out the benefits from the running?" Millie teased him, as usual.

"Haven't you ever heard the theory that strong muscles need to be fed?" he countered.

"I'll take your word for it. You do look like you know what you're talking about." She raised one eyebrow as she moved on to the next customer.

He looked down at the meal she'd put in front of him. It looked delicious, and he'd just begun piling the eggs onto the warm flour tortilla, anticipating how good it was going to taste, when Annie appeared out of nowhere, sinking into the seat across from him and sighing with relief.

"I'm so glad I found you here," she said, grabbing his glass of water and taking a long drink. "I'm dying of thirst."

She looked hot and tired, but still managed to be beautiful. He loved the way her hair curled wildly about her face. He loved how bright her dark eyes were, so interested in everything around her—the way her hands moved when she talked, the way...

He pulled himself up short. This was no time to let his feelings run away with him. She'd obviously come looking for him with a purpose in mind.

"What happened?" he asked.

"Oh, I had to walk all the way over here. My car broke down again and—"

"Damn it, Annie, I've told you to let me take that junker over to Al's Garage."

"No," she said sharply. "It's my responsibility. I'll take care of it."

He shrugged. It was on the tip of his tongue to point out that words weren't keeping the old heap from letting her down every other day, but he held it back. He knew how firmly she cherished her independence.

"So what's up?" he asked, positioning his fully stuffed tortilla for his first bite. "How did you know I was here?"

"I called Rafe's apartment and he said you might be here."

He paused, tortilla in the air. "Is something wrong?"

"Not exactly, but—" she hesitated, licking her lips "—I had an interview with your father."

The tortilla dropped back down onto his plate. "Oh, my God. What did he say? Did he do anything?"

"Well, first he wanted to know if you had done this." She looked down at her pregnant form.

Matt groaned.

"I told him no, that this baby had nothing to do with you."

Matt grinned. He could picture their encounter now. "Did that disappoint him?"

"No. I don't know." She shook her head, looking distracted. "That didn't really upset me." Reaching across the table, she put her hand on his. "But…oh, Matt, I feel like I need to be more honest with you. There's something I haven't told you. And now it's so late."

His heart went cold inside him. "What are you talking about, Annie?"

She shook her head and her face was full of misery. "I've been too scared to tell you," she began, then her eyes welled with tears. "It's going to be hard to explain."

"Okay," he said decisively, pushing his plate away. "Let's get out of here. Let's go somewhere where we can talk."

"But you just started eating," she protested.

"Forget it." He threw some money on the table, slid out of his seat and reached for her hand to help her out. "My car's right outside."

They walked out past the barbecue pit. A brand-new

shiny stainless steel grill was being erected by workmen in preparation for the Allman family prewedding party scheduled for Friday night. There was going to be Texas barbecue to die for. Matt opened the car door to help her in. He had no idea what she was about to reveal to him but he was pretty sure he wasn't going to like it. Still, he knew it wasn't going to change anything. He was crazy about her.

A few minutes later they were pulling up into a protected area off the highway, under a stand of junipers. Matt switched off the engine and turned to look at Annie. She'd settled down and was looking cool and composed now.

"You okay?" he asked.

She nodded. "Oh, yes, of course. Sorry I sort of fell apart there. That is so not me, but these pregnancy hormones keep undermining me."

He reached out and brushed a couple of wild curls back behind her shell-like ear. He couldn't help it. He just had to touch her.

"You said you had something to tell me?"

"Yes." Her gaze was troubled as it met his. "Your father recognized who I am. He knew my mother. And I think I should tell you before he does."

Alarm raised the hair on the back of his neck but he managed to stay outwardly calm. "Annie, I don't know what the hell you're talking about."

Taking a deep breath, she visibly set her shoulders and forced herself to speak. "Matt, my father was William McLaughlin. Josh and Kenny and Jimmy McLaughlin are all my half brothers."

He was usually pretty quick on the uptake but for some reason, this one had him stumped. "What?"

She folded her hands tightly together. "Remember when I told you that my mother fell in love with the young man of the family where she worked? She was working at McLaughlin Ranch at the time."

The fog began to clear. "You've got to be kidding. That means you're a McLaughlin."

"Yes." She closed her eyes as though she expected a torrent of anger from him.

He stared at her for a long moment, and then he started to laugh.

Her eyes popped open. "You're laughing?" she said indignantly. "You find this funny?"

He grabbed her hand and held it firmly in his. "Annie, I have to either laugh or cry. This is so bizarre. That you would turn out to be a member of the family I'm sworn as an Allman to hate forever... It's just too weird."

"Weird or not, it's true."

"And my father knew it?"

She nodded. "As soon as he heard my name, he recognized me. He told me about how your mother was the one who helped my mother get out of town when the McLaughlins kicked her out for being pregnant."

He shook his head. "It's a small world, isn't it?"

"And Chivaree was a small town back then."

"So that's why you felt this compulsion to keep going out to the McLaughlin Ranch." His gaze sharpened. "Do they know?"

She shook her head. "Cathy and Josh? No. I haven't

had the nerve to tell them yet. I wanted to get to know them before…"

He waited but she didn't complete the sentence.

"I don't get it. Why didn't you tell them from the beginning?"

She sighed, looking miserable. "That's what I'm asking myself now. I realize I should have. But I wanted to get the lay of the land and see what kind of people they were. I wanted to find out how they might accept that from me." She shook her head. "And now I'm wondering if I should even intrude on their happiness with my sad little tale. What does it really have to do with them?"

"Everything." He tugged on her hand. "Let's go and tell them. I'll go with you."

She shook her head, startled and resistant. "No! Not now." She looked confused. "Matt, they're such nice people. I like them so much. How can I just swoop down and ruin their picture of their father like that?"

"Don't worry about that," he said grimly. "Everyone knows Josh's father was a playboy. It's common knowledge around town." Too late, he realized he was talking about her father, too.

But it didn't seem to bother her. "I know that," she said. "But to confront them with it so directly seems cruel. Maybe we can just let this die down." She looked at him hopefully.

He shook his head. "You have to tell them. My father knows and he won't keep your secret for long."

She seemed so miserable, his heart went out to her and he leaned forward and dropped a tender kiss on her lips. She turned toward him as though he'd done some-

thing special and he was tempted to take things a little
further. But he resisted. She was torn and weak now and
it was no time to push it.

"Come on," he said. "I'll drive you over and go in
with you."

Her sigh seemed to come from deep inside her. "All
right," she said softly, but she looked as though she was
going to her doom.

"What do you want?"

Josh had looked happy enough to see Annie, but
when he caught sight of Matt standing behind her, his
face changed. Now he stood squarely in the opening, not
leaving any room for entrance.

"I need to tell you something," Annie said, her pulse
pounding. "Can we come in?"

"*You* can come in," Josh said, staring coldly at Matt.
"But I'd rather he stayed out here."

Cathy had come up behind him by now and she was
appalled at his attitude.

"Josh McLaughlin, you will not leave our guests
standing out on the porch." She gave him a push to get
him out of the way and smiled out at them. "Please.
Won't you both come inside?"

They did so and Emily ran straight for Annie with a
cry of joy. Annie curled the child into her arms and
kissed her cheek, then set her down and turned back to
face Josh who was glowering darkly.

"Won't you sit down?" Cathy offered.

Annie shook her head. "Thanks, but we won't be
here long. I've just got something I have to tell you. It's

a hard thing to do, and I'm afraid you're going to be very angry. And you have every right to be."

Cathy looked alarmed and took Emily up in her arms, carting her off to her playroom, then returning without her.

"Josh… Cathy…" Annie made a gesture almost of supplication with both hands. "I've been coming to your house under false pretenses."

"What are you talking about?" Josh demanded.

"I… uh…" Words stuck in her throat and she licked her dry lips. How could she do this? She looked at Matt. He looked like he might step forward and do the talking if she didn't hurry up and take care of it herself. Turning back, she steeled herself to the task.

"First I want to tell you both how much I love coming here and how welcome you've made me. I never would have dreamed you would turn out to be such a wonderful couple. I think the world of you. And Emily…" Her voice choked and she fought back the tears.

"Annie, what are you trying to say?"

"I never told you that my father was from Chivaree and that I partly grew up here. I never really knew him, though I did see him around town a few times when I was young."

She swallowed hard and glanced at Josh. From the look on his face she could see that he was withdrawing from her. The warmth was completely gone now. Was he beginning to realize what this was about?

"You see, my mother once worked here at McLaughlin Ranch. As a live-in housekeeper. And she fell in love with…with your father."

Josh groaned, turning away.

"I think you probably know where I'm going with this," she said quickly. "Your father was my father, too." She looked up at him.

But Josh was glaring at Matt. "Did he put you up to this?" he demanded.

"No! He didn't know anything about it until today."

"Look, this really has nothing to do with me," Matt said firmly. "I'm just here to support Annie. That's all I care about."

"He encouraged me to come and tell you. To get it over with."

Josh looked completely unconvinced. "Okay, wait a minute. This is all just a little too convenient. You come to town and start living with the Allmans, and all of a sudden, you've got a claim on the McLaughlin estate?"

Annie eyes opened wide in horror. "I'm not making any claim."

"What do you call this? Of course you are."

"No!"

"Then why are you here?"

Words failed her. Why was she here? She stared at him mutely. How could she possibly explain the loneliness she'd felt? The need for connection?

"I didn't come here to get anything from you, Josh," she said at last. "And I don't have any grievance against you. The only person I could possibly have a grievance against would be our father if he was still alive. But he isn't. And you didn't have anything to do with what happened, any more than I did."

Matt stepped forward to help out. "Look, she's come

to tell you and that's that. If you need proof of what she's saying, we can have a DNA test done right away. It'll take about a week to get the results."

Josh sneered. "Why should I trust your DNA test?"

Matt grimaced. "Fine. Call in anyone you like. Listen, I hope she turns out to be wrong. I don't want her to be a McLaughlin." He sneered right back. "And anyway, she doesn't need you to take care of her. We'll take care of her."

Josh glared at him. "If she's really a McLaughlin, *we'll* take care of her."

Annie stepped between them, angry at them both now. "Nobody needs to take care of me. I can take care of myself!"

"Annie..."

They both said it at the same time, but she turned to Matt.

"Please, Matt. I appreciate your support, but your being here is just confusing the issue. I wish you'd wait outside for a minute."

That shocked him but he quickly realized she was right. He and Josh would be at loggerheads no matter what. "Okay. I'll go outside on the porch while you talk. You give a holler if you need me."

"I will."

Matt stood out on the porch, swearing softly to himself and trying to calm down. What was it about the McLaughlins that always got his back up no matter how much he tried to avoid it? Now here he was out on the McLaughlin Ranch for the first time ever. He'd lived in Chivaree most all his life and he'd never been to the biggest ranch in the territory.

It looked like rumors were true, anyway. Josh was fixing the place up. It looked pretty good. From what he'd heard it had been a wreck just a few short years ago when William had died. The older McLaughlin had been considered a loser as far as ranching was concerned. He was pretty good at running off to New York and dating showgirls, but ranching hadn't really been his line. The McLaughlins were lucky Josh had figured out how to do it right before they lost the whole operation.

A movement from the window caught his eye. He turned. A little face surrounded by bouncing auburn curls was peering out at him. He'd seen the little girl in the house when they'd first entered, but Cathy had whisked her away. Now she was back and grinning at him through the glass.

What a little sweetheart. He grinned back at her. She stuck out her tongue at him and he made a monster face in return. Throwing back her head, she laughed with delight. And darned if he didn't, too.

What a darling. He fell in love with her immediately and it made him ache to find his own child.

Then Annie was coming out the door, hurrying toward the car. "Let's go," she said.

He caught up with her in two quick strides and helped her into the seat, then went to the driver's side. In another moment they were back on the highway.

"You've been crying," he said after glancing her way and noting the tearful evidence. "He didn't hurt you, did he?"

"No, of course not." She sighed. "It's just the darn

old hormones. I swear, once this baby comes, I'm never going to cry again."

He laughed. "Oh, sweetie, from what I've heard about raising kids, the crying has only just begun."

She looked at him mutely. She wasn't going to pretend any longer that she was sure she was going to put this baby up for adoption.

"So what happened?" he said. "Did you get that jackass to calm down and listen?"

She stared at him for a long moment, then she started to smile. "That's my half brother you're talking about," she reminded him. "Though whether he's ever going to admit it, I don't know." Shaking her head, she looked out her window at the passing fence posts. "But that's not important, I guess. I told him what I had to tell him. If he wants to have any sort of relationship, that's up to him. I've done my part. And I'm going to stop worrying about it."

Easier said than done, she knew, but at least this was a step in the right direction.

She didn't think she could face the others right now so she was glad when Matt suggested they go to dinner at a steak place out on the interstate where they weren't likely to run into anyone they knew. They ate filet mignon that melted in their mouths and lingered over crème brûlée for dessert. Matt kept the evening light, telling stories about how he and his brothers used to put gray hair on their parents' heads with their antics through the years. Annie laughed more than she'd laughed in years and told a few stories of her own.

It was late by the time they headed back. When they

reached the Allman house, Matt pulled the car to the side under the trees and shut off the engine and the lights, then turned to her instead of getting out.

Watching her tonight, he'd tried to remember why he'd decided that he couldn't fall in love with her. Whatever those reasons were, they were gone now, and the ones he could remember didn't seem to make sense anymore. She'd filled his life with sunlight over the past few weeks and he couldn't imagine going on without her.

"Annie," he said, leaning toward her and taking her hands in his, "I don't want to leave you here. I want to take you with me. I want to fall asleep with you curled up against me. I want…"

She kissed him passionately, mostly to stop whatever he was about to say, and then his arms were around her and he was gathering her to him. And she wanted to go with him. She wanted to be in his arms more than she wanted anything.

She moaned as she arched against him. Her breasts felt full and when he cupped them, she gasped at how wonderful his touch was. He pushed away the fabric of her shirt, then the lace of her bra, and she was fully exposed to his caress.

"Annie, Annie," he breathed against her breast. "You make me crazy."

She knew that feeling. Her hand slid underneath his shirt, molding the hard muscles of his chest, the tight nipple, the light sprinkling of wiry hair. She wanted to follow her hand with her mouth, her tongue. She wanted to touch every part of him, to taste him, too.

And then a surge of sensation came over her and she knew that she wanted much more than that. She wanted to make love to this man, needed him almost as much as she needed to breathe. And if she didn't exert a little self-control, things were going to get way out of hand.

"Stop," she said, but he didn't seem to hear her. His tongue was traveling down to the tip of her breast and she was going to go mad if he didn't stop. "Matt, stop," she cried, pushing as hard as she could to get his attention.

He groaned, drawing back and catching his breath. He watched as she pulled her clothes together. "You are so beautiful," he said huskily. "You can wrap me around your little finger anytime."

She gave him a mischievous smile. "I'll keep that in mind."

"Annie." He sat up straighter and got serious. "I was thinking. You know what? Maybe we should get married."

"What?"

Her reaction wasn't quite what he'd hoped.

"Well, why not? We like each other pretty well and you need a husband."

She stared at him in the darkness of the car. How lovely it would be to relax and let herself believe that would solve everything.

The only reason he says he wants to marry you is to help you and to make sure you don't give your baby up for adoption, she reminded herself. *It's not like he loves you. He hasn't said a word about love.*

She turned from him. "I'm never getting married," she murmured.

"What are you talking about?"

"My life. Thanks for the dinner, Matt. Good night." She opened the car door and was off up the path to the house like a flash. Anyone watching would hardly be able to believe that she was almost eight months pregnant.

Matt watched her go, frowning and wondering if he was ever going to be able to understand her.

It didn't take long to find out the answer to Annie's question as to whether or not Josh was interested in pursuing a family connection. In fact, family relationships seemed to be breaking out all over.

The wedding was less than two weeks away and that very morning, Kurt and Jodie had announced that they had decided to make it a double wedding with Shelley and Rafe.

"We just can't wait any longer," Jodie had told her beaming family. "Katy needs us to be an official family and we've decided that's more important than trying not to hurt the feelings of people who aren't even here."

She was talking about Kurt's mother who was in New York and his sister, Tracy, who was with her latest fiancé in Dallas. Meanwhile, his father was still somewhere in Europe and no one had heard from him in months. None of these family members showed any signs of ever coming back to Chivaree.

"I've got a couple of uncles hanging around," Kurt added. "But I'm not close to any of them. The only cousin I would like to have come would be Josh. Maybe we'll send him an invitation and see if he's got the guts to brave the feud."

Rita had tears in her eyes. "I'm so glad," she said, hugging them both. "This is going to be the most wonderful wedding ever."

Annie had been happy for them all, but the comment about Josh had hit home. She was pretty sure she'd sabotaged any hope they had of getting that branch of the McLaughlins to come to the wedding. Looking up, she'd met Matt's gaze and knew he was thinking the same thing.

Later that day, she was working on a scheduling problem and had papers set in piles all over her desk when she sensed someone in the doorway. Turning, she found herself face-to-face with Josh.

"Oh!" she said, one hand going to her mouth in surprise.

"Hi," he said. His eyes were dark and troubled. "I guess we'd better talk."

Chapter Ten

Matt was there, supporting her with an arm around her waist, before she had time to turn and look for him.

"How about we take this to the boardroom?" he suggested quietly. "That way you two won't be disturbed."

They took the ancient elevator. As the three of them stood in the swaying car as it creaked its way to the boardroom floor, Annie realized she was standing between the two men she cared for most in the world. She said a quick prayer that they would both still care for her when all this was over.

The recently remodeled boardroom had a hushed atmosphere, as if only important things should happen there. One wall was lined with impressively ornate bookcases full of beautifully bound volumes while the other was paneled in elegant mahogany and decorated with framed awards the company had won. The table was long and heavy and the chairs that lined it were richly upholstered.

"Would you like me to wait outside?" Matt asked, turning toward Annie, but looking at Josh.

Josh shook his head. "No, you might as well stay."

The three of them slipped into chairs at one end of the table. Josh leaned forward, his gaze on Annie.

"I want to tell you right up front that I've talked to some old-timers who back your story all the way. In fact, Hiram, who's been our head wrangler for thirty years, said he knew who you were the moment he saw you."

Annie breathed again. It was such a relief to have him believe her. "Why didn't he say anything?" she asked.

Josh shrugged. "He said 'it weren't none of his business' and he thought we would work it out ourselves. I hope we can do that."

She nodded. "Oh, yes."

"I've got to ask you one question that is still bothering me. What exactly did you come here for?"

Very quickly she explained to him about what had happened with her mother. She went right on into her own experience with Rick, talking quickly, getting it over with and hoping she would never have to go into it again. But she wanted him to know how lost and alone she'd felt, how she'd longed for a family, even a distant one.

"My mother was dead. My uncle had moved back to Mexico long ago and hadn't been heard from since. Chivaree was always my only home. I didn't know where else to go. And since you are the only family I felt I had in the world, I wanted to make contact. When I saw your ad, it felt like an answer to a prayer."

His eyes were still troubled. "Why didn't you approach us directly?"

"I didn't know if I really wanted to do that. I thought I ought to get to know you first. I really didn't want to create a problem. And actually, I'd about decided I wasn't going to tell you after all, but someone recognized me and I knew it would get to you eventually. So Matt finally convinced me that I'd better go ahead and tell you." She shook her head. "Now I realize it would have been better to tell you from the first. I'm sorry. I never meant to hurt anyone."

He stared at his own folded hands for a long moment, then looked up. "I guess we need to negotiate some kind of settlement for you."

"Settlement?" She was horrified. "I don't want a settlement. I don't want a penny from you." She rose from her seat, so determined to convince him. "Really, Josh. Not a penny."

He rose as well and looked at her. "Okay, Annie. But how about a little love?" And suddenly he opened his arms. "Please. Be part of our family."

With a cry, she flew into his arms and he held her tightly, looking over her head at Matt, then back down at her dark hair. "Cathy misses you. How about coming to dinner Wednesday night?"

"I'd love to," she said, her eyes shining with happiness.

"And why don't you bring him along?" Josh said, gesturing toward Matt. "I have a feeling that we might as well get to know him, too."

The dinner went beautifully. After a wary start, Josh and Matt found more and more things in common, and by the time Annie and Matt said good night, the men were both close to admitting they could actually become good friends if they tried. In fact, things seemed to be going so smoothly, Annie felt bold enough to ask if they had received the wedding invitation from Jodie and Kurt.

"We'll be there," Cathy told her, laughing. "With bells on."

"Do you think the great Allman-McLaughlin feud is finally going to crumble?" Annie asked hopefully.

"No crumbling just yet," Josh warned. He exchanged glances with Matt. "But a few major cracks are definitely appearing."

Matt got so enthused he invited them to the family prewedding dinner at Millie's the next night. And they agreed to come to that, too.

Driving home, Annie was in heaven.

"William," she said, loud and clear, like a royal pronouncement.

"What?" Matt looked over at her in surprise.

"William. I'm going to name my baby William. After my father."

He nodded, his eyes on the road, and a slow smile grew on his handsome face. "We'll call him Billy," he said. "I'll teach him how to ride and how to throw a fast ball." He glanced at her. "He can call me Uncle Matt."

She nodded happily. "You've got a deal," she told him.

"Or…" He pulled into the driveway and turned off the engine, then reached for her. "He could call me Dad. It's up to you."

She didn't answer, losing herself in his kiss. For the

first time, she dared to open up and give him clear evidence of what she felt for him. This time it wasn't laced with the driving physical hunger she'd had in the past. It was much more than that, much deeper, much more important. Could he tell that she was in love?

Maybe. Maybe not. But he kissed her with the same cherishing emotion. And when he pulled back, his smile was loving, even if he didn't say the words. But what he did say was pretty good.

"You are the best thing in my life right now."

Her heart skipped. "You too? I thought I was the only one."

He grinned and chucked her under the chin, then thought of something else. "The second best part of the evening was getting to see that adorable little girl again. How old is she?"

"Emily? About eighteen months."

"That's what I thought. Probably about the same age as my baby should be."

"Yes, that's right."

"Looking at her I was thinking that my baby might look very similar."

"Yes, very likely."

She was about to point out that Emily was adopted, just to score another point or two on his arguments, when a realization hit her like a thunderbolt. And once it had hit, she couldn't believe she hadn't thought of it before.

Her heart began to beat very fast. The things he'd told her about his baby—how his girlfriend had given birth in San Antonio and then possibly given up the baby for adoption, how the private detective was searching for a filing out of state—came back to her. Cathy had said they had adopted Emily privately in San Antonio and that Emily's birth mother requested someone from Chivaree, but that they'd had to file over the border to expedite things.

Surely there couldn't be a connection. Could there? No, that would be too much of a coincidence. Wouldn't it?

The night was long and lonely when sleep wouldn't come. Annie spent most of it at her bedroom window, looking out at the moon. What was she going to do?

The more she thought about it the more she was afraid it was a very good possibility that Emily was Matt's biological child. On the one hand, that would end Matt's desperate search. On the other, that was sure to destroy the wonderful new relationship between Matt and Josh—not to mention hers with them both. Would there be a court case? Would Matt insist on asserting his parental rights? Knowing Matt as she did, knowing his passion to find his child, she was afraid he would. And she knew Josh and Cathy would fight that tooth and nail.

Of course, she had to tell Matt what she suspected. And if she'd learned anything over the last few weeks, sooner would be better than later. In fact, she wished she'd gone ahead and told him the moment she thought of it. Well, she would tell him first thing in the office. And though she dreaded what was going to happen next, it would be a relief to get it off her chest.

Unfortunately, quick relief was not to be. Once in the office she found a message from Matt. A drug he needed for one of his private patients was stuck in a mail room in San Antonio and he was on his way to pick it up personally. He would be with his patient all afternoon and wouldn't see her until that evening at Millie's.

Annie worked all day with the apprehension of what was next hanging over her. To add to the misery, by afternoon she was feeling strange, sort of depressed and unsettled. She began to think that maybe she wouldn't tell him until after the party was over. After all, with Josh and Cathy sitting there in Millie's, just starting to get to know the Allmans, how could she ruin it all?

She was preparing to leave the office and head over to the café when Matt's private line rang in his office. She was only half listening to the message being left on his answering machine when she realized who it was.

"Hey, Matt. It's Dan Kramer. I've got good news. I found your baby. And the wacky thing is, she was adopted by a couple right there in the same town where you live. I'll try to catch you on your cell, or at your brother's apartment, but in case I don't, call me back. Later."

She stood frozen to the spot, unable to breathe. It was true, then. It was true and she hadn't told him. He wasn't going to forgive her for that. She had to find him right away. Maybe he was already at Millie's.

She raced over, nursing her sick car, which just barely chugged to life. Millie's was already filling up. The Allmans had taken it over for the night and relatives were driving in from all over the county. Searching quickly, she didn't see Matt at first, but there were Josh and Cathy waving to her from a booth, Emily sitting between them. She waved back, trying not to look as stricken as she felt, and then she saw Matt. He saw her and his eyes lit up. But just as he started toward her, Rafe stopped him and she could just make out what he was saying.

"Hey, Matt, that private eye called just before I left the apartment. He's got news and wants you to call him right away."

Matt turned toward the telephone and Annie's heart sank. That was it. Now he would know. She'd made such a mess of everything. Would he go right up to Josh and Cathy and tell them? Was it fair for her not to warn them? But wouldn't it be a betrayal to Matt if she did? Would they gather Emily up in their arms and head for home to call their lawyer? Would Matt want to know why Annie hadn't told him what she knew?

She felt light-headed, as though she might faint right here in the middle of Millie's again.

"Hey, honey," Millie said. "Are you okay?"

She grabbed Millie's hand. "He'll never understand," she muttered, looking at her wildly. "I should have told him sooner. It's all going to fall apart and it's all my fault."

Turning blindly, she headed for the door. She had to get out of there. Houston was looking good. Could she make it by midnight?

Once the contractions really got going she realized that the odd, queasy, achy way she'd been feeling all afternoon had been her body setting the stage for the big event. She just hadn't paid enough attention to realize what was going on. After all, her due date wasn't for a few weeks yet.

One thing was for sure—she wasn't going to make it to Houston. She wasn't even going to make it to Austin.

In fact, she was lucky she'd made it to Coyote Park before her car died. She'd only meant to drive by the place, just one last look in tribute to her past. But by the time she got there, her car was sputtering. She pulled into the parking lot just in time to hear the death rattle. The car had stopped and it just wasn't going to go anymore. No matter what she did she wasn't going to get it started again.

So here she was with no car, no cell phone, no nothing. The park was dark and empty. There was no sign of another human being for miles. And she was going into labor.

She wasted a couple of minutes in disbelieving anguish, then got down to work. She needed a good, clean place to have her baby. She went quickly to the building that housed the bathrooms and the meeting room. The bathrooms were open and relatively clean, but the meeting room was locked.

"It's a good thing I grew up in this park," she said. As she remembered, there used to be an extra key hidden above the door. Pulling over an old plastic milk crate, she used it to climb up and feel behind the top brick on the right. Sure enough, the key was still there.

"After all these years," she muttered to herself, amazed and thankful.

She unlocked the door and went inside. It looked very much the same as it had in her childhood, with floor-to-ceiling cupboards holding crafts supplies on one side of the room and a stack of folding chairs along with a long worktable on the other. The electricity worked. There was even a sink with running water. Luckily, someone was keeping it all clean. Making her way back out to the car, she had to stop and do the breathing she'd learned in nursing school while a contraction hardened her belly like a rock before she could move on to collect part of a pile of clothes she kept in the trunk. Gathering them up in her arms, she went back to the meeting room and began making a nest for herself in the corner.

She'd also picked up a pad of paper and a pen and she began writing down her contractions, using the time on her watch. To her surprise, a lot of her nursing training was coming back to her and she began to feel confident. She could do this.

"Pioneer women did this all the time," she told herself bracingly. "And they didn't have any nursing experience."

One hour went by. She got herself a drink of water and tried to walk during the contractions. Another hour went by, and now walking was not an option. It was dark outside, but the single bulb in the center of the room was keeping out the night. She wondered if anyone would see the light from the highway and come down to investigate. She wondered what Matt was doing right now. And what he was thinking.

She couldn't believe she'd muddled things up so badly. If only she'd been up front with everyone about everything right from the first, she probably wouldn't be in this predicament.

"Oh, Billy-boy," she said breathlessly as another contraction took over. They were getting overwhelming now. She was actually moaning, something she'd sworn she wouldn't do. And a little bit of doubt as to whether she could pull this off was creeping in. But when the need to push came, she was ready to give it her all. Once the baby started coming, she wanted him out and breathing as fast as possible.

"Oh!"

This contraction was like a vise. She was puffing away at the breathing and it wasn't doing any good at all. She wasn't sure she could handle this. It ended but another one started before she had time to catch her breath, and this one was even worse. She couldn't take it.

"Oh, Matt!" she cried out in despair.

And then, like a miracle, he was there.

"Annie, Annie, my sweet Annie." He took over, examining her dilation at the same time he whipped out his cell phone and barked into it with directions for an ambulance. "Just hold on, darling. I know you're going to want to push. Try to hold it back until I can get you ready."

Hold it back! That would be like telling the earth to hold off on that next rotation thing. Nothing was holding this baby back. He was coming now!

But she did manage to put him off for a couple of contractions, much to her own amazement.

"I can't," she told Matt, panting as the second one diminished for a moment. "I can't!"

"You're doing beautifully, Annie. We've got the head crowned." He put a hand on her belly and nodded. "Here comes another one. You can push this time, Annie. I'm ready for him."

She pushed with a growl that must have shaken the walls of the place.

"Okay, we've got the head. One more push."

She gave it everything she had left and felt the baby sliding out into the world.

"Here he is," Matt said joyfully. He held him up where she could see. He was long and stretched and covered with white stuff and the most beautiful thing she'd ever seen. "Meet Mr. William."

"Billy," she reminded him weakly, reaching out to touch his tiny fingers. Pride and joy burst inside her. "Billy Matthew Torres."

He grinned at her. "Are you sure?"

"I'm sure."

He leaned down and kissed her. She wanted to respond but she was just too tired. Still, she was drowning in happiness.

"How did you get here? How did you know?"

"It took awhile. Much too long. Everything was so confused. I didn't know you'd taken off until Millie told me. Then I started to worry. I went back to the house looking for you. When you weren't there, I started to get crazy. And then I remembered the attachment you had to this park, and I came here."

She could hear the siren coming. The ambulance was here. The image of her newborn baby was imprinted on her brain and she didn't want to see anything else. Closing her eyes, she slept.

She woke up in a hospital room. Matt was sitting beside the bed, waiting for her to come back from dreamland. She smiled at him.

"I have a baby," she said with groggy wonder.

"Yes, you do," he said, reaching out to take her hand in his. "You turned out to be a champ at this baby-delivery thing."

"Did I?"

"First class. And you produced one great baby. Eight pounds, four ounces, ready to rumble."

She laughed, then stopped herself. "Ouch. I'm really sore."

"No wonder. You ran a marathon last night, Annie. And you won the race."

She closed her eyes as it all flooded back to her—Emily, Josh and Cathy, the feud.

"Are you mad at me?" she asked him.

"Actually, I'm furious with you."

Her eyes snapped open and she stared at him. "Really?"

"Yes. For many things." He kissed her fingers. "But they might not be what you think they are."

"What, then? Tell me."

"Okay. First, I'm really ticked off about you running into the night without telling anyone where you were going. You got yourself into a very dangerous situation. That was just plain crazy."

"You know, I was a little crazy last night. I guess it was going into labor and all. I didn't think straight. But you're right. I'm very sorry." She looked contrite for a moment, then gave it up. "What else?"

"Okay. The other thing I'm angry about is that you had so little faith in me."

"What do you mean?"

"Annie…" He raised her fingers to his lips again. "What did you think I was going to do when I found out about Emily?"

She didn't answer. He waited a moment, then went on.

"Annie, Annie, how could you think I would be prepared to rip that family apart? I would be harming my own baby if I did that. I was obsessed with finding her in order to make sure she was okay. Unless I found her in some sort of distress, I never planned to try to gain custody just for my own selfish needs if she was in a good family situation. How could I do a thing like that? But I had to see for myself that she was thriving."

"Of course." She frowned, looking at him searchingly. "Then you're not going to try to get custody?"

"No. Josh and Cathy and I went head-on right there at Millie's. In fact, if it hadn't been for that, I would have found you sooner. They were shocked at first, shocked and a little scared. But I reassured them right away. We'll be working out more of the details over the next few days." He dropped a kiss into her palm. "All I want is to be able to be a part of her life. I'll be her uncle Matt. It'll all work out." He smiled down at her. "And it will work out even better once we get married."

"Married? Wait a minute…"

"No, Annie. I'm not waiting any longer." He cupped her cheek with one hand. "I love you. I want to marry you. Billy needs a dad, you need a husband—and I need a lover."

But Annie hadn't heard anything beyond his third sentence. "You love me?" she asked in a quavering voice, just wanting to be sure.

"Oh, God, woman, couldn't you tell? I thought females were the intuitive ones who knew all this stuff. Yes, I love you. I've loved you since the first moment you threw yourself at my feet."

"Well, guess what," she came back at him, shimmering with joy. "I've loved you ever since that day you tripped me in Millie's. When you picked me up and carried me out of there, I fell head over heels. I've always wanted a caveman for a husband."

"Then you'll marry me?"

"Do I have any choice?"

He laughed. "No," he said as he bent down to kiss her lips. "No choice at all."

Epilogue

The wedding day arrived and all the hard work paid off stunningly. The Allmans' yard looked like a magical land. Flower garlands were strung from the trees, white birdcages filled with white doves hung from posts, and the wedding cake on the patio table looked as big as the house. Three wedding arches stood at the end of the yard, each sporting a different color climbing rose. White wooden chairs were set out for the assembly. And the place was packed with people.

On a large chair, Jesse Allman sat waiting. In his mind he was going over the history of his family—and the McLaughlin family, too. He thought about the early days when his grandfather Hiram and Theodore McLaughlin founded the town of Chivaree and were partners until Theodore kidnapped Jesse's grandmother and tried to seduce her. To get her back, Hiram had to gather enough men and weapons to storm the ranch house where Theodore was holding her. That had been before his time, but he remembered—as though it was just weeks ago—the day his own father, Hank Allman, found out Calvin McLaughlin had stolen the lease to his good bottom land out on the Bandito River and there was no way he could prove it. Then there were the everyday fights, including the time William and Richard McLaughlin had tied Jesse himself to a post in front of the city hall in his underwear for everyone in town to see and laugh at. And the times his own boys had been harassed by that scummy crew. Not to mention the better times when the Allmans had found ways to get the McLaughlins back.

Over the years he'd developed a grudge against just about every McLaughlin there was for having done something bad to someone in his family. And the more he thought back over all those incidents, the more he grinned. Where were all those people now? William was dead. Richard was hiding out overseas. And the others were scattered here and there. Only a few McLaughlins still lived in Chivaree, and the good ones of those were coming more and more under Allman influence.

"Ready, Pop?"

"Ready as I'll ever be."

David had come to help him get to the proper placement. He let his son assist him to his feet and guide him into position. The people were all sitting in the white wooden chairs. The minister was standing between the three arbors. The music started up, the assembly rose and the three brides started coming out of the house, one by one, each looking beautiful in a lacy white gown.

He smiled at them all. The smiles he got in return were dazzling. He offered his daughter his arm and she slipped her hand in. Then he noticed Josh McLaughlin and Millie had joined them. The minister gave a short prayer and it was time to begin.

"Who gives this woman, Annie Torres, to be married to Matthew Allman?"

"Her brother, Josh McLaughlin," was the answer. Annie beamed at him as he presented her to Matt, who stood waiting.

"Who gives this woman, Shelley Sinclair, to be married to Raphael Allman?"

Millie stepped forward. "Her mother does," she said simply, kissing her daughter on the cheek before withdrawing.

"Who gives this woman, Jodie Allman, to be married to Kurt McLaughlin?"

It was Jesse's turn. "That would be me," he said, stepping forward proudly, presenting his beloved daughter to the world as he escorted her to Kurt's side. "Me and my Marie up in heaven." Jodie left him, but he wasn't finished. "Hey, Marie and me are giving our two boys, too, Matt and Rafe. Just so y'all don't forget."

"Pop!" all his children snapped at him at once.

"Oh, all right," he grumbled, heading back for his big chair.

The ceremony was over soon and the couples were kissing. The doves were released and they hovered around nicely before flying off. Celebration was in the air.

"We done it, Marie," Jesse whispered, looking up toward the bright blue sky. "We done it good. Gol'darn if we didn't go and win the feud."

* * * * *

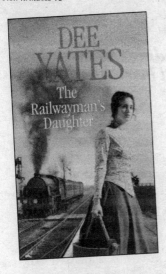

In 1875, a row of tiny cottages stands by the tracks of the newly built York – Doncaster railway…

Queens of Romance

The Marriage Risk

Sensible secretary Lucy transforms her prim image to catch her sexy boss's interest and is thrilled when he sweeps her into an intense affair. But when passion leads to pregnancy…dare she risk marriage?

The Hot-Blooded Groom

When Bryce Templar meets Sunny, the attraction is like a bolt of electricity – business is forgotten and passion takes over… But even more stunning is Bryce's proposal the very next morning! Will she be his convenient bride?

Available 16th March 2007

Collect all 4 superb books in the collection!

When three very different women fall in love with three military men, they face becoming Soldiers' Brides

Featuring

5-B Poppy Lane by Debbie Macomber

When a chance Christmas card develops into a love affair for student Ruth Shelton and Sergeant Paul Gordon, Ruth needs to ask herself – is she prepared to become the wife of a soldier?

The Apple Orchard by Katherine Stone

Elizabeth arrives at her family home needing comfort – which is exactly what she finds with her childhood friend, Nick Lawton. But Nick wants to offer Elizabeth more than just his friendship…

Liberty Hall by Lois Faye Dyer

When Chloe Abbot finds herself caught in a mystery, she turns to her grandmother, a wartime code-breaker. What she doesn't need is suggestions about her love-life – all of which involve ex-marine Jake Morrissey!

Available 6th April 2007

www.millsandboon.co.uk